Let's Get Biblical!
Why Doesn't Judaism Accept the Christian Messiah?

Volume 1

By Rabbi Tovia Singer

With deep gratitude to Patricia Deneen for her thoughtful insights and unbridled devotion to refining and editing this work.

I thank Emily Goldberg and Leah Ornish for proofreading this manuscript, and Svetlana Raivich for her insightful cover design.

Let's Get Biblical! Why Doesn't Judaism Accept the Christian Messiah? Volume 1 Copyright ©2014 by Tovia Singer

All rights reserved. No part of this book, *Let's Get Biblical! Why Doesn't Judaism Accept the Christian Messiah?* may be copied, reproduced, stored in a retrieval system or transmitted in any form or by any means—electronic, mechanical, photocopy, recording or otherwise—without the prior written permission of the copyright owner.

Dedication

In each epoch of Jewish history, an uncommon luminary emerges to nourish his generation with the sacred oracles treasured by our people.

Rabbi Dr. Leon Katz was an extraordinary talmudic scholar, born to one of the most aristocratic families in the world of Judaism before the Holocaust. He was the son of the "Degel Reuven," Rabbi Reuven Katz, the renowned Chief Rabbi of Petach Tikva.

How was Rabbi Katz able convey the fire of Torah to American Jewry, and inspire generations who were struggling against the sweeping tides of assimilation? How did this unusual, revered sage draw so many souls to the warmth and beauty of the Jewish faith, imparting the teachings of spiritual giants of the past to his countless disciples in the West? How was he able to radiate the fire of Torah to his community at his Congregation Adas Israel, which he led for more than sixty-three years, without ever compromising the eternal teachings of our nation?

I watched the special fire that this saintly rabbi carried.

Fire comes in two kinds: one is the fire that is characteristic of the altar; it is a fire that consumes the sacrifice that is laid upon it. The second is the fire of the menorah, the candelabrum. This fire does not consume; it illuminates and enlightens.

Rabbi Katz's flame was that of the menorah. It was not the fire of zealotry, but that of love which, as King Solomon taught us, "Many waters cannot extinguish such love" (Song of Songs 8:7).

His flame was not raging, but soft. He sought not to overwhelm, but to persuade, not to frighten, but to inspire.

Rabbi Dr. Leon Katz possessed the more personal, deliberate, subtle, softer, glowing light of the menorah that will continue to guide us who cherished him so dearly.

His fire remains my constant companion.

I humbly thank the Almighty for enabling me to raise and sanctify His Holy Name with this work, in memory of my teacher, Rabbi Dr. Leon Katz. May the memory of the pious be for a blessing.

My deep gratitude to Rebbitzin Rhea Katz, Shimon and Nancy Katz, and Avi and Dr. Nadine Katz for dedicating this volume.

Tovia Singer

Preface

The last thing I ever expected to be was a Torah-observant Jew. Growing up poor in a broken home with little religious influence, I embraced the Christian gospel at 16, partly through a Calvary Chapel-related commune for former street people during the early "Jesus movement" in Southern California. We were a rag-tag group—burnt out from the sex, drugs, and rock-and-roll influences of the free love culture. But through faith in a personal lord and savior, hundreds of thousands of us united around the Great Commission in a collective effort to evangelize a lost and dying world before it was too late—before hundreds of millions of believers would be divinely snatched off the planet in the Rapture, the precursor event to the seven year Great Tribulation period in which the world would be ruled—and ultimately tyrannized—by the Antichrist.

I became a member and eventually a minister of the International Church of the Foursquare Gospel, a rapidly growing Pentecostal-charismatic denomination—very similar to the Assemblies of God. I was a close disciple of such leaders as Roy Hicks, Jr. and Dr. Jack Hayford. While my evangelical professors had taught me that the gospel must be proclaimed "to all the world," they placed a premium on reaching Jewish people. (This book will explain why.) My passion for winning Jewish souls led me to living four years in Israel, first as a student of Hebrew and later as an English teacher, using my professional skills as a cover for my missionary activities.

Over time, my studies of Hebrew caused fractures in my faith. As I examined missionary proof texts in Hebrew to share them with spiritually illiterate Israelis, I noted that something seemed "off." The English translations I knew so well appeared either mistranslated or taken out of context when compared with the Hebrew original. How could this be? Wasn't the Bible—the Old and New Testaments—a seamless, divinely inspired work? Wasn't Jesus the fulfillment of some 300 Old Testament prophecies by which we could surely identify the promised Redeemer? Hadn't the Jews rejected their own Messiah and for 2,000 years paid the price of exile for rejecting him? I was less and less sure.

The few friends I spoke to of my doubts diagnosed I was under the influence of demons. But having done graduate studies in linguistics, I couldn't argue with the Hebrew texts; they didn't support the missionary interpretations. Questions tugged at me: Was Christianity true because I believed it—or did I believe it because it was true? Grasping to get back on more solid footing, I left Israel to take up a position in a large California church.

Two years later, I left the ministry. There was no gracious way to leave. I was hurting and I hurt a lot of people. For eight years, I wondered and wandered, spiritually and geographically, including a two and half year stint as an English teacher in Saudi Arabia.

Having dabbled with a veritable stew of spiritual alternatives, I had an intuitive sense that Judaism was unique among the world's faith systems, but I wasn't quite sure why. Curiously, I discovered an article by Rabbi Tovia Singer, which challenged me to objectively examine the textual evidence for the resurrection of Jesus. Jesus' resurrection is the most cardinal doctrine in the New Testament; without it, all else unravels. Rabbi Singer recommended an approach of self-study. I took it. And I let go of Jesus.

Now that I was free to examine Judaism with a clearer eye and a freer heart, I entered the Jewish world through a liberal Jewish movement (which actually reminded me of liberal Protestantism). But within a couple of years, I concluded that if Judaism was a house, I was living on the porch. My experience, while warm and culturally stimulating, was spiritually thin.

Around this time, a former Messianic rabbi told me that Rabbi Tovia Singer was lecturing in our area. I attended and left duly challenged to help other Jews influenced by missionaries. I went through another conversion, a more rigorous and demanding Orthodox process, and on the 23rd of Kislev 5760—two days before Chanukah in December 1999, I emerged from the waters of the Los Angeles *mikveh* with a new name—Gavriel Aryeh ben Avraham. Now fourteen years later, I can affirm that it's been a whole new, multi-faceted life—as rewarding as it's been challenging.

I've crossed paths with Rabbi Singer a number of times since. I've been a guest on his broadcasts and he was guest on mine when I was on New York radio. We spent challenging days together as part of a support mission to Gush Katif in the summer of 2005. We've shared in lectures together, and like many former evangelical Christians who've embraced Torah observance, I've attentively absorbed his lectures and study materials.

For more than a quarter of a century, Rabbi Singer has traveled the world helping Jews discover the richness and beauty hidden in their own spiritual heritage. Many of them had taken a detour into missionary Christianity and the Messianic movement in a quest for spiritual satisfaction. The book you hold now contains compelling biblical truths which brought them out of the Church and back home to the faith of Abraham, Isaac, Jacob, David, Solomon, the Hebrew prophets, and millions of anonymous Jews who dared cling to the Torah despite all efforts to convert them away. If it hadn't been for these brave and faithful souls, those Jews who believe in Jesus today wouldn't even know they are Jewish! Ironically, missionaries will study this book in an effort to sharpen their counter-arguments. Sincere students of the Bible will pore through it to understand why Jews have said "no" to the overtures of evangelicals for centuries. But earnest seekers will employ this book to connect with the unbroken chain of Torah learning and living.

While an easy book to read, this is a hard book to master. It chiropractically adjusts misaligned beliefs. That's not comfortable. But it's necessary as we proceed into these days our Sages regard as "*ikveseh d'meshicha*"—the footsteps of messiah. As Rabbi Singer indicates in these pages, the ultimate redemption and revelation of the Jewish people as the historical torchbearers of the Almighty is near. May this book serve as a homing beacon for many who, like I did, wondered and wandered, yet never stopped looking for the path.

B'vracha—with blessing

Gavriel Aryeh ben Avraham
(formerly Rev. Mark W. Sanders)

Invite Rabbi Tovia Singer to your community and experience his eye-opening lectures live!

Rabbi Tovia Singer is well known as the founder and director of Outreach Judaism, an international organization dedicated to countering the efforts of fundamentalist Christian groups and cults who target Jews for conversion. As a renowned public speaker, Rabbi Singer addresses many audiences each year. Through his stimulating and provocative appearances, Rabbi Singer has been an inspiration to thousands. Lecturing on college campuses and synagogues throughout the world is an integral part of his work.

Schedule a program with Rabbi Tovia Singer in your community. Contact him at toviasinger1@aol.com or call Outreach Judaism at (800) 315-5397.

www.OutreachJudaism.org

www.OutreachJudaism.org

Your financial support makes it possible for Outreach Judaism to provide much needed counseling, essential programs, and fascinating lectures throughout the world. The work of bringing the Jewish people back from the Church is an expensive one.

Please support Outreach Judaism. Your generous contribution makes it possible for us to help lost souls in the Church return to the truth and beauty of the Jewish faith.

Outreach Judaism is a non-profit organization and all contributions are tax-deductible.
Visit us online to support our work,
or send your contribution to:

Outreach Judaism
75-02 113th Street
Forest Hills, NY 11375
(800) 315-5397

Authors's Introduction

The vast, in-depth study of both Jewish and Christian Scriptures explored in this multi-volume book is not typical of Jewish literature. Rather, this work was written in response to the growing and unyielding effort of numerous fundamentalist Christian organizations which aggressively target Jews for conversion. All too often my brethren feel battered and helpless when confronted by missionaries and critics of their faith.

Let's Get Biblical! Why Doesn't Judaism Accept the Christian Messiah? therefore delves into the fundamental reasons why Judaism does not accept the Christian messiah. The pages that follow illustrate why the core teachings and doctrines of the Church are spiritually incompatible with the cornerstone principles expressed by the Prophets of Israel, and are opposed by the most cherished tenets conveyed in the Jewish Scriptures.

Moreover, this book demonstrates how the Church systematically and deliberately altered the Jewish Scriptures in order to persuade potential converts that Jesus is the promised Jewish messiah. To accomplish this feat, Christian "translators" manipulated, misquoted, mistranslated, and even fabricated verses in the Hebrew Scriptures so that these texts appear to be speaking about Jesus. Consequently, Jewish people who are most vulnerable to Jewish evangelism are those who know least about the faith they have been asked to abandon. The distinctiveness of *Let's Get Biblical! Why Doesn't Judaism Accept the Christian Messiah?* is in its eye-opening articles and probing expository notes, which explore and illuminate this thought-provoking subject.

Tragically, over the past two millennia, the church's faithful have been completely oblivious to this Bible-tampering because virtually no Christian can read or understand the Hebrew Scriptures in its original language. Since time immemorial, earnest parishioners blindly and utterly depended upon manmade Christian "translations" of the "Old Testament" in order to understand the "Word of God." Understandably, churchgoers are deeply puzzled by the Jewish rejection of their religion's claims. They wonder aloud why Jewish people, who are reared since childhood in the Holy Tongue, and are the bearers and protectors of the sacred Oracles of God, do not accept Jesus as their messiah. How can such an extraordinary people dismiss such an extraordinary claim? Are they just plain stubborn? The central goal of this work is to thoroughly answer these nagging, age-old questions.

Finally, this book was written in a manner that uses Christianity as a foil to reflect back the truth and beauty of the Jewish faith. Included in this volume are the extensive passages, references, and charts cited in the twenty-four-part *Let's Get Biblical* audio series, available online at www.OutreachJudaism.org.

Tovia Singer

Contents

Part I

Evangelizing the Jews. 1-33

"Communications Card" Instructs Missionaries
   How to Convert Jews;
   Paul's Advice on Effective Jewish Evangelism.. 3

The Reformers' Attitude Toward the Jews;
   Memorial of *Kristallnacht* 4-5

Words that Kill: What did Famed Christians
   Say About the Jews?. 6-9

Evangelizing the Jews. 11

Churches that Pose as "Messianic synagogues". 11

Evangelicals use Jewish Traditions
   to Lure Jews into the Church. 13

Gentile Christian laymen most Effective in
   Evangelizing Jews. 15

Why do Evangelicals Prioritize Jews for Conversion?. 17

Jewish Evangelism Poses
   Unique Challenges for the Church. 22

"Messianic Passover Haggadah" and "Training Manual"
   Effective Witnessing Tools. 23

Why are we so Vulnerable?. 26

Does Pastor John Hagee Believe in
   "Dual-covenant Theology?". 32

Part II

**How do Missionaries Paint Jesus
   into the Jewish Scriptures?.** 35-65

Taking a Verse out of Context. 36

Changing the Meaning of a Word. 37

Inventing a Verse. 37

**Matthew Claims Jesus' Virgin Birth Was Foretold in the
   Book of Isaiah.** 38

Matthew Mistranslates Isaiah 7:14. 38

Matthew Ripped Isaiah 7:14 Out of Context. 42

Why did Matthew Omit the Definite Article?. 44

Matthew Changes the Timeframe of the Pregnancy. 45
Who Will Call His Name 'Immanuel'?. 45
The Significance of the Name 'Immanuel'. 46
Would a Natural Conception be Called a 'Sign'?. 48
Missionaries Cite the Septuagint for Support. 49
Christians Question Meaning of the Hebrew Word *Betulah*. 51
Did Matthew Employ a 'Midrashic' Method?. 52
Why did the Church Adopt the Belief in the Virgin Birth?. 54
Christian Translations of Isaiah 7:14 that
      Do Not Render עַלְמָה (*alma*) as Virgin. 62
The *Septuagint* and the Greek Word *Parthenos:*
      Biblical and Christian Sources. 63
Articles Related to "How Do Missionaries Paint Jesus
      Into the Jewish Scriptures?" in Volume 2. 65

Part III
Sin and Atonement. 67-89
All You Need is Blood?. 68
Is Blood Sacrifice the Only
      Method to Atone for Sin in Tanach?. 71
Repentance and Prayer is Better than a Sacrifice.. 75
King Solomon Implores Future Exiled
      Generations to Atone with Prayer Alone. 76
Ezekiel Slams the Doctrine of Vicarious Atonement. 77
Tanach: 'Charity Atones for sin'. 79
Jeremiah Condemned Those Who Believed that
      Blood Sacrifices Could Save Them. 80
Did Jesus' Crucifixion Mark the
      End of Animal Sacrifices. 81
Jewish Scriptures Foretell that the Sacrificial System
      Will be Restored in the Messianic Age. 81
Hosea: There Will Be No King, High Priest, or
      Sacrifice During Israel's Long Exile –
      Until the Messianic Age.. 84
Why is the Sacrificial System So Appealing?
      Why are Sinners Attracted to this Ritual?. 85
According to Christian Theology, God Could Not
      have Forgiven the People of Nineveh. 86
Articles Related to "Sin and Atonement" in Volume 2. 89

Part IV

Isaiah 53: Who is the Suffering Servant?........ 91-129

- Introduction to the world's most debated chapter............. 92-93
- Masoretic Text and Translation of Isaiah 53.................. 94-95
- Who Is Speaking and Who is the "Servant" in Isaiah 53?.......... 96
- Isaiah Identifies the Jewish People in the Singular
  Throughout his Servant Songs........................ 97
- Isaiah 52:14 *(Stuermer* articles depicting the Jew)................ 98
- Isaiah 53:1-2.. 99
- Isaiah 53:3-7.. 100-103
- Isaiah 53:8 – Examining the Hebrew Word לָמוֹ *(lamo)*:
  "Why Tamper with an Original?".................. 103-107
- Isaiah 53:9-10... 108
- Isaiah 53:11-12...................................... 109-110
- John Adams, 2nd President of the USA, *On the Jews,* and
  What Is a Jew? by Leo Tolstoy......................... 111
- How Does the Church Respond?:
  Talmudic and *Midrashic* Texts on Isaiah 53............... 112
- Origen (Church Father) Attests to the Jewish
  Response to Isaiah 53................................ 113
- Prominent Annotated Christian Bibles Insist that the
  "Servant" of Isaiah 53 is Speaking of Israel.......... 114-115
- **Who is God's Suffering Servant?**
  The Rabbinic Interpretation of Isaiah 53. .... **116**
- Articles Related to Isaiah 53 in Volume 2...................... 129

Part V

The Trinity and Isaiah 9:5-6....................... 131-189

- Scriptures On the Unity of God............................... 132
- The Second of Maimonides' Thirteen Principles of Faith........... 136
- Genesis 1:26 ("Let us make man....")........................ 137
- Did the Authors of the New Testament
  Believe in the Doctrine of the Trinity?................... 138
- **What is the Origin of the Doctrine of the Trinity**............... **144**
- How many gods did early Christians believe in?
  It depended on who you asked........................ 150
- Does the Messianic movement reflect the beliefs of the
  original Jewish followers of Jesus?..................... 151
- 'Orthodox' Christianity emerges........................... 154

How can there be one God if Jesus is also God?
     Christians struggle for a solution. 155
Tertullian's opposition to Modalism forced him to
     invent the doctrine of the Trinity. 157
Under Constantine's guidance, Council of Nicea
     settles the clash over Jesus' nature. 160
Constantine's role at the Council of Nicea. 161
Why did Christianity abandon its monotheistic roots?. 164
What does it mean to be the 'Son of God'?
     It depended on who you asked. 167
When did Jesus become the 'Son of God'?. 169
Pagan origins of the doctrine of the Trinity. 174
Why didn't the Torah discuss the doctrine of the Trinity?. 176
Isaiah 9:5-6 ("For a child has been born to us...."). 182
Articles Related to 'The Trinity' in Volume 2. 189

Part VI
Zechariah 12:10 (Who 'Pierced' Whom?). 191-204
   **Did Zechariah Predict that the Jews Will
        Finally Accept Jesus, Whom they Crucified?. 193**
   The Christian interpretation of Zechariah 12:10
        at odds with the Book of John. 194
   Why does the story of the Roman soldier
        appear only in the Book of John?. 196
   The Book of John misquotes the Hebrew Bible. 197
   Would anyone mourn over someone who resurrected from the dead?. 199
   Church interpretation of Zechariah 12:10 anti-Semitic. 200
   'Messiah the Son of Joseph'. 202

Part VII
The Law of Moses and the New Covenant. 207-213
   Contrasting Jewish and Christian Scriptures on the
        Observance of the Law in the Messianic Age. 208-209
   Paul Rejects Torah Observance. 210-211
   Jeremiah's Promise of a "New Covenant". 212-213
   Concerning the Jews, by Mark Twain. 213
   Righteous People in the Bible. 214
   Articles Related to "The Law of Moses and the
        New Covenant" in Volume 2. 215

Part VIII
Daniel 9's "70 Weeks," Psalm 110:1, and 2:12................ 217-227
    Psalm 110:1 ("The Lord said to my master")..................... 219
    Psalm 2:12 ("Kiss the Son" or "Desire purity")................. 219
    Daniel 9 and Related Texts................................ 220-221
    Chart of Christian Translators of Daniel 9:25.................. 222
    Daniel 9 in the Original 1611 *King James Version*:
        Who Tampered with the KJV?............................ 223
    Chronological Chart of Daniel's "70 Weeks"................ 224-225
    Articles Related to Psalm 110 in Volume 2...................... 227

Part IX
Confused Texts and Testimonies........................ 229-243
    Messianic Age in the Jewish Scriptures.................... 230-233
    Is the New Testament Reliable? (Acts 7:14-16)............. 234-235
    Jesus' Genealogies Examined.............................. 236-237
    Luther on Jesus' Genealogy (and the Jews)..................... 237
    Chart of the Conflicting Crucifixion and
        Resurrection Accounts in the Gospels............... 238-239
    Why did later Gospels contradict the Passion
        narrative of earlier Gospels?...................... 240-243
    The Uniqueness of the Torah:
        The National Revelation at Mt. Sinai................... 244
    Glover on Judaism's Unique Historical
        Influence on World Religions........................... 244
    Articles Related to "Confused Texts and
        Testimonies" in Volume 2............................... 245

Part X
The Oral Law... 247-318
Oral Torah and the Church.............................. 248-299
    What is the Oral Torah, and why was it
        later recorded in writing?......................... 248-250
    Why was the Oral Law Necessary?........................... 250-257
    Oral Law was conveyed before the Written Torah................ 257
    The Church's attitude toward the Oral Law..................... 258
    The Oral Law in the Christian Bible....................... 259-262
    The Oral Law is vital to exegesis of the Christian Bible.. 262-268

Rabbinic prohibitions in the Christian Bible.	268-272
Why did Christendom reject the Oral Law?.	272-275
When did the Church officially reject the Oral Law?.	276
The precision of the Jewish Calendar depends on information contained in the Oral Torah.	276-280
The great schism between the Latin and Eastern Church over the date of celebrating Easter.	280–281
Constantine's Council of Nicaea officially rejected the Jewish Calendar and thereby the Oral Torah.	282-283
The Roman Catholic Church discovers the Talmud.	283-284
The Talmud on Trial: Contrasting two 13th century Christian-Jewish debates.	284-286
Paris debate of 1242.	286-288
Barcelona debate of 1263.	288-292
A Christian scholar defends the Talmud against the damning charges of an apostate Jew.	293-294
The Messianic movement's attitude toward the Oral Law.	294
Vague Sabbath and Festival Commandments.	300
The Prohibition of Drinking Non-kosher Wine in *Tanach*.	301
The Obligation to Pray Three Times a Day in *Tanach*.	301
Shechitah — Jewish Ritual Slaughtering.	302
The Unique Design of *Tefillin* and the Oral Law.	302
The New Testament and the Oral Law.	303
The Prophets Warned the Jewish People To Keep the Oral Law.	304
Kosher Animals in the Written Law: Information Only God Could Have Known.	305
Fish in the Oral Law: Information Only God Could Have Known.	306
The Precise Length of a Lunar Month in the Oral Law.	307-309
Historically, the Abrahamic Covenant Passed On only through the Remnant Who Observed Both the Written and Oral Law.	310-315
Pascal and Berdyaev on the Unique Imperishable Nature of the Jewish People.	316
620 Letters in the Ten Commandments reflect The Sum of Scriptural and Rabbinic Commandments.	317
Riskin: 'The Eternal Nation of Israel Throughout History'.	318

Part XI

Bethlehem and the Messiah:
What's the Connection?........................ 321-334
Two Christmas Stories in Bethlehem..................... 322-329
A Christian Bible Comments on Micah 5:2..................... 330
Micah 5:2 and the Time Line................................ 331
How many animals did Jesus ride during his
    Triumphal Entry into Jerusalem?....................... 332
מִימֵי עוֹלָם (me'may olam) in All Other Parts of Tanach........... 333
Chart of Christian Bibles that Correctly Translate Micah 5:2........ 334

Part XII

Who is the Messiah?............................... 337-345
Did the Patriarch Jacob Predict that the Davidic Kingdom
    would Continue, Uninterrupted?..................... 338-340
The Prophets of Israel Conveyed the Salvation
    plan of God to the Jewish Nation.................... 3341-343
Why Doesn't Judaism Accept The Christian Messiah?............. 344
Articles Related to "Who is the Messiah" in Volume 2............ 345

Part XIII

Judaism and Christianity on Satan:
Why We Differ. 347-353
Is Satan the Servant or Arch Enemy of God?.............. 348-354
In Whose Merit Will Israel Be Saved?:
    Compare Isaiah 59 to Romans 11. 355
Isaiah's Reference to the Morning Star (Lucifer). 356
The Devil and the Jews. 356
Articles Related to "Judaism and
    Christianity on Satan" in Volume 2..................... 357

Part XIV
Paul and the Christian Corruption Of the Jewish Scriptures. **359-364**
- Why Did Luke Tamper with the Words of Isaiah?. 360
- Paul's Misuse of Hosea's Prophecy. 360
- The Names of the Children of the Prophets were
  "Signs" for the Jewish People. 361
- **Were Paul's Teachings Divinely Inspired?. 362-363**
- Paul Tampers with the Words of the Torah. 364

Part XV
Bearers of the Torch. **367-384**
- "Jew Go Home!" A Letter by William Eiken. 368
- "You Are My Witnesses": A Nation Bears Testimony. 369
- "Remember! — Do Not Forget". 370
- Holocaust Revisionism. 371
- Trials of War Criminals Before the
  Nuremberg Military Tribunals. 372
- Adolf Hitler and the Big Lie. 372
- Historical Parallels — "Our Eyes Have Seen!". 373
- Lucy Dawidowicz on Questioning the Holocaust. 373
- Photograph of the World Gathering at the Western Wall. 374
- The "Remembrance Document" of the
  World Gathering of Holocaust Survivors. 375
- Text of "The Legacy" Read by Six Survivors. 376
- Six Survivors Reading "The Legacy". 377
- The Second Generation Accepts "The Legacy". 378
- Transmission to Future Generations: "The Testimony". 379-380
- The Integrity of the Torah: *Kri* and *Kesiv*. 381
- Transmission to Future Generation:
  The International Network. 382-383
- 1948 UN Speech by Ben Gurion. 384

Index of Scripture References. **387**

A NOTE TO THE READER

In addition to the immense body of information which thoroughly explores why Judaism does not accept the Christian messiah, this book contains fascinating reference material supporting the 24-part *Let's Get Biblical* audio series. This supplemental material has been vastly expanded since its last publication, and includes easy-to-understand charts and informative illustrations which are indispensable aids to a complete understanding of the lecture topics.

Using this material while listening to the lectures will immeasurably enrich your reading experience. There is no charge for these lectures! You may download the entire lecture series for free. Go to www.OutreachJudaism.org, click on "Let's Get Biblical," and you will see the lecture titles that correspond to the topics discussed in this book.**

For those who would like the lecture series on CDs, the complete bound set of 24 lectures is available at www.OutreachJudaism.org.

Long before you have finished listening to the lectures and reading both volumes of this work, you will grasp the importance of having intimate knowledge of the Jewish Scriptures, without which even the Christian Bible cannot be understood.

—Tovia Singer

**The lecture, "What Are We Doing Wrong? What Are They Doing Right?" corresponds to Volume 1, Part I, "Evangelizing the Jews."

Part I

Evangelizing the Jews

MESSIANIC SOUL-WINNER'S CARD

"The fruit of the righteous is a tree of life, and he that wins souls is wise!" – Proverbs 11:30

A. BECOME "AS A JEW, TO THE JEWS!" (1 Cor. 9:20)

DO SAY	DON'T SAY
(1) MESSIAH YESHUA, MESSIAH JESUS, THE MESSIAH	(1) JESUS CHRIST
(2) MESSIANIC JEW, COMPLETED JEW, FULFILLED JEW	(2) CONVERT
(3) A BIBLE BELIEVER	(3) A CHRISTIAN
(4) COME TO A MEETING OF BIBLE BELIEVERS	(4) COME TO CHURCH
(5) 2ND PART OF BIBLE, NEW COVENANT	(5) NEW TESTAMENT
(6) TREE, EXECUTION STAKE	(6) CROSS

EXPLANATION

(1) The term "CHRIST" does NOT have *ANY* Jewish connotation to the average Jew.
(2) "Convert" means to TAKE AWAY Judaism and to become a "goy," a Gentile. "MESSIANIC JEW" means to BUILD UPON OR ADD TO his Jewish heritage by *gaining* the atonement, *gaining* the Messiah and *GAINING A MORE PERSONAL RELATIONSHIP WITH GOD!* He does not have to give up his wonderful Biblical Jewish heritage. Emphasize what he gains!
(3) ALL non-Jews are considered CHRISTIANS, even Hitler.
(4) The term "CHURCH" is too Gentile to be desirable to a Jewish person.
(5) "New Testament" is considered a NON-JEWISH book. *Don't emphasize its name.* USE IT!
(6) The "CROSS" has been a symbol of Jewish persecution for centuries.

(OVER)

Communications Card used to train missionaries to convert Jews

---

Though I am free and belong to no man, I make myself a slave to everyone, to win as many as possible. ²⁰To the Jews I became like a Jew, to win the Jews. To those under the law I became like one under the law (though I myself am not under the law), so as to win those under the law. ²¹To those not having the law I became like one not having the law (though I am not free from God's law but am under Christ's law), so as to win those not having the law. ²²To the weak I became weak, to win the weak. I have become all things to all men so that by all possible means I might save some.

I Corinthians 9:19-22

The Reformers Offer

On The Jews and Their Lies
By Martin Luther — 1543

What then shall we Christians do with this damned, rejected race of Jews? Since they live among us and we know about their lying and blasphemy and cursing, we can not tolerate them if we do not wish to share in their lies, curses, and blasphemy. In this way we cannot quench the inextinguishable fire of divine rage nor convert the Jews. We must prayerfully and reverentially practice a merciful severity. Perhaps we may save a few from the fire and flames [of hell]. We must not seek vengeance. They are surely being punished a thousand times more than we might wish them. Let me give you my honest advice.

First, their synagogues should be set on fire, and whatever does not burn up should be covered or spread over with dirt so that no one may ever be able to see a cinder or stone of it. And this ought to be done for the honor of God and of Christianity in order that God may see that we are Christians, and that we have not wittingly tolerated or approved of such public lying, cursing, and blaspheming of His Son and His Christians.

Secondly, their homes should likewise be broken down and destroyed. For they perpetrate the same things there that they do in their synagogues. For this reason they ought to be put under one roof or in a stable, like gypsies, in order that they may realize that they are not masters in our land, as they boast, but miserable captives, as they complain of incessantly before God with bitter wailing.

Thirdly, they should be deprived of their prayer-books and Talmuds in which such idolatry, lies, cursing, and blasphemy are taught.

Fourthly, their rabbis must be forbidden under threat of death to teach any more....

Fifthly, passport and traveling privileges should be absolutely forbidden to the Jews. For they have no business in the rural districts since they are not nobles, nor officials, nor merchants, nor the like. Let them stay at home...If you princes and nobles do not close the road legally to such exploiters, then some troop ought to ride against them, for they will learn from this pamphlet what the Jews are and how to handle them and that they ought not to be protected. You ought not, you cannot protect them, unless in the eyes of God you want to share all their abomination...

To sum up, dear princes and nobles who have Jews in your domains, if this advice of mine does not suit you, then find a better one so that you and we may all be free of this insufferable devilish burden—the Jews.... Let the government deal with them in this respect, as I have suggested. But whether the government acts or not, let everyone at least be guided by his own conscience and form for himself a definition or image of a Jew. When you lay eyes on or think of a Jew you must say to yourself: Alas, that mouth which I there behold has cursed and execrated and maligned every Saturday my dear Lord Jesus Christ, who has redeemed me with his precious blood; in addition, it prayed and pleaded before God that I, my wife and children, and all Christians might be stabbed to death and perish miserably. And he himself would gladly do this if he were able, in order to appropriate our goods....

Such a desperate, thoroughly evil, poisonous, and devilish lot are these Jews, who for these fourteen hundred years have been and still are our plague, our pestilence, and our misfortune. I have read and heard many stories about the Jews which agree with this judgment of Christ, namely, how they have poisoned wells, made assassinations, kidnaped children, as related before. I have heard that one Jew sent another Jew, and this by means of a Christian, a pot of blood, together with a barrel of wine, in which when drunk empty, a dead Jew was found. There are many other similar stories. For their kidnaping of children they have often been burned at the stake or banished (as we already heard). I am well aware that they deny all of this. However, it all coincides with the judgment of Christ which declares that they are venomous, bitter, vindictive, tricky serpents, assassins, and children of the devil, who sting and work harm stealthily wherever they cannot do it openly. For this reason, I would like to see them where there are no Christians. The Turks and other heathen do not tolerate what we Christians endure from these venomous serpents and young devils...next to the devil, a Christian has no more bitter and galling foe than a Jew. There is no other to whom we accord as many benefactions and from whom we suffer as much as we do from these base children of the devil, this brood of vipers.

Translated by Martin H. Bertram, *On The Jews and Their Lies*, Luther's Works, Volume 47; Philadelphia: Fortress Press, 1971.

For the complete text of Luther's *On The Jews and Their Lies*, go to:
http://www.outreachjudaism.org/luther1543new.html

Some Advice on the Jews

Of The Unknowable Name and The Generations of Christ
By Martin Luther — 1543

But your [God's] judgement is right, justus es Domine. Yes, so shall Jews, but no one else be punished, who held your word and miracles in contempt and ridiculed, insulted and damned it for such a long time without interruption, so that they will not fall, like other humans, heathens and all the others, into sin and death, not up in Hell, nor in the middle of Hell but in the pit of Hell, as one cannot fall deeper....

Even if they were punished in the most gruesome manner that the streets ran with their blood, that their dead would be counted, not in the hundred thousands, but in the millions, as happened under Vespasian in Jerusalem and for evil under Hadrian, still they must insist on being right even if after these 1,500 years they were in misery another 1,500 years, still God must be a liar and they must be correct. In sum, they are the devil's children, damned to Hell....

The Jews too got what they deserved. They had been called and elected to be God's mouth as Jeremiah says...Open your mouth wide and I will fill it; they however, kept tightly closed their muzzles, eyes, ears, nose, whole heart and all senses, so he polluted and squirted them so full that it oozes from them in all places and devil's filth comes from them. Yes, that tastes good to them, into their hearts, they smack their lips like swine. That is how they want it. Call more: 'Crucify him, crucify him.' Scream more: 'His blood come upon us and our children.' (Matthew 27:25) I mean it came and found you...

Perhaps, one of the merciful Saints among us Christians may think I am behaving too crudely and disdainfully against the poor, miserable Jews in that I deal with them so sarcastically and insultingly. But, good God, I am much too mild in insulting such devils....

A Response To Questions and Objections of a Certain Jew
By John Calvin

Their [the Jews] rotten and unbending stiffneckedness deserves that they be oppressed unendingly and without measure or end and that they die in their misery without the pity of anyone.

<small>Excerpts from *Vom Schem Hamphoras und vom Geschlecht Christi*, By Martin Luther and an excerpt from *Ad Quaestiones et Objecta Judaei Cuiusdam Responsio*, by John Calvin; *The Jew in Christian Theology*; Jefferson, NC and London, 1931: Gerhard Falk, McFarland and Company, Inc.</small>

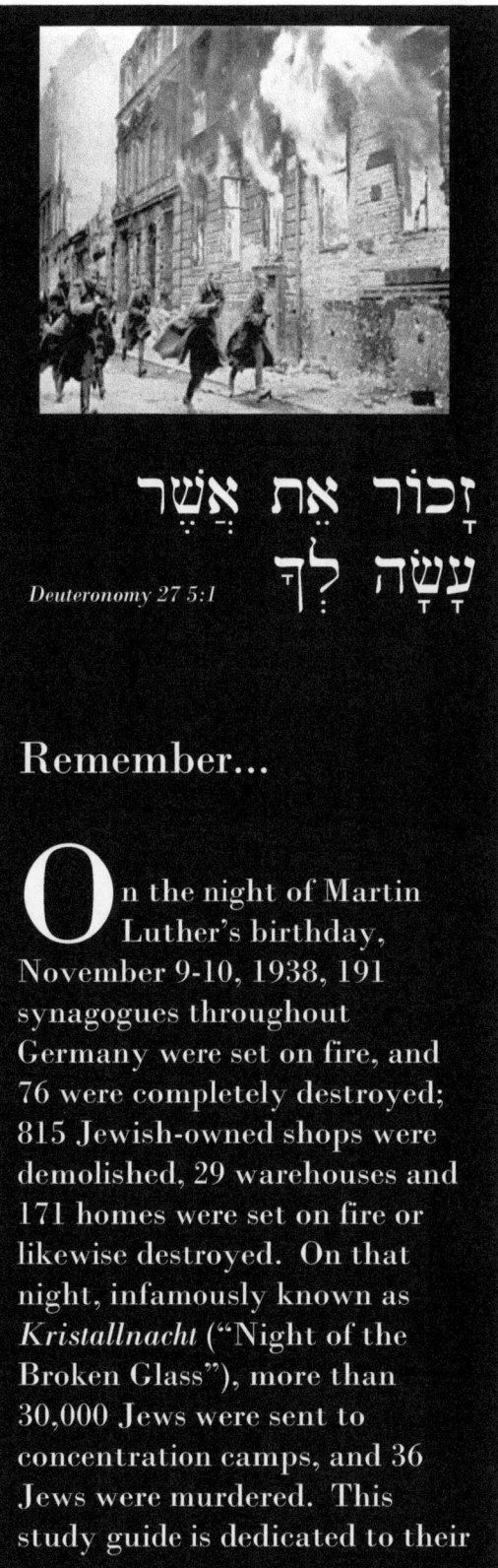

זְכוֹר אֵת אֲשֶׁר
עָשָׂה לְךָ

Deuteronomy 27 5:1

Remember...

On the night of Martin Luther's birthday, November 9-10, 1938, 191 synagogues throughout Germany were set on fire, and 76 were completely destroyed; 815 Jewish-owned shops were demolished, 29 warehouses and 171 homes were set on fire or likewise destroyed. On that night, infamously known as *Kristallnacht* ("Night of the Broken Glass"), more than 30,000 Jews were sent to concentration camps, and 36 Jews were murdered. This study guide is dedicated to their memory.

What did Famed Christians Say About the Jews?

St. Justin Martyr – Christian apologist (ca 103-165 CE)

We too, would observe your circumcision of the flesh, your Sabbath days, and in a word, all your festivals, if we were not aware of the reason why they were imposed upon you, namely, because of your sins and the hardness of heart. The custom of circumcising the flesh, handed down from Abraham, was given to you as a distinguishing mark, to set you off from other nations and from us Christians. The purpose of this was that you and only you might suffer the afflictions that are now justly yours; that only your land be desolated, and your cities ruined by fire, that the fruits of your land be eaten by strangers before your very eyes; that not one of you be permitted to enter your city of Jerusalem. Your circumcision of the flesh is the only mark by which you can certainly be distinguished from other men... as I stated before it was by reason of your sins and the sins of your fathers that, among other precepts, God imposed upon you the observance of the Sabbath as a mark.

(Dialogue with Trypho)

St. Melito (d. 180 CE) – Bishop of Sardis, leading early Church authority who coined the term "Old Testament," charges that in murdering Jesus, the Jews are guilty of killing God

Pay attention, all families of the nations, and observe! An extraordinary murder has taken place in the center of Jerusalem, in the city devoted to God's law, in the city of the Hebrews, in the city of the prophets, in the city thought of as just. And who has been murdered? And who is the murderer? I am ashamed to give the answer, but give it I must.... The one who hung the earth in space, is himself hanged; the one who fixed the heavens in place, is himself impaled; the one who firmly fixed all things, is himself firmly fixed to the tree. The Lord is insulted, God has been murdered, the King of Israel has been destroyed by the right hand of Israel.... Why was it like this, O Israel? You forsook the Lord; you were not found by him. You dashed the Lord to the ground; you, too, were dashed to the ground, and lie quite dead.

(Paschal Homily 94-99)

Constantine the Great – First Christian Roman emperor, who convened the Council of Nicea in 325 CE, where it was firmly concluded and established that Jesus was fully Equal with God, and worthy of divine worship.

We wish to make it known to the Jews and their elders and their patriarchs that if, after the enactment of this law, any one of them dares to attack with stones or some other manifestation of anger, another who has fled their dangerous sect and attached himself to the worship of God [Christianity], he must speedily be given to the flames and burnt together with all his accomplices. Moreover, if any one of the population should join their abominable sect and attend their meetings, he will bear with them the deserved penalties.

(Laws, Oct. 18, 325 – J. R. Marchus, The Jew in the Medieval World, p.4)

The Council of Nicea rejected the Jewish roots of Christianity

It separated the celebration of Easter from the Jewish Passover, stating, "For it is unbecoming beyond measure that on this holiest of festivals we should follow the customs of the Jews. Henceforth let us have nothing in common with this odious people..."

St. Gregory of Nyssa – 'Chief Defender of the Doctrine of the Trinity' (Eastern Church Father, ca. 335-394 CE)

The Jews are slayers of the Lord, murderers of the prophets, adversaries of God, haters of God, men who show contempt for the law, foes of grace, enemies of their father's faith, advocates of the devil, brood of vipers, slanderers, scoffers, men whose minds are in darkness, leaven of the Pharisees, assembly of demons, sinners, wicked men, stoners, and haters of righteousness.

(Homilies on the Resurrection, 5)

St. John Chrysostom – Because he was renowned for his eloquence in preaching, he was given the Greek surname Chrysostomos, meaning "golden mouthed," rendered in English as Chrysostom. (Church Father ca. 344-407 CE)

Of what to accuse the Jews? Of their rapine, their cupidity, their deception of the poor, of thieveries, and huckstering? Indeed, a whole day would not suffice to tell all... How can Christians dare have the slightest converse with Jews, most miserable of all men... (*Homily* 4:1)

Who are lustful, rapacious, greedy, perfidious bandits... Inveterate murderers, destroyers, men possessed by the devil whom debauchery and drunkenness have given them the manners of the pig and the lusty goat. They know only one thing, to satisfy their gullets, get drunk, to kill and maim one and another... They are impure and impious... (1:4). They have surpassed the ferocity of wild beasts, for they murder their offspring and immolate them to the devil (1:6)... The synagogue is a place of shame and ridicule (1:3)... The domicile of the devil, as is also the soul of the Jews (1:4, 6); their house of worship and assembly of criminals, a den of thieves, a cavern of devils, an abyss of perdition. Their rites are criminal and impure; their religion is a disease (1:3)... I hate the synagogue precisely because it has the law and prophets, I hate the Jews also because they outrage the law (6:6).

St. Augustine, Church Father, Bishop of Hippo (ca 354-430 CE)

How hateful to me are the enemies of your Scripture! How I wish that you would slay them (the Jews) with your two-edged sword, so that there should be none to oppose your word! Gladly would I have them die to themselves and live to you!

(Confessions, 12.14)

The true image of the Hebrew is Judas Iscariot, who sells the Lord for silver. The Jew can never understand the Scriptures and forever will bear the guilt for the death of Jesus.

(Tractatus Adversus Iudaeos)

Martin Luther – German founder of the Protestant Reformation (1483-1546)

Now behold what a fine, thick, fat lie they pronounce when they say that they are held captive by us. Jerusalem was destroyed over fourteen hundred years ago, and at that time we Christians were harassed and persecuted by the Jews throughout the world for about three hundred years, as we said earlier. We might well complain that during that time they held us Christians captive and killed us, which is the plain truth. Furthermore, we do not know to the present day which devil brought them into our country. We surely did not bring them from Jerusalem.

In addition, no one is holding them here now. The country and the roads are open for them to proceed to their land whenever they wish. If they did so, we would be glad – it would be good riddance. For they are a heavy burden, a plague, a pestilence, a sheer misfortune for our country. Proof for this is found in the fact that they have often been expelled forcibly from a country, far from being held captive in it. Thus they were banished from France, which was an especially fine nest. Very recently they were banished by our dear Emperor Charles from Spain, the very best nest of all. This year they were expelled from the entire Bohemian crownland, where they had one of the best nests, in Prague. Likewise, during my lifetime they have been driven from Regensburg, Magdeburg, and other places.

If you cannot tolerate a person in a country or home, does that constitute holding him in captivity? In fact, they hold us Christians captive in our own country. They let us work in the sweat of our brow to earn money and property while they sit behind the stove, idle away the time, fart, and roast pears. They stuff themselves, guzzle, and live in luxury and ease from our hard-earned goods. With their accursed usury they hold us and our property captive. Moreover, they mock and deride us because we work and let them play the role of lazy squires at our expense and in our land. Thus they are our masters and we are their servants, with our property, our sweat, and our labor. And by way of reward and thanks they curse our Lord and us! Should the devil not laugh and dance if he can enjoy such a fine paradise at the expense of us Christians? He devours what is ours through his saints, the Jews, and repays us by insulting us, in addition to mocking and cursing both God and man.

(On the Jews and their Lies, Chapter 14 – 1543)

Charles H. Spurgeon – British Particular Baptist preacher, revered by Christians of different denominations, among whom he is still known as the "Prince of Preachers." (1834–1892)

Do you not know, that to this day the Jew walks through the earth a wanderer, without a home and without a land? He is cut off, as a branch is cut from a vine — and why? Because of unbelief. Each time you see a Jew with a sad and somber countenance — each time you mark him like a dweller of another land, treading as an exile in this, our country — each time you see him, pause and say, "Ah, it was unbelief which caused you to murder Christ and now it has driven you to be a wanderer. And faith alone — faith in the crucified Nazarene — can fetch you back to your country and restore it to its ancient grandeur."

(The Sin of Unbelief, No. 3, Section 5 – a sermon delivered on January 14, 1855 at New Park Street Chapel, Southwark)

Evangelizing the Jews

No Sunday services take place in this church. This congregation meets only on Friday evenings and Saturday mornings.

You will never see a cross or an altar.

Evangelical Christian churches use traditional Jewish symbols to entice vulnerable Jews.

Instead, there is an *Aron Kodesh* (holy ark) with a star of David adorning its velvet cover, and a *Bimah* (stage for prayer services) in the center of the sanctuary.

The majority of the men who worship here wear *kipot*, and their *tzitzit* hang down the sides of their pants.

Most of the women are modestly dressed.

This congregation's rabbi, among many other functions, reads from the Torah and makes *Kiddush* every *Shabbat*.

Joyous shouts of *"Shabbat Shalom"* and *"Baruch Hashem"* can be heard as young couples greet each other. The sanctuary pulsates to a modern Israeli musical beat.

If this sounds like a description of a traditional Jewish house of worship, think again. It is actually a description of any one of hundreds of Messianic "synagogues" which flourish throughout the world.

Confused?

Many Jews are.

Such congregations are designed to appear Jewish, but they are actually fundamentalist Christian churches that use traditional Jewish symbols to lure the most vulnerable of our Jewish people into their ranks.

Messianic "rabbis," many of whom are Jewish by birth, are committed to bringing the Jewish people to

In effort to evangelize the elderly, missionaries distribute this Yiddish-Hebrew New Testament. A translation of the first chapter of the Book of John appears above in Yiddish (L) and Hebrew (R).

know Jesus. Their agenda is to make Christianity more palatable to the uneducated Jew, and to the astonishment and horror of the Jewish community, their marketing ploys are proving to be successful.

If the estimates are correct, more than 8,000 Jews cross over to the "Hebrew-Christian" movement each year!

Only a few decades ago, there were just a handful of Messianic congregations throughout the United States. But today, many hundreds actively attract and recruit Jews who, because they lack a sound Jewish education and support system, are buying the manipulative rhetoric and persuasive techniques of the Hebrew-Christian missionary movement.

Well over 1,000 missions are dedicated to converting the Jewish people. It is estimated that there are more than 250,000 Hebrew Christians in North America and Israel.

As an exit-counselor who works with families to reclaim their Jewish family members from these churches, I can testify that the cost in terms of Jewish souls is dear.

It is important to understand who these missionaries are in order to comprehend the dynamics of the missionary problem.

To the Jewish community, the word *missionary* is a negatively-charged word, with a multitude of misconceptions attached to it. It typically brings to mind people who stand on street corners, annoyingly and ubiquitously distributing literature, seeking to persuade individuals to believe in Jesus.

What comes to mind is a well-organized, highly centralized, clearly identifiable missionary organization with zealous members, large mailing lists, motivated secretaries, and a building to which we can point and say, "You see that place on 31st Street, between Lexington and Park Avenue? That's the New York headquarters of Jews for Jesus. They are the missionaries."

This is merely one of a variety of misconceptions we have about the inner workings of Jewish evangelism.

I. WHAT IS THE PURPOSE OF THIS TRAINING?

THE PERPOSE OF THIS TRAINING IS TO SHOW YOU HOW TO HELP YOUR JEWISH FRIEND TO PRAY WITH YOU TO INVITE THE MESSIAH INTO HIS HEART AND LIFE.

II. HOW CAN YOU HELP YOUR JEWISH FRIEND TO PRAY WITH YOU TO INVITE THE MESSIAH INTO HIS HEART AND LIFE?

A. YOU MUST KNOW WHO THE REAL SOUL-WINNER IS, *THE HOLY SPIRITY*, (Ru-ach Ha-Kodesh.)
B. You must understand your Jewish friend.
C. You must avoid that which will keep him away from the messiah.
D. You must emphasize that which will draw him to the Messiah.
E. You must create an interest in spiritual things.
F. You must make him want "what you (and others) have."
G. You must clearly explain the plan of atonement in the Messiah.
H. You must ask him to pray to invite the messiah into his heart and life.
I. You must show him how to pray to invite the Messiah into his heart and life.
J. You must pray with him to invite the Messiah into his heart and life.
K. You must follow-up with him.
L. You must be prepared to answer his questions.

III. HOW CAN YOU UNDERSTAND YOUR JEWISH FRIEND?

A. WHAT YOUR JEWISH FRIEND DOESN'T WANT AND DOESN'T KNOW...
B. HE HAS NO DESIRE TO BECOME A "CHRISTIAN" ("A *GOY, A GENTILE")
C. Even the very worst Jew, in his "heart-of-hearts" will say, "I was born a Jew, and I'll die a Jew!"
D. Becoming a "Christian to him means converting (changing his religion) and becoming a "*Goy" (a gentile. It means giving up his wonderful Jewish heritage and no longer being a Jew!
E. So-called "Christians" have always persecuted him.
F. He probably is more moral than most of his "Christian" friends' therefore, his religion must be better than their religion. So, why give up his better religion for something inferior (especially at the risk of being ostracized – cut off – from his Jewish family and friends).

*"*Goy*" comes from the Hebrew word "*Goyim*" and refers to "The non-Jews, the nations, the heathen."

The opening page of the Messianic Jewish Movement International's *Training Manual on How to Share the Messiah with a Jew.*

Who are these missionaries?

While lecturing at a large university in Ohio, I discussed my work with a campus dean. He assured me that Jewish evangelism ceased at his university. "Years earlier," he recalled, "missionaries were frequently on our campus, distributing pamphlets that misused traditional Jewish symbols for the purpose of evangelizing. But we don't have that here anymore," he insisted.

"Tell me," I asked, "are there any fundamentalist born again Christians on your campus?"

"What? Are you kidding? This is the Midwest! We're packed with them!," he quickly snapped. I informed him that in fact he had a serious missionary problem on his campus because, with rare exceptions,[1] fundamentalist, born-again Christians are dedicated to bringing every Jew to the Cross.

There is a tendency in Jewish community to view the Christian world as a monolithic group of gentiles who all essentially believe the same thing. This is a serious mistake.

> C. Avoid displaying pictures of Jesus or statues (which Jewish people consider as idolatry. Exodus 20:4)
> D. Avoid displaying crosses (which Jewish people consider as symbols of persecution – the Crusades, the Spanish Inquisition, the Holocaust, etc.).
> E. Avoid jokes about the Jewish people (their money, etc.). Some Jewish people are very sensitive about this. It's permissible for them to tell jokes on themselves; but, it may be offensive for another to do it. (Ephesians 5:4)
> F. Avoid saying "Jews" or "You Jews," which are hard terms. It is better to say "The Jewish People."
> G. Avoid using the names of Jewish missionary organizations. The word "Missionary" is interpreted by the Jewish people as "we're out to get you heathen Jews!"
> H. Avoid saying "Jesus Christ, the Messiah." The term "Christ" does NOT have any Jewish connotation AT ALL to the average Jewish person and only "turns him off!"
>
> Since "Christ" means "Messiah," you are only really saying "Jesus the Messiah the Messiah," and are being redundant.
>
> It is much better to say "The Messiah" or "Messiah Yeshua" (The term "Yeshua" comes from the Hebrew and means "Salvation") or "Messiah Jesus" (in that order of preference).
>
> I. Avoid anti-Semitic (anti-Jewish) term; such as... "Jewing-down"... "kikes"... "Christ-killers"... "dirty-Jew"... "Jew-boy"... etc. (Terms of prejudice and hate of ANY minority do not belong in the vocabulary of a child of God – I John 4:20!).
>
> **V. WHAT CAN YOU EMPHASIZE TO DRAW YOUR JEWISH FRIENDS TO HIS MESSIAH?**
>
> **EMPHASIZE THE FOLLOWING IN YOUR SHARING...**
>
> A. Emphasize that one becomes a MESSIANIC JEW (a completed, fulfilled Jew) when he invites the Messiah into his heart and life.
>
> One does not give up his wonderful Jewish heritage; rather, he gains the atonement, he gains the Messiah and he gains a MORE personal relationship with the God of Abraham, Isaac and Jacob!
>
> It's not what he gives up. It's what he gains!!!
>
> B. Emphasize that the Messiah makes one a better Jew and a better Person! There's no need to go home and stir up trouble!
>
> One should go home and QUIETLY show by his IMPROVED LIFE that GOD has made him a better Jew and a better person.
>
> Jewish believes are often among the most respected members of their families. Their marriages are happier and they don't have the problems of drug, divorce, etc.

Page 5 of the *Messianic Training Manual on How to Share the Messiah with a Jew*

> **A serious missionary problem exists on any campus with evangelical, fundamentalist Christians**

The Christian world is far more variegated than the Jewish world. In fact, the Church is composed of a dizzying number of competing denominations which differ on numerous fundamental theological issues.

At a baseball game, it is sometimes difficult to know who the players are without a scorecard. So let's break down the Christian world for a moment so that we know precisely to whom we are referring.

> **Sorting out the complex Christian world: Roman Catholics and liberal Protestants are generally not interested in Jewish evangelism**

The Roman Catholic Church, with more than one billion members worldwide, is by far the largest denomination in Christendom. Despite Rome's past bitter relationship with the Jewish people, today's Catholic Church is, for the most part, not interested in converting Jews.

I need not worry that a Catholic priest is going to evangelize a Jewish patient at a hospital. If anything, he is one of the people who will show me where I can secure a kosher meal!

Another particularly important segment of the Christian world, especially in North America, is the Protestant community. For our purposes, we will overgeneralize and divide the Protestant world into two groups: mainline and fundamentalist Christians.

Mainline or liberal Protestant denominations (Methodist, Episcopalian, Unitarian, etc.) are not at all interested in converting Jews. Liberal-leaning Protestant denominations tend to shy away from Jewish evangelism.

The other group within the Protestant community, however, is motivated and vocal. These are the fundamentalist, "born-again" Christians, who are unyielding in their staunch commitment to convert Jews to their zealous brand of Christianity.

There are two rules about Jewish evangelism that must always be kept in mind.

The Christian who makes the very first critical and successful contact with the Jew is almost never a professional missionary. It will not be a paid staff member of Jews for Jesus or Chosen People Ministries.

Rather, it is most likely to be a layperson—perhaps a secretary at the office, a roommate in college or someone on the same swim team—who makes that initial, effective connection. Only after the lay evangelical Christian has made this preliminary contact will the professional missionary step into the conversion process.

Second, the Christian layperson who makes that all-important first contact with the Jew is invariably a gentile. It is extremely rare for a "Hebrew-Christian" to successfully make that initial contact with a Jew.

> Gentile parishioners, rather than Hebrew-Christians, are most effective in evangelizing the Jews

The perceived betrayal of the Jewish people by the Hebrew-Christian's apostasy discredits his message in the mind of a Jew. *Gentile* Christians, on the other hand, do not repel Jews.

Only after the lay, gentile born-again Christian has made that first crucial and successful encounter with a Jew will the Hebrew-Christian missionaries step in to finalize the conversion.

In essence, the central role that Christian missions like Jews for Jesus play is to act as a clearinghouse and support system for evangelical churches worldwide.

As a result, these Jewish missions spend much of their resources and manpower teaching gentile churchgoers the art of Jewish evangelism. Missionaries, therefore, spend considerable time in churches encouraging Christians who are reluctant to preach the gospel to their Jewish neighbors, classmates, and coworkers.

How serious a problem are these Protestant, fundamentalist Christians? How many born-again Christians are there in the United States?

Their numbers are not small. They are the largest voting block in the United States. According to most estimates, there are well over 70 million Americans who identify themselves as "born-again Christians." That is, nearly one in five Americans is part of this army of lay people dedicated to share their faith with a Jew. When I spoke at a Nashville synagogue a number of years ago, an Assemblies of God minister bluntly told me that he would rather convert one Jew than 50,000 gentiles!

Several reasons why fundamentalist Christians are obsessed with converting the Jews

The question that naturally comes to mind is: Why us? Why the overzealous effort to convert Jews? Why are these fundamentalist Christians so consumed with bringing the Jewish people to know Jesus? Why has the largest Protestant denomination in the United States—the Southern Baptist Convention—repeatedly passed numerous resolutions, encouraging its more than 15 million members to target and evangelize the Jewish people?

To begin with, the New Testament specifically prioritizes Jews for conversion. In the book of Matthew, when Jesus is instructing his apostles, he warns them:

Christian Bible prioritizes Jews

> "Go not into the way of the gentiles...but only go to the lost sheep of the house of Israel."
>
> (Matthew 10:5)

The Apostle Paul echoes the identical sentiment when he declares:

> "For I am not ashamed of the gospel of Christ, for it is the power of God to salvation for everyone who believes, for the Jew first and also for the Greek [gentile]."
>
> (Romans 1:16)

We find a unique emphasis on reaching the Jews in the New Testament, especially in the Gospels, almost to the exclusion of the gentiles.

A second reason for this obsession relates to the Church's fascination with eschatology—the study of the End Times.

Fundamentalist Christians are consumed by the prophecies surrounding the End of Days. Are we living in these times? They want to know when the Messiah will come/return. How will this take place? To which nations did the prophet Ezekiel refer when he described how apocalyptic nations would wage war against Jerusalem before the final hour leading to the messianic age (Ezekiel 38-39)?

Christian bookstores typically set aside an entire section dedicated to eschatological inquiry.

Of course, the Jewish people eagerly await the "End of Days," and the coming of The Messiah. This faith is one of Maimonides' "Thirteen Fundamental Principles of Faith." However, the Jewish concept of The Messiah (*Mashiach* in Hebrew) is entirely different from that of Christians.

> Evangelical Christians widely believe that the mass conversion of the Jews will bring about Jesus' "second coming"

How does all this apocalyptic speculation relate to our subject?

At the end of the Book of Matthew, Jesus is quoted as making a very important statement:

> "I will not return until you say, 'Blessed is he who comes in the name of the Lord.'"
>
> (Matthew 23:39)

Since Jesus was addressing a Jewish audience at the time he made this statement, Christians have often understood this proclamation to have one meaning: Jesus will not make his second coming until large numbers of Jews embrace the Church.

The Jews, in a sense, are holding up the show. Many evangelicals believe that Jesus' second coming is imminent and the Jews must be converted posthaste and *en masse* in order to enable Jesus' return.

Finally, the most significant reason for the Church's preoccupation with the Jews stems from the unique credibility problem that only Judaism presents to Christendom.

Jesus was a Jew, and Christians claim that he is the promised Messiah about whom all the prophets spoke.

The idea of the Messiah—a man who will come at the End of Days to usher in a utopian society of love, peace, and the universal knowledge of God—is an exclusively Jewish idea.

Fundamentalist Christians insist that if the Jews would only look in their own Hebrew Scriptures, they would discover that Jesus is bouncing off every page.

It stands to reason, therefore, that if, in fact, Jesus had been the prophesied Messiah, the Jews should have been the first to follow Jesus and his teachings. They should have overwhelmingly embraced the claims of the Church.

Instead, the very people who brought the idea of a Messiah to the world, and the only people who can read their Scriptures in its original language, are the very people who rejected the claims of the Church. This has always been a troubling reality to Christendom since its inception.

> **Only the conversion of the Jew to Christianity lends credibility to the Church**

It is for this reason that only the conversion of a Jew to Christianity can lend credibility to the Church—never the conversion of the gentile.

Peering back into world history, it would probably be quite difficult to imagine another program that has been a more miserable failure than the Church's persistent effort to convert the Jews to Christianity.

Christianity swept through Europe and Latin America almost overnight. Yet the Jews, despite the unyielding persecution and forced exile that they endured rather than embrace Christianity, still would not convert.

Christians have always been puzzled why it has been so difficult for the Church to persuade the Jews to embrace Jesus as their messiah. They wonder why the Jews fail to grasp that their own Bible predicted that the messiah would die for the sins of the world. Are they just plain dense?

> **Evangelicals sought to understand why it was so difficult to convert the Jews**

In recent times, with the approach of the end of the second millennium, evangelicals were faced with a serious dilemma: How could they successfully induce the Chosen People to choose the Cross? This quandary presented a considerable challenge to the Church.

With the year 2000 in sight, two critical conferences were convened during the mid-1970s. The most significant symposiums were held in Switzerland and Thailand. The mystery they sought to unravel at these gatherings was simple:

1) Why has the Church been so unsuccessful in their past efforts to convert the Jews? And more importantly,

2) What new techniques can the Church employ to finally attract masses of new, unclaimed Jewish souls?

> **Christian leaders grasped that the Church had a considerable PR problem with the Jews**

It was at these unlikely locations that devout evangelists placed the Jewish people under a microscope. It was at these symposiums that these Christian leaders grasped that the Jews posed a number of unique, serious challenges.

The first problem they discovered was that the Church had to overcome a significant public relations problem.

They concluded that Jewish people historically tend to equate Christianity with persecution. Jewish people often feel somewhat uncomfortable just hearing the words "Jesus Christ," and when they see a Cross or a Church icon, it rarely conjures up warm, affectionate feelings.

On the contrary, whereas Christians tend to feel quite comfortable in synagogues, or observing Jewish ceremonies, Jewish people tend to feel alienated by the church and its rituals.

"We love the Jews!"

Tackling this public relations problem head-on, these evangelists embarked on a nearly unprecedented, clever strategy. It goes something like this: "You're Jewish? We Christians just *love* the Jewish people! Persecution? Oh, no! Any Christian who persecuted a Jew in the name of Jesus couldn't be a real Christian. A real Christian only *loves* the Jewish people!"

This novel technique enabled Christians to freely evangelize Jews while distancing themselves from their Christian forbearers. This way, potential Jewish converts will not feel as uncomfortable by their aggressive evangelism.

Evangelicals recognized that Jews did not want to stop being Jewish

These evangelicals realized, however, that Jews would not start converting to Christianity simply because evangelicals condemned anti-Semitism and are staunchly pro-Israel. Smothering us with love would not go far enough to achieve their ambitious goals.

They concluded that the essential reasons why Jews resist conversion are that:

- We are proud of our ethnic identity and do not want to stop being who we are, and

- We view Christianity as completely alien to the Jewish faith.

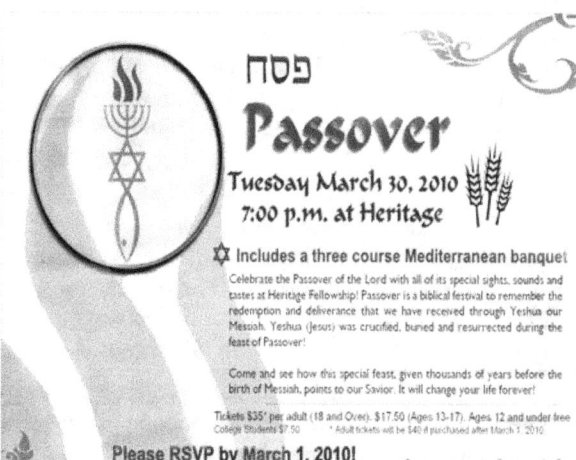

Armed with these new insights, these zealous Christians developed a fresh and simple approach to Jewish evangelism.

The new sales pitch sounds like this: "When you're becoming a believer in Jesus, you are not converting to another religion. On the contrary, you're becoming a 'fulfilled Jew' or a 'completed Jew.' After all, Jesus was a Jew and his followers were Jewish; therefore, it stands to reason that believing in Jesus is the most Jewish thing you can do!"

They also developed the slick idea of "Messianic synagogues," which are designed to look nothing like a church. They are deliberately built, furnished, and decorated to resemble a typical synagogue.

Their members make it clear that they do not observe Christian holidays. A Messianic congregation never features a Christmas Tree or blinking colored lights around the end of December. Instead, these missionaries celebrate Jewish holidays with a Christological spin.

Christian doctrines were meticulously inserted into every Jewish tradition.

For example, Messianic congregations hold elaborate and well publicized Passover Seders throughout the world.

The Messianic "Passover Seder"

At first glance, a Messianic Seder table appears traditionally Jewish, with all of the customary essentials: Seder plate, matzah, and wine.

Once the ceremony begins to unfold, however, even the most uninitiated will immediately grasp that something is askew.

Participants are told that the wine at the Seder represents the blood of Yeshua/Jesus, and the matzah represents his body. "Do you know the real reason why Jews have three matzoth at the Seder table?" they are asked. "To represent the Holy Trinity: the Father, Son, and Holy Ghost."

All
Don't you know that a little yeast **works through the whole dough? Get rid of the old yeast that you** may be a new batch without yeast — as you really are. For Messiah, our Passover lamb, has been sacrificed. (I Corinthians 5:7)

During this season of Passover, let us break our old habits of sin and selfishness and begin a fresh, new, and holy life.

Leader
(Lifting the plate which contains the three *matzot*)
This is the bread of affliction, the poor bread which our fathers ate in the land of Egypt. Let all who are hungry come and eat. Let all who are in need share in the hope of Passover.

Three *matzot* are wrapped together for Passover. There are various explanations for this ceremony. The rabbis call these three a "Unity." Some consider it a unity of the patriarchs — Abraham, Isaac, and Jacob. Others explain it as a unity of worship — the priests, the Levites, and the people of Israel. We who know Messiah can see in this the unique *tri*-unity of God — Father, Son, and Spirit. Three in one. In the *matzah* we can see a picture of Messiah. See how it is striped.

All
But he was wounded for our transgressions, he was bruised for our iniquities: the chastisement of our peace was upon him; and with his *stripes* we are healed. (Isaiah 53:5)

Leader
See how the *matzah* is pierced.

All
And I will pour upon the house of David, and upon the inhabitants of Jerusalem, the spirit of grace and of supplications: and they shall look upon me whom they have *pierced*, and they shall mourn for him as one mourns for his only son . . . (Zechariah 12:10)

Leader
(Removing and breaking the middle *matzah* in half)
Just as the middle piece of the bread of affliction is broken, Messiah, too, was afflicted and broken. One half is now called the *afikomen* — "the coming one." It is wrapped in a white cloth just as Messiah's body was wrapped for burial. (Wraps the *afikomen*)

Above pages 12-13 in the "Messianic Passover Haggadah" illustrate how missionaries insert Christian theology into Jewish traditions.

Why is this widely sold "Passover Seder Dinner" set different from all others? Although it is difficult to tell from the packaging, it is a Messianic Seder kit available on online bookstores.

"Messianic Soul-winners Card" used to train missionaries how to convert Russian Jews to Christianity

Other Christian doctrines that are typically inserted into the Messianic Passover Seder include: "Do you know why the *matzahs* are perforated? Because Jesus was pierced through when he was crucified. Why does the *matzah* have stripes? Because Jesus had stripes across his back as a result of the scourging that he endured during his trial. Why is the middle *matzah* broken? Because Jesus was brutally broken on the cross. Why is the *matzah* wrapped in a white towel? Because Jesus was wrapped in a white burial shroud. Why is this middle matzah hidden? Because Jesus was hidden away in the tomb following his crucifixion. Why is the *matzah* brought back at the end of the meal? Because Jesus will return in the Second Coming at the End of Days."

Messianic congregations are rarely listed in the Yellow Pages as "Churches." They try their hardest to be listed with the synagogues. Additionally, the Messianic movement has created a remarkable tool for Jewish evangelism called a "communications card." This card carefully teaches evangelicals how to talk to a Jew in a manner that will not alienate them as a potential convert. A two-column card which is usually wallet-sized for easy transport and access reads:

> **"Don't say 'Jesus Christ'—Do say Messiah 'Yeshua.' Don't say 'convert'– do say 'Messianic, completed, fulfilled Jew.' Don't say 'Christian'—do say 'Bible believer'"** (see page 3)

To the horror of the Jewish world, this is a tactic that has achieved remarkable success with the most vulnerable segments of our community—the very young, the very old, and our brethren of the former Soviet Union.

Why are these at-risk Jews so extremely susceptible to this current missionary assault? How do evangelicals cull our Jewish youth with relative ease?

> **Christianity had to be portrayed as Jewish**

The Messianic movement's fundamental approach seeks to blur the distinctions between Judaism and Christianity in order to lure Jews who would otherwise resist a straightforward Christian message.

There is little doubt that the intense obsession fundamentalist Christians have with Jewish evangelism contributes to the success of groups like Jews for Jesus.

If we were doing our job, however, a Christian mission to the Jews—no matter how creative, well staffed, and well funded—would pose little threat to the spiritual integrity of our community. But, a lethal combination of circumstances and factors contribute to the spiritual frailty of Jewish youth.

> **Teenagers and college-age youth are often curious and wide open to spiritual suggestions**

Young men and women are particularly vulnerable to evangelicals because all too often these adolescents are unsure of themselves, the world around them, and the adulthood that awaits them. Teenagers and college-age youth are seekers by nature; they are searching for an identity of their own.

They are often intrigued by spiritual suggestions and striking ideas—especially those that controvert and challenge their family's beliefs. Moreover, adolescents may not be emotionally well-grounded, and they often struggle with a low self-esteem.

For most emerging adults, the university campus is the place where they experience full autonomy for the first time in their lives. A paltry few of our kids are sent off to a university campus armed with a strong Jewish education. Missionaries are well aware of how lethal this combination is for Jewish youth and, as a result, they devote a great deal of their vast resources to Jewish evangelism on campus.

Jewish IQ Test

Typical Messianic jewelry displays the "Jesus fish" with Jewish symbols

I frequently give the young students a Jewish IQ test when I lecture at Hebrew Schools.

"Tell me," I ask, "what was Jesus' mother's name and what was Moses' mother's name?"

They all know that Mary was the mother of Jesus, yet few know the name of Moses' mother.

Asking for the names of any two books in the Talmud and any two books in the New Testament will invariably elicit the same type of response. Typically, the kids could rattle off the names of all four Gospels in the Christian Bible, yet are clueless about the names of the Tractates of the Talmud.

For the most part, we raised a generation of children who know little about the faith they are being asked to abandon.

A number of years ago, I received a hysterical phone call from a distraught mother. She had just discovered a New Testament hidden between her daughter's mattress and box spring. A terrible confrontation followed. Her daughter stormed out of the house, and the mother knew she desperately needed help.

We spoke for quite a while. It turned out that her daughter was involved in a local Messianic congregation on Long Island called "Olive Tree."

I explained to her that if I were going to help, I had to meet with her daughter, so we set a date and time to meet. Elizabeth was not happy about meeting with someone like me, but after some well-placed motherly prodding and pressure, an appointment was arranged.

When I first met Elizabeth, she seemed friendly. It didn't take her long before she began to tell me all about her new-found religion. She was a freshman student at Boston University, and it didn't take long before her roommate gave her a pocket-sized New Testament as a gift. "I didn't read it at the time," she said, "I just tossed it aside."

She told me how one night she was feeling depressed after an unexpected breakup with her boy friend, "and it was then that I decided to look for some solace from her little New Testament," she quipped. "I began to thumb through it, and I came upon a verse that moved me in a very special way," she explained. "It penetrated my soul in such a unique way that I knew that this New Testament had to be the word of God."

"Which verse in the New Testament did you read that was so inspiring?" I asked.

> **She quoted words of the New Testament that touched her, yet these words were first spoken by Moses!**

Elizabeth picked up the Bible from the table, and her index finger began to flip through the pages. Suddenly she said, "This is it!" She began to read this verse from the Book of Mark, "And you shall love the Lord your God with all your heart, and with all your soul, and with all your might...."

This young woman had no idea that this sacred phrase is the most precious creed of the Jewish people, and is written in the Five Books of Moses.

It wasn't long after this memorable meeting with Elizabeth that she returned to the faith of her ancestors. Less than a month later, Elizabeth left for Israel to study at a Jewish women's college for a full year.

Fundamentalists Prey on the Vulnerable: The Young, the Elderly, and Russian Jews

Like Elizabeth, many Hebrew-Christians will tell you that the first time they considered believing in Jesus was in college.

A university campus is one of the primary places that young people are invited to fundamentalist Christian retreats, prayer meetings, and Bible classes. What they will witness there is like nothing they have ever witnessed in their synagogue. People stand in their pews, crying to Jesus. Healings take place in the aisles.

Messianic Jews are exceedingly friendly. Visit a Messianic congregation—if you are a new face, members of the congregation, with big smiles and friendly words of introduction, will immediately approach you. They will want to know who you are, what do you do, and if you have a place to eat.

Messianic congregations abound in South Florida where many Jewish elderly reside

The elderly are also perilously vulnerable to Jewish evangelism. It is little coincidence that there are more Messianic congregations tightly packed into the peninsula of South Florida than any other similarly-sized region in North America.

Even more than from physical ailments, the aged suffer from chronic loneliness. The Christian mission's volunteers who seek out and witness to the Jewish elderly in nursing homes are met with little resistance to their aggressive activities by these facilities or their residents.

A pretty smile and a warm touch are priceless commodities to those who are waiting to die. With minds that have slowed down due to the passing of time, and a soul hungry for companionship, our grandparents are falling prey to the Jesus movement.

It is well known that Russian Jews are a prime target and easy prey for evangelical missionaries. Their upbringing in the former Soviet Union under communism robbed them of any Jewish education or understanding of their rich heritage.

Messianic training manual designed to evangelize Portuguese-speaking Jews

Few of these new immigrants are familiar with even the fundamentals of their heritage, such as the Passover Seder or connecting with the State of Israel. This has proven devastating to the Russian Jewish community.

As a result, Christian missions have invested extraordinary resources and manpower in large Russian communities in Israel and neighborhoods like Brighton Beach, Brooklyn.

It is ironic that although Jews of the former Soviet Union resisted harsh spiritual conditions under both Czarist and communist Russia, they rapidly succumbed to Christian missionaries in the West.

The Cry for Help from Fellow Jews is Heard—
What You Can Do

A number of years ago it became clear to me that although my lectures were being heard by many throughout the nation, and although there have been numerous young men and women like Elizabeth whom I have counseled away from these Christian groups over the years, the vast majority of the Jewish people have not been reached.

Many former Hebrew-Christians complained that very few resources were available to them that would have helped them counter the persuasive arguments used by groups like Jews for Jesus.

Something more needs to be done. It is for this reason that our organization, Outreach Judaism, works tirelessly with far-reaching and multifaceted outreach programs specially designed to counter the efforts of fundamentalist Christian groups and cults who specifically target Jews for conversion.

> Estimates are that more than 8,000 Jews will be crossing over to the Hebrew-Christian movement this coming year

Our special Role-Play for teens is regarded as the most effective tool to inoculate adolescents against pernicious evangelicals who seek to rob these youngsters of their faith.

For more information on this special program for teens, go to www.outreachjudaism.org.

Preventive medicine is always preferred to doing surgery after the patient has become ill, and keeping Jews Jewish by helping them develop an "immunity" to unhealthy outside forces is no different.

Christianity is called "the Church;" Judaism, however, is never called "the synagogue." The center of Jewish life has always been a Jewish home. This rich source of our heritage, along with a secure Jewish education, must be restored among our people. The place to begin is with our Jewish youth. They are our future.

Footnote:

1. Not all conservative Christians support attempts to convert Jews. There are some conservative Christians who espouse a theology often referred to as "Dual-covenant Theology," which teaches that Jews should not be evangelized but rather remain obedient to the Law of Moses.

    This belief gained some acceptance among a few fundamentalist Christian leaders who hold that the "covenant" between God and the Jewish people is everlasting, and therefore insist that Jews should not convert to Christianity.

    The vast majority of the evangelical world strongly rejects this idea.

    One pastor who is strongly opposed to evangelizing Jews is Kenneth W. Rawson, pastor of the Bible Students Congregation of New Brunswick for over 40 years. He is a strong proponent of this theology. Rawson wants to challenge Jews who are assimilating to embrace their Jewish heritage. Pastor Rawson is an outspoke critic of Jews for Jesus and other such organizations which engage in Jewish evangelism.

    It is widely speculated that Reverend John Hagge, senior pastor of Cornerstone Church in San Antonio, Texas, and founder of Christians United for Israel, embraces Dual-covenant Theology.

    Fundamentalist Christian organizations strongly criticized Hagee's book, *In Defense of Israel* (2007), for apparently arguing that Jesus did not claim to be the Messiah for the Jews, only the Savior for the Christian Church, and therefore attempts should not be made to convert Jews. Hagee issued a statement denying the first of these allegations and revised one chapter in a new edition of his book.

    Apparently, as a result of harsh criticism and strong pressure emanating from evangelical leadership over the years, the Christian Zionist pastor has had to retract numerous statements articulating his strong opposition to Jewish evangelism and his apparent support for Dual-covenant Theology.

In a *Houston Chronicle* interview, however, Hagee said:

> "I believe that every Jewish person who lives in the light of the Torah, which is the word of God, has a relationship with God and will come to redemption... In fact, trying to convert Jews is a waste of time."

> "The Jewish person who has his roots in Judaism is not going to convert to Christianity. There is no form of Christian evangelism that has failed so miserably as evangelizing the Jewish people. They (already) have a faith structure. Everyone else, whether Buddhist or Baha'i, needs to believe in Jesus," he says. "But not Jews. Jews already have a covenant with God that has never been replaced by Christianity."

> ("San Antonio Fundamentalist Battles Anti-Semitism," *Houston Chronicle*, April 30, 1988, sec. 6, pg. 1)

Part II

How do Missionaries Paint Jesus into the Jewish Scriptures?

A Verse Quoted Out of Context

Matthew 2:13-15
And when they were departed, behold, the angel of the Lord appeareth to Joseph in a dream, saying, "Arise, and take the young child and his mother, and flee into Egypt, and be thou there until I bring thee word, for Herod will seek the young child to destroy him." ¹⁴When he arose, he took the young child and his mother by night, and departed into Egypt. ¹⁵And was there until the death of Herod, that it might be fulfilled which was spoken of the Lord by the prophet, saying, "Out of Egypt have I called my son."

Hosea 11:1
When **Israel** was a child, then I loved him, and called my son out of Egypt.

A person who is really seeking to know the truth about God is not going to search the Bible hoping to find a text that he can construe as fitting what he already believes. He wants to know what the Tanach itself says. Yet this is not the path that the writers of the New Testament followed. Instead, without exception, every verse missionaries use as a "proof" text to bolster their claim that Jesus is the messiah is unsupported by the Jewish Scriptures, and quoted completely out of context.

For example, the author of the Book of Matthew claims that the last phrase of Hosea 11:1, "Out of Egypt have I called my son," demonstrates that Jesus' childhood escape into Egypt was foretold in the Jewish Scriptures. This verse cited by the New Testament author, however, was recklessly torn out of its original context (read pages 322 - 329 for an extensive study of Matthew's nativity narrative). The Children of Israel are specifically identified as God's "son" in Hosea 11:1, not Jesus, as Matthew would have us believe.

Moreover, Hosea recalled the past Exodus of the Jewish people from Egypt in this passage, not a future child/messiah fleeing into Egypt. Matthew ripped this phrase out of context for one purpose: he sought to persuade his readers that the prophet Hosea made a fantastic prediction about Jesus. Compare Hosea 11:1 and Matthew 1:15 for yourself!

Missionaries cite Zechariah 13:6 in order to prove that one who was "wounded in his hands" was foretold by the Hebrew prophet (see below). Oddly, this passage is describing a false prophet who will publically confess his iniquity, not a crucified messiah. In essence, to be correct about the interpretation of a verse in the Bible, you must be certain that the explanation of a text agrees with the context and is consistent with the rest of Tanach.

Zechariah 13:1-6
In that day there shall be a fountain opened to the house of David and to the inhabitants of Jerusalem for sin and for uncleanliness. ²And it shall be in that day, saith the Lord of hosts, that I will cut off the names of the idols out of the land, and they shall no more be remembered; and also I will cause the prophets and the unclean spirit to pass out of the land. ³And it shall come to pass, that when any shall yet prophesy, then his father and his mother that begot him shall say unto him, "Thou shalt not live; for thou speakest lies in the name of the Lord." And his father and his mother that begot him shall thrust him through when he prophesies. ⁴And it shall come to pass in that day, that the prophets shall be ashamed every one of his vision when he hath prophesied, neither shall they wear a rough garment to deceive. ⁵But he shall say, "I am no prophet, I am a husbandman, for man taught me to keep cattle from my youth." ⁶**And one shall say unto him, "What are these wounds between your hands?" Then he shall answer, "Those with which I was wounded in the house of my friends."**

"What are these wounds between your hands?"

בַּיּוֹם הַהוּא יִהְיֶה מָקוֹר נִפְתָּח לְבֵית דָּוִיד וּלְיֹשְׁבֵי יְרוּשָׁלַם לְחַטֹּאת וּלְנִדָּה: ²וְהָיָה בַיּוֹם הַהוּא נְאֻם ה' צְבָאוֹת אַכְרִית אֶת־שְׁמוֹת הָעֲצַבִּים מִן־הָאָרֶץ וְלֹא יִזָּכְרוּ עוֹד וְגַם אֶת הַנְּבִיאִים וְאֶת־רוּחַ הַטֻּמְאָה אַעֲבִיר מִן הָאָרֶץ: ³וְהָיָה כִּי־יִנָּבֵא אִישׁ עוֹד וְאָמְרוּ אֵלָיו אָבִיו וְאִמּוֹ יֹלְדָיו לֹא תִחְיֶה כִּי שֶׁקֶר דִּבַּרְתָּ בְּשֵׁם ה' וּדְקָרֻהוּ אָבִיהוּ וְאִמּוֹ יֹלְדָיו בְּהִנָּבְאוֹ: ⁴וְהָיָה בַּיּוֹם הַהוּא יֵבֹשׁוּ הַנְּבִיאִים אִישׁ מֵחֶזְיֹנוֹ בְּהִנָּבְאֹתוֹ וְלֹא יִלְבְּשׁוּ אַדֶּרֶת שֵׂעָר לְמַעַן כַּחֵשׁ: ⁵וְאָמַר לֹא נָבִיא אָנֹכִי אִישׁ־עֹבֵד אֲדָמָה אָנֹכִי כִּי אָדָם הִקְנַנִי מִנְּעוּרָי: ⁶וְאָמַר אֵלָיו מָה הַמַּכּוֹת הָאֵלֶּה בֵּין יָדֶיךָ וְאָמַר אֲשֶׁר הֻכֵּיתִי בֵּית מְאַהֲבָי:

Christian Bibles mistranslate the Hebrew Word כָּאֲרִי (ka'ari), which means "like a lion," not "pierced"

Psalm 22:16 (17) King James Version	Psalm 22:17 Original Hebrew	Psalm 22:17 Jewish Translation
For dogs have compassed me; the assembly of the wicked have inclosed me; they **pierced** my hands and my feet.	כִּי סְבָבוּנִי כְּלָבִים עֲדַת מְרֵעִים הִקִּיפוּנִי כָּאֲרִי יָדַי וְרַגְלָי׃	For dogs have encompassed me; a company of evildoers have inclosed me; like a **lion**, they are at my hands and my feet.

Examine the Surrounding Passages of Psalm 22:17 (16)

Psalm 22:12-13 (13-14) King James Version	Psalm 22:20-21 (21-22) King James Version	Psalm 17:11-12 King James Version
Many **bulls** have compassed me; strong **bulls** of Bashan have beset me around. ¹³They gaped upon me with their mouths, as a ravening and a roaring **lion**.	Deliver my soul from the sword; my darling from the power of the **dog**. ²¹Save me from the **lion's** mouth; for thou hast heard me from horns of the wild **oxen**.	They have now compassed us in our steps: they have set their eyes bowing down to the earth; ¹²Like a **lion** that is greedy of his prey, and as it were a young **lion** lurking....

King David is pleading with God for salvation from his relentless foes in these famed passages. Throughout the twenty-second chapter, the Psalmist characterized his fierce enemies as lions, dogs, and bulls. This violent animal motif is a common theme in the verses both before and after Psalm 22:17. Psalm 17:11-12 and 35:17 are sister passages to 22:17, and Christian translators correctly render the Hebrew word "lion" in those parallel verses. The Church deliberately mistranslated and lifted numerous verses in Psalm 22 and placed them in the mouth of Jesus. Accordingly, Christendom refers to Psalm 22 as the "Crucifixion Psalm" (see Volume 2, page 17-31).

Why in Isaiah 38:13 does the King James Version correctly translate the exact same word כָּאֲרִי "as a lion"?

King James Version - Isaiah 38:13	Hebrew - Isaiah 38:13
I reckoned till morning, that *as a lion*, so will he break all my bones; from day even to night wilt thou make an end of me.	שִׁוִּיתִי עַד־בֹּקֶר כָּאֲרִי כֵּן יְשַׁבֵּר כָּל־עַצְמוֹתָי מִיּוֹם עַד־לַיְלָה תַּשְׁלִימֵנִי׃

Matthew 2:23

And he came and dwelt in a city called Nazareth; that it might be fulfilled which was spoken by the prophets, *"He shall be called a Nazarene."*

Contrary to Matthew's claim, there is no prophecy anywhere in the Jewish scriptures which suggests that the messiah will reside in Nazareth. In fact, the city of Nazareth is never mentioned in the Hebrew Bible.

Matthew Claims Jesus' Virgin Birth Was Foretold in the Book of Isaiah

There is a good reason why the virgin birth of Jesus[1] is not mentioned in any of the earliest writings of the New Testament: The notion that Jesus was miraculously conceived was a later Christian invention.

Paul, whose epistles are the oldest and most extensive writings in the Christian canon, did not believe that Jesus was born of a virgin. Accordingly, he never mentioned his birth. Moreover, Paul appears to express a negative view of developing virgin birth stories and their variant genealogies, and considered them fanciful and harmful to faith. He urges his followers not to "occupy themselves with myths and endless genealogies which promote speculation...." (I Timothy 1:4). The author of the Book of Mark, the oldest and least embellished Gospel, was also unaware of Jesus' virgin birth, and begins by introducing us to Jesus as an adult at his baptism.

> **Matthew 1:20-23**
> But when he had considered this, behold, an angel of the Lord appeared to him in a dream, saying, "Joseph, thou son of David, do not be afraid to take Mary as your wife; for that which has been conceived in her is of the Holy Spirit. [21]And she will bear a son; and you shall call his name Jesus, for it is he who will save his people from their sins." [22]Now all this took place that what was spoken by the Lord through the prophet might be fulfilled, saying, [23] **"Behold, a virgin shall be with child, and shall bear a son, and they shall call his name Immanuel,"** which translated means, "God is with us."

Isaiah 7:14 Original Hebrew Text:
לָכֵן יִתֵּן אֲדֹנָי הוּא לָכֶם אוֹת הִנֵּה הָעַלְמָה הָרָה וְיֹלֶדֶת בֵּן וְקָרָאת שְׁמוֹ עִמָּנוּאֵל:

Did Paul and Mark just forget to mention that Jesus was supernaturally conceived?

The Gospel of Matthew mistranslated Isaiah 7:14

The Book of Matthew (80-85 CE), written about 15 years after the Book of Mark, is one of two Gospels which claim that Jesus was miraculously conceived without a human father.[2] To support this assertion, the first Gospel famously misquoted Isaiah 7:14 to read, "Behold, a virgin shall be with child, and shall bring forth a son, and they shall call his name 'Emmanuel,' which means, 'God is with us'" (1:23). Matthew, quite dramatically and very deliberately, mistranslated the original Hebrew text of Isaiah 7:14. What compelled the author of the Book of Matthew to change the original words of Isaiah? He sought to prove that Isaiah predicted that Jesus would be conceived miraculously, and was therefore quite literally the son of God.

Isaiah	וְקָרָאת	הָרָה	הִנֵּה הָעַלְמָה
Translation	and she shall call	is with a child	Behold, the young woman
Matthew	and they shall call	shall be with a child	Behold, a virgin

Furthermore, in an effort to insure that Matthew 1:23 and Isaiah 7:14 appear consistent, numerous Christian Bibles purposely mistranslated Isaiah 7:14 to comport with Matthew's mistranslation of this verse.[3] For example, the word "virgin" appears nowhere in the original text of Isaiah 7:14. Matthew rendered the Hebrew word הָעַלְמָה (*ha'almah*) as "a virgin" in order to bolster his assertion that Jesus was miraculously conceived. This Hebrew word, however, means "the young woman," conveying only age/gender, not sexual purity. The only word in both biblical and modern Hebrew that specifically and clearly encapsulates the idea of certain virginity is בְּתוּלָה (*betulah*). To be sure, the Book of Proverbs employs the same word as Isaiah, עַלְמָה, to describe an adulterous wife, a woman who also clearly cannot be said to be a virgin.

> There are three things which are too wonderful for me, four which I do not understand: ¹⁹the way of an eagle in the sky, the way of a serpent on a rock, the way of a ship in the middle of the sea, and the way of a man with a young woman (בְּעַלְמָה *b'alma*). ²⁰This is the way of an adulterous woman: she eats and wipes her mouth, and says, "I have done no wrong."
>
> (Proverbs 30:18-20)

In these passages, King Solomon compares a cheating wife's infidelity to other things that leave no trace behind: a bird flying in air, the movement of a snake over a rock, navigation of a ship through the sea, and a man with an עַלְמָה (*alma*). The sense conveyed in this text is that a promiscuous young woman having illicit sexual relations leaves no trace of her fornication just as a bird leaves no trace in the air through which it passed, a snake leaves no trace on rocks it crosses, and a ship leaves no trace after crossing the sea. Clearly, the Hebrew word עַלְמָה does not mean a "virgin."

The Septuagint therefore mistranslated Proverbs 30:19 as, "and the way of a man in his youth," which bears no resemblance to the original text. Why did the Septuagint employ such a bizarre translation of Proverbs 30:19? The answer is simple: Christian editors of the Septuagint did not want its readers to grasp that the Hebrew word עַלְמָה is unrelated to virginity or chastity.[4] We will later explore the origin of the Septuagint, and examine the methods Christian redactors employed to revise this Greek "translation" of Tanach. What motivated Church editors to alter passages in the Greek Septuagint? The answer to this question is simple as well: They had to ensure that *their* tailor-made version of the Septuagint—which eventually became everyone's version—harmonized perfectly with the New Testament (see "*Does Alma Mean a Virgin?*" Vol. 2, page 33).

Moreover, the Hebrew noun עֶלֶם (*elem*), which means "young man," is the masculine form of the word עַלְמָה (*alma*), and appears twice in the Jewish Scriptures.[5] Without exception, all Christian Bibles correctly translate עֶלֶם as "young man," "lad," or "stripling," never a "virgin." This raises an important question: Why did the King James Version of

> **I Samuel 17:56 *KJV***
> And the king said, "Enquire thou whose son the stripling (הָעֶלֶם) is."
>
> **I Samuel 20:22 *KJV***
> But if I say thus unto the young man, (לָעֶלֶם)...
>
> The above verses are the only passages where the masculine form of the Hebrew word עַלְמָה appear in Tanach. Predictably, the King James Version, the most esteemed English translation of the Bible, correctly translated this word indicating age/gender, not virginity. If the word עַלְמָה can only mean "virgin," as missionaries insist, why isn't there a single Christian Bible in the world —in any language—that translates this word as a virgin in the above two verses? Look it up yourself!

the Bible accurately translate the masculine Hebrew noun לָעֶלֶם (*la'elem*), as "to the young man," in I Samuel 20:22, and yet in Isaiah 7:14 it translated the feminine form of the exact same Hebrew noun הָעַלְמָה as "a virgin?" Why don't Christian Bibles translate לָעֶלֶם in I Samuel 20:22 as "to the virgin"? What would prompt the world's most esteemed English translation of the Bible to render the identical word so differently in two different books in the Bible? The answer is obvious: Christian Bibles had no need to mistranslate I Samuel 20:22 because this verse was not misquoted in the New Testament to support its creeds. Matthew 1:23, on the other hand, poses an existential problem for Christendom: If the word הָעַלְמָה does not mean "a virgin," Matthew deliberately misquoted the prophet Isaiah, and both a key tenet of Christianity and the credibility of the first Gospel would be shattered. The veracity of the Church rests entirely on the legitimacy of the Christian Bible.

> ## Isaiah 7:1-16
>
> ¹And it came to pass in the days of Ahaz son of Jotham, son of Uzziah, king of Judah, that Retsin, king of Aram, and Pekah son of Remaliah, king of Israel, marched on Jerusalem to wage war against it, and he could not wage war against it. ²And it was told to the House of David, saying, "Aram has allied itself with Ephraim," and his heart and the heart of his people trembled as the trees of the forest tremble because of the wind. ³And the Lord said to Isaiah, "Now go out toward Ahaz, you and Shar-Yashuv your son, to the edge of the conduit of the upper pool, to the road of the washer's field. ⁴And you shall say to him, "Feel secure and calm yourself, do not fear, and let your heart not be faint because of these two smoking stubs of firebrands, because of the raging anger of Ritsin and Aram and the son of Remaliah. ⁵Since Aram planned harm to you, Ephraim and the son of Remaliah, saying: ⁶"Let us go up against Judah and provoke it, and annex it to us; and let us crown a king in its midst, one who is good for us.' ⁷So said the Lord God, 'Neither shall it succeed, nor shall it come to pass. ⁸For the chief city of Aram is Damascus, And the chief of Damascus is Retsin; and in another sixty-five years Ephraim shall be shattered as a people. ⁹The chief city of Ephraim is Samaria, And the chief of Samaria is the son of Remaliah. If you will not believe, you cannot be trusted." ¹⁰And the Lord continued to speak to Ahaz, saying, ¹¹"Ask for yourself a sign from the Lord, your God; ask it either in the depths, or in the heights above." ¹²And Ahaz said, "I will not ask, and I will not test the Lord." ¹³And he said, "Listen now, O House of David, is it little for you to weary men, that you weary my God as well? **¹⁴Therefore the Lord, of His own, shall give you a sign; behold the young woman is with child, and she shall bear a son, and she shall call his name Immanuel. ¹⁵Cream and honey he shall eat when he knows to reject bad and choose good. ¹⁶For, when the lad does not yet know to reject bad and choose good, the land whose two kings you dread, shall be abandoned."**

A cursory examination of the Hebrew text in Isaiah 7:14 reveals that Isaiah had in mind only a normal conception by a young mother: his own wife. Matthew manufactured a made-to-order 'proof' that Isaiah predicted the messiah was destined to be miraculously conceived of a virgin. He accomplished this task in his infancy narrative by misquoting a verse from Isaiah. The first Gospel did not set the best example for countless Christian Bible translators in later centuries. Following in Matthew's footsteps, they also wove many christological messages into their "translations" of the Hebrew Bible. Matthew 1:20-23 is only one of his eleven "fulfilment citations," which are heavily doctored proof-texts, and are not mentioned in any other Gospel.

Matthew Ripped Isaiah 7:14 Out of Context

It is clear to anyone reading this entire passage in Isaiah that there is nothing in this text that was intended to be a messianic prophecy, destined to be fulfilled in the distant future. Rather, this chapter is clearly speaking only of the Syro-Ephraimite War, which occurred during the lifetime of the Prophet Isaiah and the rule of King Ahaz (reigned c.732/731-716/715 BCE). In fact, this chapter would be nonsensical if it were discussing an event that was set to occur more than 700 years later.

Isaiah's seventh chapter begins with a detailed description of events surrounding the military crisis that confronted Ahaz, the king of the Southern Kingdom of Judah.

The Syro-Ephraimite War:

Isaiah 7:14 is found in an elaborate section of the Book of Isaiah which describes in detail the Syro-Ephraimite War.

In the 8th century BCE, Assyria was a great regional power, ruled by King Tiglath-Pileser III (reigned c. 745—727 BCE). The smaller nations of Syria (often called Aram), ruled by king Retsin, and the Kingdom of Israel (often called Ephraim because it was the leading tribe of the Northern Kingdom of Israel), under king Pekah, had been vassal states of Assyria. In 735 BCE, however, both of these kingdoms decided to break away from the Assyrian Empire. Ahaz, the king of the Southern Kingdom of Judah, was loyal to Assyria and refused to join them, so Retsin and Pekah prepared to invade Jerusalem in order to depose him and install their own choice of king.

In the face of the invasion, Ahaz and his citizens were understandably petrified by what appeared to be their impending doom. God sent Isaiah along with his family to assure Ahaz that his enemies will fail. Ahaz was reluctant to accept the prophecy, and was told to ask God for a sign showing that the oracle is a true one. Feigning piety, however, Ahaz refused to ask for a sign, claiming that he would not test God. Isaiah censured the king and replied that he will have his sign whether he asks for it or not. Isaiah made it clear that he was sending a "sign" in the days of Ahaz (who lived more than 700 years before Jesus was born). Isaiah wanted King Ahaz to wait for God to rescue him instead of relying on his alliance with the king of Assyria.

Ahaz, a wicked king, did not deserve divine protection. Despite this, the Almighty rescued him because of the covenant He forged with his father David (II Sam. 7:12-16). It is for this reason that Isaiah frequently addressed him as the "house of David" in this chapter rather than by name. For Ahaz was protected in the merit of the promise that God made to King David, rather than as a result of his own virtue. In the following chapters (8-10), Ahaz' son, Hezekiah, a righteous king, will be saved from the hands of Assyria in a far more spectacular and miraculous fashion. The Church mistranslated critical passages from those texts as well (see page 184).

Around the year 732 BCE,[6] two massive armies—the Northern Kingdom of Israel, led by King Pekah, and the Kingdom of Syria (Aram), led by King Retsin—threatened to destroy King Ahaz and the House of David.

Isaiah identified Ahaz's implacable enemies: two kings whose fierce military forces besieged Jerusalem (7:1-8). In the face of the invasion, Ahaz and his subjects were gripped with fear. God therefore sent Isaiah to assure King Ahaz that divine protection was at hand; God would shield him and his kingdom. The prophet pledged to Ahaz that his deliverance was certain, his people were safe, and these two hostile armies would fail to subjugate Jerusalem.

Matthew 1:23	Isaiah 7:14
Behold, a virgin shall be with child, and shall bring forth a son, and they shall call his name Emmanuel, which being interpreted is, God with us.	Therefore the Lord, of His own, shall give you a sign; behold the young woman is with child, and she shall bear a son, and she shall call his name Immanuel.

The prophet gave Ahaz a timetable for this lifesaving event: the crisis would end while Isaiah's soon-to-be born son was yet an infant.

It is clear from the traumatic events recounted in this chapter that Isaiah's prophecy related to the siege of Jerusalem by the two northern armies of Kings Pekah and Retsin (7:14-16). The prophet assured his weary nation that by the time this child (whose imminent birth was foretold in Isaiah 7:14) reached the age of maturity ("…he knows to reject bad and choose good…"), the kings of the two enemy nations will be destroyed (7:15-16).

Two additional passages in the Bible, II Kings 15:29-30 and II Kings 16:5-9, confirm that this prophecy was fulfilled contemporaneously when both of these leaders were assassinated.

There is nothing in this chapter that even hints at a birth of a future messiah who would be conceived 700 years later. Moreover, the meaning and significance of Isaiah's seventh chapter would be nonsensical if it were discussing an event in the distant future.

Bearing this in mind, we can now begin to grasp the full scope of how the Book of Matthew misquoted a famed passage from the Book of Isaiah.

The boy's name עִמָּנוּאֵל (*Immanuel* "God is with us") in Isaiah 7:14, consists of two Hebrew words: אֵל (*El*), meaning "God," and עִמָּנוּ (*immanu*), meaning "with us." The name is a sign that points to the divine protection over King Ahaz and his people. Had God not intervened in the Syro-Ephraimite War, the combined armies of Syria and the Northern Kingdom would have destroyed the Davidic dynasty and devastated the Southern Kingdom of Judah.

For the past two millennia, the fundamentalist Church has been in an unenviable predicament as it sought to rescue the Book of Matthew's spurious claim that Isaiah predicted Jesus' virgin birth. How could a miraculous birth more than seven centuries later be a source of comfort to King Ahaz, as he was surrounded by two armies poised to destroy him? Clearly, Isaiah 7:14 is a near-term prophecy that was part of a historic narrative, and was fulfilled in the immediate time frame, not hundreds of years in the future.

In summary, a cursory reading of the entire seventh chapter of Isaiah makes it plain that the prophet is not discussing any miraculous birth, let alone one that would occur seven centuries later.

Why did Matthew omit Isaiah's definite article?

Keeping this in mind, it is easy to grasp why the author of the Book of Matthew felt compelled to ignore the implications of the Hebrew grammar of Isaiah 7:14, the conspicuous, definite article, "*ha*," which means "the."

Isaiah is speaking of his wife, a prophetess in her own right (8:3), a woman well known to Ahaz. She was likely present at the washer's field, and accompanied their son Shar-Yashuv (7:3). Isaiah's address to the "house of David," and his use of second-person plural grammatical forms when speaking with King Ahaz likely indicates that other people were present as well.

In Hebrew grammar, the letter ה (*hay*) at the beginning of a word, which is the prefix of the word הָעַלְמָה, is the definite article called the "*hay hayiddiah.*" This means that the letter ה in this word indicates that the noun is *known* to both the speaker and the listener.

Isaiah used this indiscreet grammatical device to convey that both he and Ahaz knew the identity of the mother, Isaiah's wife. In Isaiah 7:14, the Hebrew word *ha'almah* therefore means "*the* young woman." The presence of this definite article, however, creates an enormous problem for the first Gospel. Mary was unknown to Isaiah and

Ahaz. Matthew was therefore compelled to remove the definite article in Jesus' infancy story. After all, how could these men have been aware of the identity of a virgin who would save them from their siege seven centuries later?

Accordingly, the author of the first Gospel deleted the definite article and rendered הָעַלְמָה as "a virgin." Note that Matthew inserted an indefinite article, which indicates that its noun is not identifiable to the listener. The indefinite article, however, does not exist as a part of speech in the Hebrew language.

As mentioned above, the strength of this definite article indicates that the mother accompanied her husband, Isaiah, and their son, Shar-Yashuv, to the encounter with Ahaz. The Hebrew article can therefore be understood as a demonstrative pronoun ("this young woman") in order to bring out its force and emphasize to whom Isaiah was referring. It is likely that Isaiah pointed to his wife—who was present at the scene of the prophet's interview with Ahaz—because, as we will soon see, there are instructions for her in this prophecy as well.

Did Matthew alter the time frame of the pregnancy?

The woman who is addressed in Isaiah 7:14 is already pregnant. This is clearly evident from Isaiah's use of the adjective הָרָה (*hara*), "is pregnant," which appears in the perfect/past tense, in order to convey the sense that the woman had already conceived. The dramatic events that are described in Isaiah's seventh chapter, however, do not support Matthew's elaborate infancy narrative. According to Matthew, the mother-to-be addressed in Isaiah will not conceive for another seven centuries. The first Gospel therefore mistranslates the word הָרָה as well, launching it into the future tense and rendering it in Matthew 1:23 as "*shall be* with child," instead of "*is* with child." In essence, Matthew rewrote Isaiah 7:14 so that this passage appears to be a prophecy of a conception that will take place in the future rather than one which has already occurred.

Who will call his name Immanuel?

The author of the first Gospel tampered with other words in Isaiah 7:14 that he considered inconsistent with his virgin birth story. Isaiah uses the word וְקָרָאת (*v'karat*). This is a third-person, feminine, singular verb in the future tense that means, "and she will call" or "and she will name," meaning the mother of the boy will name her child Immanuel.

The difficulty that this feminine, singular pronoun "*she*" poses for the Church cannot be overstated. Throughout the entire corpus of the New Testament, Mary never calls

Jesus "Immanuel." In fact, we are told in the Book of Luke that the angel Gabriel specifically instructed Mary to name her son Jesus, not Immanuel.

> And the angel said to her, "Fear not, Mary: for you have found favor with God. ³¹And, behold, you will conceive in thy womb, and bring forth a son, and you shall call his name 'Jesus.'"
>
> (Luke 1:30-31)

Furthermore, there is not a single instance in the New Testament where anyone calls Jesus by the name, "Immanuel!" Matthew deflected this problem by altering the third-person pronoun, which we find in the original Hebrew text of Isaiah, from the singular to the plural, thereby masking the one who is to name the child.

In other words, instead of translating the verb וְקָרָאת correctly as, "and she will call," Matthew changes the meaning of the word to read "and they shall call." In so doing, Matthew disguises the mother's role in naming the child. While the text of the original Hebrew makes it clear that the mother was assigned the divine task to name her son Immanuel, Matthew has the third-person, plural pronoun "*they*" replace "*she*." Who are Matthew's "they" who are to name Jesus "Immanuel"? "They" do not exist. Yet by altering the original pronoun, Matthew shifted this task away from Mary and assigned it to an anonymous group. Look it up for yourself!

For the most part, Christian Bibles do not support Matthew's mistranslation of this word in their rendering of Isaiah 7:14. Instead, almost all Christian Bibles translate וְקָרָאת as "she will call" in Isaiah 7:14.

No Christian translator in history apparently possessed the temerity to correct the first Gospel's mistranslation in Matthew 1:23.

The significance of the name 'Immanuel'

Why do the Hebrew Scriptures place such a strong emphasis on the names of Isaiah's children? For example, why does Isaiah record that his son, Shar-Yashuv, accompanied him to the washer's field to relay to King Ahaz the prophecy of deliverance? (7:3) After all, this child is not mentioned in any other place in the Bible. The Talmud teaches us that there are no extra words in Tanach. What role did he play in the Syro-Ephraimite War?

In Isaiah 7:14, the wife of the prophet is told that she will name her unborn son "Immanuel." Given the strength of the definite article in Isaiah 7:14, it is likely that

Isaiah pointed to his wife, who was present at the scene of the prophet's encounter with Ahaz to receive her instructions. Why was she given this Divine mandate? What is the significance of her child's name?

In the following chapter, Isaiah's wife gives birth to the promised child. Isaiah is commanded to call the boy "Maher-shalal-hash-baz," which means "Hasten the loot — quicken the booty." (8:2-3) Maher-shalal-hash-baz is a redundant name, because *Maher-shalal* and *hash-baz* mean essentially the same thing. The double name signifies the destruction of the two armies that attacked Ahaz, Syria and Samaria, led by Kings Retsin and Pekah, respectively (8:4). In other words, the mother is required to call her son Immanuel, and the father, Isaiah, is commanded to name his child Maher-shalal-hash-baz.

The naming of a child is ordinarily a profound spiritual moment. According to Jewish tradition, the naming of a baby is a statement of the child's special character and path in life: "For at the beginning of life we give a name, and at the end of life a 'good name' is all we take with us" (Talmud - Brachot 7b). The naming of a prophet's child, however, conveys a national portent. It is a sign that is significant for the Jewish people. Isaiah expresses this principle in the same chapter,

> "Behold, I and the children whom the Lord hath given me shall be for signs and for wonders in Israel from the Lord of hosts, who dwells in Mount Zion."
>
> (Isaiah 8:18)

Isaiah's Hebrew name יְשַׁעְיָהוּ (*Yishayahu*) means "The salvation of God." The Almighty gave the prophet a mandate to convey his visions of deliverance regarding Jerusalem, the capital of the Kingdom of Judah (Isaiah 1:1). The names of both of his children also were signs and portents for the Jewish people. Shar-yashiv, the name of the prophet's elder son, literally means, "the remnant will remain." This child's name conveys the promise that the Southern Kingdom of Judah will be preserved. Isaiah's wife is to name her second child Immanuel, which means, "God is with us." Like his elder brother, Immanuel's name signifies that God will stand guard over the Kingdom of Judah. Isaiah is commanded to name that same child Maher-shalal-hash-baz, which describes the destruction that will befall both of the enemies of the Southern Kingdom of Judah. In essence, the names of Isaiah's family are all portents that signify that God will shelter, protect and save the Southern Kingdom of Judah. In contrast, Isaiah's contemporary, Hosea, a prophet who primarily preached to the Northern Kingdom, was given children whose names made them like walking prophecies of doom—predicting the fall of the 10 northern tribes and their severed covenant with God. The name of Hosea's daughter, "Lo-ruhamah," which translates as "not pitied," was also chosen by God, but as a sign of His displeasure with the people of Israel for following other gods. (In Hosea 2:23 she is redeemed, shown "mercy" with the term *Ruhamah*.). The name of Hosea's son, "Lo-ammi," which translates as "not my people," is also chosen by God as a sign of the Almighty's displeasure with the people of Israel for following other gods (see Hosea 1:8-9). Unlike Isaiah's wife, who was a prophet of God, Hosea's wife was a faithless prostitute, a seamy portrait of the Northern Kingdom which was unfaithful to the God of Israel.

In short, God instructed prophets to give their children unusual names, which served as signs to the nation to whom they preached. When Matthew changed the meaning of the word וְקָרָאת from "she shall call" to "they shall call," he tampered with the instruction that God gave to His prophetess, the wife of Isaiah, not Mary.

Would a natural conception be called a 'sign'?

Missionaries frequently argue that the ordinary conception of a child by a mother and father does not fit the description of the "sign" in Isaiah 7:14. After all, they ask, what sort of sign is the natural conception of a boy to healthy parents? A miraculous conception to a virgin, untouched by a man, is truly a sign, they contend. Is this argument valid? Does a sign in the Bible indicate a supernatural event: a perceptible interruption of the laws of nature? Not at all. A "sign," however, is always something that can be seen. How can a virgin birth be seen?

To be sure, there is nothing miraculous about a rainbow; it is simply an optical and meteorological phenomenon that causes a spectrum of light to appear in the sky when the sun shines onto droplets of moisture in the earth's atmosphere. Yet the rainbow after Noah's flood gained meaning in the Torah as the first "sign" of God's promise that terrestrial life would never again be destroyed by flood (Genesis 9:13—17). There is certainly nothing miraculous about circumcision, yet this is the sign of the covenant between Abraham and God in Genesis 17:11.

A sign is not necessarily miraculous. It is, however, *always* something that can be witnessed. A virgin conception fails this test because it cannot be seen. By definition, therefore, a virgin birth can never be a sign.

In fact, the sign in the seventh chapter of Isaiah is not the birth of the child, but rather his maturity. The verses that follow the famed passage (7:15-16) state that, by the time this child (whose imminent birth was foretold in Isaiah 7:14) reaches the age of maturity ("…he knows to reject bad and choose good…"), the kings of the two enemy nations will be vanquished. Thus, the child's lack of maturity is the sign from God, not his conception or birth. The sign means that two armies seeking to destroy the Kingdom of Judah will be destroyed before the boy can distinguish good from evil.

This message is repeated again in Isaiah 8:4, where the Almighty promises Isaiah: "For, when the lad does not yet know to call 'father' and 'mother,' the wealth of Damascus and the plunder of Samaria shall be carried off...." Often a little boy can call his parents "daddy" and "mommy" by the time he is a year old. This prophecy of the destruction of both Syria and Ephraim, was therefore set to be fulfilled imminently, not 700 years later. In fact, neither the Kingdom of Syria nor the Northern Kingdom of Israel even existed during the lifetime of Jesus!

Missionaries defend Matthew by citing the Septuagint

Christian apologists frequently defend Matthew's translation of the Hebrew word עַלְמָה as "virgin" by citing the Septuagint version of Isaiah. They argue that the Septuagint, a Greek translation of the Hebrew Scriptures rendered by Jewish scholars approximately 2,200 years ago, employed the Greek word for "virgin," παρθενος ("*parthenos*") in Isaiah 7:14. They conclude, therefore, that the original text must have been understood to mean "virgin," and Matthew, who was writing in Greek about the virgin birth of Jesus, was quoting the passage from the Septuagint rather than the Hebrew text.

This is one of those explanations that sounds plausible until you dig a bit and think a bit more. It is an argument that is erroneous and misleading. The original Septuagint was a Greek translation of only the Torah (the *Five Books of Moses*), nothing else. Therefore, the Book of Isaiah was not even part of the Septuagint translated by learned Jews thousands of years ago, as missionaries routinely claim. Rather, this book of Tanach is a part of the Prophets, the second section of Jewish Scriptures, and was forged by the Church many centuries later.

It is universally accepted by all scholars—both Jewish and Christian—that the original Septuagint, or "Proto-Septuagint," was a translation only of the *Five Books of Moses*.[6] The Letter of Aristeas, the earliest attestation to the Septuagint, dating back to the second century BCE, affirms that the Septuagint was a translation by Jews only of Genesis, Exodus, Leviticus, Numbers, and Deuteronomy. The first century Roman historian, Josephus Flavius, similarly states that under Ptolemy Philadelphus, only the Law was translated,[7] and the same is stated in the Talmud.[8] (See page 63 for other attestations.)

In a section below, I illustrate that the Septuagint which is presently in our hands—including the Pentateuch—is almost entirely a Christian work. (See Volume 2, page 51, entitled '*A Christian Defends Matthew, author of the first Gospel, by Insisting that He Used the Septuagint in His Quote of Isaiah to Support the Virgin Birth*')

Moreover, in his preface to the Book of Chronicles, the Church father, Jerome,[9] who was the primary translator of the Vulgate, concedes that in his day, there were at least three variant Greek translations of the Bible:

- The edition of the third century Christian theologian, Origen
- The Egyptian recension of Hesychius
- The Syrian recension of Lucian.

Thus there were numerous Greek renditions of the Jewish Scriptures, and each of them were revised and edited by non-Jews. All Septuagints in our hands are derived from the revisions of Hesychius, as well as the Christian theologians, Origen and Lucian. The Septuagint published in our day was tailor-made by the Church in order to produce an "Old Testament" that was consistent with Christian teachings. As a result, the Jewish people never use the Septuagint in their worship or religious studies, because it is recognized as a thoroughly corrupt text.

While the Septuagint in our hands is a product of the Church, a fundamental question must be asked of Christian apologists: Why would God quote from a Greek translation of the Bible? No fundamentalist Christian believes that the Book of Matthew was a human creation. Missionaries insist that the first Gospel was divinely inspired—Heaven-breathed. "Matthew was nothing more than a glorified secretary," a pastor once quipped to me. The Church insists that the Holy Ghost dictated to Matthew every word that the evangelist penned. This claim therefore raises a monumental question: Why did the Holy Spirit require a Septuagint? Did the third Person of the Trinity really need to consult a Greek translation of the Jewish Scriptures in order to understand a Hebrew passage? The claim that the Book of Matthew was divinely inspired, yet the Holy Ghost had to look up a translation of the Bible is preposterous.

Did the Holy Spirit forget how to read Biblical Hebrew?

Finally, the Greek word παρθενος *(parthenos)* does not necessarily mean "virgin." In fact, the Septuagint uses this same word in Genesis 34:2-4 in reference to Dinah after she was raped. How then could Dinah be described as a virgin?

Missionaries question the meaning of the word בְּתוּלָה

Missionaries are frequently confronted with the following glaring question: If Isaiah meant to prophesy of the miraculous conception of a woman who had never been touched by a man, why didn't the prophet employ the common Hebrew word בְּתוּלָה (*betulah*), which is the only word—in both biblical and modern Hebrew —that clearly encapsulates the clear and certain meaning of virginity? After all, Isaiah used the word *betulah* in numerous other places in his book,[10] and בְּתוּלָה appears more than 100 times throughout the Jewish Scriptures (*alma* or the masculine *elem* appear only nine times in Tanach). Why didn't the prophet employ the word *betulah* instead of *almah* to predict a supernatural, virgin birth?

An unexpected Christian reaction to this question has emerged in recent years, which employs a scorched-earth approach to respond to this perennial conundrum that has vexed the Church since the publication of the first Gospel. In order to defend the integrity of the Book of Matthew, some evangelicals attempt to blur the definition of the common Hebrew word *betulah* by questioning its meaning. They argue that the meaning of *betulah* is not necessarily clear because in one instance in the Hebrew Scriptures this word is used where the passage could not have possibly been speaking about a virgin. Missionaries cite the following passage where Joel bemoans,

> Lament like a **virgin** (כִּבְתוּלָה — *k'vesulah*) girded with sackcloth for the **husband** of her youth.
>
> (Joel 1:8)

Pointing to this verse, some Christian apologists insist that since the virgin mentioned in this passage has a husband, this proves that the word *betulah* doesn't necessarily mean a virgin. After all, missionaries contend, a betrothed woman cannot be a virgin. Strangely, Christians who make this claim believe that Mary did not lose *her* virginity, in spite of the fact that she was betrothed to Joseph.

Is there, then, a married virgin in the Jewish Scriptures? The Book of Joel opens with the prophet calling upon his nation—both young and old—to listen carefully as he describes a devastating vision of their imminent exile. Joel uses a series of powerful metaphors to describe a people who possessed great potential, yet lost innumerable blessings. Joel sees the massive locust plague (1:4) and a fierce lion (1:6) as a picture of the mighty enemies of the Jewish people who ravage their land and set in motion their bitter exile. To further illustrate the depth of the catastrophic consequences of Israel's sin, Joel draws our attention to the devastating picture of a woman betrothed to a man, yet, tragically, never consummated her relationship with him. Whereas in our modern day, such a calamity would be unlikely, in ancient days, after a couple was married before witnesses, the husband would leave his bride for a time without having consummated their marriage in order to build a home and prepare for a life and family together. A year later, the couple would leave their parents' home to live together.

Imagine if during that time the man died, what the anguish would be of a virgin who buried her husband, never having experienced their marital love. A field unharvested, a wine untasted, a wife unloved—these are the bitter metaphors of the consequences that Joel's nation endured because it turned its back on its Creator.

Confronted with this crisis, Joel calls on the masses—old and young (1:2-3), drunkards (1:5), farmers (1:11), and priests (1:13)—to return to God. Restoration and blessing will come, Joel promises, following repentance.

This argument that seeks to diffuse the meaning of the word *betulah* was not well thought out. Christian apologists who make the assertion that the Hebrew word *betulah* does not necessarily mean "virgin" deliberately ignore the fact that every Christian Bible—in all languages—translates בְּתוּלָה in Joel 1:8 as a "virgin."

Did Matthew employ a '*midrashic*' method?

Missionaries often employ a novel and rather surprising response when confronted by Matthew's ill-conceived rendition of Isaiah 7:14.

While reluctantly agreeing that Matthew's translation of Isaiah is not entirely accurate, and readily conceding that the context of the seventh chapter of Isaiah doesn't seem to support any future miraculous birth of the messiah, Christian apologists suggest that Matthew may have utilized some *midrashic* expository techniques that might have allowed for some flexibility.

After all, they ask, did not the rabbis engage in a homiletic method of biblical exegesis? Are there not interpretations of Scripture that are inconsistent with the literal meaning of a passage ensconced in rabbinic traditions and literature? Matthew, they argue, applied this same *midrashic* method in his interpretation of Isaiah 7:14, as well as other texts in the Jewish Scriptures.

There are numerous problems with this response that render it untenable. To begin with, the missionaries who engage in Jewish evangelism are ardent Protestants who utterly reject the notion that there can be any legitimate tradition outside of the literal interpretation of Scripture.

Although the missionary groups that target Jews for conversion generally avoid identifying themselves formally with the Protestant movement, in virtually all cases they completely embrace the fundamental creeds of the Reformation. As such, they fully espouse the Reformation's doctrine of *Sola Scriptura* (*Lat.* "by Scripture alone"), which holds that the Bible alone contains all information necessary for salvation. As a consequence, this doctrine demands that the only teachings that are to be confessed are found directly and literally within Scripture. This principle was a foundational doctrinal principle of the Protestant Reformation. It was also an utter rejection of the Catholic Church's teaching that Church tradition is equal to Scripture, and the notion that Scriptures are not the only infallible source of Christian doctrine.

As mentioned, the missionaries who are committed to converting the Jewish people to Christianity tenaciously hold to the doctrine of *Sola Scriptura*. Therefore, they cannot seek refuge in some sort of elastic, *"midrashic"* method of interpretation to shelter Matthew from criticism over the reckless manner in which he misquoted passages from the Hebrew Bible.

Christian apologists are vehement opponents of the authority of the Oral Law and rabbinic traditions precisely because they hold to the doctrine of *Sola Scriptura*. How, then, can these apologists possibly appeal to rabbinic *midrashic* interpretation to explain away Matthew's stunning misquotes of the Jewish Scriptures?

Moreover, if Christian apologists give Matthew *midrashic* license to misquote Isaiah, how can they discredit any innovation in the Church that is not founded on the literal meaning of the Bible? Every heresy of Christianity can then claim that it is employing a *midrashic* interpretation of the Christian Bible. On what basis can any modernization and contrivance of the Church be rejected?

Finally, and most importantly, this argument that Matthew employed *midrashic* expository techniques when quoting the Tanach completely shatters the central claim of the Church against its elder rival, Judaism.

Christendom insists, and its missionaries loudly proclaim, that the Hebrew Scriptures demonstrate that Jesus was the promised messiah. "Jesus is literally and clearly prophesied in every book of the Old Testament," they argue. "Don't be afraid! Pick up your Bible and read the Book of Isaiah for yourself!" they insist. Each year, missionary groups spend millions of dollars, and commit untold resources worldwide in order to bring their message to the Jewish people. They proclaim that it was clearly and undeniably foretold throughout the passages of Tanach that Jesus fulfilled hundreds of messianic prophecies openly outlined in the Jewish Scriptures.

Yet, what do we find when we open our Bible and explore these sacred texts that missionaries cite to prove that Jesus is the messiah? We discover that the authors of the New Testament egregiously misquoted the Jewish Scriptures, and deliberately mistranslated passages that were completely ripped out of context! Although convenient interpretations of Scripture were fashioned by the Church, it cannot expect us to permit these crafted traditions to adjudicate the Eternal Truths of God. Tanach is our authority, not the traditions spawned by Matthew and Paul.

Why did the Church adopt the belief in the virgin birth?

The author of the Book of Matthew clearly went to great lengths to rewrite Isaiah 7:14 so that this passage would appear to be foretelling Jesus' virgin birth. Although these methods were crude, they were deliberate and thought out.

This raises an important question: What prompted the authors of Matthew and Luke to promote the creed that Mary was untouched by a man when Jesus was conceived? Why did the Church adopt the doctrine of the virgin birth as the first century was coming to a close? While the notion of a savior born to a virgin was endemic in the pagan world, the idea is completely alien to the Jewish mind.

Moreover, the Torah clearly states that *the father alone* conveys the tribal identity to his son, never the mother.[11] Accordingly, the New Testament's claim that Jesus was born of a virgin completely disqualifies him from being the messiah and sitting on the royal throne of David. Ironically, the opening chapter of the New Testament undermined the Church's most central creed.

What changes were rapidly unfolding in the early Church that provoked the authors of Matthew and Luke to claim that Jesus was conceived in the womb of a virgin if this assertion disqualified Jesus from being the messiah? Furthermore, why is the notion that Jesus was born of a virgin mentioned only in the Gospels of Matthew and Luke, which are chronologically among the last books to be written in the New Testament? Why wasn't Paul or Mark aware of this central tenet?

Did they just forget to mention it?

As we have seen, the notion that Jesus was born to a virgin is a later Christian invention and is therefore not found anywhere in the epistles of Paul or the Gospel of Mark, which are the earliest writings in the New Testament. The Books of Matthew and Luke (85 CE) were written about 35 years after Paul's first letters (I Thessalonians, 50 CE). This raises two important questions: Why did the Christian movement introduce the belief in Jesus' miraculous birth if Jews never anticipated a messiah born to a virgin? Moreover, why did it take so long for the Church to adopt doctrine which was so alien to Jewish thought?

To understand why the belief in Jesus' virgin birth arose in Christian teachings only toward the end of the first century, it is important to grasp that although the Church initially vigorously sought to lure Jews into its new fold, it was largely an unsuccessful endeavor.

The zealous effort of Jesus' followers to sway the Jewish mind deteriorated rapidly. The plan failed. On the other hand, the young Church was enjoying rapid growth among spiritually-disgruntled gentiles in Asia Minor, Mediterranean countries in Europe, North Africa, Syria, and as far east as India. It was clear to the proponents of Christianity that if the new, Jesus-centered religion was to appeal to the masses, their emerging religion would have to appeal to gentiles, not the Jews. The message of the Church had to be expressed in language that made sense to pagans. While the notion of a god/man savior born of a virgin was completely foreign and bizarre to the Jewish world, it was appealing and commonplace in the pagan world. The belief in the ancient pagan world that great men were born of a mortal virgin and divine fathers was widespread. For example, Alexander the Great was believed to be the son of the Greek god, Zeus, and a virgin. Rome's founder, Romulus, was also said to be the son of the god, Mars, and a mortal virgin. Augustus, Rome's first emperor, was thought to have been born from a miraculous conception by the divine and human conjunction of the god, Apollo, and his mother, Atia.

This belief dominated the landscape of Eastern religions as well. The Hindu deity, Krishna, was said to have been conceived when the divine spirit of Vishnu descended into the womb of Devaki and was born as her son, Vasudeva (i.e., Krishna). We are told that the "Supreme Buddha" was born of his virgin mother, Maya. The Persian prophet, Zoroaster, the Egyptian deity, Horus, the Persian god, Mithra, the Greco-Roman deities, Perseus, Apollo, Dionysus, Persephone, Hercules, Pan, Ion, Asclephius, and Helen were all widely believed to have been conceived of a revered, pure, virgin mother. It was claimed the Greek deity, Adonis, was born of the virgin, Myrrha, centuries before Jesus. He was said to have been born "at Bethlehem, in the same cave that Christians later claimed as the birthplace of Jesus."[12]

While Judaism teaches that conceiving a child in a marriage is a sacred act in which God Himself is a partner, the pervasive, driving theology that satisfied the dualistic pagan thought was one of complete separation between the physical and spiritual. The sacred and sexuality were completely incompatible to the mind of much of the ancient world. It was therefore inconceivable to the pagan psyche that saviors and deities could enter this world through the carnal relationship between a man and a woman. The pagan masses craved a savior who was miraculously conceived by an undefiled woman, untouched by a mortal man.

Following the destruction of the Second Temple and the annihilation of Jerusalem's Jewish life by the Roman legions of Titus and Vespasian in the year 70 CE, the Church adopted the myth of the virgin birth, which was enormously popular in the pagan world. It was a highly successful attempt to appeal to the new target audience of gentiles. These largely illiterate, yet spiritually hungry people were abandoning paganism and Gnosticism, in which they had been reared since childhood. With few exceptions, these religions were filled with legends of various deities who were born to virgin mothers.

By the 90's, the belief in Jesus' miraculous conception was well established and widespread throughout the Roman Empire and beyond. It had emerged as full-blown Christian orthodoxy. By the second century, those who questioned Jesus' virgin birth were regarded as heretics.

The Egyptian virgin Isis holding her son, the god Horus (left), and the Virgin Mary holding her divine son, Jesus (right). Both Isis and Mary were hailed as the "Queen of Heaven" and "Mother of God."

The authors of the later books of Matthew and Luke accordingly incorporated this prevalent belief into their Gospels. As mentioned above, prior to the destruction of Jerusalem, not a single New Testament author had adopted this persistent feature found in other religions.

In the traumatic centuries that followed the birth of Christianity, the Church incorporated many other pagan ideas into its teachings, including belief in the triune nature of God, which was firmly established by the Church as an orthodox doctrine by the fourth century.

By the third century, the Church had adopted the celebration of Christmas on December 25th from the Roman Empire, which had assigned that date to honor the winter solstice. After all, December 25th was the date on the ancient calendar that marked the first detectable lengthening of daylight hours. The citizens of Rome joyfully commemorated this holiday with wild festivities.

Until this day, the most identifiable Christmas adornment is the Christmas tree. This ancient, well-known pagan practice is expressly condemned in the Hebrew Scriptures (see Jeremiah 10:1-5). As late as the year 1800, some devout Christian sects, like the Puritans, forbade their members from celebrating Christmas, because they recognized its pagan origins.

Today, Christian scholars universally concede that Jesus' birth did not occur on December 25th. They are uncomfortably aware that the Church borrowed this date from ancient pagan winter festivals. Although Christmas is the most popular holiday on the Christian calendar, all Christian scholars acknowledge that Christmas was initially selected to correspond with the Roman solar holiday *Dies Natalis Solis Invicti*, the birthday of the "Unconquered Sun." The Unconquered Sun was a Roman god in the later Roman empire who, with Sol, was accompanied with the epithet "*invictus*," meaning "unconquered," that was commonly assigned to Sol. Sol Invictus originated from the god Mithras, a Persian deity, said to be born of a virgin,[13] and was introduced to Rome from the Alexandrian Empire. Many parishioners are unaware that the origins of Christmas were pagan and were celebrated in Europe long before the Jesus movement emerged. Modern Christmas customs—all borrowed from the pagan world—include gift-giving and merrymaking from Roman Saturnalia; greenery and lights from the Roman New Year; and Yule logs and various foods from Germanic feasts.[14]

Mistletoe, which is commonly used as a Christmas decoration and figured prominently in Greek mythology, is borrowed from an ancient Druid custom at the winter solstice. Mistletoe was widely considered a divine plant that symbolized love and peace. The tradition of kissing under the mistletoe is also of Druid origin.

Pagan Scandinavians celebrated a winter festival called "Yule," held in the late December until the early January period. As Northern Europe was the last part of the continent to adopt the Christian religion, its pagan traditions had a major influence on Christmas. Scandinavians still call Christmas "*Jul*." In English, the word Yule is synonymous with Christmas,[15] a usage first recorded in 900.

During the past two millennia, Christendom emerged as the repository of pagan dogmas, rites, and rituals. With almost no hesitation, the Church increasingly adopted popular pagan rituals and beliefs that were opposed by the prophets of Israel. The idea that a god/man was conceived by a virgin was the most widespread among these pagan beliefs.

In essence, Rome did not convert to Christianity; Christianity converted to Rome.

Footnotes:

1. The Christian doctrine of the virgin birth of Jesus (i.e., Mary's virginal conception of Jesus) is not to be confused with the Roman Catholic doctrine of the Immaculate Conception, which concerns Mary's mother's conception of Mary. This is thought to have occurred in the normal way, not miraculously. The Roman Catholic doctrine of the Immaculate Conception holds that when Mary herself was conceived, she came into existence without the "stain" (Latin, *macula*) of original sin. In general, missionaries who engage in Jewish evangelism are Protestants, and therefore reject this doctrine.

2. Like Matthew, Luke (*c.* 85-90 CE) includes a virgin birth narrative; however, he does not quote Tanach to support this claim, and the details of the two accounts vary greatly. For example, according to Matthew, Joseph and Mary were in Bethlehem when Jesus was born (2:1) and moved first to Egypt, to avoid the wrath of Herod the Great (2:13-14), then later to Nazareth, in order to avoid living under Herod's son Archelaus (2:22). According to Luke, however, the couple first lived in Nazareth and only then traveled to Bethlehem, in order to comply with a Roman census (2:4).

3. Numerous Christian translators do not support Matthew's misquote of Isaiah 7:14 and correctly translate *almah* as "young woman" in Isaiah 7:14. These Christian translators include:

    - Revised Standard Version
    - New English Bible
    - Revised English Bible
    - New Revised Standard Version
    - The Message of the Bible
    - The Layman's Bible Commentary
    - The Bible: A New Translation
    - The Bible: An American Translation
    - The New Jerusalem Bible (Catholic)
    - International Critical Commentary
    - Good News Bible
    - World Biblical Commentary
    - The Bible in Basic English

    See page 62.

4. Although the original Septuagint, which is no longer extant, was a Greek translation of the *Five Books of Moses*, rendered by Jewish hands more than 2,000 years ago, all versions of the Septuagint published today are a product of the Church (see page 49 and Volume 2, page 51).

5. I Samuel 17:56 and 20:22

6. The dating of 732 BCE for the Syro-Ephraimite War is based on Herodotus' expanded estimate of the length of the Persian Empire. According to all Jewish sources, including the *Tanaic* work *Seder Olam Rabbah* (meaning "The Long Order of the World") and numerous records in the Talmud, the Syro-Ephraimite War occurred in the year 563 BCE.

    While it is beyond the scope of this book to present a detailed explanation of the various ancient chronologies, I will briefly explain the dating systems used by Jewish and modern historians.

    As mentioned above, the Jewish dating system is taken primarily from a book called *Seder Olam Rabbah*, dating back to the second century CE, and attributed to Rabbi Yosef ben Halafta. The sources for the dates in this book come from records contained in the Talmud, as well as from numerous chronologies recorded in the Bible (most notably, Daniel 11:2, because this passage relates directly to the length of the Persian Empire).

Bear in mind that traditional Jewish chronologies (since the beginning of the Jewish calendar almost 6,000 years ago), have always been based on absolute and highly accurate astronomical phenomena: the movement of the moon around the Earth (months) and that of the Earth around the sun (years). A combination of an unbroken tradition of the Bible and a precise astronomical, time-based system gives traditional Jewish chronology a high degree of accuracy, especially when it comes to the major events of Jewish history.

Contrary to what one might think, the chronology used by modern historians is far from exact. It was not until the twentieth century that the entire world recognized a universal calendar system—the Christian calendar (also known as the Gregorian calendar).

If we go back in time, however, the calendar situation was far more chaotic. Accurate historical records were almost unheard of, and every empire used its own calendar system which was often based on totally different criteria. With no unbroken historical tradition and no universally accepted standard for how to calculate time, there is no non-Jewish equivalent to *Seder Olam Rabbah*, nor to the Jewish calendrical calculation system passed down from antiquity.

So how do we get the chronology that historians generally use today?

Historians in the late nineteenth and early twentieth centuries worked backwards and pieced it together.

The assertions of the controversial Greek historian, Herodotus (who has been called "The Father of History" by Cicero, and "The Father of Lies" by the historian/philosopher, Xenophon, student of Socrates) and data from records of ancient Rome, Greece, Mesopotamia, and Egypt (including chronicles of major events such as battles between empires) were combined with archaeological finds and major astronomical phenomena such as solar eclipses, and dates were then calculated by applying various scientific dating methods.

7.   See page 63

8. Tractate Megillah 9a

9. Jerome repeats this statement in his *Apology Against Rufinus* ii, 27 (Migne, P.L. 23, 471).

10. Isaiah 23:12, 37:22, 47:1, 62:5

11. Numbers 1:18

12. B.B. Walker, *The Woman's Encyclopedia of Myths and Secrets*, Harper & Row, (1983), p. 10.

13. *The Catholic Encyclopedia*: Mithraism; S.E. Hijmans, "*Sol, the sun in the art and religions of Rome,*" 2009, pp. 587—588. See also S.E. Hijmans, *"The sun that did not rise in the east,"* Babesch 71 (1996) p.115—150.

14. Coffman, Elesha. "*Why December 25?*" *Christian History & Biography, Christianity Today*, 2000.

15. "Yule." *The American Heritage Dictionary of the English Language, Fourth Edition*. Retrieved December 3, 2006.

The Christian translators below reject Matthew's mistranslation of Isaiah 7:14 and accordingly render the Hebrew word עַלְמָה (*almah*) as a "young woman"

Revised Standard Version Therefore the Lord himself will give you a sign. Behold, a **young woman** shall conceive and bear a son, and shall call his name Immanuel.	**New English Bible** Therefore the Lord himself shall give you a sign: A **young woman** is with child, and she will bear a son, and will call him Immanuel.
Revised English Bible ...because you do, the Lord of his own accord will give you a sign; it is this: A **young woman** is with child, and she will give birth to a son and call him Immanuel.	**New Revised Standard Version** Therefore the Lord himself will give you a sign. Look, the **young woman** is with child and shall bear a son, and shall name him Immanuel.
The Message of the Bible He will give you a sign. A **young woman** shall bear a son who shall truly represent the hopes we have inherited from the days of David. His very name, "God-is-with-us," shall express the secret of his power.	**The Layman's Bible Commentary** In reply, Isaiah says that the Lord will provide a sign. It will be a most unusual and remarkable event. A **young woman** shall bear a son and name him "Immanuel," meaning "God is with us."
The Bible: A New Translation An omen you shall have, and that from the Eternal himself. There is a **young woman** with child, who shall bear a son and call his name "Immanuel" (God is with us);	**The Bible: An American Translation** Therefore the Lord himself will give you a sign: Behold! A **young woman** is with child, and is about to bear a son; and she will call him "God is with us."
The New Jerusalem Bible The Lord will give you a sign in any case: It is this: The **young woman** is with child and will give birth to a son whom she will call Immanuel.	**International Critical Commentary** Therefore the Lord himself will give you a sign. Behold, a **damsel** is with child, and shall bring forth a son, and call his name Immanuel.
Good News Bible Well then, the Lord himself will give you a sign: A **young woman** who is pregnant will have a son and will name him "Immanuel."	**World Biblical Commentary** Therefore my Lord himself will give you (pl) a sign. Behold, the **woman** shall conceive and bearing a son — she shall call his name "Immanuel."
The Bible in Basic English For this cause the Lord himself will give you a sign; a **young woman** is now with child, and she will give birth to a son, and she will give him the name Immanuel.	

Did the Word 'Virgin' Appear in the Original Septuagint?

The Oxford Companion to the Bible discusses the definition of the Hebrew word *alma*, the Septuagint's use of the Greek word *parthenos*, and rejects Matthew's application of Isaiah 7:14 to the virgin birth.

Isaiah's intent in discussing this child is clearly to set a time frame for the destruction of Israel. There is nothing miraculous about the mother or the conception process. The Hebrew word used, *almâ*, means simply "young woman," without any implication of virginity. The Greek word *parthenos* used to translate *alma* can mean either a young woman or a virgin. Matthew used a Greek Bible, so he naturally reinterpreted Isaiah 7:14 as a prophecy referring to the virgin birth of Jesus. For the evangelist, Isaiah's original meaning was superseded by the identification of Jesus as Immanuel (Grk. *Emmanouēl*).

Daniel N. Schowalter, *The Oxford Companion To The Bible.* Excerpt from "Virgin Birth of Christ," New York: Oxford University Press, 1993, pg. 790.

An example of the word παρθένος (*parthenos*) in the Septuagint where it is clearly not referring to a virgin

Genesis 34:2-4 (King James Version)
And when Shechem the son of Hamor the Hivite, prince of the country, saw her, he took her, and lay with her, and defiled her. ³And his soul clave unto Dinah the daughter of Jacob, and he loved the *damsel* (Septuagint: παρθένου) and spake kindly unto the *damsel* (Septuagint: παρθένου). ⁴And Shechem spake unto his father Hamor, saying, Get me this damsel to wife.

The Anchor Bible Dictionary on the 'Original' Septuagint

The word "Septuagint," (from Lat *septuaginta* = 70; hence the abbreviation LXX) derives from a story that 72 elders translated the Pentateuch into Greek; the term therefore applied originally only to those five books.

The Anchor Bible Dictionary. Excerpt from "Septuagint," New York. Vol. V, page 1093.

Josephus attests that the Jewish interpreters of the Septuagint translated the Law [Of Moses] alone

I found, therefore, that the second of the Ptolemies was a king who was extraordinarily diligent in what concerned learning and the collection of books; that he was also peculiarly ambitious to procure a translation of our law...into the Greek tongue...for he did not obtain all our writings at that time; but those who were sent to Alexandria as interpreters gave him only the books of the law, while there were a vast number of other matters in our sacred books.[1]

[1] Josephus, *Preface to Antiquities.* For Josephus' detailed description of events surrounding the original authorship of the Septuagint, see Josephus, *Antiquities of the Jews*, XII, ii, 1-4.

Jerome: The original Septuagint was only a translation of the Five Books of Moses

Add to this that Josephus, who gives the story of the Seventy Translators, reports them as translating only the five books of Moses; and we also acknowledge that these are more in harmony with the Hebrew than the rest.

St. Jerome, *Preface to the Book of Hebrew Questions*, Nicene and Post-Nicene Fathers, Volume 6. Pg. 487. Hendrickson.

The following related articles can be found in Volume 2 of *Let's Get Biblical! Why doesn't Judaism Accept the Christian Messiah?*

I.   A Lutheran Doesn't Understand Why
Rabbi Singer Doesn't Believe in Jesus:
A Closer Look at the 'Crucifixion Psalm'..... Page 17

II.   Does the Hebrew Word *Alma* Really
Mean 'Virgin'?......................... Page 33

III.   Dual Prophecy and the 'Virgin Birth'........ Page 39

IV.   How Do Missionaries Paint the Virgin
Birth into the Mouth of Rashi?.............. Page 47

V.   A Christian Defends Matthew by Insisting
That the Author of the First Gospel Used
the Septuagint in His Quote of Isaiah to
Support the Virgin Birth................... Page 51

Part III

Sin and Atonement

All You Need is Blood?

Christians are surprised to discover their church's cornerstone creed, "without the shedding of blood there is no atonement," which famously appears in Hebrews 9:22, is not found anywhere in the Jewish Scriptures. Although the footnote for Hebrews 9:22 in every annotated Christian Bible references Leviticus 17:11 as the source and authority for this doctrine, this idea is unbiblical and denounced by the Jewish prophets.

Leviticus 17:10-11	Hebrews 9:22
If any person, whether of the family of Israel or a proselyte who joins them, eats any blood, I will direct My anger against the person who eats blood and cut him off from his people. ¹¹**This is because** the life force of the flesh is in the blood; and I gave it to you to be placed on the altar to atone for your lives. **It is the blood that atones for a life** (כִּי־הַדָּם הוּא בַּנֶּפֶשׁ יְכַפֵּר).	And almost all things are by the law purged with blood; **and without the shedding of blood there is no atonement.**

The author of the Book of Hebrews manipulated and misquoted Leviticus 17:11 completely out of context in order to bolster the cardinal Christian doctrine that there can be no remission of sin without the shedding of blood. Why did the author of the epistle tamper with this passage in the Torah? Because if it were widely understood that God will forgive sins without a blood sacrifice, the Church would have little to offer its parishioners.

To be sure, the Church would be hard-pressed to point to a single incident in the Hebrew Scriptures in which a sacrifice atoned for an egregious sinner. The same, however, cannot be said of the manifold forgiveness granted to sinners following repentance and prayer, which occurs frequently in Tanach.

For example, the numerous sins of the inhabitants of Nineveh were forgiven as a result of their repentance alone (Jonah 3:10), King David was forgiven for his sin with Batsheva with only his heartfelt confession before the prophet, Nathan (II Samuel 12:13). Furthermore, even if one committed an unintentional sin, for which the sin sacrifice was the prescribed atonement, human sacrifices were never permitted. On the contrary, this odious, pagan ritual was practiced by Israel's neighbors, and was harshly condemned as an abomination by the God of Israel.

Leviticus 17:11, the verse that was deliberately misquoted by the Book of Hebrews, does *not* suggest that a blood sacrifice must be offered to atone for sin. Without exception, missionaries who claim to be quoting Leviticus 17:11 are instead quoting Hebrews 9:22, which distorts the passage from Leviticus. Remarkably, Christians rarely compare these two passages side-by-side.

Even more surprising, parishioners are completely unaware of the context of Leviticus 17:11. This is perplexing, given that Leviticus 17:11 begins with the unambiguous conjunctive phrase, "This is because..." In any language, whenever a sentence begins with the words "This is because," it is *always* explaining the preceding statement. In the previous verse (Leviticus 17:10), the Torah states that it is forbidden to consume blood. Leviticus 17:11 explains the reason for this prohibition. Blood was set aside for only one purpose: to make an atonement on the altar for sin. The Torah prohibits the use of blood for any other function.

> **Sin Sacrifice (קָרְבָּן חַטָּאת)**
>
> People are often surprised when they discover that the Sin Sacrifice did not atone for most wrongdoings. Although the New Testament suggests that blood sacrifices atoned for just about any kind of sin (Heb. 9:22), in fact, this offering could only expiate man's least egregious sin: those iniquities that were committed unintentionally. Read the fourth chapter of the Book of Leviticus for yourself! This offering could not atone for the iniquity of the defiant sinner. Only heartfelt confession and repentance can cleanse the person who seeks forgiveness from God for sins which were committed deliberately.
>
> **Leviticus 4:1-2**
> The Lord said to Moses, "Speak to the children of Israel saying: If a person sins **accidently** in anything God commanded not to be done, and commits any of them..."
>
> **Numbers 15:24-31**
> If this is done **unintentionally without the community being aware of it**.... The priest is to make atonement for the whole Israelite community, and they will be forgiven, for it was not intentional.... **But anyone who sins defiantly**.... that person must surely be cut off; his guilt remains on him.

Leviticus 17:11 does *not* imply that the only method of atonement is the shedding of blood. This verse explains that when a sin sacrifice is offered, every ritual associated with the blood must be conducted properly, in order for the offering to be valid. (The four separate rituals of the עֲבוֹדַת הַדָם (*avodas hadam*), "the service of the blood," include: slaughtering an animal, collecting its blood, carrying the blood, and sprinkling the blood on the altar).

In other words, there are rituals associated with a sin sacrifice that are not related to blood. For example, the person who is offering the sacrifice must lean his hands on the animal before it is slaughtered. If this ritual is not carried out with the proper intentions, the offering is still valid. On the other hand, if elements connected to the blood ritual itself are not carried out properly, then the offering becomes invalid.

Few sinners, however, could avail themselves of the sin sacrifice for atonement, because this offering expiated only the *most minor* form of transgressions, those committed unintentionally (Leviticus 4).

Another sacrifice that was offered for sin included the guilt offerings (Leviticus 5). Through this unique offering—in a few specific cases—the Torah made an exception for the penitent who came forward to confess his transgression that he had committed either intentionally or unintentionally. Under these unique, clearly-defined circumstances outlined in the Torah, the sinner weakened the severity of his original act, and the guilt offering emerged as an acceptable form of atonement.

Furthermore, this offering did not necessarily require a blood sacrifice, because the poor were permitted to instead offer a vegan, grain offering as atonement, which, of course, involved no blood. This offering not only attests to the greatness of confession, but also illustrates again that sacrifices can atone for sin only when the weight of the iniquity has been lessened, as in the case of the Guilt Offering through the noble act of confession.

Missionaries frequently point to the Yom Kippur sacrifice described in Leviticus 16:7-22, during which lots were cast on two goats by the High Priest. The first goat was designated "For God."

The second goat, which symbolically carried the sins of the people, was sent to an uninhabited area (16:22). In the second case, however, the goat that carried the sins of the Jewish people was not slaughtered on the altar. Rather, the Torah states, it was sent away "...to the wilderness, far from the camp of Israel."

The goat designated "For God," on the other hand, was only an atonement for "the Sanctuary" (16:16), not for the general sins of the nation. This meant that this unique, Yom Kippur sacrifice was not a substitute or vicarious sacrificial offering.

It was rather a *targeted*, contrite repentance only for those who had specifically defiled the Sanctuary while they were in a state of contamination.

Thus, if during the previous year a person had entered the Temple and offered a sacrifice of any kind while in a state of impurity, the appropriate repentance required that a sacrifice be brought on his or her behalf on Yom Kippur while he or she was in a state of purity. This offering was not a vicarious atonement. Accordingly, it did not expiate any sins committed outside the Temple.

For example, the sacrifice of the goat designated "For God" did not atone for those who violated the Sabbath or oppressed the stranger. It specifically expiated sins that violated the sanctity of the Temple (16:16). Repentance and the "affliction of one's soul" atoned for all other iniquities (16:30-31). Therefore, the Yom Kippur sacrifice described in Leviticus could not serve any purpose when the Temple is not standing.

Oddly, the New Testament identified Jesus with the Passover offering (1 Cor.5:7). *The Passover sacrifice is unrelated to sin or atonement.* Quite the contrary, the lamb was venerated and worshiped as a deity in Egypt. Thus, the Jews who sanctified the Almighty in defiance of the Egyptian authorities by slaughtering this Egyptian god publicly, demonstrated that they merited redemption.

According to Christian theology, however, this would have been an impossible achievement. For the Church claims that man, without an intercessor, is spiritually lost and utterly hopeless. In virtually all of his epistles, Paul vehemently denounced the principle that man can save himself through his own initiative. For if man can save himself and repent directly to God, who needs Jesus?

Is Blood Sacrifice the Only Method to Atone for Sin in Tanach?

Psalm 40:7 (6)	Hebrews 10:5
Sacrifice and offerings You did not desire; **but my ears you opened for me** (אָזְנַיִם כָּרִיתָ לִי). Burnt offerings and sin offerings You have not required.	Sacrifice and offering you did not desire, **but a body you have prepared for me** (σῶμα δὲ κατηρτίσω μοι·).

The foundation of the Church stands on its core doctrine that the blood sacrifice alone expiates iniquity and reconciles man with God. According to this teaching, Jesus' death covers the iniquities only of the "believers." The rest of sinful mankind, the New Testament claims, can do nothing to merit redemption.[1] Every person born into the world is totally depraved, therefore lost and destined to hell. Without the Cross, he has no conduit to salvation.[2]

This doctrine of substitutionary atonement—the notion that only unblemished sacrificial blood can propitiate God's wrath and atone for sin—has no greater foes than the prophets of Israel, for Christendom's central creed is denounced by the clearest utterances of Tanach. With one warm voice, the Book of Psalms and the prophets Isaiah, Micah, Hosea, and Jeremiah discourage sinners from relying on blood sacrifices as a method to atone for their sins.

> ### Vicarious Death in Greco-Roman Mythology
>
> The notion that someone could vicariously suffer and die in order to rescue others from death was not invented by Christians. They merely borrowed the idea. Ancient pagan literature frequently portrays how someone would endure agony and death in order to save others long before the advent of the Christian movement.
>
> One of the most striking examples occurs in Euripides' stirring play, *Alcestis*. Alcestis is the beautiful wife of Admetus. Although he is destined to die in his youth, the god Apollo offers him a special deal: someone else can die in his place. Admetus fails to persuade his parents to suffer his fate in his stead. Finally, Alcestis consents to give her life for her husband. Naturally, Admetus is gripped with grief and shame following her death.
>
> The god Heracles then comforts him by going down into Hades in order to rescue Alcestis from the agonies of death and brings her back alive to her heartbroken husband. Thus, Euripides' narrative is about a person who voluntarily dies in someone else's place and is then honored by a god who overcomes the grave by resurrecting the blameless victim from the dead. Sound familiar?

Rather, the prophets of Israel call upon lost souls to return to God with confession and repentance. The truly penitent are assured that God will freely forgive their sins.[3] These texts in the Hebrew Scriptures are not widely studied in Christian seminaries. As a result, Christian Bible students are largely unaware that substitutionary blood atonement is the only ritual whose importance is diminished in the Tanach. Accordingly, the prophets of Israel repeatedly warned sinners not to rely on the sacrificial system for their atonement. As mentioned earlier, the Torah harshly denounced human sacrifice, in particular.

There is no Christian voice in the Jewish Scriptures.

Moreover, the Psalmist's clear, compelling treatise on the inadequacy of sin sacrifices so utterly contradicts the base tenets of the New Testament that the author of the Book of Hebrews deliberately changed the words of the Jewish Scriptures in order to conceal the verse's unambiguous message and advance a Pauline theology. The cherished prophetic sermon on atonement is found in Psalm 40:7 (40:6 in a Christian Bible). This exposition, which was personally meaningful to King David, is laid bare for any child of God to grasp. A thousand years before the Church emerged, the Psalmist assailed Christendom's most fundamental doctrine with his clear message,

> "Sacrifice and offerings You did not desire; but my ears you opened for me; burnt offerings and sin offerings You have not required."
> (Psalm 40:7 – 40:6 in a Christian Bible)

The Book of Hebrews, however, brazenly misquoted and deleted the words, "...my ears You opened for me" when it quoted from the Book of Psalms, and replaced them with the words, "...but a body you have prepared for me" (Hebrews 10:5). The meaning of the simple Hebrew words אָזְנַיִם כָּרִיתָ לִי (*aznayim karitah lee*) is not open to debate. The average Jewish schoolchild knows that אָזְנַיִם means "ears" and כָּרִיתָ means "you have opened." The author of the New Testament's most argumentative epistle boldly interpolated the words "body" and "prepared," which appear nowhere in Psalm 40:6 or in any other part of the Hebrew Scriptures. How can the Book of Hebrews change the Word of God? There was a strong incentive for the author of the Epistle to the Hebrews to claim that the words, "...but a body you have prepared for me...." appeared in the Jewish Bible. As mentioned, the prophets of Israel frequently belittled the sacrificial system in favor of repentance. This biblical message is a direct assault on Christian teachings, which argues that substitutionary sacrifice was indispensable to atonement. Thus, by deliberately altering the message of the Psalmist, the author of the Book of Hebrews concocted the notion that animal sacrifices were an antitype and precursor to the human sacrifice of Jesus on the Cross.

While the authors of the New Testament frequently tampered with the words of the Jewish Scriptures in order to support a christological message, this example is especially striking. In other instances in which Hebrew texts were altered by the Christian Bible to make them appear as though they were speaking about Jesus, Christian translators routinely conceal these mistranslations by purposely changing the translation of the Jewish Bible to conform to the mistranslation in the New Testament. In Psalm 40:7, however, virtually all Christian translators render King David's words correctly, abandoning the Book of Hebrews' mistranslation.

For example, as was discussed in a previous chapter, the King James Version mistranslated the Hebrew word הָעַלְמָה *(ha'almah)* as "a virgin" in Isaiah 7:14 in order to conceal this deliberate mistranslation in Matthew 1:23. The word הָעַלְמָה, however, means "the young woman," with no implication of virginity. In Psalm 40:7, however, the King James Version—and most other Christian Bibles—provide no shelter for this obvious misquote in the Book of Hebrews. They correctly translate אָזְנַיִם כָּרִיתָ לִּי as "my ears you have opened." Therefore, in virtually any Christian Bible in the world, Psalm 40:6 and Hebrews 10:5 contradict each other! In the end, the author of the Book of Hebrews deliberately sought to mask King David's teaching, and advance the Pauline notion that the entire animal sacrificial system was never truly efficacious (Hebrews 9:22;10:4-5), and merely foreshadowed[4] the Cross. Although this twisting of Scripture successfully persuaded the gentile masses, it failed to satisfy the Jewish mind.

Footnotes:

1. "Total Depravity" is a Christian doctrine that derives from the Augustinian concept of Original Sin. It is the teaching that, as a consequence of the Fall of Man, every person born into the world is enslaved to the service of sin and can do nothing to choose or merit his own salvation. New Testament verses cited to support this doctrine include Mark 7:21-23, John 3:19, 6:44, Romans 3:10-11, 8:7-8, I Corinthians 2:14, and Ephesians 2:1-3. The driving theology that lies at the center of this doctrine is entirely contravened by clear teachings expressed in the Jewish Scriptures.

   Man is endowed with complete and unfettered choice as a gift from God to freely choose between good and evil (Deuteronomy 30:15-19). If free will did not exist, Abraham, Calev, Josiah, and Daniel's vertue would have been irrelevant and impossible (see page 216 and Volume 2, page 251).

2. Mark 16:16; John 3:14-16; 14:6; Acts 14:2; II Corinthians 5:21; I Peter 2:24; 3:18; I John 2:23

3. Isaiah 56.7-8; Micah 6:6-8; Hosea 6:6; 14:2-3; Jeremiah 7:7-23; Psalms 40:7 (Psalm 40:6 in a Christian Bible); 51:16-19

4. Colossians 2:16-17; Hebrews 8:5; 10:1

❖Repentance

II Samuel 12:13

So David Said to Nathan, "I have sinned against the Lord." And Nathan said to David, "The Lord has already forgiven your sin; you shall not die."

Psalms 51:16-19

Rescue me from blood-guilt, O God, God of my salvation. [17] My Lord, open my lips, that my mouth may declare Your praise. [18] For You desire no offering, else I would give it, a burnt offering You do not favor. [19] The offerings of God are a broken spirit, a heart broken and crushed O God, You will not despise.

> God forgave King David for his sin with Batsheva as a result of his brief, heartfelt, confessional prayer (II Sam. 12:13). He was deeply affected by this profound, personal experience, and this epic event shaped his prophetic message in the Book of Psalms.
>
> King David grasped that a blood sacrifice could not atone for sin. He declares in Psalm 51 that the Almighty favors humble repentance rather than sacrifice. This revelation, however, is utterly incompatible with the Church's central doctrine of substitutionary atonement.

❖Devotion to God Better than a Sacrifice

I Samuel 15:22

And Samuel said, "Has the Lord as much desire in burnt offerings and peace-offerings, as in obeying the voice of the Lord? Behold, to obey is better than a peace-offering; to hearken is better than the fat of rams."

> Contrary to the explicit teachings of the Jewish Scriptures, the New Testament insists that God will accept only the vicarious shedding of innocent blood to atone for the sins of the wicked (Heb. 9:22). Oddly, the Book of Hebrews argues that the entire animal sacrificial system was intrinsically worthless.
>
> *continued*

Micah 6:6-8

"With what shall I come before the Lord, bow before the Most High God? Shall I come before Him with burnt offerings, with yearling calves? [7] Will the Lord be pleased with thousands of rams, with myriad streams of oil? **Shall I give my firstborn for my transgression**, the fruit of my body for the sin of my soul? [8] He has told you, O man, what is good, and what the Lord demands of you: 'Do justice, love loving-kindness, and walk discreetly with your God.'"

> Instead, the sacrifices prescribed in the Torah were merely intended only to foreshadow a human sacrifice, i.e., the crucifixion of Jesus (Heb. 5; 10:1-6). This strange teaching is widely condemned as an abomination throughout the Jewish Scriptures.
>
> Both the Books of Samuel and Micah declare that obedience to God is far superior to a blood sacrifice for sin.

❖Sacrifices Replaced by Prayer

Hosea 14:2-3

Return, O Israel, to the Lord your God, for you have stumbled in your iniquity. [3] Take with you **words** and return to the Lord. Say: "You shall forgive all iniquity and teach us the good way, and let us **render for bulls the offering of our lips**."

> Hosea's divine message to the children of Israel is clear: Heartfelt prayer can replace any blood sacrifice.
>
> The New International Version Bible (NIV) translators found the theological message contained in the final phrase of Hosea 14:3 ("...let us render for bulls the offering of our lips") so deeply problematic that they altered the last words of the text to instead read, "...that we may offer the fruit of our lips."
>
> In essence, the NIV —one of the most popular Christian Bibles in the English speaking world— deliberately twisted and concealed the prophet's original message (see page 338 and Volume 2 page 77).

King Solomon Implores Future Exiled Generations to Atone with Prayer Alone

At the height of the inauguration of the First Temple (I Kings 8:46-50), in a prophetic supplication, King Solomon described future tumultuous events that would befall the Jewish People during their bitter exiles.

Anticipating and refuting the most central claims of Christendom that would emerge centuries later, King Solomon assured future Jewish exiles that confession and prayer alone will atone for all transgressions when that Temple no longer stands, and the nation would be driven into exile.

Nowhere in his entire uplifting sermon does King Solomon suggest that future generations would have to accept or believe in a crucified savior for atonement and salvation.

If, as the authors of the New Testament insist, the sovereign plan of God for the redemption of mankind culminated in the death and resurrection of the messiah, why didn't King Solomon, the wisest prophet in history, even suggest anywhere in this epic chapter of the Bible that this event would occur?

King Solomon's prophecy completely contradicts the teachings of Paul, who repeatedly insisted that repentance alone could not atone for sin.

> **I Kings 8:46-50**
> "If they sin against You, for there is no man who does not sin, and You will be angry with them, and deliver them to the enemy, and their captors will carry them away captive to the land of the enemy, far or near. ^{47}And they shall bethink themselves in the land where they were carried captive, and repent, and make supplication to You in the land of their captors, saying, 'We have sinned, and have done perversely, we have committed wickedness.' ^{48}And they shall return to You with all their heart, and with all their soul, in the land of their enemies, who led them away captive, and pray to You toward their land, which You gave to their fathers, the city You have chosen, and the house which I have built for Your name. ^{49}And You shall hear their prayer and their supplication in heaven, in Your dwelling place, and maintain their cause. ^{50}And forgive Your people for what they have sinned against You, and all their transgressions that they have transgressed against You...."
>
> *(see also Deut. 4:26-31; II Chron. 6:36-39)*

> *King Solomon warns future Jewish exiles that confession and repentance alone will atone for all their sins. The fundamental Christian doctrine of Jesus' substitutionary death is contravened by the words of the prophet/king.*

The apostle's astounding claim, however, is expressly contravened and condemned by the core principles of the Jewish Scriptures.

How can Paul insist that there is no deed or act of devotion that would be acceptable in God's sight,[1] when King Solomon explicitly states that the Almighty will forgive and save any man who confesses and repents of his sins?

Paul argues in virtually every one of his epistles that no initiative of man can bring about atonement for his sins. He insists that penitence cannot save man, because his lost and condemned condition is the direct result of Adam's disobedience.[2]

Does the Hebrew Bible ever state that Adam's sin prevents his descendants from repenting and enjoying the warm forgiveness of God?

Paul's ideas on atonement have had a greater influence on Christian theology than any other New Testament author. Yet his teachings have no greater foe than the prophets of Israel.

There is not a word or a hint in King Solomon's epic oracle that supports the notion that the death of a crucified savior can atone for sin, although this is the centerpiece of Pauline theology.[3]

Why is the most touted doctrine of Christianity unknown to the author of three books in the Hebrew Scriptures?

There can be little doubt that King Solomon would have been the Church's chief opponent, had he lived during the first century.

[1]Rom. 3:23 11:6, Eph. 2:8-9 [2]Rom. 5:27, I Cor. 15:22 [3]Tit. 3:5-6

Ezekiel Slams the Doctrine of Vicarious Atonement

Ezekiel harshly condemns the doctrine of vicarious atonement, which is the foundation of Christian theology. "The righteous man cannot die for the sins of the wicked," the prophet warns!

Yet the creed that innocent Jesus died for the sins of wretched man is the central doctrine of the Christian religion. "He made Him who knew no sin to be sin on our behalf, so that we might become the righteousness of God in Him" (II Cor. 5:21).

In contrast, the Prophet Ezekiel preached that contrite repentance alone atones for sin.

Throughout this famed chapter, which exclusively addresses the doctrine of sin and atonement, Ezekiel does not mention a word about a blood sacrifice or crucified messiah for the expiation of iniquity.

Paul claims that "the wages of sin is death" (Rom. 6:23), which means that spiritual death is the irrevocable paycheck for the sins of mankind. Outside of the Cross, the Church insists, there is nothing man can do to atone for his manifold sins, and find favor in the eyes of God.

Sola fide (Latin: by faith alone), also historically known as the doctrine of justification by faith alone, is a cherished, Protestant theological doctrine which asserts God's pardon for guilty sinners is granted to and received through faith alone, excluding all "works." We are told by the Church that mankind is under the curse of God because of the "original sin." Man is hopelessly depraved and sinful—incapable of saving himself from the wrath and curse of God.

> **Ezekiel 18:1-4,19-23**
>
> The word of the Lord came to me, saying: [2]"What do you people mean by quoting this proverb about the land of Israel, saying: 'The fathers eat sour grapes, and the sons' teeth are set on edge?' [3]As I live, declares the Sovereign Lord, you will no longer quote this proverb in Israel. [4]For every living soul belongs to Me—the father as well as the son—they are Mine. Which ever soul sins, it shall die....
>
> [19]Yet you ask: Why did the son not bear the sin of the father? But the son, justice and righteousness did he do, all My decrees did he safeguard and perform them. He shall surely live. [20]**The soul that sins, it shall die! The son shall not bear for the sin of the father, nor the father bear for the sin of the son. The righteousness of the righteous person shall be upon him, and the wickedness of the wicked person shall be upon him.** [21]As for the wicked man, if he should turn away from all his sins which he did, and safeguard all My decrees, and do justice and righteousness; he shall surely live. He will not die. [22]All his transgressions which he committed will not be remembered against him. For the righteousness which he did, he shall live.
>
> [23]**"Do I desire at all the death of the wicked man"—the words of my Lord, God—"is it not rather his return from his ways, that he might live?"**
>
> *(see Ez. 33:10-11)*

This central Church creed, however, is nowhere to be found in the Jewish Scriptures. Read it for yourself! In fact, this notion was vehemently opposed by the prophets of Israel, as expressed in the unequivocal teachings of Ezekiel.

Ezekiel confronted this aberrant idea head on:

> "Do I desire at all the death of the wicked man? Is it not rather his return from his ways, that he might live?"
>
> (Ezekiel 18:23)

Charity Atones for sin

Although the Hebrew Scriptures explicitly state that feeding the hungry, clothing the naked, and giving charity to the poor wipes away sin, parishioners are unaware of this central biblical principle. While Christians are encouraged to give charity, they are not taught that feeding the hungry atones for iniquity.

Hosea 6:6 and Proverbs 21:3 state explicitly that it is preferable to God that one gives charity rather than rely on a sacrifice. Why don't Christian ministers teach that giving alms to the poor washes away sin? After all, this is a core Biblical teaching. The answer is simple: there would be little need for churchgoers to believe in Jesus if they were convinced that God would forgive their sins if they gave charity.

Judaism teaches that charity money was never yours to begin with. Rather, it always belongs to God, who merely entrusts you with it so that you may use it properly. Hence, it is your obligation to ensure that it is received by those deserving of it. Charity is considered to be one of the main acts that can annul a less than favorable Heavenly decree. According to Jewish tradition, therefore, the spiritual benefit of giving to the poor is so great that a beggar actually does the giver a favor by giving a person the opportunity to give charity.

Proverbs 10:2
Treasures of wickedness will not avail, but charity will save from death.

Proverbs 11:4
Riches will not avail on the day of wrath, but charity will save from death.

Proverbs 16:6
With loving-kindness and truth will iniquity be expiated, and through fear of the Lord one turns away from evil.

Proverbs 21:3
Performing charity and justice is preferred by God to a sacrifice.

Hosea 6:6
For I desire loving-kindness, and not sacrifices, and knowledge of God more than burnt offerings.

Daniel 4:24 (4:27 in a Christian Bible)
Nevertheless, O king, let my advice be agreeable to you. Redeem your error with charity, and your sin through kindness to the poor, so that your tranquility will be prolonged.

Jeremiah Condemned Those Who Believed that Blood Sacrifices Could Save Them

Jerusalemites did not believe the rebuke of Jeremiah who preached that Israel had a misplaced sense of confidence that the merit of the blood sacrifices would somehow prevent God's wrath against their unacceptable behavior. They were skeptical about the prophet's warning of the coming destruction of Jerusalem.

The people foolishly believed, as the missionaries preach today, that a blood sacrifice would surely atone for their sins. They blindly relied on what would emerge as the widespread Christian doctrine of substitutionary atonement—the notion that sacrificial blood alone can propitiate God's wrath and atone for sin. They were certain that a priestly mediator, one who would intercede on their behalf, would save them from the consequences of their iniquity. They were confident that the blood would save them.

In an effort to demonstrate to his wayward generation that the sacrificial system could do nothing to rescue them, Jeremiah reminded his people that God did not even discuss blood offerings with the children of Israel during their Exodus. Rather, He desires repentance and faithfulness alone.

In essence, Jeremiah warns sinners not to rely on sacrificial blood for salvation, and berates those who claim that offerings will atone for their manifold sins.

> **Jeremiah 7:3-7, 21-23**
>
> So said the Lord of Hosts, the God of Israel "Improve your ways and your deeds, I then will allow you to dwell in this place. ⁴Do not rely on false words, saying: 'The Temple of the Lord, the Temple of the Lord, the Temple of the Lord are they.' ⁵ For if you improve your ways and your deeds, if you perform judgment between one man and his fellow man, ⁶you do not oppress the stranger, an orphan, or a widow, and you do not shed innocent blood in this place, and you do not follow other gods for your detriment, ⁷I will then allow you to dwell in this place, in the land that I gave your forefathers from days of yore to eternity...." ²¹So says the Lord of Hosts, the God of Israel: "Add your burnt offerings upon your sacrifices and eat flesh. **²²For neither did I speak with your forefathers nor did I command them on the day I brought them out of the land of Egypt concerning burnt offerings or sacrifice. ²³But this thing did I command them saying: Listen to Me so that I am your God and you are My people, you walk in all the ways that I command you...."**

Church Insists that Jesus' Crucifixion Was the Final Atonement for mankind, and Marked the End of Animal Sacrifices

Romans 6:10
   The death he died, he died to sin once for all...

Hebrews 7:27
   Unlike the other high priests, he does not need to offer sacrifices day after day, first for his own sins, and then for the sins of the people. He sacrificed for their sins once for all when he offered himself.

Hebrews 9:12
   He did not enter by means of the blood of goats and calves; but he entered the Most Holy Place once and for all by his own blood, having obtained eternal redemption.

> Paul's teachings rest on his claim that Jesus' death was once for all—in that a sacrifice for sin would never be repeated. The Greek adverb εψἂτταξ (*ephapax*) in Romans 6:10 denotes "once only," meaning that it is never to be done again.
>
> As the early Christian apologist, Justin Martyr (d. 165), stated in his *Dialogue with Trypho*:
>
> "No longer by the blood of goats and of sheep, or by the ashes of a heifer...are sins purged, but by faith, through the blood of Christ and his death, who died on this very account."

Hebrews 10:10, 18
   And by that will, we have been made holy through the sacrifice of the body of Jesus Christ once for all... where these have been forgiven, there is no longer any sacrifice for sin.

Jewish Scriptures Clearly Foretell that the Animal Sacrificial System Will be Restored in the Messianic Age

Unused ancient Jewish floor plans for the third and final Temple are found in chapters 40 – 47 of the Book of Ezekiel. In order to grasp the prophet's multilayer image of the End of Days, carefully examine this eye-opening prophecy. These passages vividly describe, in extraordinary detail, the epoch when the Jewish exile will come to an end, a new city and Temple will be built, and the children of Israel will be gathered and blessed as never before.

The final chapters of the Book of Ezekiel clearly state that the full order of the sacrifices will be resumed upon the rebuilding of the Temple. If, as Paul claims, Jesus was the final sacrifice "once and for all,"[1] and the animal sacrificial system was merely a temporary "foreshadowing" of Calvary,[2] then why will animal sacrifices be restored in the messianic era?[3] Why will the sin sacrifice return in the End of Days?[4]

The restoration of the sin sacrifice is entirely consistent with the traditional Jewish faith because this sacrifice was offered by those who only committed unintentional sins.

Accidental sins were committed frequently in the Temple. After all, masses of people who were unaware that they were ritually impure would inadvertently defile the Temple as they trod through its courtyard. This error occurred on a regular basis in the past, and, undoubtedly, will be repeated many times in the future messianic Temple.

The final chapters of the Book of Ezekiel, therefore, create a monumental conundrum for the Church.

The animal sacrificial system will be restored in the Messianic Age

Isaiah 56:7
Even them will I bring to My holy mountain, and make them joyful in My house of prayer; their burnt offerings and sacrifices shall be accepted upon My altar: for My house shall be called a house of prayer for all people.

Jeremiah 33:17-18
For thus saith the Lord: David shall never be without man to sit upon the throne of the House of Israel. [18]Neither shall the priests, the Levites, be without man before me to offer burnt offerings, and to kindle meat offerings, and to do sacrifice continually.

Zechariah 14:21
Every pot in Jerusalem and Judah will be holy to the Lord Almighty, and all who come to sacrifice will take some of the pots and cook in them...

Ezekiel 43:22-25
On the second day you are to offer a male goat without defect for a sin offering... [25]For seven days you are to provide a male goat daily for a sin offering...

In Ezekiel 45:22, the prophet envisions that the "Prince will offer a bull for a sin offering for himself and on behalf of the nation." Ezekiel discusses the "Prince" 17 times in his final messianic chapters, and many Christian scholars regard this Prince as the messiah.[5] To be sure, the Prince is explicitly identified as the messiah in 34:24 and 37:24-25.

According to Christian teachings, why would Jesus have to bring a bull as a sin offering in the future Temple? Church teachings clearly state that Jesus was sinless,[6] and was himself the sin sacrifice![7]

Why would the messiah have to bring a lamb offering (46:4), if, as the New Testament insists, Jesus was himself the lamb offering?[8]

Even more perplexing, the prophet Ezekiel explicitly states that the messiah will have a family and children (46:16-18), yet the Church teaches that Jesus bore no children.

For these reasons, numerous Church commentators concede that they were forced to abandon the notion that the Prince is the messiah.

Regardless of the identity of the Prince, Christian apologists are left with a colossal problem: How can they explain the restoration of the sacrificial system, which the New Testament insists will never return in the future? Some missionaries seek to dismiss this problem by claiming that the restoration of the sacrifices in the future messianic age will serve as a memorial to the past. This claim, however, is completely erroneous because Ezekiel explicitly states that the future sin sacrifice offered by the Prince in the Third Temple will atone for unintentional sins (Ezekiel 45:20).

Furthermore, why is the Prince the most prominent person in what are universally regarded the most detailed messianic passages in all of the Hebrew Bible?

Finally, why isn't there even a hint of Jesus or a whiff of Christian teachings in these famed eschatological chapters?

[1]Rom. 6:10; Heb. 10:10, 18   [2]Heb. chs. 9-10   [3]Ez. 44:27-31, 45:17-25   [4]Ez. 43:22, 44:27, 45:17, 19, 22-23; 46:20   [5]Christian scholars who hold that Jesus is the "Prince" of Ezekiel 44-47 include John Gill, Matthew Henry, Frederick Charles Cook, and Albert Barnes.   [6]Jn. 8:46; II Cor. 5:21; Heb. 4:15, 7:26, 9:14; I Pet. 1:19; 2:22, I Jn. 3:5   [7]Heb. 9:26-28; 10:10, 12, 14; I Pet. 1:18-20; I Jn. 2:2, 4:10   [8]Jn. 1:29, 36; I Cor. 5:7; I Pet. 1:19; Rev. 5:6-8, 6:1-16, 7:9-17

There Will Be No King, High Priest, or Sacrifice During Israel's Long Exile – Until the Messianic Age

In one of the most eye-opening, pre-messianic prophecies recorded in the Jewish Scriptures, the Book of Hosea predicted that the mass exile, which would precede the Messianic Age, would span a vast period of time.

During this epoch, the prophet foretold that the Davidic king, sacrificial system, and the role of the high priest would be suspended until its complete restoration in the Messianic Age.

Hosea 3:4-5
> For the children of Israel shall abide many days without king or prince, without sacrifice or sacred pillar, without *ephod* [sacred linen garment worn exclusively by the High Priest] or *teraphim*. ⁵Afterward, the children of Israel shall return and seek the Lord their God and David their king. They shall fear the Lord and His goodness in the latter days.

This unambiguous prophecy completely refutes Christian theology, which holds that no suspension of these roles ever occurred.

Missionaries argue that Jesus is the king, high priest, and sacrifice for eternity.[1]

In essence, the Church claims that there was never an interruption of the Davidic kingdom and priesthood. It argues that Jesus is the sole heir to all of these roles. We are told that Jesus was both high priest and king.[2]

Moreover, in Hebrews 9-10, Paul insists that Jesus' death marked the permanent end of animal sacrifices (see page 81 and Volume 2 page 311).

Hosea's precise vision of Israel's destiny, however, is perfectly aligned with history, and consistent with the core principles of the Jewish faith. Judaism teaches that the throne of David as well as the Temple's ecclesiastical functions were interrupted in the year 70 CE, when the Romans destroyed the Sanctuary, and will resume during the future Messianic Age.

[1] Mt. 4:23; 9:35; 24:14; Mk. 1:14; Lk. 1:32-33; 19:14, 27; Jn. 19:14; Col.1:13; I Tim. 6:17; Heb. 2:17; 3:11; 4:14-16; 6:20; 9:7-14; 10:19-22   [2] Heb. 5:1-10

Why is the Sacrificial System So Appealing? Why are Sinners Attracted to this Ritual?

The Church creed, which espouses that God's wrath against the sinner can only be propitiated through the blood of the Cross, and therefore only the death of Jesus can reconcile man with God, is completely alien to the manifest teachings of the Jewish Scriptures.

> **Isaiah 55:6-9**
> Seek the Lord when He is found, call Him when He is near. [7]The wicked shall give up his way, and the man of iniquity his thoughts, and he shall return to the Lord, Who shall have mercy upon him, and to our God, for He will freely pardon. [8]"For My thoughts are not your thoughts, neither are your ways My ways," says the Lord. [9]"As the heavens are higher than the earth, so are My ways higher than your ways and My thoughts higher than your thoughts."

While this point has been clearly illustrated above, it is vital to grasp why Christian teaching on substitutionary atonement is so attractive to the sinner. Why, in general, has the sacrificial cult attracted such great popularity among the masses in countless religions throughout history?

After all, the parent who punishes an obedient child for the misdeeds of another is considered cruel. A society that pardons its criminals while imprisoning the innocent is considered unjust.

Yet the notion that only Jesus' death can expiate iniquity is widely appealing to the wayward soul who feels that God could never erase his manifold sins. Despondent, the sinner who feels hopeless and lost says, "If I am unable to forgive others who treated me unfairly, how can God ever forgive all of my failings?"

Isaiah answers this nagging question while revealing that God's ability to forgive is infinitely greater than our own. Contradicting entirely Christendom's most espoused doctrine, the prophet comforts the sinner by assuring him that if he abandons his wicked ways, God will freely forgive him through heartfelt repentance alone, because "My ways are higher than your ways!"

Christians must wonder aloud why the prophet Isaiah, in his clearest exposition on sin and atonement, neither guides the sinner to believe in a crucified messiah for salvation, nor encourages the wicked to offer blood sacrifices for atonement.

According to Christian Theology, God Could Not have Forgiven the People of Nineveh

When the reluctant prophet Jonah finally enters Nineveh crying to its inhabitants, "In forty days Nineveh shall be overthrown," the people believed his word, proclaimed a fast, and repented with great contrition.

Because they demonstrated sincere remorse for their sins, the Almighty forgave the people and spared the city.

According to Church teachings, however, the epic repentance of the inhabitants of Nineveh was theologically inconceivable.

The people of Nineveh did not offer blood sacrifices to atone for their atrocious behavior. No intercessor saved them, and the Cross did not cover their iniquities. Their sins were expiated because they repented. They accomplished what Paul claimed was unthinkable, and what Augustine and Calvin argued is inconceivable. Christian doctrine plainly states that it would have been impossible for Nineveh's spiritual transition to have occurred!

Based primarily on the teachings of Paul,[1] the Church insists that man can do nothing to cleanse his own iniquities or make himself right with God through his own initiative. Instead, he is hopeless without a sacrificial, substitutionary atonement. Since his rebellious nature was spawned by the Original Sin, missionaries argue that he is spiritually lost and forever condemned without the Cross.[2]

> **Jonah 3:5-10**
> So the people of Nineveh believed God, proclaimed a fast, and put on sackcloth, from the greatest to the least of them. Then word came to the king of Nineveh; and he arose from his throne and laid aside his robe, covered himself with sackcloth and sat in ashes. And he caused it to be proclaimed and published throughout Nineveh by the decree of the king and his nobles, saying, "Let neither man nor beast, herd nor flock, taste anything; do not let them eat, or drink water. But let man and beast be covered with sackcloth, and cry mightily to God; yes, let every one turn from his evil way and from the violence that is in his hands. Who can tell if God will turn and relent, and turn away from His fierce anger, so that we may not perish?" Then God saw their works, that they turned from their evil way; and God relented from the disaster that He had said He would bring upon them, and He did not do it.

Christian apologists claim, therefore, that atonement is unattainable without the shedding of blood; no sinner can save himself with repentance alone; no effort or "work" of man can propitiate God's wrath.

The Book of Jonah disagrees.

The dramatic change that occurred in the hearts of the people of Nineveh[3] thoroughly impeach the core teachings of Paul.

Although the Books of Matthew[4] and Luke[5] identify Jonah as a precursor of Jesus, the Gospels abandon the central message contained in the Book of Jonah. Instead, Jesus compares Jonah to himself by proclaiming that "Just as Jonah spent three days and three nights in the belly of the fish; the Son of man will spend three days and three nights in the ground" (Although all four Gospels claim that Jesus spent only two nights in the ground!).

Predictably, the 13 epistles attributed to Paul, which are almost entirely consumed with the apostle's ideas on sin and atonement, completely ignore the epic story of sin and atonement contained in the Book of Jonah.

Why didn't Paul mention the Book of Jonah in his many letters?

There can be little doubt that Paul deliberately refused to acknowledge the repentance of Nineveh's inhabitants because that event is utterly inconsistent with the doctrines that he desperately sought to advance.

Moreover, in the Gospels, Jesus angrily compares and contrasts his generation to the people of Nineveh. Although Jesus fulfills his role as a type of Jonah, his generation fails to fulfill its role as a type of Nineveh. Jesus bitterly complains that the people of Nineveh successfully repented, yet his generation, "which has seen and heard one even greater than Jonah," fails to repent.[6]

Jonah's success and Jesus' failure with their respective generations, however, is more likely attributed to the message rather than the messenger.

Whereas the Church called upon sinners to believe in Jesus, Jonah called upon sinners to believe in the God of Israel.

[1]Rom. 3:10-18; 4: 1-4; 2 Tim. 1:9; Eph. 2:8-9; Tit. 3:5 [2]Mk. 1616; Eph.1:7; Col. 1:14 [3]Jonah 3:5-10 [4]Mat. 12:38-41; 16:1-4 [5]Lk. 11:29-32 [6]*Ibid*.

The following related articles can be found in Volume 2 of *Let's Get Biblical! Why doesn't Judaism Accept the Christian Messiah?*

I. Sin and Atonement.........................Page 59

II. Did the Passover Lamb Sacrifice
    Foreshadow the Crucifixion of Jesus..........Page 69

III. Could Jesus' Death Atone for Any Sin?.......Page 73

IV. Does Judaism Believe in Original Sin
    What Does the Bible Really Say?.............Page 81

V. Why Didn't the Red Ribbon on the
    Head of the Scapegoat Turn White on
    Yom Kippur, 30 C.E.?......................Page 91

VI. When a Pastor Demands Charity............Page 103

VII. Outreach Judaism Responds to
    Jews for Jesus.............................Page 301

Part IV

Isaiah 53: Who is the Suffering Servant?

Why did Isaiah 53 emerge as the most debated chapter in the Jewish Scriptures?

Christians are so convinced that Jesus is the messiah, they are utterly astounded that the Jews, of all people, consider this claim preposterous. Christians are bewildered by this rejection because it appears so obvious to them that every aspect of Jesus' life—from his miraculous conception to his crucifixion and resurrection—was clearly predicted in the Jewish Scriptures. They wonder why the Jews then fail to embrace Jesus as their messiah. Can't they grasp that the prophecies in their own Bible predict that the messiah would suffer and die and then rise from the grave? How can a people who produced so many Nobel Prize winners be so dense? Are they just plain stubborn?

Why then did the Jews reject the claim that the messiah would suffer and die for the sins of the world? The answer is quite simple: Jewish messianic expectations are firmly rooted in hundreds of prophecies recorded throughout the Hebrew Bible. And Jews who are anticipating a messiah are not looking for anyone remotely like Jesus. They are awaiting the messiah who will destroy the enemies of God, usher in worldwide peace, the universal knowledge of God, the ingathering of the exiles, the resurrection of the dead, and the rebuilding of the Temple in Jerusalem (see pages 232-235).

Who then was Jesus?

While it is difficult to answer this question with certainty because no contemporaneous historian mentioned Jesus, it is possible that he was one of hundreds—perhaps thousands—of obscure, itinerant preachers during the first century who came from the backwoods of the Galilee, wound up on the wrong side of the law, and was summarily executed by the empire. He then would have been one of hundreds of thousands of Jews who were crucified by the Romans during the turbulent first century. For Jews, calling Jesus the messiah and God, Creator of the universe, is foolish and blasphemous.

But doesn't Isaiah 53, which Christians frequently cite, predict that the messiah would be tortured and killed for the sins of mankind?

The answer to this question is simple as well: the messiah is never mentioned in Isaiah 53. Look it up for yourself! As you will see in the pages that follow, originally this passage had nothing to do with a future messiah. This chapter was ripped out of context and key words were mistranslated. Prior to the advent of Christianity, there was not a single prediction by anyone that the messiah would be executed for the sins of mankind.

This raises an important question: If there was no expectation that the messiah would die for the sins of the world, how did Jews, who were among the earliest Christians, come to believe in a suffering messiah? It is not difficult to figure out how this belief could have developed. If Jesus was proclaiming that the tyranny of Rome would soon come to an end—which would explain what got him into trouble with the empire—some people may have considered him to be the messiah in a traditional Jewish sense: he would fulfill prophecies which predict that a final Davidic ruler would drive Israel's oppressors out of the Holy Land and restore the complete sovereignty of God on earth. This hope would have been shattered when Jesus failed to fulfill this dream, and instead was summarily executed by the Romans. While some of his followers presumably concluded that their belief was therefore unfounded, others came to believe that Jesus somehow rose from the dead and was the son of God. This was their line of reasoning: Jesus is the messiah. Jesus was crucified. Therefore the messiah had to be crucified.

But this belief raised a monumental problem for these zealous believers: There were no prophecies in Tanach that suggested that the messiah was to suffer and die. They solved this problem by searching the Bible for any support for their new belief. The verses they came up with, however, do not refer to the messiah, but rather the suffering of God's faithful remnant. When they tried to convince fellow Jews that Isaiah 53 was speaking about Jesus the messiah, the sparks began to fly!

It is precisely for this reason that until this day Christians are baffled by the Jewish rejection of Jesus, and Jews are bewildered why Christians would even entertain the notion that Jesus is the messiah.

The belief that the messiah was to suffer and die is an idea that early Christians invented. Not surprisingly, years after Christians concocted this idea, Paul viewed this notion as the greatest "stumbling block" for Jews, and because Jews considered this belief so foolish it had to be true (I Corinthians 1:18-25).

Isaiah 52:13 – 53:12

13. Behold, My servant shall prosper; he shall be exalted and lifted up, and shall be very high.

14. As many wondered about you, "How marred his appearance is from that of a man, and his features from that of people!"

15. So shall he cast down many nations; kings shall shut their mouths because of him; for what had not been told to them they shall see; and that which they had not heard they shall consider.

1. Who hath believed our report? And to whom is the arm of the Lord revealed?

2. And he came up like a sapling before it, and like a root from dry ground, he had neither form nor comeliness; and we saw him that he had no appearance that we should have desired him.

3. Despised and forsaken by men, a man of pains and accustomed to illness: and as one who hides his face from us; despised, and we esteemed him not.

4. Indeed, he bore our illnesses, and our pains – he carried them, yet we accounted him as plagued, smitten by God and oppressed.

5. But he was pained from our transgressions, crushed from our iniquities; the chastisement of our welfare was upon him, and with his wound we were healed.

6. We all went astray like sheep, we have turned, each one on his own way, and the Lord accepted his prayers for the iniquity of all of us.

7. He was oppressed, and he was afflicted, yet he would not open his mouth; like a lamb to the slaughter he would be brought, and like a sheep that is mute before her shearers, and he would not open his mouth.

8. From imprisonment and from judgment he is taken, and his generation who shall tell? For he was cut off from the land of the living; because of the transgression of my people, a plague befell them.

9. And he gave his grave to the wicked, and to the wealthy with his kinds of deaths, because he committed no violence, and there was no deceit in his mouth.

10. And the Lord wished to crush him, He made him ill; if his soul makes itself restitution, he shall see seed, he shall prolong his days, and God's purpose shall prosper in his hand.

11. From the toil of his soul he would see and be satisfied; with his knowledge My servant would vindicate the just for many, and their iniquities he would bear.

12. Therefore, I will allot him a portion in public, and with the strong he shall share plunder, because he poured out his soul to death, and with transgressors he was counted; and he bore the sin of many, and interceded for the transgressors.

יְשַׁעְיָהוּ נב:יג – נג:יב

יג הִנֵּה יַשְׂכִּיל עַבְדִּי יָרוּם וְנִשָּׂא וְגָבַהּ מְאֹד: יד כַּאֲשֶׁר שָׁמְמוּ עָלֶיךָ רַבִּים כֵּן־מִשְׁחַת מֵאִישׁ מַרְאֵהוּ וְתֹאֲרוֹ מִבְּנֵי אָדָם: טו כֵּן יַזֶּה גּוֹיִם רַבִּים עָלָיו יִקְפְּצוּ מְלָכִים פִּיהֶם כִּי אֲשֶׁר לֹא־סֻפַּר לָהֶם רָאוּ וַאֲשֶׁר לֹא־שָׁמְעוּ הִתְבּוֹנָנוּ: א מִי הֶאֱמִין לִשְׁמֻעָתֵנוּ וּזְרוֹעַ ה' עַל־מִי נִגְלָתָה: ב וַיַּעַל כַּיּוֹנֵק לְפָנָיו וְכַשֹּׁרֶשׁ מֵאֶרֶץ צִיָּה לֹא־תֹאַר לוֹ וְלֹא הָדָר וְנִרְאֵהוּ וְלֹא־מַרְאֶה וְנֶחְמְדֵהוּ: ג נִבְזֶה וַחֲדַל אִישִׁים אִישׁ מַכְאֹבוֹת וִידוּעַ חֹלִי וּכְמַסְתֵּר פָּנִים מִמֶּנּוּ נִבְזֶה וְלֹא חֲשַׁבְנֻהוּ: ד אָכֵן חֳלָיֵנוּ הוּא נָשָׂא וּמַכְאֹבֵינוּ סְבָלָם וַאֲנַחְנוּ חֲשַׁבְנֻהוּ נָגוּעַ מֻכֵּה אֱלֹהִים וּמְעֻנֶּה: ה וְהוּא מְחֹלָל מִפְּשָׁעֵנוּ מְדֻכָּא מֵעֲוֺנֹתֵינוּ מוּסַר שְׁלוֹמֵנוּ עָלָיו וּבַחֲבֻרָתוֹ נִרְפָּא־לָנוּ: ו כֻּלָּנוּ כַּצֹּאן תָּעִינוּ אִישׁ לְדַרְכּוֹ פָּנִינוּ וַה' הִפְגִּיעַ בּוֹ אֵת עֲוֺן כֻּלָּנוּ: ז נִגַּשׂ וְהוּא נַעֲנֶה וְלֹא יִפְתַּח־פִּיו כַּשֶּׂה לַטֶּבַח יוּבָל וּכְרָחֵל לִפְנֵי גֹזְזֶיהָ נֶאֱלָמָה וְלֹא יִפְתַּח פִּיו: ח מֵעֹצֶר וּמִמִּשְׁפָּט לֻקָּח וְאֶת־דּוֹרוֹ מִי יְשׂוֹחֵחַ כִּי נִגְזַר מֵאֶרֶץ חַיִּים מִפֶּשַׁע עַמִּי נֶגַע לָמוֹ: ט וַיִּתֵּן אֶת־רְשָׁעִים קִבְרוֹ וְאֶת־עָשִׁיר בְּמֹתָיו עַל לֹא־חָמָס עָשָׂה וְלֹא מִרְמָה בְּפִיו: י וַה' חָפֵץ דַּכְּאוֹ הֶחֱלִי אִם־תָּשִׂים אָשָׁם נַפְשׁוֹ יִרְאֶה זֶרַע יַאֲרִיךְ יָמִים וְחֵפֶץ ה' בְּיָדוֹ יִצְלָח: יא מֵעֲמַל נַפְשׁוֹ יִרְאֶה יִשְׂבָּע בְּדַעְתּוֹ יַצְדִּיק צַדִּיק עַבְדִּי לָרַבִּים וַעֲוֺנֹתָם הוּא יִסְבֹּל: יב לָכֵן אֲחַלֶּק־לוֹ בָרַבִּים וְאֶת־עֲצוּמִים יְחַלֵּק שָׁלָל תַּחַת אֲשֶׁר הֶעֱרָה לַמָּוֶת נַפְשׁוֹ וְאֶת־פֹּשְׁעִים נִמְנָה וְהוּא חֵטְא־רַבִּים נָשָׂא וְלַפֹּשְׁעִים יַפְגִּיעַ: ס

[1]
Who Is Speaking?

Isaiah 52:15-53:1

¹⁵ So shall he cast down many nations; the kings shall shut their mouths because of him; for that which had not been told to them they shall see, and that which they had not heard they shall consider.

¹"Who hath believed our report? And to whom is the arm of the Lord revealed?"

> **K**ings of nations are speaking here in numbed astonishment, for what they will witness in the messianic age will contradict everything they had ever heard or considered in the past.
>
> "Who would have believed our report?" the astonished and contrite world leaders wonder aloud in their dazed bewilderment (53:1). The humbled kings of nations (52:15) will finally grasp and confess that Jewish suffering occurred as a direct result of "our own iniquity," (53:5) i.e., depraved, reckless Jew-hatred, rather than, as they previously thought, the stubborn blindness of the Jews.
>
> They are utterly astounded that the Jewish People, whom all their nations have together despised and molested, are finally vindicated to enjoy the promised salvation of God. The palpable shock that Israel's neighbors will express in the End of Days is a common theme in the Hebrew Scriptures.
>
> There is not a single instance in Tanach in which prophets foretell that in the messianic age the Jewish People will be surprised or astonished. They will not seek out the gentiles for spiritual guidance. On the contrary, the Bible reveals that in the End of Days, ten gentiles of different languages will grasp the shirt of a Jew and say, "Let us go with you, for we have heard that God is with you" (Zechariah 8:23).

Micah 7:15-16
According to the days of thy coming out of Egypt will I show unto them marvelous things. ¹⁶**The nations shall see and be confounded at all of their might; they shall lay their hands upon their mouth**, their ears shall be deaf.

Isaiah 41:11
Behold! All those who were incensed against you shall be **ashamed and confounded**; those who quarreled with you shall be as naught and be lost.

Jeremiah 16:19-20
O Lord, my strength, my fortress, and my refuge in the day of affliction, the **gentiles** shall come unto thee from the ends of the earth and say, "Surely our fathers have inherited lies, vanity, and things wherein there is no benefit. ²⁰ Shall a man make gods unto himself, and they are no gods?"

[2]
Who is the 'Servant' in Isaiah 53?

Isaiah 41:8-9
You, **Israel, are My servant,** Jacob whom I chose, the seed of Abraham My friend. ⁹ Whom I grasped from the ends of the earth, and from its nobles I called you, and I said to you, **"You are My servant"**; I chose you and I did not despise you.

Isaiah 44:1-2
Yet hear now, O Jacob **My servant** and Israel, whom I chose. So said the Lord your Maker, and He who formed you from the womb shall aid you. ²Fear not, **My servant** Jacob, and *Jeshurun,* whom I chose.

> **W**ho is the "servant" in Isaiah 53? If you never read the chapters that precede it, this text will appear quite puzzling. These passages were never meant to be confusing or mysterious. The prophet presupposed, however, that the reader of Isaiah 53 is already familiar with the chapters that introduce it.
>
> Isaiah 53 is the last of four powerful and inspiring Servant Songs. The identity of the servant is clearly established as the nation of Israel throughout the first three Servant Songs, which begin in chapter 41.

Isaiah 44:21
Remember these, O **Jacob and Israel, for thou art My servant**; I have formed thee; thou art **My servant, O Israel**; thou shalt not be forgotten of Me.

Isaiah 45:4
For the sake of **My servant Jacob, and Israel My chosen one**, and I called to you by your name....

Isaiah 48:20
Leave Babylon, flee from the Chaldeans; with a voice of singing declare, tell this, publicize it to the end of the earth; say, "The Lord has redeemed His **servant Jacob**."

Isaiah 49:3
And said to me, thou art **My servant, O Israel** in whom I will be glorified!

Psalms 136:22
Even a heritage unto **Israel His servant**; for His mercy endures forever.

Jeremiah 30:10
Therefore fear not, O **My servant Jacob**, says the Lord. Neither be dismayed, O Israel, for behold, I will save you from afar....

Jeremiah 46:27-28
"Do not be afraid, **Jacob my servant**; do not be dismayed, Israel. I will surely save you out of a distant place, your descendants from the land of their exile. Jacob will again have peace and security, and no one will make him afraid. ²⁸ Do not be afraid, **Jacob My servant**, for I am with you," declares the Lord..."

---

[3]
Isaiah Identifies the Jewish People in the Singular Throughout his Servant Songs

> Missionaries contend that the repeated references to the servant in the singular as "he" and "his" in Isaiah 53 prove that this chapter is speaking of a single individual, rather than the nation of Israel.
>
> *Continued*

> This argument collapses when the entire context and surrounding poetic motif of Isaiah 53 are examined.
>
> Christian commentators all concede that the chapters which encircle Isaiah 53—52 and 54—describe the Jewish people as a single, afflicted individual who is finally vindicated by God. Accordingly, the fourth Servant Song begins in 52:13.
>
> Additionally, the prophet refers to the servant in Isaiah 53 in both the singular and plural (see pages 104-107).
>
> Isaiah 54 continues to speak of the Jewish People as a single, anguished individual. The moving portrait of this chapter is that of a despised and afflicted barren woman (54:1-11). Following the uplifting theme of the Servant Songs, God assures His tormented people that their oppressors will finally witness their vindication and redemption in the End of Days.
>
> In essence, anyone who read Isaiah 41 through 54 would find it inconceivable that the "suffering servant" in Isaiah 53 is the messiah.
>
> Moreover, in Isaiah 43:10 (below), the prophet clearly identifies the "servant" (singular) as God's "witnesses" (plural).

Isaiah 43:10
Ye are My **witnesses,** saith the Lord, and My **servant** whom I have chosen, that you may know and believe Me, and understand that I am He. Before Me there was no god formed, neither shall there be after Me.

Isaiah 52:1-2
Awaken, awaken, put on your strength, **O Zion**. Put on the garments of your beauty, Jerusalem the Holy City, for no longer shall the uncircumcised or the unclean continue to enter you. ²Shake yourselves from the dust, arise, sit down, O Jerusalem. Free yourself of the bands of your neck, **O captive daughter of Zion**.

> The chapter that precedes and follows Isaiah 53 describes the nations who oppressed the Jewish people, not a messiah. In both Isaiah 52 and 54, the nation of Israel—identified in the singular—is finally vindicated and redeemed.

Isaiah 54:1-8

"Sing, you **barren woman** who has not borne; burst out into song and jubilate, you who have not experienced birth pangs, for the children of the desolate one are more than the children of the married woman," says the Lord.... [4]"Fear not, you shall not be ashamed. Do not cringe, you shall not be disgraced. For you shall forget the reproach of your youth and remember no more the shame of your widowhood. [5]For He who made you will espouse you—His name is "Lord of Hosts." The Holy One of Israel will redeem you—He is called "God of all the Earth." [6]The Lord has called you back as a wife, forlorn and forsaken. "Can one cast off the wife of his youth?" said your God. [7]"For a little while I forsook you, but with vast love I will bring you back. [8]In slight anger, for a moment, I hid My face from you. But with kindness everlasting I will take you back in love," said the Lord, your Redeemer.

> When Missionaries misquote Isaiah 53, they employ the identical method that Matthew used when he misquoted the Jewish Scriptures to support his nativity narrative (see page 36).
>
> In the Book of Hosea (11:1), the prophet is clearly speaking of the nation of Israel in the singular as God's "son." The author of the first Gospel, however, deliberately misapplied the "son" to Jesus in Matthew 2:15. You would never discover this if you only read the Book of Matthew! There is only one way to reveal the identity of the "son": look up the context of the original passage in the Book of Hosea.
>
> Employing precisely the same technique as Matthew, missionaries misquote Isaiah 53 out of context. They deliberately ignore that the "servant" is identified the as the nation of Israel in the singular in the preceding chapters, and routinely cite this chapter as though it speaks of Jesus. Read Isaiah 41:8-9, 44:1, 44:21, 45:4, 48:20 and 49:3 for yourself! Even a cursory glance of Isaiah's Servant Songs illustrates that the servant of Isaiah 53 is Israel, not the messiah.
>
> **Hosea 11:1**
> When Israel was a child, then I loved **him**, and out of Egypt I called my **son**.
>
> **Exodus 4:22**
> Then you shall say to Pharaoh, "Thus saith the Lord, **Israel is My son**, My firstborn."

[4]
Isaiah 52:14

As many wondered about you, "How marred his appearance is from that of a man, and his features from that of people!"

A typical *Stuermer* feature in the issue of December 29, 1942. The text reads, "In the secret Jewish law book, the Talmud, it is written: 'Only a Jew is a human being. Non-Jewish people should not be called human beings: they should be depicted as animals...' About human beings according to the Talmud this can only mean Jews—the scholar Darwin said in 1859 that man is descended from the ape. Whether this is correct or not, we do not wish to decide. Perhaps the reader will take the trouble to compare the features of the ape from the New York Zoo (left) and the face of the Jewish old-cloths dealer from the New York ghetto (above) and draw his own conclusions.

The Kaftan Jew and the German peasant woman. The text under these two pictures in the *Stuermer* reads, "The racial mixing of Germans of Nordic stock with the Asiatic-oriental-Negroid Jews—which is preached and blessed by liberal circles and religious denominations—is the greatest cultural disgrace in this world."

[5]
Kings of Nations Will Be Dumbfounded When They Witness the Final Vindication and Salvation of Israel

Isaiah 53:1
Who hath believed our report, and to whom is the arm of the Lord revealed?

> The anthropomorphic reference to the "arm of the Lord" appears frequently throughout Tanach, and points to the salvation of Israel from its gentile oppressors by the hand of God. The shank bone, which appears on every Seder plate, signifies the redemption of the Jewish people throughout their troubled history. The stunned reaction of the gentiles as they behold Israel's final vindication and deliverance is the central theme of the last 27 chapters of the Book of Isaiah.

Isaiah 52:9-12
Break forth into joy, sing together, ye waste places of Jerusalem, for the Lord hath comforted His people... He hath redeemed Jerusalem. [10]The Lord hath made bare His **Holy Arm** in the eyes of all the nations; and all the ends of the earth shall see the salvation of our God! [11]Turn away, turn away, get out of there, touch no unclean one. Get out of its midst, purify yourselves, you who bear the Lord's vessels. [12]For not with haste shall you go forth, and not in a flurry of flight shall you go, for the Lord goes before you, and your rear guard is the God of Israel.

> Throughout the chapters which surround Isaiah 53, the prophet describes the salvation of the Jewish people from the world's nations, their unrelenting tormentors.

Isaiah 54:7-10
"For a small moment have I forsaken you, and with great mercy will I gather you. [8]With a little wrath did I hide My countenance for a moment from you, and with everlasting kindness will I have compassion on you," said your Redeemer, the Lord. [9]"For this is to Me as the waters of Noah. As I swore that the waters of Noah shall never again pass over the earth, so have I sworn neither to be wroth with you nor to rebuke you. [10]For the mountains shall depart and the hills totter, but My kindness shall not depart from you. Neither shall the covenant of My peace totter," says the Lord, Who has compassion on you.

Deuteronomy 7:19
...the great miracles that you saw with your own eyes: the signs, the wonders, the mighty hand and the outstretched arm with which God brought you out of Egypt. (See also Exodus 14:31; 15:6)

[6]
Throughout History, the Survival of the Jewish People Seemed as Bleak as a Young Tree Planted in Dry Land

Isaiah 53:2
And he came up like a sapling before it, and like a root from dry ground: he had neither form nor comeliness. And we saw him, that he had no appearance that we should have desired him.

Hosea 14:6-8
I will be as the dew unto Israel: **he** will grow as the lily, and cast forth **his** roots as Lebanon. [7]**His** branches will spread, **his** beauty will be as an olive tree, and **his** smell as Lebanon. [8]They who dwell under his shadow shall return; they shall revive as the corn and grow as the vine. The scent thereof shall be as the wine of Lebanon.

> Can a young, feeble tree planted in dry ground survive? This has been the miserable predicament of the Jewish people during her 2,000-year exile: a nation teetering on the brink of destruction. This people, which faced annihilation in every generation, will be uplifted in the messianic age, to the surprise and bewilderment of the world's nations.

[7]
The World's Nations Despised and Afflicted the Jewish People Without Cause

Isaiah 53:3

Despised and forsaken by men, a man of pains and accustomed to illness. We hid our faces from him. He was despised and we did not esteem him.

The 49th chapter of Isaiah contains one of the most stirring dialogs in Scripture, and sets the stage for Isaiah 53. The Jewish people are explicitly identified as God's 'servant' in its opening verses (49:3). This chapter is filled with a moving conversation between God and His covenant nation, Israel. As in all the Servant Songs, Isaiah repeatedly refers to Israel in the singular, highlighting the singular destiny of the servant-nation.

The faithful servant cries out to God throughout this moving chapter. The nation feels forsaken, afflicted, and abandoned: the identical descriptions of the Servant in Isaiah 53. The remnant is reluctant, and considers itself unworthy of its mandate.

Despite their humble protest, they are assigned to carry out this divine mission as a "light to the gentiles" and restore the rest of the Jewish people, "the tribes of Jacob," who have lost their way (49:6).

In response, the Almighty assures His people that His steadfast love for them exceeds the affection a new mother feels for her nursing infant (49:15). As in Isaiah 53, the chapter's central theme is the final vindication and salvation of the Jewish people.

Isaiah 49:3, 7-8, 13-15

And He said to me, "Thou art **My servant, O Israel** in whom I will be glorified!" ⁷...for so said the Lord, the Redeemer of Israel, his Holy One, about **him** who is despised of men, about him whom the nation abhors, about a slave of rulers. "Kings shall see and rise, princes, and they shall prostrate themselves, for the sake of the Lord Who is faithful, the Holy One of Israel, and He chose you." ⁸So said the Lord, "In a time of favor I answered you, and on a day of salvation I helped you. And I will watch you, and I will make you a **people of a covenant**, to establish a land, to cause to inherit the desolate heritages.... ¹³Sing, O heavens, and rejoice, O earth, and mountains burst out in song, for the Lord has consoled His people, and He shall have mercy on His **afflicted**." ¹⁴But Zion said, "The Lord has **forsaken** me, and the Lord has **forgotten** me." ¹⁵Shall a woman forget her suckling child, from having mercy on the child of her womb? These too shall forget, but I will not forget you.

Isaiah 54:4-7, 11, 14, 17

Fear not, for you shall not be ashamed, and not embarrassed, for you shall not be put to shame. For the shame of your youth you shall forget, and for the humiliation of your widowhood you shall no longer be remembered. ⁵For your maker is your husband; the Lord of Hosts is His name. Your Redeemer, the Holy One of Israel, shall be called "God of all the earth." ⁶For like a wife who is **forsaken** and **afflicted** in spirit has the Lord called you, and a wife of one's youth who was **rejected**, said your God. ⁷ "For a small moment have I forsaken you, and with great mercy will I gather you. ¹¹O **thou afflicted**, who was not consoled, behold I will lay thy stones with fair colors and lay thy foundations with sapphires. ¹⁴With righteousness shall you be established, for you will be far from oppression, for you will not fear and from ruin, for it will not come near you. ¹⁷No weapon that is formed against you will prosper, and any tongue that rises against you in judgement you shall condemn. This is the heritage of the **servants of the Lord**, and their righteousness is from Me," says the Lord.

If a verse can grammatically be understood in more than one way, what is the correct rendering? One that is in agreement with the rest of the Hebrew Scriptures. If a person ignores vital portions of the immediate context of a passage, and builds his belief around a favorite rendering of a particular text, then what he believes really reflects, not the Word of God, but rather his own ideas, and perhaps those of another imperfect human.

Students of the Bible who explore the last 27 chapters of the Book of Isaiah grasp the identity of the "Suffering Servant." These stirring chapters triumphantly reveal God's sovereign plan for His "servant Israel."

Israel's neighbors will be dumbfounded by the startling events that will unfold in the messianic age. Together, they will comprehend that their age-old assessment of the Jew was wrong.

Continued

Throughout Israel's long and bitter exile, the nations mistakenly attributed the miserable predicament of the Jew to his stubborn rejection of the world's religions. In the End of Days, however, the gentiles will finally discover what was until then unimaginable: The unwavering Jew was, in fact, all this time faithful to the true God.

On the other hand, "We despised and held him of no account" (53:3). In contrast, Christians who ignore the context of the fourth Servant Song, erroneously conclude that Isaiah 53 refers to Jesus.

Isaiah 60:14-15

The sons of them who **afflicted you** will come bending unto you; and all they who **despised you** shall bow themselves down at the soles of your feet; and they shall call you, the city of the Lord, Zion of the Holy One of Israel. ¹⁵Whereas **you have been forsaken and despised**, with no passerby, I will make you an everlasting pride, the joy of every generation.

> Throughout the latter chapters of the Book of Isaiah, the Jewish people are repeatedly identified as afflicted, despised, and forsaken.
>
> The prophet assures Israel, however, that at the End of Days they will be redeemed and vindicated.

Isaiah 40:2

Speak to the heart of Jerusalem and call to her, for she has become full from her host, **her iniquity has been appeased; for she has taken from the hand of the Lord double for all her sins**.

Zechariah 1:15

I am very angry with the nations that are at ease, for I was wroth a little, and they helped to do harm.

Isaiah 52:4-5

The Lord God said, "My people went to Egypt to sojourn there, but Assyria oppressed **him without cause** (וְאַשּׁוּר בְּאֶפֶס עֲשָׁקוֹ). ⁵And now, what have I here," says the Lord, "that My people have been taken for nothing; **his** rulers (מֹשְׁלָו) boast," says the Lord, "and constantly, all day, My name is blasphemed."

> Christian Bibles deliberately concealed the pronouns in Isaiah 52 that clearly identify the nation of Israel in the singular by changing the pronouns into the plural.

Isaiah 62:2-4, 12

The gentiles shall see your righteousness, and all kings your glory, and you shall be called a new name, which the mouth of the Lord shall pronounce. ³And you shall be a crown of glory in the hand of the Lord and a Kingly crown on the land of your God. ⁴No longer shall **"Forsaken"** be said of you, and "Desolate" shall no longer be said of your land, for you shall be called "My desire is in her," and your land, "Inhabited," for the Lord desires you, and your land shall be inhabited.... ¹²And they shall call them "The holy people, those redeemed by the Lord," and you shall be called, **"Sought, a city not forsaken."**

> Isaiah 62 mirrors the famed Isaiah 53. When the gentiles "see your righteousness," they will no longer regard you as forsaken and smitten by God. In the messianic age, the Jewish people will be vindicated before the world, to the astonishment of Israel's neighbors.

Christian Bibles tampered with the text of Isaiah 52 in order to conceal that Isaiah consistently addressed the nation of Israel in the singular, as he does in Isaiah 53. These Christian translators sought to completely sever the umbilical relationship between Isaiah 52 and 53, which would otherwise be impossible to ignore. Both the linguistic structure of Isaiah 52 and 53 contain the same theme and motif. In addition, the chapter break between 52 and 53 is artificial and unwarranted. Christian translators grasped that most readers would notice the striking similarities between these two consecutive chapters if Isaiah 52 were rendered correctly.

For example, in both Isaiah 52 and 53, the victim suffers as a result of the unprovoked aggression of the gentile nations. In both of these epic chapters, the oppressed are referred to in the singular. In Isaiah 52, however, the prophet explicitly identifies Israel as the one who innocently suffers.

The translators of both the King James Version (KJV) and the New International Version (NIV) were therefore concerned that their readers might question the notion that Isaiah 53 is referring to Jesus. After all, Isaiah 52 clearly describes Israel as a single individual, relentlessly oppressed "without cause" by the world's nations.

To solve this problem, segments of Isaiah 52 were meticulously reconstructed so its passages do not resemble Isaiah 53's theme

Continued

and poetic language. For example, in Isaiah 52:4 the prophet recounts that "Assyria oppressed him [Israel] without cause." As stated above, the concept that the nation of Israel innocently suffered in Isaiah 52 is precisely the underlying theme of Isaiah 53. Moreover, 52:4 speaks of the Jewish people in the singular, as does Isaiah 53. Therefore, the NIV altered this text by removing a most revealing clause in this verse: the phrase in Isaiah 52:4 reads, "lately, Assyria has oppressed them." The NIV completely expunged the critical words "without cause." Moreover, the KJV as well as the NIV changed the singular pronoun "him" in this verse to the plural "them" (see below). In Isaiah 52:5, the Hebrew word מֹשְׁלָו (*moshlov*) means "his rulers," referring to Israel's rulers. The nation of Israel is, again, spoken of in the singular. Therefore, the KJV and NIV translators deliberately changed the singular reference, "his rulers," into the plural. The KJV therefore reads, "rule over them."

Ironically, Christian translators changed the singular references to Israel in Isaiah 52 into the plural, and the plural references to Israel in Isaiah 53 into the singular (see pages 104-107). Although this is a strange way to translate the Bible, it successively perpetuates the notion that the singular references to the "servant" in Isaiah 53 could not have been speaking of the Jewish people.

Verse	Hebrew	Translation	King James Version	New International Version
52:4	וְאַשּׁוּר בְּאֶפֶס עֲשָׁקוֹ	Assyria oppressed **him** without cause	the Assyrian oppressed **them** without cause	lately, Assyria has oppressed **them**
52:5	מֹשְׁלָו יְהֵילִילוּ	**his** rulers boast	they that rule over **them** make them to howl	and those who rule **them** mock

[8]
Nations Conclude That Israel Suffered as a Direct Result of Their Own Iniquity

Isaiah 53:4-5

Indeed, he bore our illness, and our pains—he carried them, yet we accounted him as plagued, smitten by God and oppressed. ⁵But he was pained because of our transgressions, crushed because of our iniquities; the chastisement of our welfare was upon him, and with his wounds we **were** healed.

In an effort to stress the ongoing atonement of Jesus, Christian Bibles incorrectly translate the Hebrew words וּבַחֲבֻרָתוֹ נִרְפָּא־לָנוּ, "with his wounds we *are* healed," in the present tense.

The astonished nations are speaking here of Israel's past suffering. Therefore the phrase correctly translated should read, "we *were* healed," in the past tense (carefully read the interlinear Bible on page 107).

Ezekiel 36:6-9, 15
Therefore, prophesy about the land of Israel and say to the mountains and the hills, to the streams and to the valleys: Thus says my Lord, God: "Behold! In My jealousy and in My anger I have spoken, because the shame of the nations you have borne. ⁷Therefore," thus says my Lord, God: "I have lifted My hand in an oath. Surely the nations that surround you will bear their shame. ⁸But you, O mountains of Israel, you shall shoot forth your branches and bear your fruit for My people Israel, when they are about to come. ⁹For behold! I am for you, and I shall turn to you. Then you shall be tilled and sown. ¹⁵And I shall no longer cause the ridicule of nations to be heard about you, and the shame of the nations you shall no longer bear, of your nations you shall never again be bereaved," the word of my Lord, God.

Jeremiah 30:8-13
"It shall be on that day," says the Lord of hosts, "[that] I will break his yoke off your neck, and I will break your thongs, and strangers shall no longer enslave them. ⁹And they shall serve the Lord their God and David their king, whom I will set up for them. ¹⁰And you, fear not, **My servant Jacob**," says the Lord, "do not be dismayed, O Israel, for behold I will save you from afar and your seed from the land of their captivity, and Jacob shall again be silent and at ease—no one will frighten them. ¹¹For I am with you," says the Lord, "to save you, for I will make an end of all the nations where I dispersed you, but of you I will not make an end, but I will chasten you in measure, and I will not completely destroy you." ¹²For so said the Lord: **"Your bruise is painful, your wound grievous. ¹³No one deems your wound to be healed**, you have no healing medicines."

[9]

The Servant Intercedes on Behalf of the Gentile Nations

Isaiah 53:6

We all went astray like sheep. We have turned, each one on his own way, and the Lord accepted his prayers for the iniquity of all of us.

Jeremiah 29:7

Seek the peace of the city where I have exiled you and pray for it to the Lord, for in its peace you shall have peace.

Psalms 44:12-22

You have delivered us **like sheep for the slaughter**, and among the gentiles you have scattered us. [14]You made us a disgrace to our neighbors, the mockery and scorn of those around us. [15]You made us a byword among the nations to shake their heads... [22]Because for Your sake we are killed all day long, **we are as sheep for the slaughter**.

> The grave plight of the righteous remnant of Israel is conveyed in Psalm 44. The language used here to describe the condition of the Jewish people precisely parallels that of Isaiah 53.
>
> As mentioned above, why is there not even one *clear*, unambiguous reference to the suffering or death of the messiah anywhere in the entire Jewish Scriptures?

[10]

The Remnant of Israel Silently Went to Their Death Like Sheep To the Slaughter

Isaiah 53:7

He was oppressed, and he was afflicted, yet he would not open his mouth. Like a lamb to the slaughter he would be brought, and like a sheep that is mute before her shearers, and he would not open his mouth.

Ezekiel 34:15-16

"I will tend **My sheep**, and lay them down"—the words of my Lord, God. [16]"The lost, I will seek out, and the banished, I will retrieve; the wounded, I will heal; and the frail, I will strengthen.

Psalms 18:28

For you will save Your afflicted nation and bring down the haughty looks.

> Although the Bible explicitly and repeatedly describes the Jewish people as afflicted and despised by the gentile nations, there is not even one *clear* reference to the messiah as afflicted or despised anywhere in all of the Jewish Scriptures.

Zechariah 11:4-7

So Said the Lord, my God: "Tend the **flock of the slaughter**, [5]whose buyers shall slay them and not be guilty, and whose sellers shall say, 'Blessed be the Lord, for I have become wealthy.' And whose shepherds shall not have pity on them... [7]And I tended the **flock of slaughter**; indeed, the poor of the flock."

> The prophets Ezekiel and Zechariah describe the Jewish people as abandoned, like sheep forsaken for slaughter. Yet there is not a single instance in Tanach where the messiah is ever called a lamb. Why does this allegory only appear in the Christian Bible?

[11]

Gentiles Confess That Israel Was Stricken as a Result of Their Own Nation's Iniquity

Isaiah 53:8

From imprisonment and from judgment he is taken, and his generation who shall tell? For he was cut off from the land of the living; because of the transgression of my people, a plague befell **them** (לָמוֹ).

The prophet's use of the Hebrew pronoun לָמוֹ (*lamo*), which means "to them," for the servant in 53:8 creates a staggering problem for Christian translators who are committed to casting Jesus as the 'servant' of Isaiah 53.

The Jewish people are frequently addressed in Tanach in the singular form in order to highlight the nation's singular destiny. The prophets, however, never speak of an individual in the plural. Therefore, the use of the Hebrew word "them" demonstrates that the "Servant" of Isaiah 53 is not a single individual. Christian Bibles escape this nagging problem by mistranslating the Hebrew word לָמוֹ as "him," in the singular, rather than "them."

Why do renowned Christian Bibles translate the Hebrew word לָמוֹ (*lamo*) as "to him" in Isaiah 53:8, and "to them" in Isaiah 48:21?

Inconsistent Translations?	Isaiah 48:21 הִזִּיל לָמוֹ מִצּוּר	Isaiah 53:8 מִפֶּשַׁע עַמִּי נֶגַע לָמוֹ
New International Version	for **them** from the rock	for the transgression of my people **he** was stricken
King James Version	out of the rock for **them**	for the transgression of my people was **he** stricken
New Living Translation	and water gushed out for **them**	But **he** was struck down for the rebellion of my people
New English Translation	out of a rock for **them**	because of the rebellion of his own people **he** was wounded.
New Jerusalem Bible	flow for **them** from the rock	at **his** having been struck dead for his people's rebellion?
Young's Literal Translation	out of the rock for **them**	By the transgression of My people **he** is plagued

Christian Bibles that mistranslate מִפֶּשַׁע עַמִּי נֶגַע לָמוֹ, which means, "for the transgression of my people *they* were stricken" (Isaiah 53:8b)

King James Version	for the transgressions of my people was *he* stricken
Modern Reader's Bible	for the transgression of my people was *he* stricken
New International Version	for the transgression of my people *he* was stricken
Living Bible	it was their sins that *he* was dying for — that *he* was suffering their punishment
English Standard Version	for the transgression of my people was *he* stricken.
New English Translation	because of the rebellion of his own people *he* was wounded.
New Jerusalem Bible (Catholic)	at *his* having been struck dead for his people's rebellion?
Young's Literal Translation	By the transgression of My people *he* is plagued.
New Living Translation	But *he* was struck down for the rebellion of my people.

Psalms 116:9
I shall walk before the Lord in the **land of the living**.

The "land of the living" is the Holy Land (see Ezekiel 32:23-32).

Why does the King James Version (KJV) correctly translate the same Hebrew word לָמוֹ as "them" in other places in the Bible?

Genesis 9:26 *(KJV)* And He said, Blessed be the Lord God of Shem; and Canaan shall be **his** (peoples of Shem) servant (לָמוֹ) (In this instance, לָמוֹ is speaking of Shem's descendants).	**Deuteronomy 32:35** *(KJV)* ...for the day of their calamity is at hand, and the things that shall come upon **them** (לָמוֹ) make haste.	**Deuteronomy 33:2** *(KJV)* ....He shined forth from Mount Paran, and he came with ten thousands of saints: from His right hand went a fiery law for **them** (לָמוֹ).
Job 6:19 *(KJV)* The troops of Tema looked, the companies of Sheba waited for **them** (לָמוֹ).	**Job 14:21** *(KJV)* His sons come to honor, and he knoweth it not; and they are brought low, but he perceiveth it not of **them** (לָמוֹ).	**Psalms 2:4** *(KJV)* He that sitteth in the heavens shall laugh: the Lord shall have **them** (לָמוֹ) in derision.
Isaiah 23:1 *(KJV)* The burden of Tyre. Howl, ye ships of Tarshish; for it is laid waste, so that there is no house, no entering in: from the land of Chittim it is revealed to **them** (לָמוֹ).	**Isaiah 16:4** *(KJV)* Let Mine outcasts dwell with thee, Moab; be thou a covert to **them** (לָמוֹ) from the face of the spoiler: for the extortioner is at an end, the spoiler ceaseth, the oppressors are consumed out of the land.	**Psalm 88:8** *(KJV)* Thou hast put away mine acquaintance far from me; thou hast made me an abomination unto **them** (לָמוֹ): I am shut up, and I cannot come forth.
Psalms 119:165 *(KJV)* Great peace have they which love Thy law: and nothing shall offend **them** (לָמוֹ).	**Psalms 78:24** *(KJV)* And had rained down manna upon them to eat, and had given **them** (לָמוֹ) of the corn of heaven.	**Psalms 44:4** *(KJV)* For they got not the land in possession by their own sword, neither did their own arm save **them** (לָמוֹ)....
Isaiah 30:5 *(KJV)* They were all ashamed of a people that could not profit **them** (לָמוֹ), nor be a help nor profit, but a shame, and also a reproach.	**Isaiah 44:7** *(KJV)* And who, as I, shall call, and shall declare it, and set it in order for Me, since I appointed the ancient people? And the things that are coming, and shall come, let them show unto **them** (לָמוֹ).	**Isaiah 48:21** *(KJV)* And they thirsted not when he led them through the deserts: He caused waters to flow out of the rock for **them** (לָמוֹ): He cleaved the rock also, and the waters gushed out.
Lamentations 1:19 *(KJV)* I called for my lovers, but they deceived me: my priests and mine elders gave up the ghost in the city, while they sought **their** (לָמוֹ) meat to relieve their souls.	**Habakkuk 2:7** *(KJV)* Shall they not rise up suddenly that shall bite thee, and awake that shall vex thee, and thou shalt be for booties unto **them** (לָמוֹ)?	**Job 24:17** *(KJV)* For the morning is to **them** (לָמוֹ) even as the shadow of death: if one know them...

Why tamper with

R. Alcalay
The Complete Hebrew-English Dictionary

1132		למד – למז״ט		1131

naught, vanity, nonentity, nothingness	²לְמָה, נ.		to judge unfavourably, to accuse, indict, arraign	לִמֵּד חוֹבָה (קטגוריה) עַל
who was reduced to nought and nothing	שֶׁהָיָה לְלָמָה וְלֹא כְלוּם		from this one may deduce that	מְלַמֵּד שֶׁ-
you are nought and your words are nought	אַתֶּם לָמָה וְדִבְרֵיכֶם לָמָה!		in order to explain to you that	לְלַמֵּד שֶׁ-, לְלַמֶּדְךָ שֶׁ-
Hama	³לָמָה, נ. [לָמוֹת]		to be trained, taught, schooled	לֻמַּד
lama (Tibet)	⁴לָמָה, ז.			מִצְוַת אֲנָשִׁים מְלֻמָּדָה ר׳ מִצְוָה
Dalai Lama	דָּלַי לָמָה		to learn by oneself, teach, train oneself, practise, be used	הִתְלַמֵּד
To what can this be likened (compared)?	למה״ד – לְמָה הַדָּבָר דּוֹמֶה?		(poet.) study, knowledge	לָמֶד, ז. [לִמְדוֹ]
(poet.) them, to them	לָמוֹ, מ״ג = לָהֶם		(to be) learned; learning, accustomed, taught; to argue, argumentative	לָמֵד, ת. [לְמֵדָה, לְמֵדִים, לְמֵדוֹת]
(poet.) to	לָמוֹ, מ״י			
trained, accustomed, experienced, used to, taught	לָמוּד, ת. [לְמוּדָה, לְמוּדִים, לְמוּדוֹת]			וְלֹא הַבַּיְשָׁן לָמֵד וְלֹא הַקַּפְּדָן מְלַמֵּד (אבות ב, ה)
instruction, learning, study, teaching; custom; disciple, accustomed, trained, taught; Yahrzeit reading in synagogue (so called by Sepharadi Jews)	¹לִמּוּד, ז. [לִמּוּדִים, לִמּוּדֵי-]		the shamefast man cannot learn and the impatient man cannot teach (Aboth 2, 5)	
				מִכָּאן אַתָּה לָמֵד, נִמְצֵאתָ לָמֵד, נִמְצֵאנוּ לְמֵדִים
			from this one (we) may deduce (learn)	
self-instruction	לִמּוּד עַצְמִי		something deducible from the context	דָּבָר הַלָּמֵד מֵעִנְיָנוֹ
classics	לִמּוּדִים קְלַסִּיִּים		something deducible from the final context	דָּבָר הַלָּמֵד מִסּוֹפוֹ
schoolroom	חֲדַר הַלִּמּוּדִים		one who comes to teach and ends by learning; teaching others teaches oneself; the best way to learn is to teach	בָּא לְלַמֵּד וְנִמְצָא לָמֵד
(obs.) mathematics, astronomy	חָכְמַת הַלִּמּוּדִים			
course of study	חֹק לִמּוּדִים			
academic language	לְשׁוֹן לִמּוּדִים		lambda (Greek letter)	לַמְדָּא, נ.
textbook	סֵפֶר לִמּוּד		lambdoid	לַמְדִּי, ת.
tuition fee	שְׂכַר לִמּוּד		sufficiently, enough	לְמַדַּי, תה״פ
school- (academic) year	שְׁנַת הַלִּמּוּדִים		learned	לַמְדָן, ז. [לַמְדָּנִית, לַמְדָּנִים, לַמְדָּנִיּוֹת]

The above page appears in the *Alcalay Hebrew-English Dictionary*. On page 1,132, the Hebrew word לָמוֹ is translated correctly as "them."

Alcalay, R. *The Complete Hebrew-English Dictionary.* Jerusalem: Chemed Books - Yedioth Ahronoth, 1990.

an original?

The Interlinear NIV Hebrew-English Old Testament

ISAIAH 53:4-12

[Hebrew interlinear text of Isaiah 53:4-12 with word-for-word English glosses, alongside NIV translation in sidebar:]

"But he was pierced for our transgressions, he was crushed for our iniquities; the punishment that brought us peace was upon him, and by his wounds we are healed. ⁶We all, like sheep, have gone astray, each of us has turned to his own way; and the LORD has laid on him the iniquity of us all. ⁷He was oppressed and afflicted, yet he did not open his mouth; he was led like a lamb to the slaughter, and as a sheep before her shearers is silent, so he did not open his mouth. ⁸By oppression and judgment he was taken away. And who can speak of his descendants? For he was cut off from the land of the living; for the transgression of my people he was stricken. ⁹He was assigned a grave with the wicked, and with the rich in his death, though he had done no violence, nor was any deceit in his mouth. ¹⁰Yet it was the LORD's will to crush him and cause him to suffer, and though the LORD makes his life a guilt offering, he will see his offspring and prolong his days,"

This is an striking example of how Christian Bible translators altered the Jewish Scriptures in order to sustain a christological reading of Isaiah 53. In these uplifting passages, the prophet alternately refers to the servant in both the singular and plural because the "servant" of Isaiah 53 is the finally elevated and vindicated nation of Israel in the messianic age. The prophets often speak of the Jewish people in this poetic fashion. For example, Isaiah identifies the nation of Israel both as God's "witnesses" (plural) and His "servant" (singular) in 43:10. In Isaiah 53, however, the prophet's reference to the Jewish people in the plural creates a significant problem for Christian Bible translators who are committed to apply this chapter to Jesus. It would be impossible to translate this chapter precisely as Isaiah wrote it while sustaining a Christological reading of the text. In simple terms, **the Hebrew Scriptures never refer to a single individual in the plural**. Christian translators, however, found a way around this problem: They altered the meaning of the original words of Isaiah 53.

The above page clearly illustrates how Christian Bible translators revised the text in this crucial chapter. This example comes from *The Interlinear NIV Hebrew-English Old Testament*—a well known word-for-word literal translation of the Old Testament by Christian scholars. Notice that the interlinear translation of Isaiah 53:8 correctly renders the Hebrew word לָמוֹ as "them" (plural), yet the NIV translation (in the sidebar, on the right) changes the translation to "he" (singular). Of course, the NIV translators had little alternative in this matter. Had the NIV Bible accurately translated this chapter, it would be clear to the reader that the suffering servant in Isaiah 53 is referring to many people rather than Jesus. The NIV translators also had no choice with regard to the translation of the next verse (53:9), where the interlinear translation correctly renders בְּמֹתָיו. as "deaths" (plural), whereas the NIV deliberately mistranslates this word in the singular as "death."

Kohlenberger III, John R. *The Interlinear NIV Hebrew-English Old Testament.* Grand Rapids: Zondervan, 1987.

[12]

The Faithful Remnant of Israel Endured Martyrdom Throughout Their Bitter Exile

Isaiah 53:9

And he gave his grave to the wicked, and to the wealthy with his kinds of **deaths** (בְּמֹתָיו); because he committed no violence, and there was no deceit in his mouth.

Isaiah 53:9 (King James Version)
And he made his grave with the wicked, and with the rich in his **death**....

> As had been done in the previous verse, Christian translators deliberately changed the plural reference to the servant into the singular. The Hebrew word בְּמֹתָיו (*b'motov*) means "his deaths," not "his death." The KJV, NIV and other Christian Bibles mistranslate this plural noun as "death" rather than "deaths" in order to conceal the identity of the servant as the Jewish people (see page 104-107).

Zephaniah 3:12-17, 19-20
And I will leave over in your midst a humble and poor people, and they shall take shelter in the name of the Lord. 13 The remnant of Israel will neither commit injustice nor **speak lies; neither shall deceitful speech be found in their mouth**, for they shall graze and lie down, with no one to cause them to shudder. 14 Sing, O daughter of Zion! Shout, O Israel!

> Here, the prophet Zephaniah vividly describes the righteous remnant of Israel in the same fashion as Isaiah did in the 53rd chapter: "The remnant of Israel shall neither speak lies; neither shall deceitful speech be found in their mouth."

Rejoice and jubilate wholeheartedly, O daughter of Jerusalem! 15 The Lord has removed your afflictions; He has cast out your enemy. The King of Israel, the Lord, is in your midst—you shall no longer fear evil. 16 On that day it shall be said to Jerusalem, "Have no fear! O Zion, let your hands not be slack. 17 The Lord your God is in your midst—a Mighty One Who will save. He will rejoice over you with joy. He will be silent in His love. 19 He will jubilate over you with song." Behold, I wreak destruction upon all those who have afflicted you at that time. And I will save the one who limps, and I will gather the stray one, and I will make them a praise and a name throughout all the land where they suffered shame. 20 At that time I will bring them, and at that time I will gather you, for I will make you a name and a praise among all the peoples of the earth when I restore your captivities before your eyes, said the Lord.

[13]

The Servant is Promised Children (זֶרַע), Long Life, and Divine Agency

Isaiah 53:10

And the Lord wished to crush him; He made him ill. **If** (אִם) his soul makes itself restitution, he shall see **seed** (זֶרַע), he shall prolong his days, and God's purpose shall prosper in his hand.

> If, as Trinitarians claim, Jesus was God, how can God promise "God" long life and children? Such a blessing is preposterous! Does God reward Himself for good behavior? Why is God talking to Himself? Furthermore, why would God bless Himself, and how can the Almighty be a servant to Himself?
>
> Moreover, the promise of "seed" to the servant is God's blessing to the faithful remnant of Israel. The Hebrew word "seed" (זֶרַע) can only mean biological children. According to Church doctrine Jesus had no physical offspring; thus, this blessing could not apply to him.

Deuteronomy 30:8-10

You will repent and obey God, keeping all His commandments, as I prescribe them to you today. ⁹God will then grant you a good surplus in all the work of your hands, in the fruit of your womb, the fruit of your livestock, and the fruit of your land. God will once again rejoice in you for good, just as He rejoiced in your fathers. ¹⁰All this will happen when you obey God your Lord, keeping all His commandments and decrees, as they are written.

Genesis 15:2-4

And Abram said, "My Lord, God, what can You give to me, seeing that I am childless, and the **son** of my house (וּבֶן מֶשֶׁק בֵּיתִי) is the Damascene Eliezer?" ³Then Abram said, "See, to me You have given no **seed** (זָרַע); and see, the **son** (בֶּן) of my house is my heir." ⁴Suddenly, the word of God came to him, saying: "That one will not inherit you. None but him who shall come forth from within your bowels shall be your heir."

Isaiah 45:11, 19

Thus says the Lord, the Holy One of Israel, and His Maker, "Ask Me of things to come concerning My signs; concerning My **children** (עַל בָּנַי). ¹⁹Not in secret did I speak, [or] in a land of darkness; I did not say to the **seed** (לְזֶרַע) of Jacob, seek Me in vain....

[14] The World is Vindicated by the Servant's *Knowledge*, Not His *Blood*

Isaiah 53:11

From the toil of his soul he would see, and would be satisfied; with his knowledge My servant would vindicate the just for many, and their iniquities he would bear.

> Does the Church teach that Jesus vindicated the world with his "knowledge"? According to Christian theology, it was not Jesus' *knowledge* that vindicated the world. It was his *blood*. This epic verse is completely inconsistent with a fundamental doctrine of the Church.
>
> *Continued*

> Isaiah, however, is not speaking of a crucified messiah in his 53rd chapter. The prophet is referring to the faithful remnant of Israel, who, by their knowledge bear witness to the world that there is no Savior other than the God of Israel (Isaiah 43:10-11). This mandate to vindicate the world as a light to the nations (49:6) is not a task for a common people. The devout remnant of Israel will be righteous (Isaiah 60:21; Zephaniah 3:12-20)
>
> In the End of Days, non-Jews will crave Israel's knowledge and turn to them in order to learn of Hashem and His Torah: Ten gentiles will grab the shirt of a Jew and cry out, "Take us with you, for we have heard that God is with you!" (Zech. 8:23) The Hebrew word עִמָּכֶם (*emachem*) in this verse means "you," in the plural.
>
> If, as the Church claims, the Jews were wrong in their assessment of Jesus, why will the gentiles seek out the knowledge of the Jews in the Messianic Age?

Exodus 19:5-6

"Now if you obey Me and keep My covenant, you shall be **My special treasure among all the nations**, because all the world is Mine. ⁶You will be a **kingdom of priests** and a holy nation to Me...."

Isaiah 61:6-7

And you shall be called **"The Priests of the Lord—Servants of our God"** shall be said of you. The possessions of the nations you shall eat, and with their glory you shall succeed (them).

> Moments before the children of Israel received the Ten Commandments, the nation was charged with the mandate to be a "Kingdom of priests" to the nations of the world (Exodus 19:5-6), as in Isaiah 61:6.

Isaiah 42:6

I am the Lord; I called you with righteousness and I will strengthen your hand; and I formed you, and I made you for a people's covenant, for a **light to the nations**.

> The term "Light Unto the Nations" is an appellation unique to the Book of Isaiah. The Jewish people are assigned the eternal role of mentor for spiritual and moral guidance for the world as a result of this special designation.
>
> The context of this mandate (Isaiah 42, 49, and 60) is one of comfort and God's promise that He will restore the Jewish nation to their land. This return will cause the rest of the nations to open their eyes, and look up to the people of Israel. Only then, in the End of Days, will the world's nations finally recognize this unique role of the Jewish people.
>
> In essence, the goal of creation is that God's glory fill the entire earth, and all mankind recognize Him. As we proclaim twice daily in the *Shema* (Deut. 6:4), our perception of the oneness of God will only be complete when God, Who is acknowledged now only by the Jewish people, will be the one God recognized by the entire world: "When God will be King over the whole world, on that day will He be One and His Name One" (Zech. 14:9).

Isaiah 49:6

And He said, "Is it too light a thing for you to be **My servant**? To establish the tribes of Jacob and to bring back the besieged of Israel, I will make you a **light of nations**, so that My salvation shall be until the end of the earth."

Isaiah 60:3

And nations shall go by your light and kings by the brilliance of your shine.

Proverbs 6:23

For a commandment is a candle, and the **Torah is light**....

Zechariah 8:13, 23

And it shall come to pass that as you were a **curse among the gentiles**, O House of Judah and House of Israel, so will I save you—and you shall be a blessing. Fear not; may your hands be strengthened! ²³ So said the Lord of Hosts: "In those days, when ten men of all the languages of the **gentiles shall take hold of the shirt of a Jewish man, saying, 'Let us go with you, for we have heard that God is with you.'"**

Numbers 18:1

And God said to Aaron, "You and your sons, and your father's house with you, you must **bear the iniquity** against the sanctuary, and you and your sons must **bear the iniquity** against your priesthood."

Isaiah 2:2-5

And it shall be at the End of Days, that the mountain of the Lord's house shall be firmly established at the top of the mountains, and it shall be raised above the hills, and all the nations shall stream to it. ³ And many **nations shall go, and they shall say, "Come, let us go up to the Lord's mount, to the House of the God of Jacob, and let Him teach us of His ways, and we will go in His paths. For out of Zion shall the Torah come forth, and the word of the Lord from Jerusalem**.... ⁵ O house of Jacob, come let us go in the light of the Lord."

[15]

Israel, the Servant of God, Is Finally Vindicated before the Eyes of the World's Nations

Isaiah 53:12

Therefore, I will allot him a portion in public, and with the strong he shall share plunder, because he poured out his soul to death, and with transgressors he was counted. And he bore the sin of many, and interceded for the transgressors.

Ezekiel 34:27-30

"And the tree on the field will yield its fruit, and the earth will yield its produce, and they shall remain securely upon their ground. Then shall they know that I am God, when I break the bars of their yoke and save them from the hands of those who enslave them.... ²⁹ And I shall establish for them a plantation of renown, and they shall no more be gathered in by famine in the land, **and they shall no more bear the shame of the nations.** ³⁰ Then they shall know that I, God their Lord, am with them, and they are My people, the family of Israel"—the words of my Lord, God.

On the Jews
By John Adams
Second President of the United States

In spite of Bolingbroke and Voltaire, I will insist that the Hebrews have done more to civilize men than any other nation. If I were an atheist and believed in blind eternal fate, I should still believe that fate had ordained the Jews to be the most essential instrument for civilizing the nations. If I were an atheist of the other sect, who believe or pretend to believe that all is ordered by chance, I should believe that chance had ordered the Jews to preserve and propagate to all mankind the doctrine of supreme, intelligent, wise, Almighty Sovereign of the universe, which I believe to be the great essential principle of all morality, and consequently of all civilization.

I have read this last fall half a dozen volumes of this last wonderful Genius' Ribaldry against the Bible. How is it possible this old fellow should represent the Hebrews in such contemptible light? They are the most glorious Nation that ever inhabited this Earth. The Romans and their empire were but a bauble in comparison to the Jews. They have given religion to three-quarters of the globe and have influenced the affairs of Mankind more, and more happily, than any other nation, ancient or modern.

From a letter to F.A. Van der Kemp (1808), Pennsylvania Historical Society

---

What is a Jew?
By Leo Nikolaievitch Tolstoy

What is a Jew? This question is not at all so odd as it seems. Let us see what kind of peculiar creature the Jew is, who all the rulers and all the nations have—together and separately—abused and molested, oppressed and persecuted, trampled and butchered, burned and hanged—and, in spite of all this is yet alive. What is a Jew, who has never allowed himself to be led astray by all the earthly possessions that his oppressors and persecutors constantly offered him in order that he should change his faith and forsake his own Jewish religion? The Jew is that sacred being who has brought down from heaven the everlasting fire and has illumined with it the entire world. He is the religious source, spring and fountain, out of which all the rest of the peoples have drawn their beliefs and their religions.

The Jew is the pioneer of civilization. Ignorance was condemned in olden Palestine even more than it is today in civilized Europe. Moreover, in those wild and barbarous days, when neither the life nor the death of anyone counted for anything at all, Rabbi Akiba did not refrain from expressing himself openly against capital punishment, a practice that is recognized today as a highly civilized way of punishment.

The Jew is the emblem of civil and religious tolerance. "Love the stranger and the sojourner," Moses commands, "because you have been strangers in the Land of Egypt." And this was said in those remote and savage times when the principal ambition of the races and nations consisted of crushing and enslaving one another. As concerns religious tolerance, the Jewish faith is not only far from the missionary spirit of converting people of other denominations, but, on the contrary, the Talmud commands the rabbis to inform and explain to everyone who willingly comes to accept the Jewish religion all the difficulties involved in its acceptance, and to point out to the would-be proselyte that the righteous of all nations have a share in immortality. Of such a lofty and ideal religious tolerance not even the moralists of our present day can boast.

The Jew is the emblem of eternity. He who neither slaughter nor torture of thousands of years could destroy, he who neither fire nor sword nor inquisition was able to wipe off the face of the earth, he who was the first to produce the oracles of God, he who has been for so long the guardian of prophecy—and who transmitted it to the rest of the world—such a nation cannot be destroyed. The Jew is as everlasting as is eternity itself.

From "Jewish World" London (1908)

Ancient Rabbinic passages below identify Israel as the "servant" of Isaiah 53. For an in-depth study of the Rabbinic interpretation of Isaiah 53, see page 115.

Zohar Genesis, *Vayerah*

Consider the **congregation of Israel, how it is called a lamb, as it said, "like a lamb to the slaughter he would be brought, like a sheep that is mute before her shearers, and he would not open his mouth."** (Is. 53:7) Why was it mute? Because while other nations ruled over it, it was deprived of speech and made mute.

Zohar Genesis, *Vayeshev*

"The Lord wished to crush him, He made him ill; if his soul makes itself restitution, he shall see seed, he shall prolong his days, and God's purpose will prosper in his hand" (Is. 53:10). If his desires to be rehabilitated, then he will see seed, for the soul hovers about and is ready to enter the seed of procreation, and thus 'He will prolong days, and God's purpose...' namely the Torah, **"will prosper in his hand."**

Zohar Leviticus *Acharai Mos*

Rav Yossi taught that on the Day of Atonement it has been instituted that this portion should be read to atone for Israel in captivity. Hence we learn that if the chastisements of the Lord come upon a man, they are an atonement for his sins, and whoever sorrows for the sufferings of the righteous obtains pardon for his sins. Therefore on this day we read the portion commencing "after the death of the two sons of Aaron," that the people may hear and lament the loss of the righteous and obtain forgiveness for their sins. For whenever a man so laments and sheds tears for them, God proclaims of him, "thine iniquity is taken away and thy sin purged" (Is. 6:7). Also he may be assured that his sons will not die in his lifetime, and of him it is written, **"he shall see seed, he shall prolong his days"** (Is. 53:10).

Midrash Rabbah Numbers XIII. 2

I have eaten my honeycomb with my honey (Song. 5:1): because the Israelites poured out their soul to die in captivity, as it is said, **"Because he poured out his soul to death, he was counted with transgressors, he bore the sins of many, and interceded for the transgressors"** (Is. 53:12)—and bruised themselves with the Torah which is sweeter than honey, the Holy One, blessed be He, will therefore in the here-after give them to drink of the wine that is preserved in its grapes since the six days of creation, and let them bathe in rivers of milk.

Babylonian Talmud, *Berachoth* 5a

Rabba states in the authority of Rav Shorah that Rav Huna said, "If the Holy One, blessed be He, is pleased with any man, He crushes him with painful sufferings. For it is said, **"And the Lord was pleased with him, hence He crushed him by disease"** (Is. 53:10). Now, you might think that this is so even if he did not accept them with love, therefore it is said, "To see if his soul would offer itself in restitution" (*ibid.*). Just as the trespass-offering must be brought by consent. And if he does accept them, what is his reward? **"he shall see his seed, he shall prolong his days"** (*ibid.*). And more than that, his knowledge of the Torah will endure with him. For it is said, "and God's purpose shall prosper in his hand" (ibid.).

Babylonian Talmud, Sabbath 105b

Whoever sheds tears for the righteous, all his transgressions will be forgiven of him.

Matthew 16:21-22

From that time forth began Jesus to show his disciples how that he must go unto Jerusalem, and suffer many things of the elders and chief priests and scribes, and be killed and raised again on the third day. Then Peter took him, and began to rebuke him saying, **"Be it far from thee, lord: this shall not be unto thee!"**

Acts 13:14-15

He went into the synagogue on the Sabbath day, and sat down. After **reading the Law and the Prophets,** the rulers of the synagogue sent unto them...

Missionaries argue that Isaiah 53 was originally understood as speaking of the messiah, and the rabbis later changed the interpretation of this chapter to refer to Israel. If this were in fact the case, why was Peter surprised to learn that Jesus would have to suffer and die?

Missionaries often claim that the Jews deliberately expunged Isaiah 53 from the synagogue service. The tradition to read the *Haftorah* on Sabbath, however, predated the Christian era (see Volume 2, page 107).

Origen Contra Celsum
Chadwick, Henry; Cambridge Press, page 50

54. Since Celsus, who professes to know everything about the gospel, reproaches the Savior for his passion, saying that he was not helped by *his father, nor was he able to help himself,* I have to affirm that his passion was that he should die for them and endure the stripe to which he was condemned. It was also foretold that the people of the Gentiles would 'take notice of him,' although the prophets have not lived among them. And it was said that he shall be seen with a form dishonorable as men regard it. The passage reads as follows:

> Behold, my servant shall have understanding, and shall be exalted and glorified and raised very high. Just as many will be astonished at thee (so inglorious will thy form be among men, and thy glory among men), even so many nations shall be amazed at him and kings shall shut their mouths; because those to whom he was not proclaimed shall see him and those who have not heard shall take notice of him. Lord, who has believed our report? And to whom was the arm of the Lord revealed? We proclaimed as a child before him, as a root in a thirsty land; there is no form nor glory in him. And we saw him, and he had not form or beauty, but his form was dishonored and not considered. This man bears our sins and suffers pain for us, and we considered him to be in trouble and in calamity and affliction. But he was wounded for our transgressions, and he was made sick for our iniquities; the chastisement of our peace was upon him; by his stripe we were healed. All we like sheep went astray, a man went astray in his path; and the Lord delivered him for our sins, and because of his affliction he opens not his mouth. As a sheep he was led to the slaughter, and as a lamb before his shearer is dumb, so he opens not his mouth. In his humiliation his judgement was taken away; who shall explain his generation? Because his life is taken away from the earth, because of the iniquities of my people he was led to death.

> **W**hy do missionaries argue that the first rabbi to say that Isaiah 53 was speaking about the nation of Israel was Rashi, the 11th century Bible commentator?
> Origen, the 3rd century church father, concedes that learned Jews of his time said that Isaiah 53 "referred to the whole [Jewish] people."

55. **I remember that once in a discussion with some whom the Jews regard as learned I used these prophecies. At this the Jew said that these prophecies referred to the whole people as though of a single individual,** since they were scattered in the dispersion and smitten, that as a result of the scattering of the Jews among the other nations many might become proselytes. In this way he explained the text: 'Thy form shall be inglorious among men.... and 'those to whom he was not proclaimed shall see him.'

Revised Standard Version (Christian) – Oxford Study Edition

The suffering Servant   ISAIAH 53

name is despised. ⁶ Therefore my people shall know my name; therefore in that day they shall know that it is I who speak; here am I."

⁷ How beautiful upon the mountains
    are the feet of him who brings
        good tidings,
  who publishes peace, who brings
        good tidings of good,
  who publishes salvation,
  who says to Zion, "Your God
        reigns."
⁸ Hark, your watchmen lift up their
        voice,
  together they sing for joy;
  for eye to eye they see
    the return of the L{ORD} to Zion.
⁹ Break forth together into singing,
    you waste places of Jerusalem;
  for the L{ORD} has comforted his
        people,
  he has redeemed Jerusalem.
¹⁰ The L{ORD} has bared his holy arm
    before the eyes of all the nations;
  and all the ends of the earth shall
        see
  the salvation of our God.

¹¹ Depart, depart, go out thence,
    touch no unclean thing;
  go out from the midst of her, purify
        yourselves,
  you who bear the vessels of the
        L{ORD}.
¹² For you shall not go out in haste,
    and you shall not go in flight,
  for the L{ORD} will go before you,
    and the God of Israel will be your
        rear guard.

¹³ Behold, my servant shall prosper,
    he shall be exalted and lifted up,
    and shall be very high.
¹⁴ As many were astonished at him[s]—
    his appearance was so marred,
        beyond human semblance,
    and his form beyond that of the
        sons of men—
¹⁵ so shall he startle[t] many nations;
    kings shall shut their mouths
        because of him;
  for that which has not been told them
        they shall see,
  and that which they have not
        heard they shall understand.

53 Who has believed what we
      have heard?
  And to whom has the arm of the
        L{ORD} been revealed?
² For he grew up before him like a
        young plant,
  and like a root out of dry ground;
  he had no form or comeliness that
    we should look at him,
  and no beauty that we should
        desire him.
³ He was despised and rejected[u] by
        men;
  a man of sorrows,[v] and acquainted
        with grief;[w]
  and as one from whom men hide
        their faces
  he was despised, and we esteemed
        him not.

⁴ Surely he has borne our griefs[x]
    and carried our sorrows;[y]
  yet we esteemed him stricken,
        smitten by God, and afflicted.
⁵ But he was wounded for our
        transgressions,

s Syr Tg: Heb *you*
t The meaning of the Hebrew word is uncertain
u Or *forsaken*   v Or *pains*   w Or *sickness*
x Or *sicknesses*   y Or *pains*

(10.7–11), Babylon (Jer.50.29). **7–8:** Tensely, all creation awaits word of God's decisive victory (Ps.125.2; 2 Sam.18.25–27; Nah.1.15; Rom.10.15). The *watchmen* see the victor returning (40.5). **11–12:** Ritually clean, people and priests return home in peace (Ex.13.21–22).
→ **52.13–53.12: The fourth Servant Song** (see 42.1–4 n.). **52.13–15:** God will exalt his brutally disfigured Servant (Israel) to the numbed astonishment of the world's rulers (49.7,23). **15:** Rom.15.21. **53.1–3:** A lament (40.12; 50.8–10). The Servant's background and appearance (52.14) are undistinguished; his person, rejected. **1:** Jn.12.38. **2:** *Young plant*, compare 11.1; *root*, 11.10, compare Jer.23.5; these are sometimes considered Messianic allusions. **3:** Like a leper, he suffers painful loneliness and rejection by the community (Job 19.13–19). **4–6:** By the Servant's vicarious suffering, he restores all people to God (Mt.8.17; 1 Pet.2.24–25). *Whole,*

Why would two prominent annotated Christian Bibles—the Revised Standard Version and the New English Bible (following page)—tell us in their commentary that the "servant" in Isaiah 53 is speaking of the nation of Israel rather than Jesus? Read their extensive notations for yourself! The Christian commentators in both of these Bibles concluded from the surrounding chapters that the "suffering servant" can only be speaking of the Jewish people.

The New English Bible (Christian) – Oxford Study Edition

ISAIAH 52, 53 *Israel a light to the nations*

6 day long, says the LORD. But on that day my people shall know my name; they shall know that it is I who speak; here I am.

7 How lovely on the mountains are
    the feet of the herald
who comes to proclaim prosperity
    and bring good news,
    the news of deliverance,
calling to Zion, 'Your God is king.'
8 Hark, your watchmen raise their
    voices
    and shout together in triumph;
for with their own eyes they shall
    see
    the LORD returning in pity to Zion.
9 Break forth together in shouts of
    triumph,
    you ruins of Jerusalem;
for the LORD has taken pity on his
    people
    and has ransomed Jerusalem.
10 The LORD has bared his holy arm
    in the sight of all nations,
and the whole world from end to end
    shall see the deliverance of our God.
11 Away from Babylon; come out,
    come out,
    touch nothing unclean.
Come out from Babylon, keep
    yourselves pure,
    you who carry the vessels of the
    LORD.
12 But you shall not come out in
    urgent haste
    nor leave like fugitives;
for the LORD will march at your
    head,
    your rearguard will be Israel's
    God.

Behold, my servant shall prosper, 13
he shall be lifted up, exalted to the
    heights.

Time was when many[c] were aghast 14
    at you, my people;[d]
so now many nations[e] recoil at 15
    sight of him,
and kings curl their lips in disgust.
For they see what they had never
    been told
and things unheard before fill their
    thoughts.

Who could have believed what we 53
    have heard,
and to whom has the power of the
    LORD been revealed?

He grew up before the LORD like a 2
    young plant
    whose roots are in parched ground;
he had no beauty, no majesty to
    draw our eyes,
    no grace to make us delight in him;
his form, disfigured, lost all the
    likeness of a man,
    his beauty changed beyond
    human semblance.[f]
He was despised, he shrank from 3
    the sight of men,
    tormented and humbled by
    suffering;
we despised him, we held him of
    no account,
    a thing from which men turn
    away their eyes.
Yet on himself he bore our 4
    sufferings,

[c] *Or* the great. [d] *See note on 53. 2.*
[e] *Or* great nations.
[f] *his form . . . semblance: transposed from end of 52. 14.*

---

of Israel's slavery by the plagues and death of its firstborn, but Babylon *paid no price* when it *carried* them *off* into Exile. 6: *That day:* see 7.18–25 n. *Know my name:* see 43.1.
52.7–12: A pilgrim victory hymn. This is a continuation of the song, interrupted after v. 2, which celebrates the joyful return of the LORD and his people to the holy city. 7: *God is king:* see 43.15 n. 8–9: *Watchmen* are the people left in the *ruins of Jerusalem* at the time of its destruction by the Babylonians in 587 B.C. (2 Kgs.25.8–12). They look for the return of *the LORD* who was considered to have gone to Babylon with the captives; compare Ezek.11.22–25; 43.1–7. 12: The Israelites on their return from Babylon did not ask for an escort of soldiers but trusted that the LORD would be their guard: see Ezra 8.21–23.
➤ **52.13–53.12: Fourth servant song. The suffering servant.** See 42.1–4 n. Israel, the servant of God, has suffered as a humiliated individual. However, the servant endured without complaint because it was vicarious suffering (suffering for others). 13–15: *Nations* and *kings* will be surprised to see the servant *exalted.* 53.1: The crowds, pagan nations, among whom the servant (Israel) lived, speak here (through v. 9), saying that the significance of Israel's humiliation and exaltation is hard to believe. 2: In traditional Hebrew thought, the good man prospers like a tree by water but the wicked is like a *plant* growing in *parched ground;* see Ps.1.3–6. 3: *Turn away their eyes:* lit. hide their faces, an expression used in relation to lepers, whose sickness, considered a sign of sin, made them *despised.* 4–5: The vicarious suffering expressed here is in contrast both to the traditional solidarity in guilt of Exod.20.5 and to individual responsibility proposed by the prophets at the time of the Exile; see Jer.31.30; Ezek. ch. 18. 5: *Health for us:* lit. "our peace," which means "general welfare." 6–7: The servant is *led like a sheep* in contrast to the peoples going their *own way.* 8: Although some legal process seems to be involved, the servant does not receive *justice;* see Jer.39.5–6. 9: The death probably refers to the destruction and Exile of Israel. Compare Ezek. ch. 37. 10–12: The theme of 52.13 is resumed. Israel, which has suffered for all mankind, will now be granted her rightful place. 10: *Long life* and *children's children* are the signs of a final vindication before God; see Job 42.16–17. 11: *Bathed in light:* enjoying God's favor; see Ps.80.3.

Who is God's "Suffering Servant"? The Rabbinic Interpretation of Isaiah 53

Despite strong objections from conservative Christian apologists, the prevailing rabbinic interpretation of Isaiah 53 ascribes the "servant" to the nation of Israel, which silently endured unimaginable suffering at the hands of its gentile oppressors. The speakers, in this most-debated chapter, are the stunned kings of nations who will bear witness to the messianic age and final vindication of the Jewish people following their long and bitter exile. "Who would have believed our report?" the astonished and contrite world leaders will wonder aloud in dazed bewilderment (53:1).[1]

The stimulus for the world's baffled response contained in this famed cluster of chapters at the end of the Book of Isaiah is the unexpected salvation of Israel. The redemption of God's people is the central theme in the preceding verse (52:12) in which the "you" signifies the Jewish people, who are sheltered and delivered by God. Moreover, the "afflicted barren woman" in the following chapter is protected and saved by God; she is also universally recognized as the nation of Israel[2] (54:1).

Christian apologists frequently advance the well-worn claim that the noted Jewish commentator, Rashi (1040CE-1105CE), was the first to identify the suffering servant of Isaiah 53 with the nation of Israel. This contention is inaccurate and misleading. In fact, Origen, a prominent and influential church father, conceded in the year 248 CE—eight centuries before Rashi was born—that the consensus among the Jews of his time was that Isaiah 53 "...bore reference to the whole [Jewish] people, regarded as one individual, and as being in a state of dispersion and suffering, in order that many proselytes might be gained, on account of the dispersion of the Jews among numerous heathen nations."[3]

The broad consensus among Jewish and many Christian commentators that the "servant" in Isaiah 52-53 refers to the nation of Israel is understandable. Isaiah 53, which is the last of the four renowned "Servant Songs," is umbilically connected to its preceding chapters. The "servant" in each of the three previous Servant Songs is plainly and repeatedly identified as the nation of Israel:

Isaiah 41:8-9

But you, Israel, My servant, Jacob, whom I have chosen, the offspring of Abraham, My friend, you whom I took from the ends of the earth, and called from its farthest corners, saying to you, "You are My servant, I have chosen you and not cast you off."

Isaiah 44:1

But now hear, O Jacob My servant, Israel whom I have chosen!

Isaiah 44:21

Remember these things, O Jacob and Israel, for you are My servant; I formed you; you are my servant; O Israel, you will not be forgotten by Me.

Isaiah 45:4

For the sake of My servant Jacob, and Israel My chosen, I called you by your name. I name you, though you do not know Me.

Isaiah 48:20

Go out from Babylon, flee from *Chaldea*, declare this with a shout of joy, proclaim it, send it out to the end of the earth; say, "The Lord has redeemed His servant Jacob!"

Isaiah 49:3

And He said to me, "You are my servant, Israel, in whom I will be glorified."

According to this widespread rabbinic opinion, Isaiah 53 contains a deeply moving narrative that world leaders will cry aloud in the messianic age. The humbled kings of nations (52:15) will confess that Jewish suffering occurred as a direct result of "our own iniquity," (53:5) i.e., depraved Jew-hatred, rather than, as they previously thought, the stubborn blindness of the Jews.

The stunned reaction of the world's nations to the unexpected vindication and redemption of the Jewish nation in the messianic age is a recurring theme throughout the Hebrew Scriptures.⁴ Israel's neighbors will be amazed when their age-old assessment of the Jew is finally proven wrong. Throughout Israel's long and bitter exile, the nations mistakenly attributed the miserable predicament of the Jew to his stubborn rejection of the world's religions. In the End of Days, however, the gentiles will discover what was until then unimaginable: the unwavering Jew was, in fact, all this time faithful to the one true God. On the other hand, "We despised and held him of no account" (53:3).

In essence, the final and complete redemption of the Jews, to which the stunned nations will bear witness, contradicts everything Israel's gentile neighbors had ever previously anticipated, heard, or considered (52:15). "Who would have believed our report?" the kings will ask with their mouths wide open in amazement (53:1). The curtain of blindness is finally lifted when the Lord reveals His holy arm before the eyes of all the nations; all the ends of the earth will witness the salvation of His people (52:10).

The unanticipated vindication of the Jews in the End of Days, however, will raise nagging, introspective questions for Israel's neighbors: How then can we explain the Jews' long-enduring suffering at our own hands? After all, the age-old reasons we contrived to explain away Israel's agony are clearly no longer valid. Who is to blame for Israel's miserable existence in exile?

In essence, why did the servant of God seem to suffer without measure or cause?

Therefore, Isaiah 53:8 concludes with their stunning confession, "...for the transgressions of my people [the gentile nations] they [the Jews] were stricken." The fact that the servant is spoken of in the third person, plural לָמוֹ (*lamo*) demonstrates beyond doubt that the servant is a nation rather than a single individual.

Accordingly, the rabbinic interpretation of Isaiah 53 fits seamlessly with its surrounding chapters, which all clearly depict the nation of Israel as "despised, afflicted" (54:6-11), and oppressed "without cause" (52:4) at the hands of the gentile nations.

According to the most ancient rabbinic commentaries, the identification of Israel as God's servant is evident throughout the four Servant Songs.⁵

Rabbinic sources from the Talmudic period identify the servant of Isaiah 53 in the plain sense as being the Jewish people, consistent with the previous three Servant Songs.

For example, commenting on Isaiah 53 the Talmud states:

> Rava said...: "Whomever the Holy One, blessed is He, desires, He crushes with afflictions." As it is stated, 'And the one whom Hashem desires He crushed with sickness (Isaiah 53:10).' One might have thought that this applies even if he does not accept [the afflictions] with love. Scripture therefore states in the continuation of the verse, 'if his soul acknowledges his guilt' (ibid.)... And if he accepts [the afflictions with love], what is his reward? He will see offspring and live long days. Moreover, he will retain his studies, as it is stated, '...and the desire of *Hashem* will succeed in his hand'" (*ibid.*).
> (Talmud Berachos 5a)

The ancient Midrash Rabba on Numbers 23 likewise attests that Isaiah 53 refers to the nation of Israel:

> I have eaten my honeycomb with my honey" (Song of Songs 5:1): because the Israelites poured out their soul to die in captivity, as it is said, "Because he poured out his soul to die."
> (Midrash Rabba – Isaiah 53:12)

The traditional Church did not completely satisfy the Christian mind with its stock interpretation of Isaiah 53. Therefore, there is a consensus among many modern, liberal Christian commentators that is in accord with this prevailing rabbinic exegesis on this most-debated chapter. For example, the commentary of the 11th-century Rashi and the 20th-century Christian Oxford New English Bible[6] are strikingly similar. Both clearly identify the "suffering servant" in Isaiah 53 as the nation of Israel, which suffered as a humiliated individual at the hands of the gentile nations.

Conservative Christians, on the other hand, strongly argue against the Jewish interpretation of Isaiah 53 for a number of expected reasons. The Church historically has relentlessly used Isaiah 53 as its most important proof-text in order to demonstrate the veracity of the Gospels. They argue that this chapter proves that Jesus' death was explicitly prophesied in the Hebrew Scriptures. In fact, the author of the Book of Acts claims that the church deacon Philip converted an Ethiopian eunuch using Isaiah 53,[7] and the authors of Luke,[8] John,[9] and I Peter[10] associate Isaiah 53 with Jesus, as well. While evangelicals routinely claim that Jesus is alluded to in several hundred verses throughout the Hebrew Bible, there are only a handful of passages in Tanach that the Church insists irrefutably identify Jesus alone as the messiah—Isaiah 53 is chief among these polemical texts.

Consequently, since time immemorial, missionaries fervently used Isaiah 53 to proclaim that the Hebrew prophet Isaiah predicted the advent of Christianity centuries before the birth of Jesus. Accordingly, the traditional Church recoils at the rabbinic interpretation of the fourth Servant Song. In order for a Christian to concede that the servant in Isaiah 53 refers to the righteous remnant of Israel rather than Jesus, he would have to abandon the Church's most cherished polemical chapter, which is a vital part of its textual arsenal used against its elder rival, Judaism.

The systemic suffering of the Jews plays no essential role in Christian theology. The suffering of Jesus, on the other hand, is the cornerstone of Church doctrine. In fact, widespread Christian teachings throughout history concluded that the suffering of the Jews illustrates the wrongness of their beliefs, while the suffering of Jesus and his followers illustrates the truth and veracity of the Cross. In fact, Augustine argued that the Jews should be left alive and suffering as a perpetual reminder of their collective act of deicide. As a result, conservative Christians are unyielding in their rejection of the Jewish interpretation of Isaiah 53.

Liberal Christian scholars, on the other hand, are frequently in accord with the classic rabbinic commentaries on Isaiah 53. Unlike their conservative co-religionists, liberal Christians do not use, or depend on, Church dogma or creedal statements to interpret the Bible. In other words, liberal Christian Bible commentators tend to interpret scripture without any preconceived notion of the correctness of Church teaching. Instead, they apply the same modern hermeneutics used to understand any ancient writings to their interpretation of the Bible. Given that Isaiah's first three Servant Songs unambiguously identify Israel as God's servant, and the chapters surrounding Isaiah 53 frequently speak of Israel as a suffering and humiliated individual, liberal Christian scholarship frequently identifies the servant in Isaiah's fourth Servant Song as the nation of Israel.[11]

Rabbinic commentaries who state Isaiah 53 refers to the messiah

According to rabbinic thought, when Isaiah speaks of the "servant," the prophet is not speaking of all the Jewish people. Rather, the "servant" in these uplifting prophetic hymns refers to the righteous remnant of Israel – the most pious of the nation. The faithful members of Israel who willingly suffer for Heaven's sake are identified in the Tanach as God's servant. These are the pious remnant who call upon the name of the Lord (43:7), who bear witness to His unity (43:11), and are therefore charged to restore the rest of Jacob (49:5).

> "You are My witnesses," declares the Lord, "and My servant whom I have chosen."
>
> (Isaiah 43:10)

In essence, God's "servant" is the cherished few—the faithful who walk in the footsteps of Abraham, whom the Almighty called "My friend."

> But you, O Israel, My servant, Jacob, whom I have chosen, you, descendants of Abraham, My friend.
>
> (Isaiah 41:8)

The Servant Songs address only the believers of Israel who emulate the first patriarch of the Jewish people. As Abraham endured trials and adversity in his walk with God, so too would His servant, the righteous remnant of Israel, endure ordeals and affliction in its sacred path (Isaiah 49:3; 51:21; 54:11; Psalm 44:11-15).

The Hebrew prophet, Zephaniah, vividly describes the cherished remnant of Israel in the following manner:

> And I will leave in the midst of thee an afflicted and poor people, and they shall take refuge in the name of the Lord. The remnant of Israel shall not do iniquity, nor speak lies, neither shall a deceitful tongue be found in their mouth. For they shall feed and lie down, and none shall make them afraid.
>
> (Zephaniah 3:12-13)

In rabbinic thought, all of God's faithful—gentiles included (Zechariah 13:8-9)—endure suffering on behalf of God (Isaiah 40:2; Zechariah 1:15). Thus, Jewish leaders of the past, such as Moses[12] and Jeremiah,[13] Rabbi Akiva,[14] as well as future eschatological figures, such as the messiah ben Joseph and the messiah ben David, are held up in rabbinic literature as individuals who exemplify the "servant" who willingly suffers on behalf of Heaven.

Therefore, when the Talmud (Sanhedrin 98a) describes the predicament of the messiah as he is waiting to be summoned by God, the rabbis cast him as:

> ...sitting among other paupers, all of them afflicted with disease. Yet, while all the rest of them tie and untie their bandages all at once, the messiah changes his bandages one at a time, lest he is summoned for the redemption at a moment's notice.

While this story may be understood allegorically, its jarring message is clear: The messiah, like other afflicted members of Israel, endures the agony and trials assigned to the faithful. Unlike the other suffering servants, however, who completely remove all their bandages before patiently replacing them with a fresh dressing, the messiah must methodically replace each bandage, one at a time. In other words, the messiah does not suffer more or less than other servants of God. According to the Talmud, the messiah is different from other men of God because he must be ready at a moment's notice to usher in the deliverance of his beleaguered people. Because he is prepared to be summoned for the redemption at all times, he is never in a predicament in which his bandages are fully removed.

Therefore, when Isaiah speaks of the suffering remnant of Israel, the messianic king is included. The final heir of David's throne is an integral member of the pious of Israel. According to rabbinic interpretation, this is the *pshat*, or the plain meaning of the text in Isaiah 52:13–53:12. Therefore, when both ancient and modern rabbinic commentators expound on the clear meaning of the text, they ascribe the suffering servant in Isaiah 53 to the nation of Israel.

Moreover, while Ezekiel warned that the righteous can never suffer or die as a sacrificial atonement for the wicked,[15] the Talmud teaches:

> Whosoever weeps over the [suffering] of the righteous man, all his sins are forgiven.
>
> (Talmud, Shabbat 105b)

In order to shed much-needed light on the famed "Servant Songs," numerous rabbinic commentators hold up Jewish heroes as a paradigm of Isaiah 53's "servant." Thus, while—on one hand—the Talmud, Zohar, and other ancient rabbinic texts state explicitly that the "servant" of Isaiah 53 refers to the faithful of corporate Jewry,[16] the same sources frequently point to renowned servants of Israel as archetypes of the Suffering Servant. These virtuous individuals include prophets such as Moses, Elijah, Jeremiah—and the messiah the son of Joseph and David. Each embodies a perfect example of God's servant, the righteous remnant of Israel.

Bear in mind that the rabbinic commentary on Isaiah 53 is not dualistic or multilateral. Meaning, the sages of old did **not** suggest that Isaiah 53 refers to **either** the righteous remnant of Israel, Moses, Jeremiah, **or** an anointed leader. Rather, the servant in all four Servant Songs are the faithful descendants of Abraham. Isaiah 53 attests to an unprecedented worldwide repentance of all of mankind: a redemptive achievement that no other righteous person has accomplished in history. Therefore, rabbinic commentators tend to proclaim the messiah's name more frequently than the names of other faithful servants of God.

While the vast majority of rabbinic commentary seeks to provide the *pshat*—the principal analysis which illuminates the plain meaning of sacred literature—there is, broadly speaking, a second and distinct stream of rabbinic commentary that explores the *drash*. In general terms, the *drash* delves into the deeply profound, yet often less precise, homiletic method of exegesis used to interpret the Hebrew Scriptures. This sacred material is often referred to as *midrashic*, literally "derived from a *drash*."

In Jewish thought, the *pshat* conveys the foundational understanding of any text in Tanach; this is the commentary which elucidates the clear and basic meaning of a verse. As the sages declare in the Talmud, "A verse cannot depart from its plain meaning." (Shabbat 63a; Yev. 11b, 24a). While the *midrashic* interpretation of a biblical verse is never intended to nullify, contradict, or injure the natural sense of a text, the *pshat* always supplies the primary meaning of a passage. Moreover, it is impossible to fully grasp the inspirational *midrashic* commentary without first comprehending and accepting the simple meaning of a text.

On the other hand, without the sublime illumination of the *Midrash*, seminal, seemingly disconnected principles throughout various passages in Tanach can be challenging to harmonize and fully comprehend. In other words, with only the *pshat* commentary, Biblical principles, when studied independently, can only be understood on a fundamental level. Yet the separate, straightforward commentaries of the *pshat* may appear incompatible and disjointed from other sections of Scripture without the *midrashic* commentary. *Midrashic* literature, generally speaking, weaves together and painstakingly merges Judaism's Written and Oral tradition into a transcendent revelation. Because the *Midrash* illuminates rabbinic thought to its fullest, holistic expression, it stands out as a vital tool for the student of sacred literature.

Few chapters in Tanach better illustrate the role the *Midrash* plays in expounding Biblical texts than Isaiah 53. The straightforward, rabbinic approach to elucidate Isaiah 53 begins by identifying the astonished speakers in Isaiah 53:1-9 and the "Servant" in Isaiah 52:13 and 53:11. The rabbinic annotations, i.e., the *pshat*, convey the clear and essential commentary. They describe how these passages record the reaction of the astonished and contrite kings of nations when they discover that the faithful members of Israel were always God's true servant. As mentioned earlier, the identities of the speakers and the servant are self-evident from the chapters surrounding of Isaiah 53.

The *Midrash*, however, illuminates a profound, yet often overlooked central theme of Isaiah 53: never before in history has any servant of God brought about the mass repentance of the gentiles. Whereas the patriarch Abraham redeemed only 70 souls in Haran, the future scion of the House of David will usher in an unprecedented epoch in which the gentile kings of nations will repent, as is vividly described in the fourth Servant Song. In other words, the messiah will bring about an age in which the most important feature of Isaiah 53 will materialize: the worldwide repentance of the gentiles.

Whereas Moses drew only a single nation from Egypt into the service of God, the messianic king will redeem the other nations as well. At this epic, redemptive moment in the future, all the nations will perceive that Judaism is the only true faith, as it is written:

> For then I will make the peoples pure of speech, so that they all invoke the name of the Lord and serve Him with one accord.
> (Zephaniah 3:9)

In the messianic age, the gentiles will cry aloud the remorseful and repentant words sketched in Isaiah 53. In essence, the sequence of events outlined in the fourth Servant Song will be an unparalleled occasion in history. Never before throughout the annals of time have "...the gentiles come to your light, and kings to the brightness of your rising" (Isaiah 60:3).

Therefore, although various rabbinic commentaries discuss the lives of people who exemplify the Suffering Servant of Israel in Isaiah 53, the future messiah is held up more frequently and prominently than any other pious Jew in this startling context, for the future anointed Davidic king will usher in this dramatic epoch in which the gentiles will repent, as outlined in Isaiah 53. In other words, the stunning narrative of the fourth Servant Song will be fulfilled by the reign of the messiah, the foremost member of God's Suffering Servant, Israel. Only the messiah will ignite global repentance in the final redemption, which neither Abraham, Moses, nor Jeremiah was able to accomplish. Only the messianic age will trigger the worldwide penitence of the nations. Therefore, the rabbis teach,

> My servant shall be high, and lifted up, and lofty exceedingly—he will be higher than Abraham, more exalted than Moses, loftier than the angels.[17]
> (Yalkut ii: 571)

In short, the messiah will ignite the contrition of Israel's neighbors as outlined in Isaiah's fourth Servant Song.

Because of the deeply esoteric and elastic nature of *midrashic* writings, these millennia-old texts are vulnerable to misuse by opponents of the Jewish faith. Isaiah 53 – the chapter in the Bible that has, for ages, formed one of the principal battlefields between Jews and their Christian opponents – is no exception to this rule.

Under ordinary circumstances, traditional Church apologists regard rabbinic commentaries with sneering derision, casting them, at best, as damaging to spiritual enlightenment. However, ancient *midrashic* annotations on Isaiah 53, which can be ripped out of context and portrayed as supportive of Christian teachings, are widely quoted and cheerfully paraded by missionaries in the hope of winning more unclaimed souls to the Cross. The fact that the Christian interpretation of Isaiah 53 is not supported by the chapters that surround it only adds to the Church's desperate feeding frenzy on these ancient rabbinic texts. It is ironic that missionaries use rabbinic texts to support Christian doctrines, given that **each and every one of the rabbis whom they zealously quote utterly rejected the teachings of Christianity**.

The most frequently quoted rabbinic text in Christian literature is, undoubtedly, the second-century Targum Yonatan ben Uziel on Isaiah 53. Although the word "*Targum*" literally means a "Translation," the Targum Yonatan ben Uziel is not at all a word-for-word translation of the Tanach.

Rather, this unique, highly regarded Aramaic annotation on the Hebrew Scriptures fuses together both *drash* and *pshat*—the homiletic and plain meaning of a text – in its running, dynamic commentary on the Prophets.

Thus, it is the messiah who is raised up as God's ideal servant in the Targum Yonatan ben Uziel on Isaiah 52:13, yet in the following verse, the Targum identifies the faithful of Israel who suffer vicariously (Isaiah 52:14).

As expected, missionaries selectively quote the Targum Yonatan ben Uziel on Isaiah 52:13, which identifies God's servant as the messiah.

The Targum's rendering of Isaiah 52:13 is as follows:

> Behold my servant messiah shall prosper; he shall be high, and increase, and be exceedingly strong.

Yet the Targum's commentary on the following verse, Isaiah 52:14, identifies Israel as the long-suffering and humiliated servant:

> As the House of Israel looked to him during many days, because their countenance was darkened among the peoples, and their complexion (darkened) beyond the sons of men.

Of course, the commentary of Targum Yonatan ben Uziel on Isaiah 52:14 is nowhere to be found in Christian missionary material. Neither is there a single church apologist who quotes the Targum's elucidation on Isaiah 53:10. In the following commentary from the Targum, these words of Isaiah—"He is crushed and made ill"—identify the suffering servant as the nation of Israel, which suffers unbearable chastisement:

> But it is the Lord's good pleasure to refine and cleanse the remnant of His people in order to purify their souls from sin. They shall see the kingdom of the messiah, they shall increase their sons and daughters, they shall prolong their days; and those who perform the Law of the Lord shall prosper in good pleasure.

Although Christian missionaries ignore Targum Yonatan ben Uziel's commentary on Isaiah 53:10, this two millennia-old message remains immortal. The nation of Israel, God's servant, suffered unimaginable torment at the hands of its gentile neighbors, so that its sins would be washed away.

> Speak tenderly to Jerusalem and declare to her: Her term of service is over, her iniquity is expiated; for she has received at the hand of the Lord double for all her sins.
>
> (Isaiah 40:2)

Simply put, there are 15 verses in the Targum's annotation on Isaiah 53 (52:13-15 and 53:1-12), yet with surgical precision, missionary conversionist tracts selectively and deliberately ignore almost all of them, with the exception of the first verse on Isaiah 52:13.

This is a well-worn technique of wielding rabbinic literature as an evangelical sledgehammer in order to promote a well-crafted message to unlettered Jews. The message? That ancient rabbis concealed the truth that Isaiah 53 is speaking of Jesus, not the nation of Israel. Nothing, of course, could be further from the truth.

Footnotes:

1. *Midrash Rabbah* (Numbers XXIII.2), Zohar (Genesis & Leviticus), Talmud (Berochos 5a), Rashi, Joseph Karo, Ibn Ezra, Joseph Kimchi, David Kimchi, Nachmanidies, Arbarbinbanel, et all

2. Ibn Ezra on Isaiah 53

3. *Origen, Contra Celsum*, Chadwick, Henry; Cambridge Press, book 1, chapter 55, page 50

4. Isaiah 41:11; Micah 7:15-16; Jeremiah 16:19-20;

5. Isaiah 41:8-9; 43:10; 44:1; 44:21; 45:4; 48:20; 49:3

6. *The New English Bible*, Oxford Study Edition, page 788-789. See also the *Revised Standard Bible*, Oxford Study Edition, page 889.

7. Acts 8:28-34

8. Luke 22:37

9. John 12:38

10. I Peter 2:22

11. *The Christian New English Bible, Oxford Study Edition*, annotation on Isaiah 52:13-53:12 explains:

    > The "fourth Servant Song, the Suffering Servant, Israel, the servant of God, has suffered as a humiliated individual. However, the servant endured without complaint because it was vicarious suffering (suffering for others). 52:13-15: Nations and kings will be surprised to see the servant exalted. 53:1: The crowds, pagan nations, among whom the servant (Israel) lived, speak here (through verse 9), saying that the significance of Israel's humiliation and exaltation is hard to believe (page 788-789). See also the *Revised Standard Bible, Oxford Study Edition*, page 889.

Walter Brueggemann Ph.D., *Isaiah 40 – 66* (Louisville: Kentucky, 1998), p. 143, states:

> "There is no doubt that Isaiah 53 is to be understood in the context of the Isaiah tradition. Insofar as the servant is Israel—a common assumption of Jewish interpretation—we see that the theme of humiliation and exaltation serves the Isaiah rendering of Israel, for Israel in this literature is exactly the humiliated (exiled) people who, by the powerful intervention of Yahweh is about to become the exalted (restored) people of Zion. Thus the drama is the drama of Israel and more specifically of Jerusalem, the characteristic subject of this poetry.
>
> Second, although it is clear that this poetry does not have Jesus in any first instance on its horizon, it is equally clear that the church, from the outset, has found the poetry a poignant and generative way to consider Jesus, wherein humiliation equals crucifixion and exaltation equals resurrection and ascension."

12. Talmud, Sotah 14a and the Sifre on Deuteronomy 355 applies Isaiah 53:12 to Moses

13. Rabbi Sadya Gaon (tenth century), Oxford, Ms. (Poc 32)

14. Jerusalem Talmud, Shekalim V.I.

15. Ezekiel 18:20-23

16. *Midrash Rabbah* (Numbers XXIII.2), Zohar (Genesis & Leviticus), Talmud (Berochos 5a),

17. *Yalkut*, ii, 571 on Zechariah 4:7

The following related articles can be found in Volume 2 of *Let's Get Biblical! Why doesn't Judaism Accept the Christian Messiah?*

I. The Haftorah and Isaiah 53:
   Are the Jews Hiding Something?. . . . . Page 107

II. Isaiah 53: Did Jesus Have Long Life?. . . . . . . Page 111

Part V

The Trinity and Isaiah 9:5-6

I believe with perfect faith that God is one...

Exodus 20:2-3 - The First of the Ten Commandments
"I am the Lord your God, who brought you out of Egypt, and of the land of slavery. You shall have no other gods before Me." (See also Deuteronomy 5:7)

Numbers 23:19
"God is not a man that He should lie, nor a mortal that He should change His mind."

Deuteronomy 4:11-12
"You came near and stood at the foot of the mountain while it blazed with fire to the very heavens, with black clouds and deep darkness. Then the Lord spoke to you out of the fire. You heard the sound of words but saw no image; there was only a voice."

Deuteronomy 4:35
"You are the ones who have been shown, so that you will know that God is the Supreme Being, and there is none other besides Him!"

Deuteronomy 4:39
"Know therefore today, and take it to your heart, that the Lord, He is God in heaven above and on the earth below; there is no other!

Deuteronomy 6:4
"Hear O Israel! The Lord is our God, the Lord is one."

Deuteronomy 6:14
"You shall not follow other gods, any of the gods of the peoples who surround you!"

Deuteronomy 32:39
"See, now, that I, I am He - and no god is with Me..."

I Samuel 2:2
"There is none holy as the Lord: for there is none beside Thee; neither is there any Rock like our God.

I Samuel 15:29
"The Eternal One of Israel will not lie nor change His mind: for He is not a man that He should change His mind."

There is no unity that is in any way like His...

I Kings 8:27
"For will God indeed dwell on the earth? Behold the heaven and heaven of heavens cannot contain Thee; how much less this house that I have built?"

I Kings 8:60
"So that all the nations of the earth may know that the Lord is God and that there is no other!"

II Kings 19:19
"Now, O Lord our God, deliver us from his hand, so that all kingdoms on earth may know that You alone, O Lord, are God." (Psalm 113:5)

Isaiah 40:18
"To whom then will you liken God? Or what likeness will you compare unto Him?"

Isaiah 40:25
"To whom will then you liken Me, that I should be his equal?" says the Holy One.

Isaiah 42:8
"I am the Lord, that is My name, and My glory will I not give to another. Neither My praise to graven images!"

Isaiah 43:10-11
"You are My witnesses," declares the Lord, "and My servant whom I have chosen, so that you may know and believe Me and understand that I am He. Before Me no god was formed, nor will there be one after Me. I, even I, am the Lord, and besides Me there is no Savior."

Isaiah 44:6-8
This is what the Lord says, Israel's King and Redeemer, the Lord Almighty, "I am the first and I am the last; apart from Me there is no God! Who then is like Me? Let him proclaim it. Let him declare and lay out before Me...Do not tremble, do not be afraid. Did I not proclaim this and foretell it long ago? You are My witnesses. Is there any God besides Me? No, there is no other Rock; I know not one."

Continued on the following page

He alone is our God.

Isaiah 44:24
So said the Lord, your Redeemer, the One who formed you from the womb, "I am the Lord Who makes everything, Who stretched forth the heavens alone, Who spread out the earth by Myself."

Isaiah 45:5-6
"I am the Lord, and there is no other; besides Me there is no God... I will strengthen you...I order that they know from the shining of the sun and from the west that there is no one besides Me; I am the Lord and there is no other!"

Isaiah 45:18-19
For this is what the Lord says – He who created the heavens, He is God; He who fashioned and made the earth, He founded it; He did not create it to be empty, but formed it to be inhabited – He says: "I am the Lord, and there is no other. I have not spoken in secret, from somewhere in a land of darkness; I have not said to Jacob's descendants, 'Seek Me in vain.' I, the Lord, speak the truth; I declare what is right."

Isaiah 45:21-22
"...who announced this before, who declared it from the distant past? Is it not I, the Lord, and there is no God apart from Me, a righteous God and Savior; there is none but Me. Turn to Me and be saved, all you ends of the earth; for I am God, and there is no other!"

Isaiah 46:5
"To whom shall you liken Me and make Me equal and compare Me that we may be alike?"

Isaiah 46:9
"Remember the first things of old, that I am God and there is no other; I am God and there is none like Me."

Isaiah 48:11
"...And My honor I will not give to another."

He was, He is, He will be.

Isaiah 48:12
"Hearken unto Me, O Jacob and Israel, My called: I am He; I am the First, I also am the Last."

Hosea 13:4
"And I am the Lord your God, Who brought you out of Egypt. You shall acknowledge no God but Me, no Savior except Me!"

Joel 2:27
"And you shall know that I am in the midst of Israel, and I am the Lord your God, there is no other; and My people shall never be ashamed."

Malachi 2:10
"Have we not all one Father? Has not one God created us? Why should we betray, each one his brother, to profane the covenant of our forefathers?"

Psalm 73:25
"Whom have I in heaven but You? And earth has nothing I desire besides You."

Psalm 81:8-9
"Hear, O My people, and I will admonish you; O Israel, if you would listen to Me! Let there be no strange god among you; nor shall you worship any foreign god.

Psalm 146:3
"Do not put your trust in princes, nor in the son of man, in whom there is no salvation!"

Nehemiah 9:6
"You alone are the Lord; You made the heavens, the heavens of the heavens and all their host, the earth and all that is upon it, the seas and all that is in them, and You give life to them all, and the heavenly host bow down before You."

I Chronicles 17:20
"O Lord, there is none like You, neither is there any God beside You, according to all that we have heard with our ears!"

Maimonidies Thirteen Fundamental Principles of Faith

1. I believe with perfect faith that God is the Creator and Ruler of all things. He alone has made, does make, and will make all things.

2. I believe with perfect faith that God is One (יָחֵד). There is no unity that is in any way like His. He alone is our God. He was, He is, and He will be.

3. I believe with perfect faith that God does not have a body – physical concepts do not apply to Him. There is nothing whatsoever that resembles Him at all.

4. I believe with perfect faith that God is first and last.

5. I believe with perfect faith that it is only proper to pray to God. One may not pray to anyone or anything else.

6. I believe with perfect faith that all the words of the prophets are true.

7. I believe with perfect faith that the prophecy of Moses is absolutely true. He was the chief of all prophets, both before and after Him.

8. I believe with perfect faith that the entire Torah that we now have is that which was given to Moses.

9. I believe with perfect faith that this Torah will not be changed, and that there will never be another given by God.

10. I believe with perfect faith that God knows all of man's deeds and thoughts. It is thus written, "He has molded every heart together, He understands what each one does." (Psalm 33:15)

11. I believe with perfect faith that God rewards those who keep His commandments, and punishes those who transgress Him.

12. I believe with perfect faith in the coming of the Messiah. How long it takes, I will await his coming every day.

13. I believe with perfect faith that the dead will be brought back to life when God wills it to happen.

Genesis 1:26-27

And God said, "Let *us* make man in *our* image, after *our* likeness..." So God created man in His image, in the image of God He created him...

I Kings 22:19
Micah continued, "Therefore hear the word of the Lord: I saw the Lord sitting on His throne *with all the host of heaven standing around Him* on His right and on His left.

Isaiah 6:1-2, 8
In the year that king Uzziah died I saw also the Lord sitting upon a throne, high and lifted up, and his train filled the temple. ²*Seraphims* stood above; each one had six wings... ⁸Also I heard the voice of the Lord, saying, "Whom shall I send, and who will go for *us*?"

Jeremiah 22:26
²⁶But which of them has stood in *the council of the Lord* to see or to hear His word?

Jeremiah 23:18, 22
¹⁸But which of them [false prophets] has stood in the *council* of the Lord to see or to hear His word?... ²²But if they had stood in My *council* they would have proclaimed My words to My people and would have turned them from their evil ways...

Job 1:6
Now there was a day when the sons of God of God came to present themselves before the Lord, and Satan came also with them.

Job 15:8
Do you listen in on God's council? Do you limit wisdom to yourself?

Christian (Trinitarian) Commentators on Genesis 1:26

G. J. Wenham
"Christians have traditionally seen [Genesis 1:26] as adumbrating [foreshadowing] the Trinity. It is now universally admitted that this was not what the plural meant to the original author."

Word Biblical Commentary on Genesis, Word Books, 1987, p. 27.

The NIV Study Bible
us...our...our. God speaks as the Creator-king, announcing his crowning work to the members of his heavenly court (see 322; 11:7; Isa 6:8; see also I Ki 22:19-23; Job 15:8; Jer 23:18)

Grand Rapids: Zondervan, 1985, p. 7.

The Ryrie Study Bible
Us...Our. Plurals of majesty.

Charles Caldwell Ryrie (Dallas Theological Seminary), Chicago: Moody Press, 1978, p. 9.

Liberty Annotated Study Bible
"The plural pronoun *us* is most likely a majestic plural from the standpoint of Hebrew grammar and syntax."

Jerry Falwell (Executive Editor), Lynchburg: Liberty Univ., 1988, p. 8.

Keil and Delitzsch
"The plural 'We' was regarded by the fathers and earlier theologians almost unanimously as indicative of the Trinity: modern commentators, on the contrary, regard it either as *pluralis majestatis*...No other explanation is left, therefore, than to regard it as *pluralis majestatis*..."

Keil & Delitzsch Commentary on the Old Test., Peabody: Hendric., 1989, Vol. I, p. 62.

Did the Authors of the New Testament Believe in the Doctrine of the Trinity?

Matthew 3:17

And suddenly a voice came from heaven, saying, "This is My beloved Son, in whom I am well pleased."

> What is the value of God indicating his pleasure in Jesus, if Jesus was God? Was God taking pleasure in Himself? And what did Jesus supposedly achieve here, if he was God and it was impossible for him to sin, or do wrong?

Matthew 20:20-23

The mother of the sons of Zebedee... ²¹said to him [Jesus], "Command that these two sons of mine may sit, one at your right hand and one at your left, in your kingdom." ²²But Jesus answered and said..., ²³ "You will drink my cup, but to sit at my right hand and at my left is not mine to grant, but is for those for whom it has been prepared by my Father."

> If Jesus was fully God, why could only the Father, and not Jesus, grant that the two sons of Zebedee sit at the right and left of Jesus?

Matthew 26:39

Going a little farther, he [Jesus] fell on his face to the ground and prayed, saying, "O my Father, if it is possible, may this cup be taken from me. Yet not as I will, but as you will.

> If the Father and Jesus were of the same substance, such a prayer would have been meaningless. Jesus would have been praying to himself, and his will, out of necessity, would have been that of the Father.

Matthew 26:53

Do you think I cannot call on my Father, and he will at once put at my disposal more than twelve legions of angels?

> If Jesus was God, why would he need to request legions of angels from God? Is there anything God lacks that He must request from another?

Mark 10:17-20

And as he [Jesus] was setting out on a journey, a man ran up to him and knelt before him, and began asking him, "Good Teacher, what shall I do to inherit eternal life?" [18] And Jesus said to him, "Why do you call me good? No one is good except God alone." [19] "You know the commandments: 'Do not murder...'" [20] And he said to him, "Teacher, I have kept all these things from my youth up."

> If, as Trinitarians insist, Jesus was God, why did Jesus rebuke the man for addressing him as "*Good Teacher*"? (Jesus believed that the title *"good"* was appropriate for God *alone*, who he considered the *only* standard of goodness).
>
> Interestingly, after the man was corrected, he addressed Jesus only as "Teacher."

Mark 13:32

But of that day and that hour knoweth no man, no, not the angels which are in heaven, neither the son, but the Father.

> If Jesus was coequal with the Father, how could the Father have information that Jesus lacked? Moreover, if, as some Trinitarians suggest, the son was limited by his human nature, why didn't the Holy Spirit know?

John 5:37

"The Father who sent me has himself borne witness about me. His voice you have never heard, his form you have never seen."

> Yet Jesus said, "The servant is not greater than his lord; neither he that is sent greater than he that sent him." (John 13:16) Jesus said on numerous occasions that, "the Father... hath sent me." (John 5:37, 6:37) The Holy Ghost was also sent by the Father (John 14:26) and Jesus (John 16:7), thus making Jesus subordinate to the Father, and the Holy Ghost inferior to both the Father and Jesus.
>
> Moreover, God is invisible and never seen, Jesus was of course seen (John 1:18, I John 4:12, I Tim. 6:16).

John 8:17-18

"In your own Law it is written that the testimony of two men is valid. [18] I am one who testifies for myself; my other witness is the Father, who sent me."

> In John 8:17-18, Jesus quotes from the Law the necessity that evidence, to be valid, must be agreed upon by two witnesses. Jesus states that the two witnesses are himself and God. Two, not one. If Jesus was God, there was only one witness, and if Jesus says there are two, then he and God are not one.

John 10:30-34

"I and my Father are **one (ἕν)**." ³¹Again the Jews picked up stones to stone him, but Jesus said to them "I have shown you many great miracles from the Father. For which of these do you stone me?" ³²"We are not stoning you for any of these," replied the Jews, "but for blasphemy, because you, a mere man, claim to be God." ³⁴Jesus answered them, "Is it not written in your Law, 'I have said you are gods?'" *(see Psalm 82:6)*

Trinitarians maintain that Jesus' statement, "I and my Father are *one*," demonstrates that Jesus was declaring himself to be God. The Greek word ἕν (one), however, does not imply being a part of the same substance. This is clearly illustrated in John 17:11 and 17:21-22, where in these passages Jesus prays to God for his disciples to be one (ἕν) as Jesus and God are. Jesus is obviously requesting that the disciples be of one *unified purpose*, not of the same substance or part of the Trinity.

Moreover, John 10:30-34 is particularly revealing. The fourth Gospel claims that when the Jews heard Jesus proclaim, "I and my Father are one," they immediately wanted to stone him to death. When Jesus asked why they wanted to kill him, the Jews responded because "you claim to be God." Upon hearing this Jesus asked, "Is it not written in your Law, 'I have said you are gods'?"

This response gives us insight into the mind of the author of the Book of John, and should be instructive to Trinitarians.

The verse quoted by Jesus is found in Psalm 82:6 where the Bible refers to judges who teach God's divine Law as gods.

> "I said, 'You are "gods"; you are all sons of the Most High.'"
> (Psalm 82:6)

Furthermore, the Torah identifies Judges as gods (אֱלֹהִים *Elohim*) as well,

> Then his master shall bring him to the judges הָאֱלֹהִים... for any kind of lost thing which ⁸ another claims to be his, the cause of both parties shall come before the judges (אֱלֹהִים); and whoever the judges (אֱלֹהִים) condemn shall pay double to his neighbor.
> (Exodus 21:6, 22:8)

This title was bestowed upon Jewish judges because they were agents of the Almighty's divine Law, not because they were actually God in any way. The Jewish Scriptures frequently refer to agents of God as a god.

For example, in Exodus 7:1 Moses is called a "god" because he was God's representative to Pharaoh. The New Testament never claims that Jesus is God, the Creator of the universe, but rather His subordinate representative.

John 12:49

For I did not speak of my own accord, but the Father who sent me commanded me what to say and how to say it.

> If God and Jesus are "one in essence," as the Trinity doctrine says, how could Jesus' accord, or will, be different from that of his Father? How can Jesus' privilege not be the same as God? Moreover, if Jesus was the same as God, why would God have to send or command God to do anything?

John 14:28

"...I [Jesus] go unto the Father, for my father is greater than I."

> This verse speaks for itself.

John 17:3

And this is life eternal, that they might know thee, the only true God, and Jesus Christ, Whom thou hast sent.

> Here Jesus insists that the Father is the "*only* true God." The Greek word used here for "only" is *monos*, which is meant to exclude all others. Clearly, the Father cannot be "the *only* true God" if there are two others who are God to the same degree as he is.

John 20:17

Jesus saith unto her [Mary], "Touch me not; for I am not yet ascended to my Father. But go to my brethren, and say unto them, I ascend unto my Father, and your Father; and to my God, and your God."

> If Jesus was God, why would he tell Mary that he considered her Father as his Father, and her God as his God? In Revelation 3:12, after the crucifixion, we continue to see Jesus calling the Father "my God." But never in the Christian Bible is the Father reported to refer to Jesus as "my God," nor does either the Father or Jesus refer to the Holy Spirit as "my God."

Did Paul believe in the doctrine of the Trinity?

I Corinthians 8:4-6
...and that is none other God but one. ⁵For though there be that are called gods, whether in heaven or in earth, (as there may be many gods, and many lords,) ⁶But to us there is but one God, the Father, of whom are all things, and we in him; and one Lord Jesus Christ, by whom are all things, and we by him.

> Paul insisted that only the Father is declared to be the one and only God. In Ephesians 1:17 Paul was still unaware of the Trinity when he says, "That the God of our Lord Jesus Christ..."

I Corinthians 11:3
But I would have you know, that the head of every man is Christ; and the head of the woman is the man; and the head of Christ is God.

> This verse does not depict Jesus as coequal with God. On the contrary, God is of superior rank to Jesus.
>
> Moreover, this statement reveals that the New Testament did not consider Jesus to be equal with God even after the ascension. Paul wrote these words around 55 C.E. — long after the crucifixion.

I Corinthians 15:28
When he has done this, then the Son himself will be made subject to him who put everything under him, so that God may be all in all.

> Here Paul unambiguously insists that Jesus was subordinate to God as His "subject." Throughout the New Testament it is claimed that God bestowed authority upon Jesus – never the other way around.

I Peter 1:3
Blessed be the God and Father of our Lord Jesus Christ...
(Not a Pauline epistle)

> As mentioned above, this concept is restated many times throughout the New Testament: the Father is Jesus' God—never the other way around (see also Matt. 4:7, 27:46; Rom. 15:6, II Cor. 1:3, I Pet. 1:3; Rev. 1:6, 3:12 (four times).

Colossians 1:15

He [Jesus] is the image of the invisible God, the firstborn of all creation.

> If the earliest Christians believed in the Trinity, why didn't the New Testament ever refer to the Father or the Holy Spirit as the "firstborn of all creation?" Understandably, the New Testament would never refer to the Father as "firstborn" because early the early Church considered the Father alone eternal. The doctrine of the Trinity was a later Christian invention.

I Timothy 2:5

For there is one God and one mediator between God and men, the man Christ Jesus.

> The fact that Paul clearly distinguished between God and Jesus places considerable strain on Trinitarianism.

Hebrews 4:15

For we do not have a high priest who cannot sympathize with our weaknesses, but one who has been tempted in all things as we are, yet without sin.

> Consider how the temptation of Jesus is portrayed throughout the Gospels. The New Testament emphatically states "Jesus was tempted in all things as we are, yet without sin." But the Church's claim that Jesus is God spawned insurmountable conundrums: Temptation without the possibility of falling to sin is meaningless. If Jesus is God, it was impossible for him to sin, and it makes no sense to say he was tempted.
>
> Moreover, James 1:13 states that God cannot be tempted!

Hebrews 5:7-8

[Jesus] offered up both prayers and supplications with loud crying and tears to the one who was able to save him from death, and he was heard. ⁸Although he was a son, he learned obedience from the things he suffered.

> Why would God need to beg and cry to God to save him from death?
> Moreover, if the author of Hebrews considered Jesus God, why does Hebrews 5:8 insist that Jesus learned obedience from suffering? Is there anything God does not know and must learn through experience?

What is the Origin of the Doctrine of the Trinity?

People frequently ask: "If the Trinity is not found in the New Testament, how did this Church teaching become a central doctrine of Christianity?" Many speculate that this creed was first expressed under the authority of the Emperor Constantine at the Council of Nicea, which he convened in 325 CE. This widespread notion, however, which was likely popularized by the book, *The Da Vinci Code*, is not accurate. There is, in fact, one famed verse in the Christian Bible which succinctly articulates the doctrine of the Trinity, that there are three divine persons in the godhead, yet these three all constitute one God. This passage appears in the anonymous epistle (letter) I John, whose authorship was ascribed by the Church to the Apostle John.[1] The King James Version of the Bible reads:

> **For there are three that bear record in heaven, the Father, the Word, and the Holy Spirit: and these three are one.** And there are three that bear witness in earth, the Spirit, and the water, and the blood: and these three agree in one.
>
> (1 John 5:7-8)

Budapest. Holy Trinity Statue (Father, Son, Holy Spirit), 18th cent.

This passage explicitly and concisely conveys the Church's core teaching on the triune nature of God, who is yet one in essence. If this verse in I John did not exist, the central doctrine of the Trinity would not be found anywhere in the New Testament. Missionaries would then be forced to rely on only a few sketchy passages in the Christian canon, which they claim infer that Jesus was a member of a triune godhead. For many centuries, Christian apologists frequently touted 1 John 5:7 to demonstrate the veracity, and most importantly, the apostolic authority of Christendom's most controversial creed.

As you might suspect, the authenticity of the Trinitarian segment in I John 5:7, which scholars have called the "Johannine Comma," is doubtful. In fact, this phrase is a forged comma (short clause) of spurious origin which later scribes deliberately inserted into John's first epistle. Virtually all Christian commentators—fundamentalist, Trinitarian scholars included—concede that the author of I John did not write the triune passage, and the Johannine Comma is a late insertion that was interpolated into the text of 1 John 5:7-8.

The Johannine Comma does not appear in any Greek manuscript prior to the 16th century. The words crept into the Latin text of the New Testament in the Early Middle Ages (approx. 800 CE) and then were back-translated into some 16th century Greek manuscripts. All of the earlier Greek manuscripts of I John 5:7 simply read:

> There are three that bear witness: the Spirit, the water, and the blood: and these three are one.

What happened to the phrase, "the Father, the Word, and the Holy Spirit: and these three are one"?

Thus, the Jewish Bible was not the only victim of the Christian editor. The first epistle of John contains a startling example of how the New Testament was doctored in order to bolster the

---

Below are the most renowned, ancient manuscripts of the New Testament. I John 5:7-8 is highlighted. The Trinitarian phrase, "For there are three that bear record in heaven, the Father, the Word, and the Holy Spirit: and these three are one" does not appear in any of these Greek texts.

Codex Vaticanus - 4th Cent.

Codex Sinaiticus - 4th Cent.

Codex Alexandrinus - 5th Cent.

notion that the earliest Christians believed in the doctrine of the Trinity. What would compel later Christian editors to tamper with their own Bible? The answer is simple: the doctrine of the Trinity is a creed which developed after the completion of the New Testament, where there is no mention of a triune godhead. As you would expect, later scribes of the New Testament found this glaring absence disturbing, and so in one place they inserted an explicit reference to the Trinity. In essence, the Trinity is a later Christian invention and therefore this doctrine is not expressed in any of the books of the Christian Bible.

To be sure, the Church Fathers, who desperately sought to defend the doctrine of the Trinity and would have loved such a reading, never quoted I John 5:7.[2] The leading apologists of the early Church, Tertullian and Origen, never quoted or referred to the passage, which they would have done if the verse was in the Bibles of that era. Jerome's extant writings from the period 380 – 420 CE give no evidence that he was aware of the Comma's existence. Augustine (354 – 430 CE), widely revered as the Church's greatest theologian, also never quoted the Comma, which provides unassailable evidence that the Comma did not exist in John's epistle during his lifetime.[3]

> **Newton: Trinitarian clause in I John 5:7 a forgery**
>
> Although Isaac Newton (1643-1727) is best known as one of the greatest and most influential scientists who ever lived, he wrote more about theology and Biblical studies than science and mathematics. Newton was a fierce opponent of the doctrine of the Trinity. In a 1690 treatise entitled, *An Historical Account of Two Notable Corruptions of Scripture*, he summed up the history of the Johannine Comma and his own belief that it was a forgery. He was convinced that the Comma was inserted into a Latin text in a later century, a time when he believed the Church to be ripe with corruption. He commented:
>
>> In all the vehement universal and lasting controversy about the Trinity in Jerome's time and both before and long enough after it, this text of the "three in heaven" was never once thought of. It is now in everybody's mouth and accounted the main text for the business and would assuredly have been so too with them, had it been in their books.[4]

Why does the King James Version contain the Comma?

Although the Authorized King James Version retained the Comma, numerous modern Bible translations such as the New International Version (NIV), the New American Standard Bible (NASB), the English Standard Version (ESV), the New Revised Standard Version (NRSV) and others omit the spurious Comma in I John 5:7 entirely because they regard it as a later interpolation. The Nova Vulgata, the modern revision of the Vulgate approved for liturgical use by the

Catholic Church, also excludes the Comma. Given that the Trinitarian phrase in I John 5:7 appears in none of the early Greek manuscripts of the New Testament, how did the Johannine Comma creep its way into the Authorized King James Version, which is one of the most revered translations of the Bible in the English speaking world?

The central figure in the 16th century history of the Johannine Comma is the humanist scholar Erasmus from Rotterdam, who was the first to produce and publish the Greek New Testament in 1516. Erasmus would ultimately produce four subsequent revised editions of this first Greek New Testament in the years that followed, which would become the standard form of the Greek text to be published by Western European printers for the next few centuries.

> **Was the King James Version divinely inspired?**
>
> In the early 20th century there emerged a popular "King James Only" movement which claims that the KJV itself was divinely inspired. They see the translation to be preserved by God and as accurate as the original Greek and Hebrew manuscripts found in its underlying texts. Members of this sect claim that the KJV is a "new revelation" or "advanced revelation" from God, and it should be the standard from which all other translations originate. Adherents to this belief also claim that the original languages, Hebrew and Greek, can be corrected by the KJV! It goes without saying the sect's members tenaciously hold that the Johannine Comma belongs in its rightful place in I John 5:7, just where Erasmus placed it in his third edition.
>
> As the old saying goes, "If the King James was good enough for St. Paul, it's good enough for me!"

Of course, when Erasmus examined his collection of Greek manuscripts of 1 John 5:7, all he found was "There are three that bear witness: the Spirit, the water, and the blood, and these are all one." The phrase, "The Father, the Word, and the Spirit: and these three are one," did not appear in any of Erasmus' manuscripts, and so, understandably, he left it out of his Greek New Testament.

As you could well imagine, the Comma's absence from Erasmus' early editions sparked intense outrage among leading churchmen and scholars of his day. They charged Erasmus with the heretical undertaking of tampering with the text in an effort to eradicate the doctrine of the Trinity. In particular, Lopez de Zúñiga, one of the chief Complutensian polyglot editors,[5] publicly accused Erasmus of attempting to eliminate the doctrine of the Trinity and thereby call into question the deity of Jesus. He demanded that Erasmus restore the Johannine Comma in his next edition of the Greek text.

Erasmus replied to his critics that the Comma did not exist in any of the Greek manuscripts he could find. Nevertheless, he promised that he would add it to future editions if his critics could produce a single Greek manuscript which contained the Johannine Comma.[6]

And so, just such a manuscript was subsequently produced just for Erasmus. As the story goes, a Franciscan copied the Greek text of the Epistle, and when he came to John 5:7-8, he back-translated the Latin Trinitarian text into the Greek.[7] Essentially, this was a custom-made 16th century Greek manuscript produced especially for the Erasmus' next publication. Erasmus then kept his promise and inserted the Comma into his third edition in 1522. Erasmus' change was accepted into the Received Text editions (*Textus Receptus*), the chief source for the King James Version, thereby fixing the Comma firmly in the English language Scriptures for centuries.[8]

Clearly, the earliest Christians did not consider Jesus to be God, and the doctrine of the Trinity was a later development in Christian thinking. After all, if the first followers of Jesus thought that Jesus was one of the three persons of the triune godhead, why didn't a single New Testament author say so? It seems like it would have been a significant feature of Jesus' identity to point out. And surely, if Jesus spent his days proclaiming that "I am the God of Abraham, Isaac, and Jacob, Who brought you out of Egypt...," one would think that all the Gospel authors would have been eager to mention it. Did the Gospel writers just forget to say anything about that part of Jesus' teachings?

Rather, the earliest Christian traditions point in a completely different direction, emphasizing that Jesus was completely human and subordinate to God, and say nothing at all about his being divine. On the contrary, the Gospels insist that Jesus denied that he was God (Matthew 19:16-17; Mark 10:17-18; Luke 18:28-29) and conceded that "the Father is greater than I" (John 14:26). The Gospels portray Jesus as praying to God (Matthew 26:36-46; Mark 14:32-42; Luke 22:39-46; John 17:1-26) and pleading for an answer to his question on the cross: "My God, my God, why have You forsaken me?" (Mark 15:34). Was God talking to Himself or asking Himself a question? Moreover, according to the Gospel narratives of Jesus' baptism, a voice from heaven declares, "You are my beloved son in whom I am well pleased" (Mark 1:11). If Mark, the author of the earliest Gospel, believed that Jesus was God, why would he have God exclaiming that He was pleased with Himself?

The answer is simple: The notion that Jesus is God and a member of a triune godhead was developed long after the inception of Christianity.

This raises a pressing and intriguing question: How did the thoroughly monotheistic Christian movement that first broke away from Judaism so rapidly transform itself into a religion that embraced the notion that God had a son who was both fully human and divine, and a member of a three-part godhead? Why did it stray so far from Judaism, and eventually espouse the pagan notion that there were multiple deities that were incorporated into one Trinity?

In order to grasp how, when, and why Christians came to regard Jesus as God we need to explore the Christian Church from its inauspicious beginnings among the few followers of Jesus in Jerusalem to the heart of the empire, the city of Rome.

Is there a religion that is more variegated than Christianity in the modern world? A Catholic priest might feel more comfortable attending a Bar Mitzvah than a Pentecostal tent revival. A Seventh Day Adventist who found himself at a Greek Orthodox Divine Liturgy, or a high-church Episcopal priest who happened upon an Amish church service would likely find the rituals unfamiliar. There are traditionalist Roman Catholics who insist on worshiping with the highly structured, centuries-old Latin Mass (Tridentine Mass), and Pentecostal churches where parishioners spontaneously speak in strange "tongues" while rolling on the floor shouting imperceptible "prophecies." There are staunch Lutherans who claim that the pope is the anti-Christ, and ultraconservative Roman Catholics who believe that Protestants are unsaved. No doubt that there are significant common beliefs among these divergent Christian movements; however, the differences between their liturgy, expression, devotion, and worship are probably more striking than their similarities.

Are these widely diverse beliefs and practices among Christians a relatively recent phenomenon? Was Christianity a uniform religion at its inception and splintered in recent centuries? This is precisely what many people think about the history of the early church. They believe that the Christian religion was originally stable, monolithic, and uniform; however, as a result of numerous divisive events, including the 11th century East-West Great Schism and the 16th century Reformation, this unity was shattered. As it turns out, however, the diversity in what Christians believe today pales in comparison with the variances that existed during the first three Christian centuries. In fact, if we go back 1,800 years, we would encounter groups identifying themselves as Christian who embraced beliefs and practices that most Christians today would hardly recognize.

What did these ancient Christian sects believe, and how did their radically divergent beliefs shape what would emerge as the doctrine of the Trinity?

How many gods did early Christians believe in? It depended on whom you asked

While it is beyond the scope of this book to present a detailed description of the many Christian sects that flourished in the ancient world, we will briefly explore those early groups whose staunch views shaped the orthodox view of Jesus' nature. This view, which emerged as the formal doctrine of the Trinity, was firmly established by the unified Church under the authority of powerful Christian Roman emperors during the 4th century.

As mentioned earlier, the notion that Jesus was divine developed long after the inception of the Christian movement. The very earliest Christians, many of whom were Jewish, did not believe in Jesus' pre-existence, divinity, virgin birth, and physical resurrection. This view is called "adoptionist" because its adherents did not believe that Jesus was born to a virgin, but rather from the sexual union between Joseph and Mary, and that God "adopted" Jesus as His son at his baptism.

The Book of Mark, the oldest and least embellished of the four Gospels, therefore says nothing about Jesus' divinity, pre-existence, virgin birth in Bethlehem, Herod's slaying of the innocents, or post-resurrection encounters with the disciples. The earliest Gospel gives no indication that the events surrounding his birth were unusual. Accordingly, Mark introduces us to Jesus as an adult at his baptism. In fact, if you read only the Book of Mark—and in the early church, this was the only Gospel that many Christians had—you would have no clue that Jesus was conceived miraculously, born in the city of Bethlehem, or appeared *physically* to any of his followers after his resurrection. The earliest gospel concludes with Jesus' burial, and the following Sunday, the two Marys and Salome discover that the stone was rolled away. Going inside, they find a man in a white robe who tells them that Jesus has risen. He instructs them to tell the disciples that Jesus will appear to them in Galilee, and does not indicate whether Jesus will appear physically, in a vision, or as a ghostly spirit (16:1-7). The women flee the tomb and say nothing to anyone, "for they were afraid" (16:8). The original Book of Mark abruptly ends without any description of Jesus encountering Mary or the disciples following the crucifixion.

Scribes in the early Church were so disappointed by Mark's unsatisfying conclusion that they added their own, appending twelve additional verses (16:9-20) that describe some of Jesus' appearances to the disciples, the signs to the believers that they will be able to cast out demons, speak in "tongues," handle poisonous snakes (this is the passage on which Christian snake handlers base their tradition), and drink anything deadly. All of the earliest Greek manuscripts of the Book of Mark end at 16:8 with the report that the women fled Jesus' empty tomb in fear and told no one what they had seen. All Christian scholars—fundamentalist evangelicals included—concede that Mark 16:9-20 is a later interpolation.

None of the writings of the adoptionist groups from the very early years of the Christian movement survived. Everything we know about them is recorded in the writings of their enemy's records. Paul, who had at least as many enemies as friends, frequently refers to these groups in his letters. The Ebionites, a group made up of Jews who had converted to Christianity, were among the most well-known of these sects. They insisted that followers of Jesus had to be Jewish or convert to Judaism. They considered the Jewish Law given by Moses, including kosher food laws and the observance of Sabbath and all Jewish holidays, as binding. This sect likely reflects the most primitive Christian thinking.

For them, Jesus was the messiah who was conceived like everyone else, from the sexual union of his parents—Joseph and Mary. Jesus, they believed, was unique in that he was more righteous in his loyalty to the Jewish law, and he was chosen by God at his baptism, where it was announced that he became God's son. In essence, even though Jesus was chosen by God, he was not himself divine. He was a righteous man, but nothing more than a man. For them, it was blatant sacrilege to call Jesus God. For if Jesus were God, and his Father were also God, there would be two Gods, not one. This they regarded as outright idolatry, for the Torah states "Hear O Israel, the Lord is our God, the Lord is one" (Deut. 6:4). Man was created by God; thus, he could not be God. They regarded Jesus as the "son of God" in the Jewish sense where this title is assigned to the nation of Israel (Ex. 4:22; Hos. 11:1) or the

---

Does the Messianic movement espouse the beliefs of the original Jewish followers of Jesus?

Messianic leaders insist that their movement's beliefs reflect the most authentic and earliest expression of the first followers of Jesus.

The early followers of the Jesus-movement should not be confused with the modern "Messianic movement," which aggressively promotes itself as embodying the beliefs and practices of the first believers in Jesus.

The Ebionites and the very earliest Christian movement, which was largely made up of Jews, would consider the Messianic movement thoroughly aberrant and completely heretical because it embraces the doctrine of the Trinity, the virgin birth, and unflinchingly follows all the teachings of Paul. In essence, the Messianic movement embraces the most embellished and evolved doctrines of Protestant Christian theology while adopting Jewish customs, icons, ethnicity, and rabbinic traditions in order to portray their beliefs as authentically Jewish. They borrow superficial Jewish culture and shy away from inconsequential Christian holidays such as Christmas in order to lure into their fold Jews who would otherwise reject a straightforward Christian message.

king of Israel (II Sam. 7:14), indicating that someone is in a special relationship with God because that individual devoted his life to perform His work on earth. This title is never bestowed on a divine being in the Jewish Scriptures.

Not surprisingly, these early "Jewish-Christian" groups were Paul's chief opponents, as is widely attested in Paul's epistles and in the Book of Acts. They considered Paul to be a complete heretic—a self-promoting, late-coming fraud rather than an apostle. Because Paul taught that Jesus brought an end to the Jewish Law, they regarded him as their archenemy and his teachings as blasphemy. And Paul explicitly states in his own letters that his avid opponents were aberrant and spreading false teachings. There was no love lost between these early Christian interlocutors. Paul's enemies saw themselves as the true followers of Jesus, as well as his brother James and the apostle Peter, who were both prominent leaders of the Jerusalem Church. For this reason, when Paul battles his staunch critics—which he does in virtually all of his epistles—he emphasizes at every turn that he is the true apostle of Jesus.

At the diametrical opposite end of the theological spectrum stands another early Christian sect called the "Marcionites," named after the scholar and evangelist Marcion. In sharp contrast to the Ebionites, Marcion insisted that Paul was the true apostle who effectively set the Gospel of Jesus over and against the God of the Jews.

Marcion, who took his cues exclusively from Paul, was an intriguing thinker who gained a huge following during the mid-2nd century. He grasped that Judaism and Christianity were completely incompatible and utterly irreconcilable. The teachings of the Law of Moses, he believed, are alien to the Gospel. He argued that the God of Jesus and Paul was not the God of the "Old Testament." He drew a logical conclusion. There were two separate and entirely incompatible Gods: the lower God of the Jews, who created the world, and the God Jesus who came into the world to save mankind from the inferior, angry, Jewish Creator God. In other words, the "God of the Old Testament" chose the Jews, gave them a Law they couldn't keep, and then condemned them when they disobeyed. These two Gods, in his opinion, were enemies and had nothing in common. Jesus could have no connection to this material world that the inferior, furious God of the Jews had made.

According to Marcion, therefore, Jesus was not really born and did not have a real physical body. If Jesus' body was not made of flesh and blood, how did he eat, drink, bleed and die? Marcionites insisted that it was all just an appearance: Jesus only seemed to be human. In reality, he never engaged in any of those mortal activities. Jesus' body was only an apparition. Jesus *appeared* to die on the cross in order to enable his followers to escape the clutches of the wrathful God of the Jews.

Marcion, therefore, completely rejected the entire Hebrew Bible. He wanted nothing to do with it. He wrote a book called *Antitheses* (literally, *Contrary Statement*) that showed the God of the Law and the God of Jesus were hostile to each other. However, his most important literary accomplishment was not a work that he had written, but one that he edited. He was the first to assemble a Christian canon. His New Testament, however, included only ten letters of Paul (he omitted the three Pastoral Epistles—1 & 2 Timothy and Titus); and since Paul made some reference to his "gospel," Marcion included a truncated version of the Book of Luke. Thus, the first known New Testament, which was assembled by Marcion, contained eleven books. What did Marcion do about all the references to the Jewish Scriptures in the Book of Luke and Paul's epistles? He insisted that they were later interpolations—adoptionist forgeries—and stripped his New Testament of those references.

The contrast between the Ebionites and Marcionites could not be more stark. One group said that Jesus was not divine, but completely human, while the other insisted that he was completely divine and not human. One group staunchly declared that there was only one God, while the other said that there were, in fact, two. One group asserted the one and only God created the world and gave the Laws of the Torah, which are eternal and binding. The other group argued that the superior God, Jesus, had nothing to do with this wretched world and demanded that Christians reject the commandments altogether.

Another of the many groups vying for converts in Christendom's early years were Gnostic Christians, so named because they claimed that a special *gnosis* (Greek for "knowledge"), not faith, was essential for salvation.

What knowledge would save you from what?

Knowledge of how this world was fashioned, and yet more important, who you really are, where you came from, how you arrived here, and how you can escape this dreadful world and return to the heavenly realm. Clearly, Gnostics felt deeply alienated from this world, which they believed was an dreadful place, and that they did not belong here. Like the Marcionites, they believed that this world and their bodies were created by an inferior god. Jesus, they believed, was one of the deities who came down from the heavenly realm to impart the secret knowledge necessary to flee this evil earth.

Gnostics were themselves a very diverse sect. Unlike the adoptionists who were strict monotheists and believed in one God, and the Marcionites, who believed in two (ditheists), all Gnostic groups were polytheists who claimed there were many divine beings in the heavenly realm. Some sects believed in a few dozen different gods, and others as many as a few hundred. Most importantly, all Gnostic sects were emphatic that the true God was definitely not the God of the Jewish Bible, who they believed is as inherently evil and inferior as the world that He created. This may not sound like the Christianity preached by TV evangelists, but it was enormously popular throughout much of the Mediterranean region during the 2nd and 3rd centuries, especially in Egypt, Syria, and Asia Minor where Gnostic groups thrived.

'Orthodox' Christianity emerges

The most important Christian group that is directly germane to understanding the formation of the doctrine of the Trinity is the one that eventually "won out" in their acrimonious debates with their opponents and determined the shape of Christianity up to the present day. Ultimately, it was this latter group of Christians who determined which doctrines would be established as "Orthodox" (from the Greek for "the true belief") and which would be regarded as "heresy" (literally meaning "choice," i.e., to "choose" a false belief). Although all of these groups, of course, considered themselves to be the true Christians and the others completely heretical, this is the group that was victorious in the end. How did they manage to win while their opponents were relegated to the trash bin of church history? Ironically, they did so by arguing against all contrary sides while paradoxically, embracing some of the beliefs of their opponents as well.

Eventually, they did so by acquiring far more converts than any of the others, and to some degree, successfully stifled their opponents. Strategically, they had the advantage over other Christian sects, for they were well-represented in the city of Rome. As such, they were able to assert their influence on other churches. The Christian church in Rome, the center of the empire, was larger, far more powerful, and better organized than the other Christian sects. As a result, when the Roman emperor Constantine converted to Christianity in 312 CE, he converted to this form of Christianity. By the end of the 4th century, it was this form that was accepted by nearly everyone—with significant variations of course.

Strangely, this sect that emerged as the church's orthodoxy fashioned the doctrine of the Trinity by both opposing and embracing the conflicting beliefs of the other groups we discussed. In essence, it blended their teachings together in order to produce one of the most enduring theological inventions of the early Christian church.

This sect agreed with the Ebionite's belief that Jesus was fully human, but disagreed with their claim that he was not divine. They agreed with the Marcionites, who said that Jesus was fully divine, but rejected their notion that he was not human. They agreed with the Gnostics, who said that Jesus taught the way of salvation, but disagreed with their assertion that he did not die as an atonement for the sins of mankind. They disagreed with both the Marcionites and Gnostics, who said that this world was evil, and agreed with the Ebionites, who said that the world is inherently good, even if flawed by sin. In turn, they agreed with the Marcionites' claim that Paul was a true apostle and opposed the Ebionites' claim that Paul was a fraud. They argued with both the Marcionites and Gnostics, who said that there was more than one God, but insisted that Jesus was both human and divine. How could you have it both ways? By declaring that Jesus was at once both God and man.

How can there be one God if Jesus is also God? Christians struggle for a solution

But this assertion that Jesus was both fully divine and fully human sparked an obvious problem: How to reject the pagan notion that there are many gods, yet retain the firm monotheism expressed in the Jewish Scriptures? After all, if God the Father is God, and Jesus the son is God, are there not two Gods? How can God and Jesus both be God if there is only one God?

This notion doesn't square with the unambiguous declarations of faith in the Jewish Scriptures, which state:

> Hear O Israel, the Lord is our God, the Lord is one!
>
> (Deuteronomy 6:4)

> This is what the Lord says—Israel's King and Redeemer, the Lord Almighty: I am the first and I am the last; apart from Me there is no God! Who then is like Me? Let him proclaim it. Let him declare and lay out before me what has happened since I established my ancient people, and what is yet to come—yes, let them foretell what will come. Do not tremble, do not be afraid. Did I not proclaim this and foretell it long ago? You are My witnesses. Is there any God besides Me? No, there is no other Rock; I know not one.
>
> (Isaiah 44:6-8)

> I am the Lord, and there is no other; apart from Me there is no God.... So that from the rising of the sun to the place of its setting people may know there is none besides Me. I am the Lord, and there is no other.
>
> (Isaiah 45:5-7)

These epic passages do not allow for much wiggle-room on the nature of God or on the notion of multiple deities in a godhead. Of course, the Marcionites and Gnostics had no difficulty in declaring that Jesus was a divine being. For them, these verses in the Jewish Scriptures posed no problem because they didn't believe in anything Jewish, especially Tanach. As far as they were concerned, the Jewish Scriptures were completely irrelevant. The God Who declared that He alone is God and "there is no other" (Isaiah 45:18) was not the true God. The adoptionists, on the other hand, loved these passages because they didn't believe that Jesus was divine in any way. They held that Jesus was only human.

But what were the other Christians to do with hundreds of passages in the Jewish Scriptures which all clearly state that there is one God and no other? Few Christians were willing to say that there was more than one God. How could they call themselves monotheists and still insist that Jesus was God? Here is where various early Christian sects had some of their most turbulent arguments among themselves, and it was these arguments that led to the Council of Nicea in 325 CE.

These intra-Christian disagreements frequently ignited fuming debates. During these same early years, Christians were in conflict with Jews and pagans over the validity of their religion. These disagreements were often heated. But the most vitriolic early Christian debates, which were often filled with insult and hatred, were with other Christians. Christians said scathing things about one another, and denied that their opponents even had the right to call themselves Christians. Little has changed in this arena; Christianity has never been a monolithic religion. The earliest author in the New Testament was Paul, and it is clear in virtually every one of his letters that he had bitter enemies on all sides.

To this day, most evangelical Christians derisively label the Church of the Latter Day Saints (the Mormon Church) and the Jehovah's Witnesses as "cults," and deny that members of these sects are Christian. They regard the teachings of these sectarian groups entirely aberrant. These clashes hinge primarily on the nature of Jesus: Is he human, divine, or both?

Prior to the Council of Nicea, Christians attempted to solve the problem of how Jesus could be both God and human while solving the ancillary problem of how Jesus and the Father could both be God—and yet there were not two gods but only one. There were various efforts to explain how Jesus could be divine if there was only one God. All of these approaches, with the exception of one, were eventually rejected, summarily labeled as heretical, and proscribed by the Church.

Tertullian's opposition to Modalism forced him to invent the doctrine of the Trinity

One popular solution was to say that Jesus was actually God the Father himself, who became a human. This response aggressively insisted that there is only one God, and Jesus was both God and man without distinction, even though Jesus was God and the Father was God, because they were the same entity. In other words, Jesus was the Father in a human form. Period. At one time this was the most popular view among Christian thinkers because it vigorously asserted the oneness of God, even though Jesus was God and God the Father was God, for they claimed that they were one and the same. This idea, however, often labeled modalism since it argues that the one God has different modes of existence, was mocked because it spawned staggering problems for Christian thinkers.

The Christian apologist Tertullian (160 – 225 CE), the early Church's famed heresy-hunter, battled modalism head on. In fact, his confrontation with this teaching led him to the accomplishment for which he was most famous: Tertullian was the first Latin theologian to use the term Trinity (Latin *trinitas*) and formulate its underlying scheme. Ironically, as we will soon see, Tertullian did not believe in the doctrine as it was eventually hammered out more than a century later at the Council of Nicea (325 CE) and Constantinople (381 CE).

Tertullian wrote extensive works refuting all sorts of sects that he deemed heretical, including modalism. Tertullian derisively labeled this view "Patripassianism"—a term that literally means "the Father suffers" (from Latin *patri-* "father" and *passio* "suffering"). He lambasted this teaching because it suggested that God the Father suffered and died on the Cross. He argued that God the Father was superior to all worldly matters and above such limitations as mortality, suffering, and death. Tertullian pointed out, for example, that when Jesus prayed (Matthew 26:36-46; Mark 14:32-42; Luke 22:39-46; John 17:1-26), he obviously wasn't talking to himself. Contemptuously, he mocked modalists with an artful challenge:

> If you want me to believe him to be both the Father and Son, show me some other passages where it is declared, 'The Lord said to Himself, "I am my own Son, today have I begotten myself."
>
> *(Against Praxeas, 11)*

Tertullian bemoaned that in his day, the end of the 2nd century, modalism was endorsed by two popes and widely embraced in the Roman church. It was in direct response to this view that Tertullian developed the idea that God the Father is somehow different from God the son. Yet, if the Father and Jesus are both God and distinct, you would have two Gods, not one. Though Tertullian conceded that this was a mystery, he struggled to form an explicable solution to this conundrum. While his ideas on the nature of Jesus' divinity were later rejected and labeled heretical, he was no doubt the most revered "heretic" of the Christian church, for his formulations on the nature of the Christian godhead laid the foundation for the doctrine of the Trinity. Nevertheless, Tertullian was one of the few Church Fathers never canonized as a saint.

How is it possible that the man who essentially invented one of Christendom's most central creeds would later be deemed a heretic? As strange as this sounds, Tertullian did not believe in the doctrine of the Trinity—at least not in the manner that it was finally accepted and officially declared more than a century later.

Although Tertullian thought that the Father is God and the Son is God, and they differ only "on the ground of personality, not substance" (*Against Praxeas*, 12), he nonetheless believed that there was a hierarchy in the godhead. The Father is greater than the Son, otherwise he wouldn't be the Father. For the designation "Father" and "Son" conveys the distinction of personality. The Father is one, the Son is one, and the Spirit is one (*Against Praxeas*, 9). According to his formulation, God is three in degree, not condition; in form, not substance; in aspect, not power (*Against Praxeas*, 2). Tertullian did not teach that the Son was coeternal with the Father. After all, he insisted, there must be a point in time when a father—any father—exists without a son. The fact that he believed that Jesus was inferior to the Father can be easily seen in his same letter *Against Praxeas*, where he states:

> Thus the Father is distinct from the Son, being greater than the Son.
> (*Against Praxeas*, 9)

> While I recognize the Son, I assert his distinction as second to the Father.
> (*Against Praxeas*, 7)

The Catholic Encyclopedia comments that for Tertullian, "There was a time when there was no Son and no sin, when God was neither Father nor Judge.[9] With regard to the subject of subordination of the Son to the Father, the New Catholic Encyclopedia comments:

> In not a few areas of theology, Tertullian's views are, of course, completely unacceptable. Thus, for example, his teaching on the Trinity reveals a subordination of Son to Father that in the later crass form of Arianism[10] the Church rejected as heretical.[11]

Ultimately, it was Tertullian's belief that the Son was subordinate and inferior to the Father that eventually created a theological uproar. Nevertheless, his writings, more than that of any other Christian exponent, were the most influential in the development of the doctrine of the Trinity. And it was his war against the modalists that forced Tertullian to develop a trinity: one God manifest in three distinct persons (Greek *hypostases*).

Origen of Alexandria (185-254 CE), who was perhaps Christendom's most prolific and famous theologian, sought to solve the problem of the paradoxical nature of the Trinity by suggesting that the mind of Jesus and God were so deeply connected that it became one with God. Just as the iron placed in a blazing fire eventually takes on all the characteristics of the fire, Jesus took on the characteristics of God. According to Origen, Jesus' disembodied mind fused together with God and eventually became human when born to a virgin (Origen, *On First Principles* 2:6). But—this is a central point—he is equal to God only by *transference* of God's being, ultimately subordinate to God, and "less than the Father" (*On First Principles* 1:3).

As you might imagine, Origen's creative solution eventually landed him in hot water with later church leaders who utterly rejected any suggestion that Jesus was in any way subordinate to the Father.

Herein lies the irony: Tertullian and Origen were not the first Christians to contend that Jesus was divine. This idea was expressed at the end of the 1st century. Although many of their predecessors made this assertion, none of them could explain how the Father and Jesus could both be God if there are not two gods. For example, the Church Father Ignatius (ca. 50—117 CE), the third Bishop of Antioch, claimed there is one God, yet both the Father and Jesus were divine (*Ign*. Eph. 7:2). How was this possible? Ignatius lacked the requisite intellect to make sense out of this monumental theological conundrum. Yet, because he left this issue hopelessly unexplained, unrefined and undeveloped, the Church later venerated him as a saint. On the other hand, Tertullian and Origen, who were Christendom's most renowned apologists, were both later denounced as heretics because they struggled to make sense out of the Trinity.

Although Tertullian and Origen employed somewhat different approaches to the problems generated by a triune godhead, both posited that although Jesus was divine, he nevertheless was subordinate, inferior, and created by the Father. Accordingly, Origen, who refers to Jesus as a creature,[12] was the other revered heretical Church Father who never achieved sainthood. Nevertheless, one solution based on the reflections of Tertullian and Origen led to the Council of Nicea.

Council of Nicea settles the clash over Jesus' nature

For well over a century after Tertullian's formulation of the Trinity, theologians continued to wrestle over the precise nature of the relationship between the Father and Jesus. In the early 4th century, at about the time that the Roman emperor Constantine converted to Christianity (312 CE), there was a famous teacher named Arius in Alexandria, Egypt, a leading center for theological reflection. By this time, the Ebionites, Marcionites, and the various groups of Gnostics had mostly been vanquished, suppressed, reformed, or marginalized by those who would emerge as Christendom's orthodoxy. Almost everyone in the Christian world subscribed to the notion that both God the Father and Jesus were divine, but there was somehow only one God. Therefore it was this surviving form of Christianity that Constantine knew and supported. But how can you call yourself a monotheist while insisting that Jesus was God as well?

Arius thought he had a simple solution: he taught that in the beginning there was only one God: God the Father. But at some point in eternity past, God brought His son into existence, and it was through this son that He created the entire universe. And even though His son was a divine being, he was subordinate to God the Father. Thus, Arius held that the Father and son are one in divine purpose, but not in substance; they were in some ways similar in substance, but not identical in essence.

This solution was extremely popular because it affirmed in the Christian mind that there is really only one supreme God, and Jesus, who was a created divine being, was subordinate to Him. This belief, called "Arianism" after its founder, is based on the passage,

> You heard me say, 'I am going away and I am coming back to you.' If you loved me, you would be glad that I am going to the Father, for the Father is greater than I.
>
> (John 14:28)

But there were other Christians who vehemently opposed Arius' teachings because it portrayed Jesus as subservient and inferior to God and not fully God himself. The best-known opponent of Arianism was Athanasius, a young deacon in an Alexandrian church who emerged as one of the most influential figures in the history of 4th-century Christianity. Athanasius' importance in Christendom cannot be overstated.[20] In the early 4th century Athanasius and his coreligionists insisted on a paradoxical understanding of Jesus as fully divine and yet human. He argued that Jesus always existed—he did not come into being at a certain point in time—and he was himself fully, not derivatively, divine. He was fully God and of the very same essence as

God the Father. They were coeternal and complete equals. He advanced this creed without providing any solution to the serious paradox that it created.

This was the theological clash that led to the Council of Nicea, and this latter view ultimately became the orthodox doctrine of the Trinity, which maintains that there are three persons who make up the one God. The paradoxical and inexplicable nature of this creed is therefore an "inscrutable mystery, beyond the grasp of human reason." Thus, the renowned Alexandrian Bishop, Athanasius, a Church Father who was the chief opponent of Arianism and a noted Egyptian Christian leader of the 4th century, exerted his influence as they formulated ideas that led to the Trinity.

To us, this confrontation may seem like trivial hair-splitting, but back then this was the issue that was hotly contested and divided the church: Was Jesus the same substance as the Father—the Greek term *homoousios* ("same substance")—or was he only of "similar substance," *homoiousios*"? That little letter *i* made all the difference in the world to 4th-century church leaders.

Contrary to popular belief, the issue to be settled at the Council of Nicea was not a vote on Jesus' divinity. By that time, the adoptionists were basically gone; they had virtually disappeared many years earlier. All of the interlocutors at Nicea believed that Jesus was a god. The only question was *how* he was a god, how long he was a god, and how divine was he? Although there were other outstanding disagreements to be settled as well, this was the central and most furious conflict that the Council of Nicea was called to resolve.

Constantine's role at the Council of Nicea

Constantine was by no means a devout Christian. It is suggested that he may have sincerely converted later in life, but he was not baptized until he lay on his deathbed in 337 CE. Constantine himself was known to worship the "invincible sun god" (Latin: *Sol Invictus*) before and after becoming Christian. Constantine frequently identified his deity with the god Apollo, also associated with the sun. Coins minted during his reign, for example, continued to portray *Sol Invictus* for another nine years after his conversion. It is no coincidence that he determined that the Christian God was to be worshiped on the day of the sun (Sunday), and that the birth of Jesus should be celebrated at the time of the winter solstice. Despite the fact that Constantine was not a devout Christian, he attributed his military victory over the emperor Maxentius near the Milvian Bridge in the autumn of 312 CE to the Christian god because of a vision in which he claimed to have seen a cross in the sun-filled sky. He insisted that it was the Christian god, rather than the other gods he worshiped, that saved him on the battlefield and enabled him to emerge as the senior emperor in the West. As Henry Chadwick, the renowned Oxford theologian, says about Constantine's conversion:

> Constantine, like his father, worshiped the Unconquered Sun;... his conversion should not be interpreted as an inward experience of grace. It was a military matter... His comprehension of Christian doctrine was never very clear, but he was sure that victory in battle lay in the gift of the God of the Christians.
> (Henry Chadwick, *The Early Church*, 1993, p. 122, 125, 127)

More than anything, Constantine wanted Christianity to help unify his empire. But how could Christianity bring unity when it was divided against itself on significant issues, mainly the nature of God and Jesus? Herein lies Constantine's central problem: in order for Christianity to unify his empire, it had to unify itself. He sought to forge one empire that worshiped the one God (the Christian God), with one emperor at its helm: one God, one religion, one doctrine, one emperor, one empire.

In an effort to solve the dispute and unify the Roman Empire under one monolithic religion, Constantine summoned all bishops to Nicea in the summer of 325 CE. Of the 1,800 Christian bishops whom he invited to the gathering, approximately 300 showed up. This council was the first effort to attain a consensus on core tenets of Christianity in a deeply divided Church. Rome's first professing Christian emperor sought to accomplish this daunting task through an assembly representing all of Christendom.

Constantine's central role at the Council of Nicea cannot be overstated. After two months of furious religious debate, the emperor intervened and decided in favor of those who said that Jesus was God. The vote wasn't even close. But why would an upbaptized emperor take any interest in the outcome of this Church debate? Certainly not because he possessed any spiritual conviction on this matter. "Constantine had basically no understanding whatsoever of the questions that were being asked in Greek theology," says the preeminent Church historian, Professor Bernhard Lohse.[13] "He keenly grasped, however, that an ecclesiastical schism on fundamental Christian teachings posed a threat to his empire, and he wanted to solidify his domain."

Encyclopædia Britannica further outlines Constantine's role at the Council of Nicea:

> Constantine himself presided, actively guiding the discussions, and personally proposed... the crucial formula expressing the relation of Christ to God in the creed issued by the council, 'of one substance with

> the Father'... Overawed by the emperor, the bishops, with two exceptions only, signed the creed, many of them much against their inclination."
> (*Encyclopædia Britannica*, 1971, vol. vi, p. 386)

Is it correct, then, that the Council of Nicea produced the doctrine of the Trinity?

Not exactly. The Council of Nicea did declare that Jesus was of the same substance as God, which laid the groundwork for later Trinitarian theology. But they did not establish the full-blown doctrine of the Trinity as it is promulgated today, for at this first ecumenical gathering the nature of the holy spirit was not contested. The bishops at Nicea were not concerned with Trinity itself; they were squabbling only over whether to equate Jesus to the substance of God. The doctrine of the Trinity did not firmly emerge as orthodoxy until more than a half-century later.

Even following Nicea, debates on the subject of Jesus' nature persisted and raged among major Christian sects. The belief that Jesus was not equal to God even came back into favor for a time. The Roman Emperors Constantius II (337—361) and Valens (364—378) were Arians or Semi-Arians.

It was not until the Council of Constantinople, convened in 381 CE by the Emperor Theodosius, when the nature of Jesus and his relationship to God and the holy spirit was finally decided and promulgated. Theodosius convened the council specifically to clarify this core theological question. He was in a unique historical position to unify disputed Church doctrine because he was the last emperor to rule over both the eastern and western halves of the Roman Empire (reigned from 379—395 CE). Accordingly, this council ended the formal argument and placed the holy spirit on the same level as God and Jesus. For the first time, Christendom declared that the doctrine of the Trinity was the established orthodoxy of the Church, and all other beliefs about the nature of Jesus and the holy spirit were formally rejected and labeled as heresy.

The paradoxical doctrine of the Trinity—that there are three distinct persons in the godhead, yet all three are of the same substance and equally God—is quite a departure from anything found in the New Testament, where there is no statement of anything of the sort. Moreover, the self-contradictory doctrine of the Trinity, formally adopted during the 4th century, forced Christendom to revert to its hopelessly inexplicable state as expressed by the first century Church father, Ignatius.

The theological war that raged at Constantine's Council of Nicea raised a monumental question: If the nature of Jesus' divinity is so clearly spelled out in the New

Testament, as missionaries argue, why was the doctrine questioned at Nicea? In fact, why was there any contention over this topic at all? Why is it that, to this day, Christians cannot agree on this crucial matter? For example, no Christian council ever had to convene to determine whether Jesus was born in Bethlehem to a virgin, was baptized or rose from the dead. No such council was necessary because, unlike the doctrine of the Trinity, the Gospels explicitly make those claims.

Why did Christianity abandon its monotheistic roots?

Until this point we explored how the doctrine of the Trinity evolved from the 2nd through the 4th century—from the time, say, between the completion of the writing of the New Testament books and the conversion of the Roman emperor Constantine, which, as we have seen, changed everything. We know a great deal about this period because of the enormous diversity of Christian beliefs and what was written about them during this era by interlocutors, such as Tertullian, and church historians, such as Eusebius. As of yet, though, we did not probe the answer to what is perhaps the most pressing question of all: Why did Christianity, which emerged as a breakaway sect from Judaism, eventually abandon the uncompromising monotheism of the Jewish faith? How did this period occur?

Although Judaism—even during the worst of times—was never as theologically variegated as Christianity, the Jews endured significant schisms. There were numerous well-known Jewish sects that broke away from Pharisaic Judaism throughout history, including the Sadducees, Essenes, and Karaites. While these bitter schisms sparked heated intra-Jewish debates and painful conflicts, none of these splinter groups ever called into question the radical and uncompromising monotheism expressed Judaism's most sacred creed, "Hear O Israel, the Lord is our God, the Lord is one!" (Deut. 6:4). None of these sects ever divided over the nature of God. Judaism, which has endured and persisted longer than any other faith in history, never required an equivalent of the Council of Nicea to settle a disagreement over the nature of God. Why did Christianity depart from its monotheistic origins? Within the span of three centuries, Jesus went from being an itinerant preacher to being God himself, a member of the Trinity. How did this happen?

Moreover, the popular solutions expressed by Tertullian, Origen, Arius, and many others to the paradoxical nature of the Trinity may seem more puzzling and incomprehensible than the doctrine itself. How could Jesus be God yet created, subordinate yet divine, inferior yet exalted? How could such a seemingly inexplicable idea gain widespread acceptance among the masses prior to the Council of Nicea? Isn't God the Prime Mover and First Cause in the universe, Eternal and Omnipotent? How can God be a created being, inferior and subordinate to anything? How can this "solution" work? What were Tertullian, Origen, and Arius thinking? In other words, we can imagine various ancient sects arguing over whether or not Jesus was God, and in fact, this disagreement remains alive and well today between Unitarians and Baptists, Christadelphians and Roman Catholics. But how can anyone believe that Jesus was a "junior" god? What sort of god is created, subordinate, and inferior to anything?

Oddly, the answer to these questions illustrates how the traditions about Jesus quickly evolved away from the monotheism rooted in Judaism. And this understanding lies in our ability to fully grasp the pagan world in which the Christian movement rapidly grew.

As strange as it may seem, in order to comprehend the ancient pagan religions that flourished during the 1st century, we have to abandon virtually everything we know about religion today, for it was primarily among pagans that Christians told most of their stories about Jesus and acquired most of their converts. This all occurred while the New Testament was being written. In order to study the early traditions told about Jesus, we must begin by situating them in their original context, in the Greco-Roman world of the 1st century.

Greco-Roman paganism shapes Christian thinking

The narratives related about Jesus were conveyed by people who could make sense of them, and the sense they made of them was within a world filled with many different gods, enormously different from the sense that we make of them in our modern, monotheistic world. Such an endeavor is quite challenging to the modern mind, because 1st century pagan traditions and world views do not translate easily into the 21st century where our reasonable assumptions are vastly different from those shared by the early converts to Christianity.

In our time, religions of the West are generally monotheistic and advocate belief in one God. For most people we encounter, it is simply common sense that there is only one Divine Being. For people in the ancient world outside of Judaism, however, this was nonsense. The Judaism from which Christianity sprang was a completely distinctive and peculiar religion in the Greco-Roman world. Throughout the entire Roman empire there was not a single religion that remotely resembled the Jewish faith. All other religions in the empire were pagan.

The masses were sure that there were many gods of all types and descriptions. They worshiped a whole host of deities of varying sorts and functions—they were the "great gods" that we learn about from Greek and Roman mythology. For example, the Greek Zeus, Ares, and Athena, or their Roman equivalents Jupiter, Mars, and Minerva. These were the most exalted gods of the state. Lesser gods, however, were local or personal, including gods of the rivers and streams, home and crops, and health and wealth. There were gods who kept the livestock fertile and gods who protected women in childbirth; there were gods who were believed to oversee all aspects of a family's life cycle, from birth to death, and beyond the grave.

In the pagan world no one insisted that if you worshiped one god, you could not also worship another. Exclusive adherence to one god was unknown outside of the Jewish faith. If you worshiped one god, that god did not care if you worshiped another god or eighteen other gods. In fact, the gods did not care what you did and how you conducted yourself when you were not worshiping them. The gods, the people believed, were only concerned about the sacrifices that you offered and the rituals that you performed. In exchange, they would provide what was within their power, whether it was your health, harvest, or fertility. It amounted to a transaction between you and the gods. You took care of their needs and they, in turn, took care of yours.

How did the pagan world understand the relationship of the great gods of the empire to those of their own locality? The people of the Greco-Roman world conceived of a hierarchy in the divine realm: the gods were not created equal. The few most important gods were at the top of the pyramid and the more numerous but less powerful deities were at the bottom. At the very peak of the hierarchy of gods was one almighty god, the Greek Zeus or the Roman Jupiter. Ordinary people considered this greatest god so powerful and unknowable that he was completely beyond human comprehension. He was all but inaccessible to mere mortals. There was little point spending much time praying for your personal needs to gods like Zeus or Jupiter because they were too busy taking care of things larger than you, like the universe. They were, however, worshiped in elaborate, mass state ceremonies by the empire.

The next tier below the great gods were powerful gods whom the pagans frequently worshiped in different areas throughout the Roman empire, such as Neptune, Juno, Diana, Ares (Latin Mars) the god of war, Aphrodite (Venus) the goddess of love, and Dionysus (Bacchus) the god of wine. These were the gods who the pagans considered worthy of praise because of their awesome might. In this pagan hierarchy of gods there were many tiers below these gods as well. These included gods of your own household, vineyard, and courtyard.

Finally, the lowest tier of gods included a host of divine beings who essentially bridged the gap between mortals and the gods. Among these great beings were humans who were considered divine, or became divine after they died. In essence, they were extraordinary people who were made immortal and venerated like the gods. This final category is particularly germane for our study because these demigods were special human beings who were widely believed to be too great to be just human. These individuals included great rulers like Alexander the Great and powerful athletes like Heracles who were both believed to be the son of the Greek god Zeus and a mortal virgin. Rome's founder, Romulus, was said to be the son of the god Mars and a mortal virgin. Roman emperors like Augustus and great philosophers like Pythagoras were widely regarded to be this kind of divine being. Each one of them was considered to be a *son of god* whose remarkable accomplishments earned them unique gifts from the gods in life as well as in death.

What did it mean to be the 'Son of God'? It depended on whom you asked

No one in the ancient world, however, considered any one of these members on the bottom level of the divine hierarchy to be equal to the one great god or even one of the twelve Olympians who were the principal deities of the Greek pantheon. These exalted men were all considered fantastically powerful but still completely subordinate to the great god(s). They were called the "son of god," whose supernatural abilities and miraculous achievements demonstrated their divine lineage.

For the Jews, however, the familiar term "son of God" meant something different—something radically different. As mentioned earlier, the Jewish Scriptures speak of many individuals and groups who were considered to be the son of God. In not one of these passages were these persons considered divine. For example, in both Exodus 4:22 and Hosea 11:1 the children of Israel are called "God's son." King David is called the son of God in Psalm 2:7, and King Solomon is called the son of God in 2 Samuel 7:14-16. This certainly didn't make the Davidic kings or the Jews divine in any way. This term in the Hebrew Bible meant only one thing: some people stood in a close relationship with God and were especially chosen by the Almighty to fulfill a sacred national mandate. This conspicuous title never refers to physical descent of God.

Herein lies the problem: Jesus is frequently called the "son of God" throughout the New Testament, including all the Gospels, the Book of Acts, and many of Paul's epistles. When the Greek mind, rather than the Jewish mind began to guide the church and convey its stories about Jesus, this title sparked a theological disaster from which Christianity has never recovered.

What would the same term, "son of God," mean to pagans who decided to believe in Jesus? These people, who made up the vast majority of converts to Christianity, told stories about Jesus' virgin birth and his miracles to other pagans. They had no difficulty understanding what it meant: Jesus was himself a divine man who came to earth. These were the people who were raised to believe that sons of God were part human and part divine—they had superhuman abilities because they had a mortal virgin mother and an immortal father. Therefore, if you emerged from the empire's pagan world, the definition of the son of God was quite simple. After all, the son of a giraffe is a giraffe, and the son of a horse is a horse.

Accordingly, in the pagan Greco-Roman world, it was presumed that the son of God could be nothing less than a god.

Moreover, these pagans found striking comparisons between Jesus and their pagan traditions. For example, compare the infancy narrative of Heracles (the Roman Hercules) to Luke's version of Jesus' birth. These semidivine people were capable of great miracles, and at the end of their lives went to live with the gods in heaven (compare this with the story of Jesus' ascension). Any pagan who adopted the Christian religion with this understanding of what it meant to be the son of God thought of Jesus in Greco-Roman terms: a semidivine being, not like the traditional Jewish son of God found in the Tanach, who was completely human.

Simply put, the term "son of God" would have meant something entirely different to Jewish people, who would have taken it as a reference to a unique mortal person, than to gentiles, for whom it meant some sort of a divine man. The early Christian communities, which possessed some Jewish leadership, believed that Jesus received this special status very late in his career.

When did Jesus become the 'Son of God'?

To be sure, we can identify when the Greek understanding of the son of God began to supplant the Jewish view by answering the following question: At which point did Jesus become the son of God? We can then trace the 1st-century timeline in the Christian Bible following the chronological order of each book's authorship.

The books of the New Testament, which were written many years after Jesus' death, were authored over the course of half a century—from about the year 50 CE (the letters of Paul) until the turn of the century. It is not difficult to identify when its authors—from the earliest to the latest—conferred the title "son of God" upon Jesus. This pattern in Christian canonical texts is clear: The earlier the New Testament author claimed that God bestowed this special status upon Jesus, the later the event transpired in Jesus' career.

Accordingly, Jesus is never spoken of as divine in the earliest New Testament statements. Rather, we find the primitive belief that it was specifically at the resurrection that Jesus became God's son.

In the Book of Romans, written about 55 CE, Paul claims that Jesus was proclaimed to be God's son following his resurrection:

> Concerning his Son Jesus Christ our Lord, which was made of the seed of David according to the flesh; and declared to be the Son of God with power, according to the spirit of holiness, by the resurrection from the dead.
>
> (Romans 1:3-4)

In one of Paul's speeches he speaks of Jesus as being rejected by the Jews, "who pleaded with Pilate to have him killed," but...

> That which God had promised to our ancestors he has fulfilled for us, their children, by raising Jesus; as also it is written in the second Psalm, "You are my son; today I have begotten you."
>
> (Acts 13:32-33)

Based on the above passages, at what point does Paul claim that Jesus came to be "begotten" as the son of God? At his resurrection: "*Today* I have begotten you."

This is a primitive and less embellished expression of the Christian religion.

Jesus was a human being, not divine, whom God empowered to do great works. According to Paul, only God can give Jesus power: he had no power of his own. And only after Jesus was executed, Paul claimed, God raised him from the dead and bestowed upon him his exalted status as the "son of God."

As time passed, members of the Christian sect found Paul's exposition unsatisfying. Soon these followers suggested that Jesus must have been the son of God during his public ministry, not just after the resurrection. They reasoned that it was Jesus' baptism that made him God's son rather than his resurrection. After all, Jesus' baptism in the Jordan River initiated his public ministry. Therefore, the earliest of the four gospels, the Book of Mark, written about 15 years after the Book of Romans, we are introduced to Jesus as an adult. The book opens with his baptism by John. We are told that as soon as he emerges from the Jordan he immediately saw the heavens open and heard a heavenly voice declaring, "You are my beloved son, in whom I am well pleased" (Mark 1:11). The Gospel of Mark gives no indication that Jesus is divine or that the events surrounding his birth were unusual. The oldest and least embellished Gospel continues to portray Jesus as completely human through his crucifixion, during which Jesus screams out, "My God, my God, why have You forsaken me?" (Mark 15:34). In this "cry of dereliction," as it is called, Mark casts Jesus as someone who is confused and genuinely wants to understand why God had abandoned him on the cross.

In about 70 CE, Christians still regarded Jesus as completely human. The march from Jerusalem to Athens, however, does not stop here. In about fifteen years, both the Book of Matthew and the Book of Luke point to Jesus' conception as the moment when Jesus became God's son—literally. According to these two Gospels, God impregnated the virgin Mary. None of the New Testament authors writing prior to Matthew and Luke say anything about Jesus' birth.

The message from the heavenly voice at Jesus' baptism in the Book of Matthew is —by necessity—fundamentally different from that of Mark. Remember, when Jesus emerged from the waters of the River Jordan in Mark's Gospel, the voice spoke directly to Jesus, making it known to him that "You are My beloved son, in whom I am well pleased" (Mark 1:11). In this Gospel, God informs Jesus that he is His son. According to Matthew, however, the heavenly proclamation expressed in Mark 1:11 is redundant because Jesus was well aware that he has been God's son his entire life. Thus, the voice from heaven in Matthew's version of Jesus' baptism informed everyone else, "This is My beloved son, in whom I am well pleased" (Matthew 3:17). In Matthew's story, God was not speaking to Jesus about his status. Rather, He informed the audience that Jesus is His son.

The Book of Luke, written at about the same time as Matthew, is very direct in its explanation of the virgin birth: God made the virgin Mary pregnant so that her son was also God's son. Jesus is literally part human and part divine. In Luke's Gospel, Jesus possessed his unique status at his birth. The angel Gabriel delivered to Mary this specific message that:

> The Holy Spirit will come upon you, and the power of the Most High will overshadow you; therefore the child to be born from you will be holy; he will be called the "Son of God."
>
> (Luke 1:35)

Note the "therefore" in this passage: because God caused Mary to conceive, Jesus can *therefore* be called the "son of God." *Therefore*, this is the point at which Jesus attains his unique status. Here, the Father literally caused Mary to become pregnant. By about the year 85 CE, Jesus's status as the son of God is pushed back about three decades before his baptism and resurrection.

The literary style of the Book of Luke is not only more polished than Matthew, but his nativity story is far more developed. Although Matthew makes no attempt to engage in theological speculation about Jesus' virgin birth (he simply and famously misquotes the Jewish Scriptures; see pages 38-61), Luke presents an elaborate nativity story in which Mary's status is by far the most highly exalted of any book in the New Testament. After all, God used her womb to produce His son. So, whereas in the Book of Matthew, the angel informed Joseph that Mary is *already* pregnant (1:18-21), in the Book of Luke, the angel informed Mary of Jesus' impending birth *before* she is even pregnant. This news is presented with an elaborate "Annunciation," in which Mary learns from Gabriel that she will conceive (1:26-38), and Mary's recital of the "Magnificat" (1:46-55), which contains central features of the prayers of Hannah (I Samuel 1:11; 2:1-10). Neither the Annunciation nor the Magnificat is found anywhere else in the New Testament. In fact, Mary's central role in carrying God's son is so glorified in the third Gospel that its nativity text is three times the length of that in the Gospel of Matthew, and in itself is longer than several of the books of the New Testament.

There is no sense that Jesus existed before his conception in either the Book of Matthew or Luke. As time went on, though, even the idea that Jesus had been the son of God from his birth failed to satisfy some Christians who thought that Jesus existed even before his conception. Therefore, the Book of John, the last of the four Gospels, pushes back Jesus' status as the son of God even further, into an unmarked moment somewhere in eternity past. According to this late view, written at the end of the 1st century (about 65 years after Jesus' death), Jesus was himself a divine being: "a god." He is introduced to us as the "Word of God" through whom God created the world, and has now become a human being. This notion is advanced in the prologue to John's Gospel (1:1-18), and is by far the most exalted portrait of Jesus in the entire Christian Bible. Although the exact meaning of these passages is also the most wrangled over, argued, and dissected in the New Testament, the author of John has certainly escorted his reader into the theological epicenter of the Greco-Roman world. There is no doubt that in John's prologue, Jesus is, for the first time, portrayed as pre-existent.

What sort of god is Jesus in John's Gospel? He is not the great god of the divine hierarchy. He is portrayed as a lower tier god, separate from God ("with God"), and then becomes a being who transcends history.

John, therefore, has no interest in discussing how Jesus came into the world, his virgin birth in Bethlehem, his baptism in the Jordan River, his temptation for 40 days in the wilderness, his transfiguration, his proclamation of the coming kingdom of God, and his use of parables to convey that warning. Although these stories form the skeleton of the narratives in the synoptic Gospels, they do not appear anywhere in John, because these stories are not relevant and do not fit into his theology.

Why discuss Mary's virginal conception if her womb played no role in Jesus' sonship? Accordingly, in stark contrast to the Book of Luke, where Mary is bestowed with the most glorified status in the New Testament, the Book of John introduces the mother of Jesus in the most derisive manner imaginable. The name of Jesus' mother is never even mentioned in the Book of John; no other book in the New Testament refers to Jesus' mother without naming her. When the "mother of Jesus" is first introduced to us at a wedding in Cana, she informs her adult son that there is no wine for the ceremony. Jesus' response to his mother is quite shocking: "Woman, what have I to do with you?" Jesus is making it very clear that she should not consider him her son. John's portrait of Mary is quite a departure from Luke. If Jesus pre-existed his mother's womb, as John insists, Mary is irrelevant. Accordingly, no aspect surrounding Jesus' birth is mentioned in the fourth Gospel.

It is likely that John rejected the idea advanced by Matthew and Luke that Jesus was born in Bethlehem. We are told in John 7:41-42 and again in 7:52 that some of the Pharisees dismissed the possibility that Jesus was the Messiah on the grounds that the Messiah must be a descendent of David and born in Bethlehem. The Jews pointed out the fact that Jesus instead came out of Galilee (as is stated in the Gospel of Mark). John made no effort to refute or correct this.

There is no need for divine beings to get baptized, gods can't be tempted by the devil, and the transfiguration story in which Jesus engages in a conversation with mortals like Moses and Elijah is unnecessary to elevate his status. John therefore expunged all these stories which appear prominently in the first three Gospels.

Moreover, Jesus' nature and mission in the Book of John is strikingly different from that of Mark. In the Book of Mark, Jesus' message is summarized in the first words he speaks: "The time has been fulfilled; the kingdom of God is near...." (Mark 1:15). Jesus says little about himself in the synoptic gospels in general. His central message is: Prepare yourself. God's kingdom is coming to earth, and it is arriving imminently. In fact, it is coming so soon that "Truly I tell you, some of those standing here will not taste of death before they see the kingdom of God having come in power" (Mark 13:30). He speaks almost nothing about himself. His focus in the Book of Mark is to prepare this generation "who will not taste of death" before they witness Jesus' return to earth in judgment, bringing with him the kingdom of God.

Jesus' teachings are very different in John, where Jesus does not stop talking about himself, who he is, where he came from, and how he can provide eternal life. John's Jesus cannot make the sweeping predictions that he made in the Book of Mark—that his own generation would still be alive when the kingdom arrives (Mark 9:1; 13:32)—because by the time John was written everyone of Jesus' generation is dead. Jesus' predictions never materialized. Therefore in John, the kingdom that is promised is no longer on earth, but rather eternal life in heaven (John 3:3; 3:16). Eventually, John would become the standard position adopted by Christians: Jesus was himself a preexistent being. But this was not the earliest Christian view, not by a long shot. This view is found in no other Gospel, and is a far cry from the relatively humble beginnings of Jesus expressed in the Book of Mark.

I would be remiss if I failed to mention the striking, paradoxical nature of the fourth Gospel. The Book of John, more than any other Gospel, goes out of its way to illustrate that Jesus, although in some sense divine, is in no way equal to God the Father, the great God: "...I [Jesus] go unto the Father, for my father is greater than I" (John 14:28). In essence, although in his prologue the author of the Book of John portrayed Jesus in the most exalted state found anywhere in the New Testament, he goes out of his way to point out that Jesus is inferior and subordinate to the Father. John's Jesus is a lower tier god in the grand pyramid of gods.

Pagan origins of the doctrine of the Trinity

About a century after the writing of the Book of John, Tertullian advanced the notion that Jesus was a member of a triune godhead. Tertullian's radical formulation, however, raises an intriguing ancillary question: Why did Tertullian invite the holy spirit into the godhead? After all, the holy spirit was

Capitoline Triad: Minerva, Jupiter, and Juno

always considered to be the active force of God, not some distinct person from the Father. In both the Jewish Scriptures and the Christian Bible it is the perceptible presence of God's power. It is not a "he," a person separate from God, but an "it," as the Almighty's dynamic operational presence that He uses to accomplish His will in creation and redemption. To be sure, in the later heated Christian debates and councils, especially at Nicea, the holy spirit was largely ignored. Christians squabbled over the nature of Jesus, not the holy spirit. Why then did Tertullian forge a trinity rather than a bianity? Why did he invent a triune model of the godhead?

The answer to this intriguing question lies in the portrait of the ancient world, as far back as ancient Egypt, where the worship of pagan gods grouped in threes, or triads, was widespread, and three major deities which were frequently considered as chief. That influence was also prevalent in India, Egypt, Greece, and Rome in the centuries before, during, and after the 1st century. Hinduism believed in one chief substance, Brahman, expressed in three personalities: Brahma, the Creator, Vishnu, the Preserver, and Shiva the Destroyer. Osiris, Isis, and Nephthys formed a triad of deities in Egypt. In Greece the three major deities on Mount Olympus were Zeus, Hera and Athena. The triad of deities that the Romans templed on the Capitoline Hill, one of the seven hills of Rome, consisted of Jupiter, Juno, and Minerva. As the Church rapidly grew, a wide range of pagan beliefs began to invade the quickly evolving Christian religion. This is the world in which Tertullian was raised.

The historian Will Durant observed: "Christianity did not destroy paganism; it adopted it... From Egypt came the ideas of a divine trinity."[14] And in the book, *Egyptian Religion*, Siegfried Morenz notes: "The trinity was a major preoccupation of Egyptian theologians... Three gods are combined and treated as a single being, addressed in the singular. In this way the spiritual force of Egyptian religion shows a direct link with Christian theology."[15]

Egypt. Triad of Horus, Osiris, and Isis (c. second millennium BCE.)

As is evident from the letters of Paul, the vast majority of converts to Christianity, even in its infancy, were gentiles. By the second century, almost all Christians were former pagans, non-Jews who understood that even though this religion was based, ultimately, on faith in the Jewish God as described in the Jewish Scriptures, it was nonetheless of a different orientation. Tertullian was not an exception.

Tertullian was not born into a Christian family. He was raised a pagan in Carthage, the Roman province in north Africa, and converted to Christianity in 197 CE. Christian converts from the pagan world, like Tertullian, told stories about Jesus in terms that resonated to them. They increasingly molded the stories so that Jesus looked more and more like the divine men commonly talked about in the Greco-Roman world: Men who were supernaturally conceived because of the intervention of a god, who were often part of a triad divine partnership, who performed miracles and ascended to heaven.

> **Luther's insights on the doctrine of the Trinity and the Jewish people**
>
> Consequently, if I had power over them [the Jews], I would assemble their scholars and their leaders and order them, on pain of losing their tongues down to the root, to convince us Christians within eight days of the truth of their assertions and prove this blasphemous lie against us, to the effect that we worship more than one true God.
>
> *On the Jews and Their Lies*, Luther's Works, vol. 47, p. 289; Philadelphia: Fortress Press, 1971.

If you wanted to describe a son of God to someone in the ancient world, these were the terms you used. Given that the spirit of God appears in both the Jewish Scriptures and Christian Bible, Tertullian incorporated the holy spirit as a distinct "person" in the godhead in order to shape a Christian triad. This enabled him to employ the language and conceptions found in the idiom of the day. What other idiom could he have used? It was the only language available to him.

As it turned out, Christians also used the striking parallels between Christianity and paganism because they wanted pagans to realize that Christianity was not all that different from what other pagans said and did in their religions thus there would be no grounds for singling out Christians for persecution.

Why didn't the Torah discuss the doctrine of the Trinity?

If, as the Church claims, the notion that the messiah would be part of a triune godhead is clearly conveyed in the Jewish Scriptures, why wasn't this puzzling creed spelled out in the Ten Commandments? Why didn't the Jewish prophets plainly express this paradoxical doctrine in their sacred oracles if they wanted the Jews to believe that God and the messiah were of the same substance?

What was God waiting for?

Do missionaries expect you to believe that for thousands of years not a single one of God's prophets clearly taught their people about the Trinity? Why didn't Moses, the Great Teacher, make the Trinity clearly understood to his nation? Would God inspire thousands of pages of Scripture and yet not use any of this instruction to clearly teach that God would come to the world to die as a human if it were a central doctrine of faith?

Are the Jewish people to believe that God would make Himself known to the children of Israel at Mt. Sinai, inspire the writing of Tanach, and then support a doctrine which contradicts His revelation on Sinai? A doctrine unknown to His prophets and servants for thousands of years? Are we to believe a doctrine which can only be explained as an "inscrutable mystery beyond the grasp of human reason" — one that admittedly has pagan origins and was forged by Rome's politics?

> God is not a man that He should lie, nor is He a mortal that He should change His mind....
> (Numbers 23:19)

Footnotes:

1. The Book of John and the three epistles that the Church attributed to John the son of Zebedee were not written by the Apostle John, the "Beloved Disciple." These books as well as five other books in the New Testament were written anonymously. In fact, one third of the New Testament books—including all the Gospels, the books of Acts and Hebrews—were written by authors who never identified themselves or even claimed that they were contemporaneous eye-witnesses.

   For example, whoever wrote the Book of John did not call it "The Gospel according to John." It was nearly a century later that Christian scribes tell us who, in their opinion, wrote it and the other Gospels. For example, at the end of the Book of John the author says of the "Beloved Disciple:" "This is the disciple who is testifying to these things and has written them, and we know that his testimony is true" (John 21:24). Pay close attention to how John's author clearly distinguishes between his own source of information, "the disciple who testifies," and himself: "We know that his testimony is true." The anonymous author of the Book of John is the not the disciple John. Here the author of the fourth Gospel claims that he received some of his information from the "Beloved Disciple" John.

2. Catholic Encyclopedia, "Epistles of St John"

3. Catholic Encyclopedia: "The silence of the great and voluminous Augustine and the variation in form of the text in the African Church are admitted facts that militate against the canonicity of the three witnesses."

4. Newton Project, *Newton's Views on the Corruptions of Scripture and the Church: Two Notable Corruptions*, p.17.

5. *The Complutensian Polyglot Bible* is the name given to the first printed polyglot (meaning a side by side version of the same text in different languages) of the entire Bible, initiated and financed by Cardinal Francisco Jiménez de Cisneros (1436-1517) and published in Complutum (Alcalá de Henares), Spain. It includes the first printed editions of the Greek New Testament, the complete Septuagint, and the Aramaic Targum Onkelos. Of the 600 printed six volume sets, only 123 are known to have survived.

6. Metzger, Bruce M., *The Text of the New Testament: Its Transmission, Corruption, and Restoration*, 2d ed., (Oxford University Press, 1968), p. 101.

7. Mann, Theodore H. (January-March 2001). *"Translation Problems in the KJV New Testament," Journal of Biblical Studies 1.*

8. This manuscript (codex 61), written by one Roy or Froy at Ireland in 1520, which contains the entire New Testament, is now housed in Dublin, Ireland. These verses were examined so often that the book now reportedly falls open naturally to 1 John 5.

9. "Tertullian," *The Catholic Encyclopedia.*

10. Arianism is the theological teaching attributed to Arius (ca. 250–336 CE), a Christian presbyter from Alexandria, Egypt, concerning the relationship of the entities of the Trinity ('God the Father,' 'God the Son' and 'God the Holy Spirit') and the precise nature of the Son of God as being a subordinate entity to God the Father. Deemed a heretic by the First Council of Nicaea of 325, Arius was later exonerated in 335 at the First Synod of Tyre, and then, after his death, pronounced a heretic again at the First Council of Constantinople of 381.

11. W. Le Saint, "Tertullian," *The New Catholic Encyclopedia*, Thompson Gale, 2003, Vol. 13, p. 837.

12. Pelikan, Jaroslav, *The Christian Tradition: A History of the Development of Doctrine*, The Chicago University Press, 1971, vol. 1, p. 191.

13. Lohse, Bernhard, *A Short History of Christian Doctrine*, 1963, p. 51.

14. Durant, Will, *The Story of Civilization*: Part III, 1944, p. 594-595.

15. Morenz, Siegfried, *Egyptian Religion*, 1973, p. 254-357.

20. In 367 CE, many years after the Council of Nicea, Athanasius was to be the first Christian in history to list the 27 books of the New Testament.

The Trinity in Reference Sources

The Church of the First Few Centuries:

The Doctrine of the Trinity was of gradual and comparatively late formation. It had its origin in a source entirely foreign to that of the Jewish and Christian Scriptures. It grew up and was ingrafted on Christianity through the hands of the Platonizing Fathers. Summing up the historical evidence, the modern popular doctrine of the Trinity derives no support from the language of Justin Martyr, and this observation may be extended to all the ante-Nicene Fathers: that is, to all Christian writers for three centuries after the birth of Christ. It is true, they speak of the Father, Son, and holy Spirit, but not as co-equal, not as one numerical essence, not as Three in One, in any sense now admitted by Trinitarians. The very reverse is the fact. Thus, the testimony of the Bible and of history makes clear that the Trinity was unknown throughout Biblical times and for several centuries thereafter. — (Alvan Lamson, 1869 edition, Horace B. Fuller, Boston, MA, p. 103-108; p. 180-183)

The New Encyclopedia Britannica:
Neither the word Trinity, nor the explicit doctrine as such, appears in the New Testament, nor did Jesus and his followers intend to contradict the Shema in the Old Testament: 'Hear, O Israel: The Lord our God is one Lord' (Deut. 6:4).... The doctrine developed gradually over several centuries and through many controversies... By the end of the 4th century... the doctrine of the Trinity took substantially the form it has maintained ever since. — (1976, *Micropoedia*, Vol. X, p. 126)

The Encyclopedia Americana:
Christianity derived from Judaism and Judaism was strictly Unitarian [believing that God is one Person]. The road which led from Jerusalem to Nicea was scarcely a straight one. Fourth century Trinitarianism did not reflect accurately early Christian teaching regarding the nature of God; it was on the contrary, a deviation from this teaching. — (1956, Vol. XXVII, p. 294)

The New Catholic Encyclopedia:
The formulation 'one God in three Persons' was not solidly established, certainly not fully assimilated into Christian life and its profession of faith, prior to the end of the 4th century. But it is precisely this formulation that has first claim to the title the Trinitarian dogma. Among the Apostolic Fathers, there had been nothing even remotely approaching such a mentality or perspective. — (1967, Vol. XIV, p. 299)

Nouveau Dictionary Universal:
The Platonic trinity, itself merely a rearrangement of older trinities, dating back to earlier people, appears to be the rational, philosophic trinity of attributes that gave birth to the three hypostasis or divine persons taught by the Christian churches.… This Greek philosopher's [Plato, 4th century B.C.E.] conception of the divine trinity…can be found in all the ancient [pagan] religions. — (Paris, 1865-1870, edited by M. Lachâtre, vol. 2, p. 1467.)

Dictionary of the Bible:

The trinity of persons within the unity of nature is defined in terms of 'person' and 'nature' which are Greek philosophical terms; actually the terms do not appear in the Bible. The Trinitarian definitions arose as the result of long controversies in which these terms and others such as 'essence' and 'substance' were erroneously applied to God by some theologians. — (John L. McKezie, New York, 1965), p. 899.

New Bible Dictionary:

The word Trinity is not found in the Bible, and, though used by Tertullian in the last decade of the 2nd century, and it did not find a place formally in the theology of the Church till the 4th century. — (J. D. Douglas & F. F. Bruce, Trinity, p. 1298)

Thomas Jefferson, third President of the United States and principal author of the Declaration of Independence:

The Shema, the creed of Israel, "Hear, O Israel, YHWH our God is one Lord" (Deut. 6:4). No historical fact is better established than that the doctrine of one God, pure and uncompounded, was that of the early ages of Christianity... Nor was the unity of the Supreme Being ousted from the Christian creed by the force of reason, but by the sword of civil government, wielded at the will of Athanasius. The hocus-pocus phantasm of a God like another Cerberus, with one body and three heads, had its birth and growth in the blood of thousands of martyrs... The Athanasian paradox that one is three, and three but one, is so incomprehensible to the human mind, that no candid man can say he has any idea of it, and how can he believe what presents no idea? He who thinks he does, only deceives himself. He proves, also, that man, once surrendering his reason, has no remaining guard against the most monstrous absurdities, and like a ship without a rudder, is the sport of every wind. With such person, gullibility which they call faith, takes the helm from the hand of reason, and the mind becomes a wreck. — *Letter to James Smith*, Dec. 8, 1822.

New Catholic Encyclopedia:

There are few teachers of Trinitarian theology in Roman Catholic seminaries who have not been badgered at one time or another by the question, 'But how does one preach the Trinity?' And if the question is symptomatic of confusion on the part of the students, perhaps it is no less symptomatic of similar confusion on the part of their professors. — (*Trinity*, 1967, p. 304)

New Catholic Encyclopedia:

The doctrine of the Holy Trinity is not taught [explicitly] in the [Old Testament], The formulation "one God in three Persons" was not solidly established [by a council]...prior to the end of the 4th century. — (1967, Volume XIV p.299)

The New International Dictionary of New Testament Theology:

The New Testament does not contain the developed doctrine of the Trinity. 'The Bible lacks the express declaration that the Father, the Son, and the Holy Spirit are of equal essence' [said Protestant theologian Karl Barth]. — (Colin Brown, 1932, God, vol 2, Three, p. 687, C. J. Hemer)

Encyclopedia Encarta:

The doctrine is not taught explicitly in the New Testament, where the word God almost invariably refers to the Father.... The term *trinitas* was first used in the 2nd century, by the Latin theologian Tertullian, but the concept was developed in the course of the debates on the nature of Christ.... In the 4th century, the doctrine was finally formulated. — (Macquarrie, John, "Trinity," *Encarta Reference Library* 2005.)

The Anchor Bible Dictionary:

One does not find in the New Testament the Trinitarian paradox of the coexistence of the Father, Son, and Spirit within a divine unity. — (Bassler, Jouette M., "God in the New Testament," *The Anchor Bible Dictionary*, Doubleday, New York 1992, 2:1055.)

Correct Translation	New American Standard	King James Version
Isaiah 9:5-6* For a child **has been born** (יֻלַּד) to us, a son **given** to us, and the authority **was placed** (וַתְּהִי) upon his shoulder, and his name **was called** (וַיִּקְרָא) Wondrous Adviser, the Mighty God, the Everlasting Father, the Prince of Peace. ⁶To him who increases the authority, and for peace without end, on David's throne and on his kingdom, to establish it and to support it with justice and with righteousness; from now and to eternity; the zeal of the Lord of Hosts shall accomplish this. ***Isaiah 9:5 in a Jewish Bible appears as 9:6 in a Christian Bible.**	**Isaiah 9:6*** For a child **will be** born to us, a son **will be given** unto us; and the Government **will** rest on His shoulders; And His name **will be** called Wonderful Counselor, Mighty God, Eternal Father, Prince of Peace.	**Isaiah 9:6*** For unto us a child **is** born, unto us a son **is given**: and the government **shall be** upon his shoulder: and his name **shall be** called Wonderful, Counselor, The Mighty God, The Everlasting Father, The Prince of Peace.

> In an effort to portray Isaiah 9:6* as a future prophecy about a divine Jesus, Christian Bibles crudely mistranslated this passage. This verse is not discussing any future event or the messiah. Rather, Isaiah is describing the exaltation of King Hezekiah and the divine names bestowed upon him following the miracle when Jerusalem was saved from the Assyrian seige 2,700 years ago. Read this passage in the original Hebrew for yourself! The KJV, NAS, and a host of other Christian Bibles meticulously changed all of the past tense verbs in this verse into the future tense so it would appear to be foretelling of an event in the distant future. Below are the Hebrew verbs which the KJV mistranslated in Isaiah 9:6, yet correctly rendered in other places in the Tanach where these identical words appear.
>
> To further conceal that Isaiah 9:6 is referring to names given to Hezekiah, the New International Version Bible completely deletes the word "name," causing the verse to read, "and he will be called." For the full record of Hezekiah's salvation from Assyria, read Isaiah 37:32 and II Kings 19:31.

In an effort to support the doctrine of the Trinity, Christian translators deliberately changed the past-tense verbs in Isaiah 9:5* into the future tense.

→ and was *called*   and it *was*   was born

כִּי־יֶלֶד יֻלַּד־לָנוּ בֵּן נִתַּן־לָנוּ וַתְּהִי הַמִּשְׂרָה עַל־שִׁכְמוֹ וַיִּקְרָא שְׁמוֹ פֶּלֶא יוֹעֵץ אֵל גִּבּוֹר אֲבִי־עַד שַׂר־שָׁלוֹם:

וַיִּקְרָא	וַתְּהִי	יֻלַּד
Leviticus 1:1 – (King James) And the Lord **called** (וַיִּקְרָא) unto Moses....	**Isaiah 5:25 – (King James)** Their carcasses **were as** (וַתְּהִי) refuse in the streets....	**Genesis 4:26 – (King James)** And to Seth, to him also there **was born** (יֻלַּד) a son; and he called his name Enos....
Isaiah 21:8 – (King James) Then **he cried** (וַיִּקְרָא), "A lion, my Lord!"	**Isaiah 23:3 – (King James)** ...**and she is** (וַתְּהִי) the marketplace for the nations.	**Genesis 10:21 – (King James)** And children **were born** (יֻלַּד) also to Shem....
Isaiah 36:13 – (King James) Then the Rabshakeh stood **and called out** (וַיִּקְרָא) with a loud voice in Hebrew....	**Isaiah 29:11 – (King James)** The whole vision **has become** (וַתְּהִי) to you like the words of a book that is...sealed....	**Genesis 35:26 – (King James)** ...these are the sons of Jacob, which **were born** (יֻלַּד) to him in....

Jewish Names Frequently Contain the Name of God

Hezekiah - The Mighty God
Tovia - Goodness of God
Elienai - God Is My Eyes
Jehoiada - Knowledge of God
Hananiah - Gracious Lord
Elisha - God Is Salvation
Elijah - Yhwh God

Gedalia - Great God
Jesse - the Lord Is
Elihu - God Is He
Eliab - God Is Father
Eli - God Is
Eliezer - Help of God
Netanyahu - God Gives

Moses is Called a "God"
Exodus 7:1
And the Lord said unto Moses, See, I have made thee a *god* (אֱלֹהִים) to Pharaoh, and Aaron thy brother shall be thy *prophet*. *(see also Exodus 4:16)*

Jerusalem is Called "Lord"
Jeremiah 33:16 (See Volume 2, page 119)
In those days shall Judah be saved, and Jerusalem shall dwell safely; and this is the name wherewith she shall be called, "***The Lord Our Righteousness***" (יהוה צִדְקֵנוּ).

Angels are Called "God"
Psalms 8:6
For you have made him a little lower than the ***angels*** (מֵאֱלֹהִים)...

An Altar is Called "God"
Genesis 33:20
And he [Jacob] erected an altar, *and called it* "***Lord, the God of Israel***" (אֵל אֱלֹהֵי יִשְׂרָאֵל).

An Altar is Called "God"
Judges 6:24
Then Gideon built an altar to the Lord, and he named it "Lord is Peace" (יהוה שָׁלוֹם)...

Judges are Called "God"
Exodus 21:6, 22:8
Then his master shall bring him to the ***judges*** (הָאֱלֹהִים)... ⁸for any kind of lost thing which another claims to be his, the cause of both parties shall come before the ***judges*** (אֱלֹהִים); and whoever the ***judges*** (אֱלֹהִים) condemn shall pay double to his neighbor.

Isaiah 37:31-35
And the remaining survivors of the house of Judah shall continue to take root below and they shall produce fruit above. ³²For from Jerusalem shall come forth a remnant, and survivors from Mt. Zion; **the zeal of the Lord of hosts shall do this** (קִנְאַת יְהוָה צְבָאוֹת תַּעֲשֶׂה־זֹּאת) ³³Therefore, so has the Lord said concerning the king of Assyria: "He shall not enter this city, neither shall he shoot there an arrow, nor shall he advance upon it with a shield, nor shall he pile up a siege mound against it. ³⁴By the way he comes he shall return, and this city he shall not enter," says the Lord. ³⁵ I will protect this city to save it, for My sake and *for the sake of My servant David*. *(see also II Kings 19:30-34)*

(see page 186)

Isaiah 10:20-27
And it shall come to pass on that day that the remnant of Israel and the survivors of the house of Jacob shall not continue to lean on him that smote them; but he shall lean on the Lord, the Holy One of Israel, in truth. ²¹The remnant shall return, the remnant of Jacob, *to the mighty God*... ²⁴Therefore, so said the Lord God of Hosts, "Fear not, My people who dwell in Zion; *Assyria, with a rod may he smite you*, and his staff may he bear over you as he did in Egypt..." ²⁶And the Lord of Hosts shall stir up a scourge against him, *like the smiting of Midian* at the Rock of Oreb, and His staff on the sea, and He shall carry him off after the manner of Egypt. ²⁷And it shall come to pass on that day, that his burden shall be removed from upon your shoulder, and his yoke from upon your neck, and the yoke shall be destroyed....

(see page 185)

Biblical Revisionism?

The chart below illustrates how Christian Bibles deliberately altered the ninth chapter of the Book of Isaiah. They tampered with these texts in order to portray these passages as speaking about a future prophecy—the birth of a divine savior—rather than a past epic event: Hezekiah prayed to God in the Temple to save Jerusalem from the Assyrians (2 Kings 19:15). Christian translators accomplish this task by changing critical past-tense verbs in these verses into the future tense.

In this chapter, Isaiah enumerated the recent traumatic exile of the 10 northern tribes by the mighty Assyrian Empire, and the miraculous salvation of Jerusalem. The events described in these passages convey the unbridled, euphoric reaction of the Kingdom of Judah, which was saved from imminent destruction at the hands of the powerful Assyrian forces. When the people of Judah awoke to discover that 185,000 enemy soldiers inexplicably perished outside of their walls, a state of spiritual ecstacy and unrestrained jubilation swept the nation. The people grasped that it was King Hezekiah who inspired them to rely on God during Assyria's horrifying siege 2,700 years ago. They recognized that the Kingdom of Judah was miraculously saved as a direct result of Hezekiah's leadership. This was the first time that the children of Israel witnessed a supernatural salvation of this magnitude since the Exodus from Egypt, nearly 700 years earlier. This epic event is discussed extensively in Isaiah 36-37, II Kings 19, and 2 Chronicles 32. This forensic textual study below illustrates how two well-known Christian Bibles employed crude Bible-tampering in order to change the past tense verbs in these passages into the future tense. They were determined to portray these passages as speaking of a divine Jesus rather than Hezekiah, who was redeemed by God.

Isaiah 9:1 *New International Version*	Isaiah 8:23 (Verse numbers are one number lower in a Jewish Bible than a Christian Bible)	Isaiah 8:23
Christian Translation	**Jewish Translation**	**Original Hebrew**
¹Nevertheless, there will be no more gloom for those who were in distress. In the past he humbled the land of Zebulun and the land of Naphtali, but in the **future** he **will honor** Galilee of the Gentiles, by the way of the sea, along the Jordan.	²³For there is no weariness to the one who oppresses her; like the first time, he dealt mildly, [exiling only] the land of Zebulun and the land of Naphtali, and the last one he dealt harshly; the way of the sea, and the other side of the Jordan, the attraction of the nations.	כִּי לֹא מוּעָף לַאֲשֶׁר מוּצָק לָהּ כָּעֵת הָרִאשׁוֹן הֵקַל אַרְצָה זְבֻלוּן וְאַרְצָה נַפְתָּלִי וְהָאַחֲרוֹן הִכְבִּיד דֶּרֶךְ הַיָּם עֵבֶר הַיַּרְדֵּן גְּלִיל הַגּוֹיִם:
Isaiah 9:2-4 (*New American Standard*)	**Isaiah 9:1-3** (*Jewish Trenslation*)	**Isaiah 9:1-3**
²The people who **walk** in darkness **will see** a great light; those who live in a dark land, the light **will** shine on them.	¹The people who **walked** in darkness, **have seen** a great light; those who dwell in the land of the shadow of death, light **has** shone upon them.	הָעָם הַהֹלְכִים בַּחֹשֶׁךְ רָאוּ אוֹר גָּדוֹל יֹשְׁבֵי בְּאֶרֶץ צַלְמָוֶת אוֹר נָגַהּ עֲלֵיהֶם:
³Thou **shalt** multiply the nation, thou **shalt** increase their gladness; they **will** be glad in Thy presence as with the gladness of harvest, as men rejoice when they divide the spoil.	²You **have** aggrandized this nation; you **have** magnified the joy for them; they **have** rejoiced over You like the joy of the harvest, as they rejoice when they divide spoils.	הִרְבִּיתָ הַגּוֹי לֹא (לוֹ) הִגְדַּלְתָּ הַשִּׂמְחָה שָׂמְחוּ לְפָנֶיךָ כְּשִׂמְחַת בַּקָּצִיר כַּאֲשֶׁר יָגִילוּ בְּחַלְּקָם שָׁלָל:
⁴For Thou **shalt** break the yoke of their burden and the staff on their shoulders, the rod of their oppressor, **as at the battle of Midian.**	³For, the yoke of his burden and the staff of his shoulder, the rod of the one who oppressed him **have** You broken, **as on the day of Midian**.	כִּי אֶת־עֹל סֻבֳּלוֹ וְאֵת מַטֵּה שִׁכְמוֹ שֵׁבֶט הַנֹּגֵשׂ בּוֹ הַחִתֹּתָ כְּיוֹם מִדְיָן:

The Context of the Ninth Chapter of Isaiah

In the tenth chapter of the Book of Isaiah we find the epilogue to the startling events described in chapter nine. In these two interconnected chapters, the prophet recounts how God saved King Hezekiah and his people when Assyria's powerful leader, Sannacherib, laid siege to Jerusalem.

By this time, the Assyrian army carried off nine and a half tribes of the Northern Kingdom of Israel, and it was poised to exile the remaining Kingdom of Judah with a massive siege of Jerusalem. The residents of the holy city faced an existential threat; only divine intervention could save them. In these chapters, Isaiah recounts how the desperate Jewish nation was miraculously delivered from the mighty Assyrian army. Thus, Isaiah begins the ninth chapter declaring, "The people who walked in darkness, have seen a great light; those who dwell in the land of the shadow of death, light has shone upon them."

The story of Hezekiah's remarkable salvation from Assyria about 2,700 years ago is related in the tenth chapter of Isaiah as well. The fact that the tenth chapter continues to speak of Hezekiah's stunning victory and Assyria's devastating defeat does not bode well for evangelical Christians who insist that the ninth chapter of Isaiah is speaking of a deified Jesus. As can be seen below, Isaiah nine and ten use identical language to convey God's miraculous intervention on King Hezekiah's behalf.

Isaiah 9	Isaiah 10
For the **yoke** of his **burden** and the **staff** of his **shoulder**, the **rod** of the one who oppressed him have You broken, **as on the day of Midian**. (9:3)	And it shall come to pass on that day, that his **burden** shall be removed from upon your **shoulder**, and his **yoke** from upon your neck, and the **yoke** shall be destroyed.... (10:27)
	Woe to Assyria, the **rod** of My anger And the **staff** in whose hands is My indignation. (10:5) Assyria, with a **rod** may he smite you, and his **staff** may he bear over you as he did in Egypt." (10:24)
	And the Lord of Hosts shall stir up a scourge against him, like the smiting of **Midian** at the Rock of Oreb.... (10:26)
...and his name was called...the **Mighty God** (9:5)	The remnant shall return, the remnant of Jacob, to the **mighty God**.... (10:21)

Identifying phrase in Tanach:
'The zeal of the Lord of hosts shall accomplish this'

Isaiah 9:6	Isaiah 37:32	II Kings 19:31
Of the increase of his government and peace there will be no end, upon the throne of David and over his kingdom, to order it and establish it with judgment and justice from that time forward, even forever. **The zeal of the Lord of hosts will accomplish this.**	For out of Jerusalem shall go a remnant, and those who escape from Mount Zion. **The zeal of the Lord of hosts will accomplish this.**	For out of Jerusalem shall go a remnant, and those who escape from Mount Zion. **The zeal of the Lord of hosts will accomplish this.**

"The zeal of the Lord of hosts shall accomplish this" is a striking expression that can only be found in passages which describe Hezekiah's miraculous victory over Assyria

The unusual phrase, קִנְאַת ה' צְבָאוֹת תַּעֲשֶׂה־זֹּאת ("the zeal of the Lord of hosts shall accomplish this"), appears only three times throughout the entire corpus of the Jewish Scriptures (Isaiah 9:6, 37:32, and in II Kings 19:31). Each of these three verses occurs in the context of the same epic event: that moment in history, about 2700 years ago, when God miraculously saved King Hezekiah and his besieged nation from certain defeat at the hands of King Sennacherib and his mighty Assyrian army.

At the time, the people of Jerusalem were terrified because the massive forces of the Assyrian empire besieged their city and threatened to destroy them. They were frightened by the Assyrians' repeated taunts because they knew that no other nation had been able to withstand their powerful military machine. Faced with an existential threat of annihilation, Hezekiah went to the temple, and there he prayed for God's intervention. He was the first king of Judah to do so since the temple had been built some 250 years earlier, during the time of Solomon. He spread out before the Lord the latest communiqué from the Assyrians, and beseeched the Holy One of Israel to defend His Name and deliver his nation (II Kings 19:14-19).

The people of Jerusalem were inspired by Hezekiah's unwavering trust in God. They were spiritually transformed and rallied around him. They refused to surrender to their enemy's powerful forces. As a result, "the zeal of the Lord of hosts" was unleashed on the first night of Passover, when an angel of the Lord killed 185,000 Assyrian soldiers in a single night. When King Sennacherib awoke the next morning and realized that his entire army had been wiped out, he fled to his capitol city, Ninevah, where he was assassinated shortly thereafter (II Kings 19:37).

God had intervened on behalf of His faithful people in a manner which had not been witnessed since the Exodus. Thus, "the zeal of the Lord of hosts" dealt a stunning defeat to Assyria and miraculously saved Hezekiah and the entire kingdom of Judah.

The following related articles can be found in Volume 2 of *Let's Get Biblical! Why doesn't Judaism Accept the Christian Messiah?*

I. Why is the Messiah Called
'The Lord Our Righteousness'?............ Page 119

II. Monotheism and Idolatry................. Page 125

III. The Trinity in the *Shema* Prayer............ Page 133

IV. Did Jesus Claim to be God?............... Page 139

V. Did Someone Find the Trinity in the
First Chapter of the Bible? To Whom
Was God Speaking When He Said,
"Let Us Make Man In *Our* Image"?......... Page 145

VI. Did Someone Find the Trinity in the
Name of God? Why is God's
Name *Elohim* in the Plural?............... Page 153

Part VI

Zechariah 12:10

John 19:34-37

But one of the soldiers with a spear pierced his side, and forthwith came there out blood and water. ³⁵And he that saw it bare record, and his record is true: and he knoweth that he saith true, that ye might believe. ³⁶For these things were done, that the scripture should be fulfilled, A bone of him shall not be broken. ³⁷And again another scripture saith, "They shall look upon him (ὄν) whom they have pierced."

Obadiah 1:17-18, 21

And on Mount Zion there shall be a remnant, and it shall be holy, and the house of Jacob shall inherit those who inherited them. ¹⁸And the house of Jacob shall be fire and house of Joseph a flame, and the house of Esau shall become stubble, and they shall ignite them and consume them, and the house of Esau shall have no survivors, for the Lord has spoken.... ²¹And the saviors shall ascend Mt. Zion to judge the mountain of Esau, and the Lord shall have the kingdom.

Zechariah 12:8-14 (King James Version)

In that day shall the Lord defend the inhabitants of Jerusalem; and he that is feeble among them at that day shall be as David; and the house of David shall be as God, as the angel of the Lord before them. ⁹And it shall come to pass on that day, that I will seek to destroy all the nations that come against Jerusalem. ¹⁰I will pour out upon the house of David and upon the inhabitants of Jerusalem a spirit of grace and supplications. And **they shall look upon me** (וְהִבִּיטוּ אֵלַי) **whom** (אֵת אֲשֶׁר) they have pierced, and they shall mourn for *him* as one mourneth for his only son. ¹¹On that day there shall be great mourning in Jerusalem, like the mourning of Hadadrimmon in the valley of Megiddon. ¹²And the land shall mourn, every family apart: The Family of the house of David apart, and their wives apart. ¹³The family of the house of Levi apart, and their wives apart; the family of the Shimeites apart, and their wives apart. ¹⁴All the remaining families — every family apart, and their wives apart.

Zechariah 12:10

And they shall look to Me **because of the one** (אֵת אֲשֶׁר) who was thrust through, and they shall mourn over him as one mourns over an only son....

וְהִבִּיטוּ אֵלַי אֵת אֲשֶׁר דָּקָרוּ וְסָפְדוּ
עָלָיו כְּמִסְפֵּד עַל הַיָּחִיד וְהָמֵר עָלָיו
כְּהָמֵר עַל הַבְּכוֹר:

The Living Bible
(Christian Translation)

Zechariah 12:10

and they will look on *him* they pierced, and mourn for him....

Isaiah 61:3

To place for the mourners of Zion, to give them glory instead of ashes, oil instead of mourning, a mantle of praise instead of feeble spirit, and they shall be called the elms of righteousness, the planting of the Lord.

Isaiah 66:10

Rejoice with Jerusalem and exalt in her all those who love her; rejoice with her a rejoicing, all who mourn over her.

II Chronicles 35:22-25

Nevertheless, Josiah would not turn his face from him, but disguised himself, that he might fight with him, and hearkened not unto the words of Necho from the mouth of God, and came to fight in the valley of Megiddo. ²³And the archers shot at King Josiah; and the king said to his servants, "Have me away, for I am sore wounded." ²⁴His servants therefore took him out of that chariot, and put him in the second chariot that he had, and they brought him to Jerusalem, and he died, and was buried in one of the sepulchers of his fathers. And all Judah and Jerusalem mourned for Josiah. ²⁵And Jeremiah lamented for Josiah; and all the singing men and singing women spoke of Josiah in their lamentations, unto this day; and they made them an ordinance in Israel; and, behold, they are written in the Lamentations.

Did Zechariah Predict that the Jews Will Finally Accept Jesus, Whom they Crucified?

Missionaries point to a passage found at the end of the Book of Zechariah, which they insist foretells an epoch that will occur during the End of Days when the Jews finally embrace Jesus, the messiah whom they crucified.

The King James Version of the Bible translates Zechariah 12:10 as follows:

> And I will pour upon the house of David, and upon the inhabitants of Jerusalem, the spirit of grace and of supplications: and they shall look upon Me whom they have pierced, and they shall mourn for Him, as one mourns for his only son, and shall be in bitterness for him, as one that is in bitterness for his firstborn.

The interpretation of nearly all Christian Bible commentators on this passage is epitomized in the words of the famed British Methodist theologian, Adam Clarke:

> This is the way in which the Jews themselves shall be brought into the Christian Church. 1. "They shall have the spirit of grace," God will show them that he yet bears favor to them. 2. They shall be excited to fervent and continual prayer for the restoration of the Divine favor. 3. Christ shall be preached unto them; and they shall look upon and believe in him whom they pierced, whom they crucified at Jerusalem. 4. This shall produce deep and sincere repentance; they shall mourn, and be in bitterness of soul, to think that they had crucified the Lord of life and glory, and so long continued to contradict and blaspheme, since that time.

Clarke's exposition of this passage is not unique.

With virtual unanimity, Christian apologists and interpreters insist that Zechariah 12:10 contains a prophecy that points to a future time when, as the contemporary American Bible commentator, John MacArthur, concludes in his popular study Bible, "Israel's repentance will come because they look to Jesus, the One whom they rejected and crucified."[1] Predictably, all Christian missionary groups celebrate and tout this passage as Scriptural proof that in the End of Days, the Jews will finally recognize their colossal error and embrace Jesus, whom they crucified thousands of years ago.

The Christian interpretation of Zechariah 12:10 at odds with the Book of John

It is surprising that this stock interpretation of this passage became so popular in the Christian world because it is contradicted by the New Testament itself!

The unflinching willingness of Church teachers to discard and subvert the Gospel interpretation of Zechariah 12:10 in order to produce an artful proof-text is unprecedented in the contentious arena of biblical polemics. No other example exists in which doctors of the Church unabashedly abandon the interpretation of the New Testament in favor of a more lethal and pungent assault on Judaism, Christendom's elder rival.

Virtually all Christian commentators on Zechariah 12:10 claim that this passage conveys the following clear prophecies:

1) The "piercing" in this passage refers to the crucifixion
2) This event will take place in the future, following the "second coming" of Jesus, when the Jews will recognize their immense error
3) With regret, the Jews will finally look to Jesus as the true messiah

All missionary tracts highlight this verse as evidence that the crucifixion and the future Jewish contrition for the rejection and execution of Jesus are explicitly foretold in the Hebrew Bible. "Other than Jesus, who was crucified at the hands of his own people," missionaries ask. "Whom else could this verse be speaking of?"

Commenting on this passage, the famed British preacher, Charles Spurgeon writes:

> So now, read these words, "They shall look upon Me Whom they have pierced." Our text is a prophecy of the conversion of the Jews. They practically pierced the Savior when they clamored for His crucifixion, although Pilate tried to make a way for His escape—and the whole Jewish race has continued to endorse their dreadful deed. Most of the Jews who are now living still reject Christ with the utmost scorn and contempt.
> (Spurgeon's sermon, "The Bitterness of the Cross," May 12, 1881)

Strangely, this stock explanation of this passage is at odds with the interpretation offered in the New Testament. According to the passion narrative in the Book of John, Zechariah 12:10 is unrelated to the piercing of hands and feet during a crucifixion, and has nothing to do with the Jews. Instead, the fourth Gospel claims that this verse was fulfilled by a brief event that occurred after Jesus had already died, when the Roman soldiers looked at Jesus after his side was punctured.

We are told in the Book of John that Roman soldiers planned to break Jesus' legs. This was a practice known as "crucifragium," a method of hastening death during a crucifixion because the crucified man could not push up on his legs to relieve the pressure on his lungs and breathe. By not breaking the criminal's legs they prolong his torment. Just before they did so, the fourth Gospel states that soldiers realized that Jesus was already dead and that there was no reason to break his legs. But to make sure that he was dead, a Roman soldier stabbed him with a lance in the side.

> So the soldiers came and broke the legs of the first, and of the other who had been crucified with Jesus; [33]but when they came to Jesus and saw that he was already dead, they did not break his legs. [34]But one of the soldiers pierced his side with a spear, and at once there came out blood and water. [35]He who saw it bore witness—his testimony is true, and he knows that he tells the truth—that you also may believe. [36]For these things took place that the scripture might be fulfilled, "Not a bone of him shall be broken" (Exodus 12:46). [37]And again another Scripture says, "They shall look on him whom they have pierced" (Zechariah 12:10).
>
> (John 19:32-37)

Clearly, John's interpretation of Zechariah 12:10 completely contradicts the explanation that missionaries and Christian commentators attribute to this verse.

Missionaries argue that the passage in Zechariah foretells that Jews will contritely gaze at Jesus. John, on the other hand, claims that Jews had nothing to do with the fulfillment of this verse. Rather, the fourth Gospel insists that Zechariah was referring to Roman soldiers who looked at Jesus' dead body; Jews were not even present in John's story.

Christian apologists claim that the "piercing" in Zechariah refers to the crucifixion nails that pierced Jesus' hands and feet. John, on the other hand, insists that the word "pierced" in this passage is unrelated to Jesus' execution, but rather the postmortem piercing to confirm death. The Jews did not recommend this method according to

John's Passion Narrative. Rather, the fourth Gospel claims that this prophecy refers to the lance used by the Roman soldier to confirm that Jesus was already dead.

We are told by missionaries that this prophecy in the Book of Zechariah will be fulfilled in the future second coming of Jesus. In this time in the future, they insist, the Jews will finally embrace Jesus, whom they pierced. The fourth Gospel, however, says that Zechariah 12:10 was fulfilled nearly 2,000 years ago!

Why does the story of the Roman soldier appear only in the Book of John?

Of the four Gospels, only John portrays Jesus as the "lamb of God," with the proclamation: "Behold the Lamb of God who takes away the sin of the world" in John 1:29 and 1:36. As a result of this unique Johannine christology, only the fourth Gospel claims that the Jews recommend *crucifragium* (19:31), and the Romans instead decided to pierce Jesus' side (19:33-34).

Contrary to the accounts in the Synoptic Gospels, the Book of John casts Jesus' death as a fulfillment of the sacrifice of the Passover lamb. This would have a significant impact on John's version of the events surrounding the crucifixion.

For example, John claims that Jesus was crucified at roughly the same time as the Passover lambs were being slain in the temple, on the afternoon of the 14th of Nisan. Accordingly, no Passover Seder transpires during John's version of the Last Supper (chapter 13). This interpretation, however, is contradicted by the chronology found in the Synoptic Gospels. The Books of Matthew, Mark, and Luke date Jesus' crucifixion on the 15th day of Nisan, which is the first day of Passover. Therefore, the synoptic's account of the Last Supper includes a Passover Seder.

Moreover, the Torah expressly states that it is forbidden to break the bones of the Passover lamb (Exodus 12:46). With this commandment in mind, John inserted a narrative into his Gospel in which a Roman soldier prevents Jesus' bones from being broken (John 19:37).

This story appears nowhere else in the New Testament.

In an effort to support this account, the fourth Gospel misquotes the passage from the Jewish Scriptures in John 19:37 by altering Zechariah 12:10, and ripping the verse completely out of its original context.

The Book of John misquotes the Hebrew Bible

Zechariah 12:10b begins with the words, "...וְהִבִּיטוּ אֵלַי אֵת אֲשֶׁר דָּקָרוּ" (*V'hebetu eylai et asher dakaru*), which means, "And they shall look to Me because of the one who was pierced..." If left unaltered, this phrase would not fit well with the story of a Roman soldier piercing the side of Jesus. John, therefore, changed the word "Me" to "him," so John 19:37 instead reads, "They shall look upon him (ὃν) whom they have pierced."

The meaning of the Hebrew word אֵלַי (*eylai*) is not ambiguous or debated, for it appears approximately 400 times throughout Tanach. אֵלַי means "to me," not "him."

Zechariah 12:10	they shall look to **Me** אֵלַי because of the one who was pierced
John 19:37	they shall look on **him** ὃν whom they have pierced

Why did the Book of John change the word of God?

The context of Zechariah 12:10 discredits John's interpretation of this passage

Furthermore, the story of the Roman soldier piercing the side of Jesus bears no resemblance to the context of Zechariah 12:10. In order to grasp why Zechariah's 12th chapter is inconsistent with the narrative in the Book of John, it is vital to explore the tumultuous setting in which Zechariah 12:10 appears.

The 12th chapter of the Book of Zechariah points to the glories that await Israel in the End of Days and the final conflict and triumph of God's kingdom in the messianic age. "Jerusalem will be saved" is the central theme of this famed chapter. Thus, the last oracle of Zechariah presents the familiar theme of Israel's ultimate deliverance from her many enemies who rise up against Jerusalem.

In this final epoch, Jerusalem will become a "cup of drunkenness" (12:2) and "a heavy stone" for all the nations who rise up against Israel (12:3). The most feeble Jew will "become like David," our greatest warrior (12:8). "In that day, all the nations that come up against Jerusalem will be destroyed" (12:9).

In these famed passages, God encourages His covenant people with a vivid description of their restoration and blessing, true to Zechariah's name, which means, "God remembers."

Although God will destroy the enemies of Jerusalem during this apocalyptic battle, tragedy will strike the heart of the nation. In the midst of this triumphant war, a deep sense of mourning will grip the people of Israel.

The prophet describes the turmoil that follows the death of a great leader slain in battle. This sorrowful event will ignite a great mourning and anguish among the Jewish people. As a result, the nation turns to God "with supplication."

> "And they shall look to Me because of the one who was pierced, and mourn for him as one mourns over a firstborn son" (12:10).

This deep mourning, interlaced with Israel's wondrous victory over her enemies in the final battlefield of human history, will turn the nation's heart to God.

Although Zechariah does not identify the slain individual by name, the prophet provides us with precise information needed to assess the exact circumstance that will bring about his tragic death and profound effect this tragedy will have on his people.

In the following verse, the prophet confirms that the future battlefield tragedy will be similar to the calamity that occurred more than a century earlier:

> In that day shall there be a great mourning in Jerusalem, as the mourning of Hadadrimmon in the valley of Megiddon.
> (Zechariah 12:11)

To which woeful event that transpired in the valley of Megiddon is the prophet referring? The bitter mourning of that future day is likened to the death of the righteous King Josiah, who was killed by the archers of Necho, king of Egypt (2 Chronicles 35:20-25).

> Then Jeremiah chanted a lament for Josiah. And all the male and female singers speak about Josiah in their lamentations to this day....
> (2 Chronicles 35:25)

These passages establish that Zechariah is not discussing an execution 2,000 years ago, but, rather, the future tragic death of a great warrior on the battlefield of the apocalyptic war of Gog and Magog. This final conflict will be the immediate precursor to the messianic age described in these final pages of the Book of Zechariah and in the Book of Ezekiel chapters 38-39.

The person slain in Zechariah 12:10 will be killed in the future, during the heat of war on the battlefield, not through crucifixion 2,000 years ago.[2]

Moreover, John's narrative of the Roman soldier who pierced the side of Jesus did not occur at a time when Jerusalem was saved, as described in Zechariah 12:1-9. Quite the contrary: the first century marked a dark period in history when Jerusalem and the temple were destroyed by the Romans, and the second Jewish commonwealth in the Holy Land was extinguished.

On the other hand, during the events in the 12th chapter of Zechariah, God displays the full force of His superior power over Israel's enemies, for He chose Jerusalem as the city of His special affection. Unlike the miserable first century which was marked by devastation in Jerusalem, in the Latter Days, the power of God will devour the armies that will attack Israel.

In essence, John completely ignored the context of Zechariah 12:10 and hoped that you did as well!

No one would 'mourn' over someone who resurrected from the dead

As mentioned earlier, in virtual unison, Christian commentators on Zechariah 12:10 insist that at the End of Days the Jews will recognize their immense error, embrace the one they pierced (Jesus), and then mourn over him. This explanation, however, raises a pressing question: Why would anyone mourn over someone who is no longer dead? The mourning in Zechariah 12:10-14 is for a dead person, not someone who resurrected 2,000 years ago.

There are numerous examples in the Tanach of people who died and were then brought back to life. Did any of their loved ones mourn after their resurrection? Did the widowed mother mourn when Elijah resurrected her son at Zarephath? (1 Kings 17:17-23) When Elisha raised the Shunammite's son from the dead, did his mother mourn following his resurrection? (II Kings 4:8-37) This idea is not even expressed in the New Testament. Are we ever told by the Gospels that the disciples mourned over Jesus after his post-resurrection appearances? Such a response would have been preposterous. People mourn over the dead, not the living.

A cardinal principle of Judaism is the belief in the resurrection during the messianic age. The final resurrection is discussed in a number of places in the Hebrew Scriptures, including: Job 14:13-15, Isaiah 26:19, and Daniel 12:2.

Maimonides, one of the greatest Jewish authorities in history, set down 13 cardinal principles of the Jewish faith, which have ever since been printed in all Jewish prayer books. The belief in the Resurrection is the thirteenth principle:

> I believe with perfect faith that there will be a revival of the dead at the time when it shall please the Creator, Blessed be His name, and His mention shall be exalted forever and ever.

When the patriarchs Abraham, Isaac, and Jacob rise from the dead at the End of Days, will the Jewish nation mourn or rejoice? When the prophets Isaiah, Jeremiah, and Ezekiel resurrect from their grave, will this be a cause for lamenting or celebration? When the millions who perished in Hitler's ovens return to life, will the Jewish people mourn, or will they thank the Almighty in gladness for keeping His promise?

Zechariah 12:10-14 prophesies that the Jewish nation will mourn over an eschatological figure who is dead, not someone who resurrected from the grave thousands of years ago. If the person had already been resurrected, there would not be "...mourning, as one mourns over a firstborn son." Rather, there would be joy, feasting, and gladness.

The notion advanced by Christian apologists that the Jews will mourn out of regret for crucifying and rejecting Jesus is ludicrous and contravened by Zechariah's prediction that the Jewish people will mourn exactly as they did over the pious Josiah, who was slain on the battlefield (2 Chronicles 35:25).

Church interpretation of Zechariah 12:10 is derived from age-old, Christian antisemitism

It would be difficult to ignore the unpleasant fact that the stock Christian interpretation of Zechariah 12:10 is rooted in the centuries-old, Christian anti-Semitic canard which holds that the Jewish people are collectively responsible for deicide, the killing of Jesus, whom Christians believe to be the son of God. In essence, this classical Christian exegesis of this passage can only make sense if you believe that both the Jews who were present at Jesus' death, as well as the Jewish people collectively and for all time, are uniquely culpable for committing the unfathomable crime of murdering God.

Throughout history, this accusation has been the most powerful warrant for anti-Semitism by Christians. This age-old prejudice against Jews for the death of Jesus can be directly attributed to the Book of Matthew:

> When Pilate saw that he was getting nowhere, but that instead an uproar was starting, he took water and washed his hands in front of the crowd. 'I am innocent of this man's blood,' he said. 'It is your responsibility!' All the people answered, 'His blood is upon us and on our children!'
>
> (Matthew 27:24-25)

This odious portrayal of the Jews collectively—throughout history—as Christ-killers is essential to the Church's interpretation of Zechariah 12:10. Moreover, Matthew assigns no blame to Pontious Pilate, who washes his hands of the whole affair.

While the Church holds that Jesus died for the sins of the world, according to this fallacious interpretation of Zechariah 12:10, the Jews of all generations are collectively and uniquely responsible for crucifying Jesus. Christendom's apologists accordingly express the notion that the Jews who witness the "second coming" are uniquely responsible for "piercing" Jesus. As the renowned French theologian and reformer, John Calvin, noted in his commentary on Zechariah 12:10:

> At the beginning of this verse the Prophet intimates, that though the Jews were then miserable and would be so in future, yet God would be merciful to them..., for they would learn to look to him whom they had previously pierced.[3]

It is easy to understand why Christians find solace in the Church's stock interpretation of Zechariah 12:10. After all, parishioners who quietly wonder, "What if the Jews were right all along?" are comforted by an exegesis of Zechariah, which suggests that in the End of Days, the Jews will confess to the world that they were wrong about Jesus, "whom they pierced." For if the Christian mind were to discover that their favorite Bible commentators deliberately mistranslated and ripped this passage out of context, they would have to consider another famous messianic passage, which appears only four chapters earlier:

> This is what the Lord Almighty says: "In those days ten men from all languages and nations will take firm hold of one Jew by the hem of his robe and say, 'Let us go with you, because we have heard that God is with you.'"
>
> (Zechariah 8:23)

If the Jews were wrong about Jesus, why would the nations of the world confess these words to the Jews at the End of Days?

Footnotes:

1. MacArthur, John; *The MacArthur Study Bible*, Thomas Nelson Pub., 2009; page 1959

2. According to a Jewish tradition, the warrior who will be slain in the future battle of Gog and Magog is an apocalyptic figure called the Messiah ben Joseph (Moshiach ben Yosef) of the tribe of Ephraim (son of Joseph). He is also referred to as "Moshiach ben Ephrayim," which means "Messiah the descendant of Ephraim."

While it is beyond the scope of this book to present a detailed explanation of the Messiah ben Joseph, bear in mind that in rabbinic literature, the title "messiah" used here is not meant in the common, pedestrian sense, as the final Davidic king who will rule over Israel. Rather, the rabbis use the lexicon of the Bible where the word "messiah"—which appears 38 times in Tanach—refers to any leader, priest or prophet. In fact, in Isaiah 45:1, this title is bestowed upon the gentile King Cyrus. While the messiah the son of David, who will rule over Israel in the messianic age is discussed in the Jewish Scriptures, **he is never actually called the "messiah" in Tanach**.

The rabbinic use of the title "Messiah ben Joseph" frequently creates confusion for those unfamiliar with this topic. Missionaries frequently marshal this confusion in order to claim that the Jews believe in two messiahs: one who suffers and another, victorious. This argument is deliberately used to mislead those who know little about the faith they are being asked to abandon. Using the language of the Jewish Scriptures, many thousands of people throughout history could be called a messiah. The word "messiah" (Hebrew: מָשִׁיחַ *moshiach*) literally means "anointed," symbolizing a position of leadership.

The description of the Messiah ben Joseph is found in numerous rabbinic sources, including the Talmud (Sukkah52a, b) and in Rabbi Saadia Gaon's work, *Emunot ve-De'ot* (ch. viii.). All of the discussion surrounding this eschatological figure is intimately linked to our passages in the twelfth chapter of the Book of Zechariah.

Generally speaking, according to this tradition, the principal and final function ascribed to Moshiach ben Yosef is of a military nature. He will wage war against the forces of evil that oppress Israel. More specifically, he will battle against Edom, the descendants of Esau. Edom is the comprehensive designation of the enemies of God's covenant nation. Israel will be triumphant in this conflict, Jerusalem will be saved, the enemies of Israel will be destroyed, and the Messiah ben Joseph will be slain during this battle.

Thus it was prophesied of old:

> The House of Jacob will be a fire and the House of Joseph a flame, and the House of Esau for stubble..." (Obadiah 1:18): the progeny of Esau shall be delivered only into the hands of the progeny of Joseph.
> (Baba Batra 123b, Targum Yehonathan on Genesis 30:23)

His death will jolt the nation. It will cause the people to mourn—as in the days when the pious king Josiah was slain in battle—and ignite the Jewish nation's full repentance, which will lead them to the Redemption (Isaiah 59:20).

This war is the precursor to the messianic age, and described in detail in the Books of Zechariah (ch. 12-14) and Ezekiel (ch. 38-39). During the resurrection of the dead, which will occur in the messianic age, the faithful, including the Messiah the son of Joseph, will be resurrected.

Interestingly enough, according to Pirkei deR. Eliezer ch. 28 (in non-censored versions), the *Ishmaelites* (Arabs) will be the final kingdom to be defeated by Moshiach ben Joseph.

Other sources say it will be "Edom and the Arabs" (see Torah Shelemah on Genesis 15:12, note 130). Note, however, that in Pirkei deR. Eliezer, ch. 44 (and cf. *Midrash Tehilim* 2:6 and 83:3) that Edom and Yishmael have become intermingled. See also *Mayanei Hayeshu'ah*, Mayan 11:8.

Rav Avraham Yitzchak HaKohen Kook, the State of Israel's first chief rabbi, was one of Judaism's greatest scholars in recent generations—a spiritual giant who blazed unique trails in Jewish thought.

In his eulogy of Theodor Herzl in 1904, Rabbi Kook, who then served as chief rabbi of Jaffa, explained, based on earlier teachings of Nachmonodies, that the Jewish defense forces embodied the role of the Messiah ben Yosef. According to this opinion, the Messiah the son of Joseph is not an individual but, rather, a moving portrait of the Jewish soldiers who while defending Jerusalem will die in battle at the End of Days. Their deaths will unite the Jewish people in repentance.

3. Calvin, John; *Commentary on the Book of Haggai and Zechariah*

Part VII

The Law of Moses and the New Covenant

> The English word "law" is a rather cold translation of the Hebrew term "Torah," which is better rendered as "teaching."
>
> Throughout history, Christians frequently misunderstood the intent and purpose of the Jewish Law. It has never been the case that the Jewish people—both ancient or modern—thought that they are bound to observe all the laws in order to earn God's favor. In stark contrast to Paul's portrayal of the Jewish faith, Judaism has never been a religion of "works" in the sense that one had to follow a laundry list of do's and don'ts in order to earn salvation. Quite the contrary, the Jewish people were always committed to following the Torah because they had already been shown favor by God. In God's wisdom and for His purpose, the Jewish people were chosen to be His special people, and the Law was given to show them how to live up to this unique calling. For this reason, keeping the Law was never a dreaded chore that everyone hated; the Jewish nation considered the Law a great joy to uphold and cherish, and God's greatest gift to his people (see Psalm 119).

Paul on Torah Observance

Romans 3:20; 7:4-6; 10:4

"Therefore, by the deeds of the law there shall no flesh be justified in his sight: for by the law is the knowledge of sin."

7:4-6 "Therefore, my brethren, ye also are becoming dead to the law by the body of Christ... ⁶But now we are delivered from the law, that being dead wherein we were held; that we should serve in newness of spirit, and not in the oldness of the letter."

10:4 "For Christ is the end of the law for righteousness to everyone that believeth."

> In the seventh chapter of Romans, Paul encouraged Jews rather than gentiles (7:1) to abandon the commandments. It is a common misconception that Paul characterized the Torah as a "curse" for gentiles alone. Here, Paul is clearly insisting that the Jewish people discard the *mitzvoth* as well.

Galatians 2:16, 21, 3:13

"For by works of the law shall no flesh be justified... ²¹I do not frustrate the grace of God: for if righteousness came by the law, then Christ is dead in vain....

³:¹³Christ has redeemed us from the curse of the law, being made a curse for us..."

Does the Torah Ever State That it Is Too Difficult to Observe the Commandments?

Deuteronomy 30:10-14

If thou shalt hearken to the voice of the Lord your God, to keep His commandments and His statutes which are written in this book of the law; if you turn unto the Lord thy God with all your heart and with all your soul. ¹¹For this commandment which I command you this day is not too hard for you neither is it too far off. ¹²It is not in heaven, that you should say: 'Who shall go up for us to heaven, and bring it to us, and make us hear it, that we may do it?' ¹³Neither is it beyond the sea, that you should say: 'Who shall go over the sea for us, and bring it unto us, and make us to hear it that we may do it?' ¹⁴But the word is very near to you, in your mouth and in your heart, **that you may do it.**

> The core teachings of Paul are not supported by Deuteronomy 30:14. Consequently, the evangelist deliberately deleted the offending text at the end of Romans 10:8.
>
> The conclusion of Deuteronomy 30:14, "that you may do it" (i.e., keep the commandments), is an anathema to every idea that Paul vigorously promoted (Gal. 3:13).
>
> Therefore, in Romans 10:8, Paul completely expunged this offense phrase. In fact, the entire 30th chapter of Deuteronomy testifies that one can keep the *mitzvoth*.

Romans 10:4-8

For Christ is the end of the law for righteousness to everyone who believes. ⁵For Moses writes about the righteousness which is of the law, "The man who does those things shall live by them." ⁶But the righteousness of faith speaks in this way, "Do not say in your heart, 'Who will ascend into heaven?'" (that is, to bring Christ down from above). ⁷Or, "Who will descend into the abyss?" (that is, to bring Christ up from the dead). ⁸ But what does it say? "The word is near you, in your mouth and in your heart."

> Where did "that you may do it" go? In Romans 10:8, Paul deliberately expunged the last phrase of Deuteronomy 30:14.

Deuteronomy 30:15-19

See! Today I have set before you the choice between life and good [on one side], and death and evil [on the other]. ¹⁶I have commanded you today to love God your Lord, to walk in His paths, and to keep His commandments, decrees and laws. You will then survive and flourish, and God your Lord will bless you in the land that you are about to occupy. ¹⁷But if your heart turns aside and you do not listen, you will be led astray to bow down to foreign gods and worship them. I am warning you today, that [if you do that] you will be utterly lost... ¹⁹I call heaven and earth as witnesses! Before you I have placed life and death, the blessing and the curse. You must choose life, so that you and your descendants will survive.

Deuteronomy 4:5-8

See! I have taught you rules and laws as God my Lord has commanded me, so [that you] will be able to keep them in the land to which you are coming and which you will be occupying. ⁶Safe-guard and keep [these commandments], since this is your wisdom and understanding in the eyes of the nations. They will hear all these rules and say, "This great nation is certainly a wise and understanding people." ⁷What nation is so great that they have God so close to it, as God our Lord is, whenever we call on him? ⁸What nation is so great that they have such righteous statutes and laws, like this entire Torah that I am presenting before you today?

Deuteronomy 10:12-13

And now, Israel, what does God want of you? Only that you remain in awe of God your Lord, so that you will follow all His paths and love Him, serving God your Lord with all your heart and with all your soul. ¹³You must keep God's commandments and decrees that I am prescribing for you today, so that good will be yours.

Deuteronomy 29:28 (29)

The things that are revealed belong unto us and our children forever, that we may keep all the words of the law.

> **P**aul argues that the observance of the Law is no longer necessary, while the Tanach clearly states that the Law is eternal.

Psalm 111:7-8

The works of His hands are truth and justice, all his commandments are sure. ⁸They stand fast **forever and ever**, done in truth and uprightness.

Psalm 19:8-9 (7-8)

The law of the Lord is perfect, it restores the soul; the testimony of the Lord is trustworthy, making the simple one wise! ⁹The statutes of the Lord are right, rejoicing the heart; the commandments of the Lord are pure, enlightening the eyes!

Psalm 119:44, 72, 97, 155, 163, 165

So shall I keep Thy Torah continually, forever and ever! ⁷²The Torah of Thy mouth is better unto me than thousands of gold and silver! ⁹⁷O how I love Thy Torah! All day long it is my conversation! ¹⁵⁵Salvation is far from the wicked: for they seek not Thy law. ¹⁶³I hate and abhor falsehood, but Thy Torah do I love! ¹⁶⁵Great peace have they that love Thy Torah; there is no stumbling block for them!

> **T**he largest chapter in the Bible has much to say about Paul's teachings, and none of it is positive.

The Jewish People will Perform the Commandments in the Messianic age

Ezekiel 11:19-20

And I will give them one heart, and I will put a new spirit within you; and I will take the stony heart out of their flesh, and will give them a heart of flesh. ²⁰That they may walk in My statutes, and keep My ordinances, and do them; and they shall be My people, and I will be their God.

Ezekiel 37:24

And David My servant shall be king over them; and they all shall have one shepherd. They shall also walk in My judgments, and observe My statutes, and do them.

Ezekiel 44:9

Thus saith the Lord God: No stranger, uncircumcised in the heart, or uncircumcised in the flesh, shall enter into My sanctuary...

> **W**hy does Paul claim that Jesus' death marked the end of circumcision (Gal. 5:2-3), when Ezekiel states that no one who is physically uncircumcised will enter the future messianic Temple?

Isaiah 2:3

And many nations shall go, and they shall say, "Come, let us go up to the Lord's mount, to the House of the God of Jacob, and let Him teach us of His ways, and we will go in His paths," for out of Zion shall the Torah come forth, and the word of the Lord from Jerusalem.

Zachariah 14:16

It shall come to pass that everyone that is left of all the nations...will keep the Feast of Tabernacles.

Malachi 3:22 (4:4)

Remember ye the Torah of Moses My servant, which I commanded unto him in Horeb, for all Israel, with all statutes and judgments!

Paul Rejects the Law of Moses

It would be easy to argue that Paul was the most important convert to Christianity. Had Paul not joined the small, inauspicious movement, if he had not engaged in his extensive missionary activity, the fledgling group would have joined the ranks of many other Jewish sectarian movements, and vanished without a trace. Instead, as a direct result of Paul's influence, Christianity was transformed into a worldwide religion across the Roman Empire and beyond. Moreover, the writings ascribed to him by the Church form a considerable portion of the Christian canon, of whose twenty-seven books, thirteen are attributed to Paul. The influence of his epistles on Christian thinking cannot be overstated.

Paul's works are rightly called "the Christian Manifesto." His ideas about God's salvation plan for mankind are not found in the Jewish Scriptures. Paul said almost nothing about what Jesus did or said during his lifetime because the two of them never met. Yet he forged some of Christendom's most enduring theological doctrines. Paul never mentioned Jesus' miraculous birth in Bethlehem, his sermon on the mount, baptism, temptation, transfiguration, etc.—all of which would have been invaluable to his followers—because these stories had not yet been invented. Remember, Paul's letters were written long before the Gospels. However, a theme scattered throughout the Gospels is founded on Paul's principal message: Reject the commandments outlined in the Torah and replace them with faith in Jesus the messiah. For most Jews, however, it was completely absurd to call Jesus "the messiah." Jesus was nothing like the powerful Davidic king promised in the Jewish Scriptures. What were Christians to do with the fact that they had trouble convincing most Jews of their claims about Jesus? Their own expectations about Jesus were shattered: Jesus was powerless to usher in the messianic age. We know from Jewish documents written from the biblical period until the time of Jesus that there was an overarching anticipation of what the messiah would be like.[1] This expectation did not remotely resemble Jesus. No Jew—Jesus' followers included—anticipated that the messiah was to be executed. Yet many of the early Christians could not concede that they were wrong. And if *they* were not wrong, who was? It had to be the Jews. Paul, therefore, introduced his own salvation plan: he insisted that man could receive redemption only by faith in the death and resurrection of Jesus. The Law of Moses was powerless to save mankind.[2] What about the messianic kingdom promised by the Jewish prophets? Those prophecies, Paul insisted, would be fulfilled during Jesus' second coming. When would this second coming occur? Both Jesus and Paul insisted that these End Time events were imminent, and were to unfold during their own generation.[3] Jesus and Paul's predictions never materialized.

To convey the idea that the Law of Torah could not bring about salvation, we are told in the Book of Acts that Peter had a recurring dream where he saw unclean animals on a sheet descending from heaven.[4] A heavenly voice instructs Peter to eat these forbidden animals.

At first, Peter rejected this command. At once, the voice from heaven rebuked him for refusing to eat "what God has cleansed."

Paul's emphatic rejection of the Mosaic Law with all its commandments, which he argued must be replaced with faith in Jesus, is stressed in the Book of Acts. The Church regards the Book of Acts as an essential "bridge" in the New Testament, linking the itinerant ministry of Jesus in the Gospels and the ministry of the apostles, when we are told that the disciples received the Holy Spirit on Pentecost. For Christendom, however, the Book of Acts plays a far more important role than an outline conveying the transition between epochs of the emerging Church. While the complete title of this work is the "Acts of the Apostles," the book really focuses on only two men: Peter (chs. 1–12) and Paul (chs. 13–28). In the Book of Acts, the guiding leadership of the Church is transferred from Peter to Paul; from a movement that splintered away from Judaism, to Christianity, a religion which supplanted Judaism.

Until the 11th chapter of the Book of Acts, Peter is cast as a Jew grappling with his Jewish faith, unsure of his conduct with others who did not share his birthright. We are told that he was reluctant to meet and eat with gentiles, and determined to resist unkosher food. Peter was prodded repeatedly to abandon his Jewish traditions. Peter's unwillingness to walk away from his Jewish practices infuriated Paul, and he sternly rebuked Peter for his stubbornness.[5] Peter is frequently portrayed as someone who blundered and floundered in his walk as a new Christian. Paul, on the other hand, is cast as infallible following his conversion to Christianity. To this day, Paul is regarded as the father of Christian doctrine, and his teachings remain the foundation of Christian theology. In his epistle to the Colossians, Paul emphatically expressed his disdain for Torah observance:

> "...he forgave us all our sins, having canceled the written code and regulations, that was against us and that stood opposed to us; he took it away, nailing it to the cross."
>
> (Colossians 2:13-14)

Paul insisted that keeping the Law was worse than irrelevant; it was an admission that Jesus' death was insufficient for salvation. We find in the Book of Acts that Saul adopted the Roman name Paul. When Saul changed his Jewish name to Paul, he illustrated his assimilationist Christian message, which is contravened by the Torah. Paul begins all of his epistles by introducing himself by name and never mentioned his former name, Saul, in any of his writings. By the time Paul was writing letters to fellow Christians he had severed his relationship to Judaism. In his own words, everything else, including the Law, "is as worthless as excrement" (Phil. 3:8).

[1] Psalm of Solomon 17:21-32 (Pseudepigrapha), 1 Enoch 69, 4 Ezra 13:1-11 [2] Rom. 3:21-22 [3] Mark 9:1;13:30; I Thes. 4:13-17 [4] Acts 10:11-16; 11:5-10 [5] Galatians 2:11-14

Jeremiah 31:30-36 (31:31-37 in a Christian Bible)

30 Behold, days are coming, says the Lord, and I will form a covenant with the House of Israel and with the house of Judah, a new **covenant** (בְּרִית). 31 Not like the covenant that I formed with their forefathers on the day I took them by the hand to take them out of the land of Egypt, that they broke My covenant, although **I was a husband unto them** (וְאָנֹכִי בָּעַלְתִּי בָם), says the Lord. 32 For this is the covenant that I will form with the house of Israel after those days, says the Lord; I will place My law (תּוֹרָתִי) in their midst and I will inscribe it in their hearts, and I will be their God and they shall be My people. 33 And no longer shall one teach his neighbor or shall one teach his brother, saying, "Know the Lord," for they shall all know Me, from their smallest to their greatest, says the Lord, for I will forgive their iniquity and their sin I will no longer remember. 34 So said the Lord, Who gives the sun to illuminate by day, the laws of the moon and the stars to illuminate at night, Who stirs up the sea and its waves roar, the Lord of Hosts is His name. 35 If these laws depart from before Me, says the Lord, so will the **seed** (זֶרַע) of Israel cease being a nation before Me for all time. 36 So said the Lord: If the heavens above will be measured and the foundations of the earth below will be fathomed, I too will reject all the **seed** (זֶרַע) of Israel because of all they did, says the Lord.

> **M**issionaries erroneously assert that the word covenant (בְּרִית), which appears in Jeremiah 31:30-31, refers to the New Testament, written nearly 2,000 years ago. The Hebrew word *brit*, however, means a promise, not a new Bible. This passage contains a clear future prophecy, not a description of an event that occurred thousands of years ago (see Volume 2 page 159).
>
> This chapter contains an irrevocable oath from God promising that the nation of Israel is eternal, and will be permanently restored to their land in the End of Days.

A Covenant is a promise from God, not a Bible. The following are covenants that God made with our forefathers and Pinchas:

Leviticus 26:42

I will remember My covenant with Jacob as well as My covenant with Isaac and My covenant with Abraham. I will remember the land.

Numbers 25:12

Therefore, tell him [Pinchas] that I have given **him My covenant** of peace.

> **A**lthough the Book of Hebrews is designated as an "epistle," more accurately, it is an elaborate argument that seeks to demonstrate that Christianity is superior to Judaism. It therefore portrays the Torah as partial and incomplete, unable to accomplish its task of setting people into a right standing before God. The anonymous author, therefore, deliberately twisted the words of the prophet Jeremiah, whom it claims to be quoting. Whereas Jeremiah 31:31 states "I was a husband unto them [the Jews]," the Book of Hebrews reversed Jeremiah's prophecy to read, "I disregarded them." Why did author of Hebrews tamper with the words of Jeremiah?
>
> The bond between God and Israel is eternal and therefore unbreakable. Jeremiah conveys this message in 31:31-36, where Israel is declared betrothed to God. This is precisely the opposite relationship conveyed in Hebrews 8:9, where the Jews are portrayed as a people that are rejected by God.
>
> Jeremiah clearly predicted a future epoch in which "no one shall teach his neighbor... for they shall all know Me!" (31:33)

Hebrews 8:7-13

7 For if that first covenant had been faultless, then should no place have been sought for the second. 8 For finding fault with them, He saith, "Behold the days come, saith the Lord, when I will make a new covenant with the house of Israel, and with the house of Judah: 9 Not according to the covenant that I made with their fathers in the day when I took them by the hand to lead them out of the land of Egypt; because they continued not in my covenant, and I regarded them not (κἀγὼ ἠμέλησα αὐτῶν – *lit. although I disregarded them*), saith the Lord. 10 For this is the covenant that I will make with the house of Israel after those days, says the Lord; I will put my laws unto their mind, and write them in their hearts: I will be to them a God, and they shall be a people to me: 11 And they shall not teach every man his neighbor, and every man his brother, saying, "Know the Lord," for all shall know me, from the least to the greatest. 12 For I will be merciful to their unrighteousness, and their sins and their iniquities will I remember no more." 13 In that he saith, "A new covenant," He hath made the first old. **Now that which decayeth and waxeth old is ready to vanish away.**

Final Redemption of Israel will Eclipse the Exodus from Egypt

Jeremiah 23:7-8 (See also 16:14-15)
Therefore, behold days are coming, says the Lord, when they shall no longer say, "As the Lord lives, Who brought up the children of Israel from the land of Egypt." But, "As the Lord lives, Who brought us up and Who brought the seed of the House of Israel from the North Land and from all the lands where I have driven them, and they shall dwell on their land."

Can So Few Be So Right? Israel's Faithful Remnant Will Remain "Few in Number"

Deuteronomy 4:27
And the Lord shall scatter you among the nations, and you shall be left few in number among the heathen, where the Lord will lead you.

The Covenant Bestowed Upon the Faithful of Israel

Deuteronomy 7:6-9, 12
For you are a holy nation unto the Lord your God. The Lord your God has chosen you to be a special nation unto Himself, above all people upon the face of the earth. [7]The Lord did not set His love upon you, nor choose you, because you were more in number than any people, for you were the fewest of all the people. [8]But because the Lord loved you, and because He would keep the oath which He had sworn unto your fathers, has the Lord brought you out with a mighty hand, and redeemed you out of the house of bondmen, from the hand of Pharaoh king of Egypt. [9]Know therefore that the Lord your God, He is God, the faithful God, **which keeps His covenant and mercy with them that love Him and keep His commandments** to a thousand generations. [12]Wherefore it shall come to pass, **if you hearken to these judgments, and keep and do them, that the Lord your God shall keep unto you the covenant** and the mercy which He swore to your fathers.

Concerning the Jews
by Mark Twain

If the statistics are right, the Jews constitute but one percent of the human race. It suggests a nebulous dim puff of star dust lost in the blaze of the Milky Way. Properly the Jew ought hardly to be heard of; but he is heard of, has always been heard of. He is as prominent on the planet as any other people, and his commercial importance is extravagantly out of proportion to the smallness of his bulk. His contributions to the world's list of great names in literature, science, art, music, finance, medicine, and abstruse learning, are also away out of proportion to the weakness of his numbers. He has made a marvelous fight in this world, in all the ages; and has done it with his hands tied behind him. He could be vain of himself, and be excused for it. The Egyptian, the Babylonian, and the Persian rose, filled the planet with sound and splendor, then faded to dream-stuff and passed away; the Greek and the Roman followed, and made a vast noise, and they are gone; other peoples have sprung up and held their torch high for a time, but it burned out, and they sit in twilight now, or have vanished. The Jew saw them all, beat them all, and is now what he always was, exhibiting no decadence, no infirmities of age, no weakening of his parts, no slowing of his energies, no dulling of his alert and aggressive mind. All things are mortal but the Jew; all other forces pass, but he remains. What is the secret of his immortality?

From the article "Concerning the Jews"; *Harpers* (1899). See "*The Complete Essays of Mark Twain*"; Doubleday (1963), page 249.

If the entire human race is infected with the "Original Sin" and mankind is "totally depraved," why does the Bible bear witness to so many saintly people in history who were faithful to the Almighty? Men who devoted every moment of their lives to Heaven and prayed directly to God, never to Jesus. The Jewish Scriptures testify that these pious men were righteous because of their obedience to God—an achievement which the Church insists is an impossible task. Christendom argues that as a result of the first sin, every person born to the world is a slave to sin. The Tanach disagrees.

Genesis 26:5
Because Abraham obeyed My voice, and kept My charge, My commandments, My statutes, and My laws.

Numbers 14:24
But My servant Calev, because he had another spirit with him, and has followed Me fully, him will I bring into the land which he went, and he will leave it to his descendants.

I Kings 15:11
And Asa did that which was just in the eyes of the Lord, as had done David his father.

II Kings 22:2
And he [Josiah] did that which was right in the sight of the Lord, and walked in all the ways of David his father, and turned not aside to the right hand or the left.

II Chronicles 29:2
And he [Hezekiah] did what was right in the sight of the Lord, according to all that David his father had done.

According to a core doctrine of Christian theology, humanity's sinful state resulted from the Fall of Man. This hopeless condition has been characterized by the Church as a "sin nature" of all humans through collective guilt. This teaching is based primarily on the epistles of Paul.[1]

Luke 1:6
"Both of them [Zechariah and Elizabeth] were upright in the sight of God, observing all the Lord's commandments and regulations blamelessly."

In Augustine's view (termed "Realism"), all of humanity was really present within Adam when he sinned, therefore all of mankind is infected with the trespass of our first parents.[2] Original sin, according to Augustine and all Protestant Reformers, consists of the guilt of Adam and Eve that all humans inherit. As sinners, humans are utterly depraved in nature, lack freedom to do good, and are unable to adequately respond to the will of God. In essence, man can do nothing to merit his salvation through his own initiative and obedience to God.

Ironically, a claim in the New Testament completely contradicts this doctrine. We are told in Luke 1:6 that Mary's cousins, Zechariah and Elizabeth, kept all the Laws of the Torah perfectly and never sinned! According the Church's teachings, Luke's claim is preposterous and heretical!

[1] Rom. 3:10, 5:12; 1 Cor. 15:22
[2] Justo L. Gonzalez (1970-1975). *A History of Christian Thought: Volume 2 (From Augustine to the eve of the Reformation)*. Abingdon Press.

In one village, a certain soldier on this occasion found a copy of the sacred Law, tore the book to pieces and threw it into the fire. The Jews, as if their whole country were in flames, flocked together, religious fervor drawing them together like an instrument.

On the first announcement of the news, they hurried together with united clamor to Cumanus in Caesarea, where they besought him not to leave unpunished the author of such an outrage to God and their Law, but punish him for what he had done. Cumanus, seeing that the multitude could not be appeased unless amends were made, agreed to send for the soldier and ordered him to be led between the lines of his accusers to his execution. Then the Jews withdrew. (Josephus, *"The Jewish Wars"* Book II, 12:2)

The following related articles can be found in Volume 2 of *Let's Get Biblical! Why doesn't Judaism Accept the Christian Messiah?*

I. Has God Divorced Israel? What is the Meaning of the "New Covenant" Promised by the Prophet Jeremiah?.................. Page 159

II. Will God Save Only the Jews?............. Page 165

Part VIII

Daniel 9's 70 Weeks, Psalm 110 and 2:12

Psalm 110
(see Volume 2, page 183)

Jewish Translation	King James Version
Of David a Psalm. The Lord (יהוה) said to my master (לַאדֹנִי), "Sit thou at My right hand, until I make your enemies a footstool at your feet."	A Psalm of David. The Lord said to my Lord, "Sit thou at my right hand, until I make thine enemies thy footstool."

Matthew 22:41-46
While the Pharisees were gathered, Jesus asked them, Saying, "What think ye of Christ? Whose son is he?" They say unto him, "The son of David." He saith unto them, "How then doth David in spirit call him Lord, saying, The Lord said unto my Lord, 'Sit thou on my right hand, till I make thine enemies thy footstool?' If David then called him Lord, how is he his son?" And no man was able to answer him a word, neither did any man from that day forth ask him any more questions.

Psalm 2:12

Jewish Translation	King James Version
Desire purity (נַשְּׁקוּ בַר) lest He become angry and you perish in the way, for in a moment His wrath will be kindled; the praises of all who take refuge in Him.	Kiss the Son, lest he be angry, and ye perish from the way, when his wrath is kindled but a little. Blessed are all they that put their trust in Him.

Why does the King James Version translate the Hebrew word בַר as "son" in Psalm 2:12, yet correctly translates the exact same word as "pure" or "clean" in every other place where this word appears in the Book of Psalms?

Psalms 18:20 (21) — King James Version
The Lord rewarded me according to my righteousness; according to the cleanness (כְּבֹר) of my hands hath He recompensed me...

Psalm 18:24 (25) — King James Version
Therefore hath the Lord recompensed me according to my righteousness, according to the cleanness (כְּבֹר) of my hands in His eyesight.

Psalm 19:9 — King James Version
The statutes of the Lord are right, rejoicing the heart: the commandment of the Lord is pure (בָּרָה) enlightening the eyes.

Psalms 24:4 — King James Version
He has clean hands, and a pure (וּבַר) heart...

Psalm 73:1 — King James Version
Truly God is good to Israel, even to such as are of a clean (לְבָרֵי) Heart.

In Aramaic, the word בַר is a conjunctive noun, and means "son of." In Hebrew, the word בַר means "pure" or "clean" (see above). The Book of Psalms does not contain any Aramaic words. If King David wished to use the word "son," he would have written the Hebrew word בְּנִי, as he did in Psalm 2:7. Look it up for yourself!

Psalm 2:7 — King James Version
I will declare the decree: the Lord hath said unto me, "Thou art My son (בְּנִי) This day have I begotten thee."

Daniel 9:1-3, 13-27

In the first year of Darius, son of Ahasuerus, of the seed of Media, who was made king over the kingdom of the Chaldeans: ²In the first year of his reign, I Daniel, contemplated with books the calculation, the number of years about which the **word** (דְּבַר) of Hashem had come to the prophet Jeremiah, to complete the seventy years from the ruin of Jerusalem. ³ And I set my face toward my Lord, God, to request prayer and supplication, with fasting, sackcloth, and ashes. ¹³ As is written in the Law of Moses, all this evil has come upon us, and we did not entreat the countenance of the Lord our God to repent of our iniquities and to contemplate Your truth.... ¹⁴And the Lord hastened with the evil and brought it upon us, for the Lord our God is righteous with all His deeds which He performs, and we did not hearken to His voice. ¹⁵ And now, O Lord our God, Who took Your people out of the land of Egypt with a strong hand, and You have made for Yourself a Name as of this day; we have sinned, we have dealt wickedly. ¹⁶ My Lord, in keeping with all Your righteousness, please let Your anger and Your fury turn away from Your city Jerusalem, Your holy mountain; for because of our sins and the sins of our ancestors, Jerusalem and Your people have become the scorn of all those around us. ¹⁷And now, pay heed, our God, to the prayer of Your servant and to his supplications, and let Your countenance shine upon Your desolate Sanctuary for my Lord's sake. ¹⁸ Incline, my God, Your ear, and listen, open Your eyes and see the desolation of ourselves and of the city upon which Your Name is proclaimed; for not because of our righteousness do we cast down our supplications before You, rather because of Your great compassion. ¹⁹O my Lord, heed; O my Lord, forgive; O my Lord, be attentive and act, do not delay; for Your sake, my God, for Your Name is proclaimed upon Your city and Your people.' ²⁰ And more I was speaking, praying, and confessing my sin and the sin of my people, Israel, and casting my supplication before Hashem, my God, for the mountain of the Sanctuary of my God. ²¹Still I was speaking in prayer, and the man Gabriel, whom I saw in the beginning vision, was lifted in flight and approached me about the time of the afternoon offering. ²² He made me understand and spoke to me. And he said, `Daniel, I have just gone to make you skillful in understanding. ²³ At the beginning of your supplications a word went forth, and I have come to relate it, for beloved are you. Contemplate the matter and gain understanding in the vision. **²⁴ Seventy weeks have been decreed upon your people and your holy city to terminate transgression, to end sin, to wipe away iniquity, to bring everlasting righteousness, to seal vision and prophet, and to anoint the Holy of Holies.**

Daniel 9:25-27

King James Version

Know therefore and understand, that from the going forth of the commandment to restore and to build Jerusalem unto **the Messiah the Prince shall be seven weeks, and threescore and two weeks;** the street shall be built again, and the wall, even in troublous times.

²⁶And **after threescore and two weeks** shall Messiah be cut off, but not for himself: and the people of the prince that shall come shall destroy the city and the sanctuary; and the end thereof shall be with a flood, and unto the end of the war desolations are determined.

²⁷And he shall confirm the covenant with many for one week: and in the midst of the week he shall cause the sacrifice and the oblation to cease, and for the overspreading of abominations he shall make it desolate, even until the consummation, and that determined shall be poured upon the desolate.

Jewish Translation

And you should know and comprehend: From the emergence of the **word** (דָּבָר) to return and build Jerusalem until **an anointed prince** (עַד מָשִׁיחַ נָגִיד) will be seven weeks (שָׁבֻעִים שִׁבְעָה); and for sixty two weeks (וְשָׁבֻעִים שִׁשִּׁים וּשְׁנַיִם) it will be rebuilt, street and moat, but in troubled times.

²⁶And after the sixty-two weeks **an anointed one will be cut off** (יִכָּרֵת מָשִׁיחַ) **and will be no more** (וְאֵין לוֹ); the people of the prince who comes will destroy the city and the Sanctuary, but his end shall come like a flood. Until the end of a war, desolation is decreed!

²⁷He will strengthen a covenant with the great ones one week; and for half of the week he will abolish the sacrifice and offering, and upon soaring heights will the mute abominations be, until extermination as decreed will pour down upon the abomination.

Isaiah 44:28-45:1, 13

Who says of Cyrus, "He is My shepherd, and all My desire he shall fulfill," and to say of Jerusalem, "It shall be built, and the Temple shall be founded." ¹So said the Lord to **His anointed one** (לִמְשִׁיחוֹ לְכוֹרֶשׁ) to **Cyrus**, whose right hand I held, to flatten nations before him, and the loins of kings I will loosen, to open portals before him, and gates shall not be closed. ¹³"I aroused him with righteousness, and all his ways I will straighten out. He shall build My city and free My exiles, neither for a price nor for a bribe," said the Lord of Hosts.

Ezra 1:1-3

And in the first year of **Cyrus**, the king of Persia, at the completion of the **word** (דְּבַר) of the Lord from the mouth of Jeremiah, the Lord aroused the spirit of Cyrus, the king of Persia, and he issued a proclamation throughout his kingdom, and also in writing, saying: ²"So said Cyrus, the king of Persia, 'All the kingdoms of the earth the Lord God of the heavens delivered to me, and He commanded me to build Him a House in Jerusalem, which is in Judah. ³Who is among you of all His people, may his God be with him, and he may ascend to Jerusalem, which is Judea, and let him build the House of the Lord, God of Israel; He is the God Who is in Jerusalem."

> ### Jeremiah's Two 70-Year Prophecies
>
> **Jeremiah 25:12**
>
> And it shall be at the completion of **seventy years**, I will visit upon the king of Babylon and upon that nation, says the Lord, their iniquity, and upon the land of the Chaldeans, and I will make it for everlasting desolations.
>
> **Jeremiah 29:10**
>
> For so said the Lord: for at the completion of **seventy years** of Babylon I will remember you, and I will fulfil My good **word** (דְּבָרִי) toward you, **to restore you to this place**.

II Chronicles 36:21-23

To fulfil the **word** (דְּבַר) of the Lord in the mouth of Jeremiah, until the land was **appeased for its Sabbaths**; [for] all the days of its desolation it rested until the completion of seventy years. ²²And in the first year of Cyrus, king of Persia, at the completion of the **word** (דְּבַר) of the Lord in the mouth of Jeremiah, the Lord aroused the spirit of Cyrus the king of Persia, and he issued a proclamation throughout all his kingdom, and put it also in writing, saying: ²³"So said Cyrus the king of Persia: all the kingdoms of the earth has the Lord God of the heavens delivered to me, and He commanded me to build Him a House in Jerusalem, which is in Judah. Who among you is of all His people, may the Lord his God be with him, and he may ascend."

Leviticus 26:18

If despite this you do not heed Me, then I shall punish you seven times for your sins **(7 X 70 years = 490 years)**.

> This blistering curse found in Leviticus 26 was Daniel's greatest, immediate concern. The prophet was gripped with fear that as a result of Israel's ongoing sins, the Almighty multiplied the seventy-year exile sevenfold. In essence, he was petrified that his people were now set to endure a 490-year exile, rather than the 70-year exile that Jeremiah originally foretold.

Leviticus 25:1-22 — *Shmittah* — The Sabbatical Year

God spoke to Moses at Mount Sinai, telling him to speak to the Israelites and say to them: When you come to the land that I am giving you, the land must be given a rest period, a Sabbath to God. For six years you may plant your fields, prune your vineyards, and harvest your crops, but the seventh year is a Sabbath of Sabbaths for the land. It is God's Sabbath during which you may not plant your fields, nor prune your vineyards. Do not harvest crops that grow on their own and do not gather the grapes on your unpruned vines, since it is a year of rest for the land. What grows while the land is resting may be eaten by you....Keep My decrees and safeguard My laws. If you keep them, you will live in the land securely. The land will produce its fruit, and you will eat your fill, thus living securely in the land. **If you ask, "What will we eat in the seventh year? We have not planted nor have we harvested crops." I will direct My blessing to you in the sixth year, and the land will produce enough crops for three years.** You will therefore be eating your old crops when you plant in the eighth year. You will still be eating your old crops until the crops of the ninth year are ripe.

> **N**otice how none of the *Christian* translations below compress the seven-week period with the sixty-two week period into one period of sixty-nine weeks in Daniel 9:25. By correctly designating an anointed prince who comes after seven weeks, or forty-nine years, and a second anointed one (9:26) who is cut off after a subsequent sixty-two weeks (four hundred and thirty-four years), these translators are accurately conveying Gabriel's message: There are *two* entirely different "anointed" individuals discussed in Daniel 9:25-26.

King James Version — 1611 Edition	1885 Revision of the King James Version — 1611 Edition	The Bible: An American Translation
Know therefore and vunderstand, *that* from the going foorth of the commandement to restore and to build Ierusalem, vnto the Messiah the Prince, *shall be* seuen weekes; and threescore and two weekes, the street shall be built againe, and the wall, euen in troublous times.	Know therefore and discern, that from the going forth of the commandment to restore and to build Jerusalem unto the anointed one, the prince, shall be seven weeks: and threescore and two weeks, it shall be built again, with street and moat, even in troublous times.	Learn, therefore, and understand: 'from the going forth of the word to restore and rebuild Jerusalem, Till there comes a prince, an anointed one, there shall be seven weeks; Then for sixty-two weeks it shall stay rebuilt, with its squares and streets;
The Modern Readers Bible Know therefore and discern, that from the going forth of the commandment to restore and to build Jerusalem unto the anointed one, the prince, shall be seven weeks: and threescore and two weeks, it shall be built again, with street and moat, even in troublous times.	**The Bible: A New Translation** Know then, understand, that between the issue of the prophetic command to re-people and rebuild Jerusalem and the consecrating of a supreme high priest, seven weeks of years shall elapse; in the course of sixty-two weeks of years it shall be rebuilt, with its squares and streets.	**The Anchor Bible** Know then, and understand this: from the utterance of the word regarding the rebuilding of Jerusalem to the coming of an anointed leader there will be seven weeks. Then during sixty-two weeks it will be rebuilt, with its streets and moat, but in a time of distress.
Revised Standard Version Know therefore and understand that from the going forth of the word to restore and build Jerusalem to the coming of an anointed one, a prince, there shall be seven weeks. Then for sixty-two weeks it shall be built again with squares and moat, but in a troubled time.	**New Revised Standard Version** Know therefore and understand: from the time that the word went out to restore and rebuild Jerusalem until the time of an anointed prince, there shall be seven weeks; and for sixty-two weeks it shall be built again with streets and moat, but in a troubled time.	**New English Bible** Know then and understand: from the time that the word went forth that Jerusalem should be restored and rebuilt, seven weeks shall pass till the appearance of one anointed, a prince; then for sixty-two weeks it shall remain restored, rebuilt with streets and conduits.
Revised English Bible Know, then, and understand: from the time that the decree went forth that Jerusalem should be restored and rebuilt, seven of those seventy will pass till the appearance of one anointed, a prince; then for sixty-two it will remain restored, rebuilt with streets and conduits. At the critical time...	**New American Bible (Catholic)** Know and understand this: From the utterance of the word that Jerusalem was to rebuilt until one who is anointed and a leader, there shall be seven weeks. During sixty-two weeks it shall be rebuilt, with streets and trenches, in time of affliction.	**The Expositor's Bible** From the decree to restore Jerusalem unto the Anointed One (or "the Messiah"), the Prince, shall be seven weeks. For sixty-two weeks Jerusalem shall be built again with street and moat, though in troublous times.
The Good News Bible: Today's English Version Note this and understand it: From the time the command is given to rebuild Jerusalem until God's chosen leader comes, seven times seven years will pass. Jerusalem will be rebuilt with streets and strong defenses, and will stand for seven times sixty-two years, but this will be a time of troubles.	**A New Commentary on Holy Scriptures** The first period lasts seven weeks, and runs from the prophesy of the restoration to the coming of the anointed prince; the second period of sixty-two weeks is that during which the restoration is duly carried out:	**The International Critical Commentary** And thou art to know and understand. From the issue of the word to build again Jerusalem unto an Anointed-Prince seven weeks. And for sixty-two weeks it shall be built again, street and moat, but in distress of times.

The Abington Bible Commentary
From the day when Jeremiah announced the future restoration of Jerusalem, i.e., from 586 B.C., to an anointed one, a prince, i.e., Cyrus the Great (538 B.C.), would be seven weeks, i.e., forty-nine years. This was the date of the formal close of the exile by the decree of Cyrus, forty-eight years from the destruction of the holy city. There would follow sixty-two weeks (434 years) during which Jerusalem was to be rebuilt with streets and open spaces, but not without experiencing many troubles.

Daniel 9:26 (RSV):
And after the sixty-two weeks, an anointed one shall be cut off, and shall have nothing...

Who Tampered with the KJV?
King James Version—1611 Edition

> **Daniels vision.**   **Chap. x.**   **He is dumbe.**
>
> *† Heb. a man of desires.*
>
> art † greatly beloued : therefore vnderstand the matter, & consider the vision.
>
> 24 Seuentie weekes are determined vpon thy people, and vpon thy holy citie, ‖ to finish the transgression, and to ‖ make an ende of sinnes, and to make reconciliation for iniquitie, and to bring in euerlasting righteousnes, and to seale vp the vision and † prophecie, and to anoynt the most Holy.
>
> *‖ Or, to restraine.*
> *‖ Or, to seale vp.*
>
> *† Heb. prophet.*
>
> 25 Know therefore and vnderstand, *that* from the going foorth of the commandement to restore and to build Ierusalem, vnto the Messiah the Prince, *shall be* seuen weekes; and threescore and two weekes, the street † shall be built againe, and the ‖ wall, euen † in troublous times.
>
> *† Heb. shall returne and be built.*
> *‖ Or, breach or ditch.*
> *† Hebr. in strait of times.*
> *‖ Or, shall haue nothing.*
>
> 26 And after threescore and two weekes, shall Messiah be cut off, ‖ but not for himselfe, and the people of the Prince that shall come, shall destroy the citie, and the Sanctuarie, and the ende thereof *shall be* with a flood, and vnto the ende of the warre ‖ desolations are determined.
>
> *‖ Or, it shall be cut off by desolations.*
>
> 27 And hee shall confirme the couenant with many for one weeke : and in the midst of the weeke he shall cause the sacrifice and the oblation to cease, and ‖ for the ouerspreading of *abominations hee shall make *it* desolate, euen vntill the consummation, & that determined, shalbe powred vpon the desolate.
>
> *‖ Or, with the abominable armies.*
> ** Mat. 24. 15. marke 13. 14. luke*
>
> ded with fine gold of Vphaz.
>
> 6 His body also *was* like the Berill, and his face as the appearance of lightning, and his eyes as lampes of fire, and his armes, and his feete like in colour to polished brasse, and the voice of his words like the voice of a multitude.
>
> 7 And I Daniel alone saw the vision : for the men that were with mee saw not the vision : but a great quaking fell vpon them, so that they fled to hide themselues.
>
> 8 Therefore I was left alone, and saw this great vision, and there remained no strength in me : for my ‖ * comelinesse was turned in me into corruption, and I retained no strength.
>
> *† Or, vigor.*
> ** Dan. 7. 28.*
>
> 9 Yet heard I the voice of his words : and when I heard the voice of his wordes, then was I in a deepe sleepe on my face, and my face toward the ground.
>
> 10 ¶ And behold, an hand touched me, which † set me vpon my knees, and vpon the palmes of my hands.
>
> *† Heb. mooued.*
>
> 11 And hee said vnto me, O Daniel, † a man greatly beloued, vnderstand the wordes that I speake vnto thee, and † stand vpright : for vnto thee am I now sent ; and when he had spoken this word vnto me, I stood trembling.
>
> *† Heb. a man of desires.*
> *† Heb. stand vpon thy standing.*
>
> 12 Then sayd hee vnto me ; Feare not, Daniel : for from the first day that thou diddest set thine heart to vnder-

Who tampered with the first edition of the King James Version (KJV)? The original KJV published in 1611 (above) correctly separates the seven weeks from the sixty-two weeks in Daniel 9:25 with a semicolon. The KJV published today, however, deceptively compresses these two separate time periods into one period of four hundred and eighty-three years. The semicolon has now mysteriously disappeared. Accordingly, the modern KJV reads, "Know therefore and understand that from the going forth of the commandment to restore and build Jerusalem unto the Messiah the Prince shall be seven weeks, and threescore and two weeks." The equivalent of a semicolon in Hebrew grammar is an *etnachta* (ʌ). The editors of the 1885 version of the KJV deliberately removed this semicolon—a critical punctuation mark in Daniel 9:25—in order to change the message conveyed in Gabriel's prophecy. By combining "seven weeks" with the "sixty-two weeks" into one period of sixty-nine weeks, the illusion is created that there is only one anointed one spoken of the ninth chapter of Daniel rather than two.

    Until 1885, however, the KJV correctly separated these two epochs with a semicolon, making it clear that the angel Gabriel spoke of two different anointed individuals. Cyrus, the first anointed ruler, arose forty-nine years after the destruction of the first temple, and a second who was removed after a subsequent four hundred and thirty-four years (the high priest). The Prophet Isaiah specifically identified Cyrus as God's "anointed," who would command the Jews to return to the land of Israel from the Babylonian exile, in order to rebuild Jerusalem and construct the second temple (Isaiah 44:28-45:1, 13; Ezra 1:1-5).

Chronological Chart of Daniel Chapter Nine

Beginning of the Kingdom of Babylon - 3319
Babylon's subjugation of Jerusalem - 3320

1 — "The prophet Jeremiah predicted (25:12) the termination of Babylon following a period of 70 years. This prophecy began when Babylon subjugated Jerusalem in the year 3320, and culminated when Cyrus called for the rebuilding of Jerusalem and a temple (Isaiah 44:28-45:1) in the year 3390."

2 — Nebuchadnezzer, king of Babylon, destroyed the First Temple in the year 3338, 18 years after he subjugated Jerusalem in the year 3320.

Destruction of the first temple - 3338

3 — **70 WEEKS (of years)** - Gabriel begins his prophecy to Daniel (9:24) with the revelation that "70 weeks" (490 years) have been decreed upon the Jewish people and Jerusalem, after which the Messianic Age can commence. The verses that follow contain a detailed description of what would transpire during this time. This period spanned from the destruction of the First Temple until the destruction of the Second, exactly 490 years (3338-3829).

4 — "Seven weeks" (of years) - Gabriel reassured Daniel that after a full "7 weeks" (49 years) passed, counting from "the going forth of the WORD [דָּבָר]" when Jerusalem was

---

Jeremiah 29:10 → "For so said the Lord: `For at the completion of **seventy** דְבָרִי toward you, **to restore you to this place**.`"

Jeremiah 25:12 → "And it shall be at the completion of **seventy years**, I will visit upon the king of Babylon and iniquity, and upon the Chaldeans, and I will make it for everlasting desolations."

Kings of Judah		Year From Creation	Kings of Babylon and Persia		Jeremiah's Prophecies Of Seventy Years
Name of King	Years of Kingship		Years of Kingship	Name Of King	
Jehoiakim	4	3319			
	5	3320			
	6	3321			
	7	3322			
	8	3323			
	9	3324			
	10	3325			
	11	3326			
Jehiachin	3-month reign	3327			
Zedekiah	1	3328	1	Nebuchad-nezzar	
	2	3329	2		
	3	3330	3		
	4	3331	4		
	5	3332	5		
	6	3333	6		
	7	3334	7		
	8	3335	8		
	9	3336	9		
	10	3337	10		
	11	3338	11		
		3339	12		
		3340	13		
		3341	14		
		3342	15		
		3343	16		
		3344	17		
		3345	18		
		3346	19		
		3347	20		
		3348	21		
		3349	22		
		3350	23		
		3351	24		
		3352	25		
		3353	26		
		3354	27		
		3355	28		
		3356	29		
		3357	30		
		3358	31		
		3359	32		
		3360	33		
		3361	34		
		3362	35		
		3363	36		
		3364	37		
		3365	38		
		3366	39		
		3367	40		
		3368	41		
		3369	42		
		3370	43		
		3371	44		
		3372	45		
			1		
			2		
			3		
			4		
			5		
			6		
			7		
			8		
			9		

---

* In the year 3390, Daniel contemplated two critical prophecies in which Jeremiah spoke of Babylon's demise following 70 years (Jer. 25:12 and 29:10). Although both of these 70-year visions foretold the termination of the Babylon Empire, it was only the second prophecy (Jer. 29:10) that spoke of the restoration of the Jewish people to the Promised Land. When Daniel considered these two texts, however, he mistakenly concluded that Jeremiah's two 70-year prophecies were speaking of an identical period of time. This misunderstanding caused him to draw three flawed conclusions. First, that the point to begin counting the 70 years for both prophecies was the year 3320, when Babylon conquered Jerusalem. Second, these prophecies must therefore end 70 years after Jerusalem's subjugation, in the year 3390, when Darius the Mede succeeded the throne. Third, because Jeremiah's second prophecy (Jer. 29:10) spoke of God restoring Israel after the completion of 70 years, Daniel concluded that the second temple would certainly be built in the year 3390, in the first year of Darius the Mede.

When Daniel realized that the year 3390 was at hand, and there was no sign of the impending redemption, he became deeply agitated. He thought that the sins of Jewry had caused the date to be delayed, or worse - canceled. This terrifying thought compelled Daniel to fast and pray (Dan. 9:4-20) for the restoration of Jerusalem and its Sanctuary.

destroyed (9:2), an anointed ruler would command the Jewish people to return and rebuild Jerusalem (9:25). Indeed, after a half century passed, Cyrus, who God declared as His "anointed one," (Isaiah 45:1), ordered the Jews to return and rebuild Jerusalem and the holy sanctuary (Isaiah 44:28-45:1, 13; Ezra 1:2-3; II Chronicles 36:22-23).

Cyrus calls for the city and temple to be rebuilt - 3391

"Sixty two weeks" (of years) - In verse 9:25, the angel reveals to Daniel how, for a nearly four and a half centuries, Jerusalem would be "rebuilt, street and moat." Gabriel adds, however, that throughout these "62 weeks," the Holy City would endure "troubled times." Accordingly, the Second Temple period was filled with spiritual and political turbulence. In verse 9:26, the angel reveals that the "62 weeks" would tragically conclude with two watershed events. First, an anointed one (the high priest) would be cut off, and would cease his ecclesiastical functions. Second, the "people of the prince" (the legions of Vespasian and Titus) would come to destroy the Holy City and its sanctuary. Both of these tragic events occurred simultaneously, shortly after the 434 years, or "62 weeks" were completed.

Building of the second temple - 3408

years of Babylon I will remember you, and I will fulfil My good **WORD** upon that nation, says the Lord, their

Final events of Purim - 3405

Evil-meridach	3373 / 10
	3374 / 11
	3375 / 12
	3376 / 13
	3377 / 14
	3378 / 15
	3379 / 16
	3380 / 17
	3381 / 18
	3382 / 19
	3383 / 20
	3384 / 21
Belshazzar	3385 / 22
	3386 / 23
	3387 / 1
Darius the Mede	3388 / 2
	3389 / 3
Cyrus	3390 / 1
	3391 / 2
	3392 / 3
	3393 / 1
	3394 / 2
	3395 / 3
Ahasuerus	3396 / 4
	3397 / 5
	3398 / 6
	3399 / 7
	3400 / 8
	3401 / 9
	3402 / 10
	3403 / 11
	3404 / 12
	3405 / 13
	3406 / 14
Darius II (Persian)	3407 / 1
	3408 / 2

Seven years before the Second Temple was destroyed, Rome permitted the Jews to offer sacrifices. This agreement, however, was broken when Nero sent Vespasian to crush Jewish life in Jerusalem in 66 CE, 3½ years before Titus razed Herod's Temple in the year 3829 (Daniel 9:27).

Sacrifice Ends

Rome's Emperor Nero goes to war against Jerusalem in 66 CE, 3½ years before Vespasian destroyed the Second Temple in the year 3829, completing 490 years of Daniel's prophecy

3½ years
½ a week

415 Years

Emperor of Rome		
Nero	3823	10
	3824	11
	3825	12
	3826	13
	3827	14
Galba; Otho; Vitellius	3828	Year of Three Emperors
Vespasian	3829	1

Messianic Age

It is therefore in this chapter that Daniel is made to understand that the two prophecies of Jeremiah are in fact not identical, and each one of them referred to a separate, but overlapping, 70-year period of time. Whereas the prophecy of Jeremiah 25:12 was in fact referring to the 70-year time span that began in the year 3320, when Jerusalem was subjugated, the prophecy that promised the restoration of the Jewish people to their land (29:10) was not to begin for another 18 years.

Accordingly, Gabriel here relates to Daniel that in order to correctly ascertain when the Second Temple would be built, he must begin counting the 70 years "from the going forth of the WORD [דבר] (9:25)," which is "the WORD [דבר] of Jeremiah" that begins at "the destruction of Jerusalem (9:2)," in the year 3338. In fact, Jeremiah's prophecy of restoration (29:10) was fulfilled in the year 3408, 18 years later than Daniel had originally thought.

**The angel Gabriel responds to Daniel's prayerful inquiry of God by carefully outlining the course of events which was to unfold over a crucial period of time that spanned 490 years, or "70 weeks" (the Babylonian exile lasted 70 years, plus the 420 years which the Second Temple stood). Thus, the angel was not only revealing to Daniel when the Second Temple would be restored, but when it would be destroyed as well.

Gabriel also reveals that once these "70 weeks" were completed, the Messianic Age could begin. Thus, in verse 24, the angel describes six elements that will characterize the world in the Messianic Age: 1) termination of transgression 2) end of sin 3) removal of all iniquity 4) ushering in of everlasting righteousness 5) sealing of vision and prophet 6) anointing of the Holy of Holies. And once these 490 years are completed, it would indeed be up to each subsequent generation to turn back to God in order to bring about the glorious arrival of the messiah.

The following related articles can be found in Volume 2 of *Let's Get Biblical! Why doesn't Judaism Accept the Christian Messiah?*

I. "The Lord Said To My Lord..."
   To Whom Was the Lord Speaking
   In Psalm 110:1?. . . . . Page 173

Part IX

Confused Texts and Testimonies

Messianic Prophecies

World Peace

Isaiah 2:4

He will judge among nations, and shall rebuke many people; and they shall beat their swords into plowshares, and their spears into pruning hooks. Nation shall not lift up sword against nation, neither shall they learn war anymore.

Isaiah 11:6-8

The wolf also shall dwell with the lamb, and the leopard shall lie down with the kid; [7]and the calf and the young lion and the fatling together....[8]And the sucking child shall play on the hole of the cobra....

Micah 4:3-7

He shall judge between many peoples, And rebuke strong nations afar off; They shall beat their swords into plowshares, And their spears into pruning hooks; Nation shall not lift up sword against nation, Neither shall they learn war any more. [4] But everyone shall sit under his vine and under his fig tree, And no one shall make *them* afraid; For the mouth of the Lord of hosts has spoken. [5] For all people walk each in the name of his god, But we will walk in the name of the Lord our God Forever and ever. [6] "In that day," says the Lord, "I will assemble the lame, I will gather the outcast And those whom I have afflicted; [7] I will make the lame a remnant, And the outcast a strong nation; So the Lord will reign over them in Mount Zion from now on, even forever."

Zephaniah 3:12-16

I will leave in your midst a meek and humble people, And they shall trust in the name of the Lord. [13]The remnant of Israel shall do no unrighteousness And speak no lies, Nor shall a deceitful tongue be found in their mouth; For they shall feed *their* flocks and lie down, And no one shall make *them* afraid. [14] Sing, O daughter of Zion! Shout, O Israel! Be glad and rejoice with all *your* heart, O daughter of Jerusalem! [15] The Lord has taken away your judgments, He has cast out your enemy. The King of Israel, the Lord, *is* in your midst; You shall see[1] disaster no more. [16] In that day it shall be said to Jerusalem: "Do not fear; Zion, let not your hands be weak."

Zechariah 8:3-6

Thus said the Lord: I have returned to Zion, and I will dwell in Jerusalem. Jerusalem will be called the City of Faithfulness, and the mount of the Lord of Hosts the Holy Mount. [4] Thus said the Lord of Hosts: There shall yet be old men and women in the squares of Jerusalem, each with staff in hand because of their great age. [5] And the squares of the city shall be crowded with boys and girls playing in the squares. [6] Thus said the Lord of Hosts: Though it will seem impossible to the remnant of this people in those days, shall it also be impossible to Me? – declares the Lord of Hosts.

Universal Knowledge of God

Isaiah 11:9

For the earth shall be full of the knowledge of the Lord, as the waters cover the sea.

Jeremiah 31:33

No longer shall one teach his neighbor or shall one teach his brother, saying, "Know the Lord," for they shall all know Me, from their smallest to their greatest, says the Lord...

Zechariah 8:20-23

Thus said the Lord of Hosts: Peoples and the inhabitants of many cities shall yet come – [21] the inhabitants of one shall go to the other and say, "Let us go and entreat the favor of the Lord, let us seek the Lord of Hosts; I will go, too." [22] The many peoples and the multitude of nations shall come to seek the Lord of Hosts in Jerusalem and to entreat the favor of the Lord. [23] Thus said the Lord of Hosts: In those days, ten men from nations of every tongue will take hold – they will take hold of a Jew by a corner of his cloak and say, "Let us go with you, for we have heard that God is with you."

Zechariah 14:9

And the Lord shall be king over all the earth: in that day shall there be one Lord, and His name one.

Zephaniah 3:9

For then I will make the peoples pure of speech, so that they all invoke the Lord by name and serve Him with one accord.

Micah 4:1-2

But in the end of days it shall come to pass, that the mountain of the Lord's house shall be established as the top of the mountains, and it shall be exalted above the hills; and peoples shall flow unto it. [2] And many nations shall go and say: 'Come ye, and let us go up to the mountain of the Lord, and to the house of the God of Jacob; and He will teach us of His ways, and we will walk in His paths'; for out of Zion shall go forth the law, and the word of the Lord from Jerusalem.

Resurrection of the Dead

Isaiah 26:19

Thy dead men shall live, together with my dead body shall they arise. Awake and sing, ye that dwell in dust, for thy dew is as the dew of herbs, and the earth shall cast out the dead.

Daniel 12:2

And many of them that sleep in the dust of the earth shall awake, some to everlasting life, and some to shame and everlasting contempt.

Ezekiel 37:12-13

Therefore, prophesy and say to them, "So says the Lord God: Lo! I open your graves and cause you to come up out of your graves as My people, and bring you home to the land of Israel. [13] Then you shall know that I am the Lord, when I open your graves and lead you up out of your graves as My people.

Ingathering of Israel

Isaiah 11:11-12

And it shall come to pass in that day, that the Lord will set His hand again the second time to recover the remnant of His people, that shall remain from Assyria, and from Egypt, and from Pathros, and from Cush, and from Elam, and from Shinar, and from Hamath, and from the islands of the sea. [12] He will hold up a signal to the nations And assemble the banished of Israel, And gather the dispersed of Judah From the four corners of the earth.

Isaiah 27:12-13

And it shall come to pass in that day, that the Lord will beat off His fruit from the flood of the River unto the Brook of Egypt, and ye shall be gathered one by one, O ye children of Israel. [13] And it shall come to pass in that day, that a great horn shall be blown; and they shall come that were lost in the land of Assyria, and they that were dispersed in the land of Egypt; and they shall worship the Lord in the holy mountain at Jerusalem.

Isaiah 43:5-6

I will bring thy seed from the east, and gather you from the west. I will say to the north, "Give up," and to the south, "Keep not back, bring My sons from far, and My daughters from the ends of the earth.

Jeremiah 16:15

But rather, "As the Lord lives who brought the Israelites out of the north land, and out of all the lands to which He had banished them." For I will bring them back to their land, which I gave to their fathers.

Jeremiah 23:3

And I Myself will gather the remnant of My flock from all the lands to which I have banished them, and I will bring them back to their pasture, where they shall be fertile and increase.

Ezekiel 34:11-16

For thus saith the Lord God: Behold, here am I, and I will search for My sheep, and seek them out. [12] As a shepherd seeketh out his flock in the day that he is among his sheep that are separated, so will I seek out My sheep; and I will deliver them out of all places whither they have been scattered in the day of clouds and thick darkness. [13] And I will bring them out from the peoples, and gather them from the countries, and will bring them into their own land; and I will feed them upon the mountains of Israel, by the streams, and in all the habitable places of the country. [14] I will feed them in a good pasture, and upon the high mountains of Israel shall their fold be; there shall they lie down in a good fold, and in a fat pasture shall they feed upon the mountains of Israel. [15] I will feed My sheep, and I will cause them to lie down, saith the Lord God. [16] I will seek that which was lost, and will bring back that which was driven away, and will bind up that which was broken, and will strengthen that which was sick; and the fat and the strong I will destroy, I will feed them in justice.

Continued

Ezekiel 36:24-28
For I will take you from among the nations, and gather you out of all the countries, and will bring you into your own land . . . A new heart also will I give you, and a new spirit will I put within you; and I will take away the stony heart out of your flesh, and I will give you a heart of flesh. [27] And I will put My spirit within you, and cause you to walk in My statutes, and ye shall keep Mine ordinances, and do them. [28] And ye shall dwell in the land that I gave to your fathers; and ye shall be My people, and I will be your God.

Ezekiel 37:21-22
And you shall declare to them, "Thus said the Lord God: I am going to take the Israelite people from among the nations they have gone to, and gather them from every quarter, and bring them to their own land. [22] I will make them a single nation in the land, on the hills of Israel, and one king shall be king of them all. Never again shall they be two nations, and never again shall they be divided into two kingdoms."

Joel 4:1 (3:1 in a Christian Bible)
For, behold, in those days, and in that time, when I shall bring back the captivity of Judah and Jerusalem

Amos 9:15
"I will plant Israel in their own land, never again to be uprooted from the land I have given them," says the Lord your God.

Micah 2:12
I will surely assemble, O Jacob, all of thee; I will surely gather the remnant of Israel; I will render them all as sheep in a fold...

Zephaniah 3:18-20
I will gather them that are far from the appointed season, who are of thee, that hast borne the burden of reproach. [19] Behold, at that time I will deal with all them that afflict thee; and I will save her that is lame, and gather her that was driven away; and I will make them to be a praise and a name, whose shame hath been in all the earth. [20] At that time will I bring you in, and at that time will I gather you; for I will make you to be a name and a praise among all the peoples of the earth, when I turn your captivity before your eyes, saith the Lord.

Zechariah 10:6-10
And I will strengthen the house of Judah, and I will save the house of Joseph, and I will bring them again, for I have mercy upon them; and they shall be as though I had not cast them off: for I am the Lord their God, and I will hear them. [7] And they of Ephraim shall be like a mighty man, and their heart shall rejoice as through wine; yea, their children shall see it, and rejoice, their heart shall be glad in the Lord. [8] I will hiss for them, and gather them, for I have redeemed them; and they shall increase as they have increased. [9] And I will sow them among the peoples, and they shall remember Me in far countries; and they shall live with their children, and shall return. [10] I will bring them back also out of the land of Egypt, and gather them out of Assyria; and I will bring them into the land of Gilead and Lebanon; and place shall not suffice them.

Building of the Third Temple

Isaiah 56:7
Even them will I bring to My holy mountain, and make them joyful in My house of prayer; their burnt-offerings and their sacrifices shall be acceptable upon Mine altar; for My house shall be called a house of prayer for all peoples.

Ezekiel 37:26-28
And I will set My sanctuary in the midst of them for evermore. [27] My temple also shall be with them. Yes, I will be their God and they shall be My people. And the heathen shall know that I the Lord do sanctify Israel, when My sanctuary shall be in the midst of them for evermore. *(See Ez. 40-48; Is. 33:20)*

Ezekiel 43:7
And He said unto me: 'Son of man, this is the place of My throne, and the place of the soles of My feet, where I will dwell in the midst of the children of Israel for ever; and the house of Israel shall no more defile My holy name...

Elijah the Prophet Ushers in the Messianic Age

Malachi 3:23-24 (4:5-6 in a Christian Bible)
Behold, I will send you Elijah the prophet before the coming of the great and dreadful day of the Lord. And he shall turn the heart of the fathers to the children, and the heart of the children to their fathers...

The Messiah

Isaiah 11:1-5
And there shall come forth a shoot out of the stock of Jesse, and a twig shall grow forth out of his roots. ²And the spirit of the Lord shall rest upon him, the spirit of wisdom and understanding, the spirit of counsel and might, the spirit of knowledge and of the fear of the Lord. ³And he shall be filled with the fear of the Lord; and he shall not judge after the sight of his eyes, neither decide after the hearing of his ears; ⁴But with righteousness shall he judge the poor, decide with equity for the meek of the land; and he shall smite the land with the rod of his mouth, and with the breath of his lips shall he slay the wicked. ⁵And righteousness shall be the girdle of his loins, and faithfulness the girdle of his reins.

Jeremiah 23:5
Behold, the days come, saith the Lord, that I will raise unto David a righteous shoot, and he shall reign as king and prosper, and shall execute justice and righteousness in the land.

Ezekiel 34:23-24
And I will set up one shepherd over them, and he shall feed them, even My servant, David, he shall feed them, and he shall be their shepherd. ²⁴And I the Lord will be their God, and My servant David prince among them; I the Lord have spoken.

Ezekiel 37:24-25
And My servant David shall be king over them, and they all shall have one shepherd; they shall also walk in Mine ordinances, and observe My statutes, and do them. ²⁵And they shall dwell in the land that I have given unto Jacob My servant, wherein your fathers dwelt; and they shall dwell therein, they, and their children, and their children's children, for ever; and David, My servant, shall be their prince forever.

Although the Messianic Age is vividly described throughout the Jewish Scriptures, very few passages in the entire Tanach discuss the messiah. Central to the Biblical message regarding the End of Days is the transformation of the world, not the messiah himself. In the handful of texts in the Hebrew Bible where the messiah is discussed, this descendants and heir of David's throne is described as a righteous king who fears God, and will inspire his people to be faithful to the Almighty as well.

In stark contrast, consider how frequently Jesus' name is mentioned during a typical church service. In Christian worship, parishioners pray to Jesus and venerate him as God. It is a cardinal Church doctrine that sinful man's only hope for salvation and eternal life depends entirely on his belief in the resurrection of Jesus.

Why is this core Christian tenet not mentioned anywhere in the Hebrew Bible? Did the prophets simply forget to point out that part of the messiah's identity? Why is there not a single verse in Tanach which clearly states that man can have salvation only if he believes that the messiah died for his sins?

The Christian concept of the messiah differs radically from the clear teachings conveyed in the Jewish Scriptures. The Tanach declared that the messiah will restore the Kingdom of Israel and usher in an era of peace, prosperity, and spiritual understanding for Israel and all of the nations.

John the Baptist: I am not Elijah
And they asked him [John], "What then? Are you Elijah?" And he said, "I am not." "Are you that prophet?" And he answered, "No." ***John 1:21***

Jesus: John the Baptist is Elijah
"I tell you the truth: Among those born of woman there has not risen anyone greater than John the Baptist... And if you are willing to accept it, he is the Elijah who is to come." ***Matthew 11:11-14***

Jesus Demands Alienation Within the Family
"Think not that I have come to send peace on earth. I came not to bring peace on earth, but a sword. For I am come to set man at variance against his father, and the daughter against her mother, and the daughter-in-law against her mother-in-law. And a man's foes shall be they of his own household." ***Matthew 10:34-36***

"If any man comes to me, and does not **hate** his father, mother, wife, children, brethren, and his sisters, yes, and even his own life also, he cannot be my disciple." ***Luke 14:26***

Acts 6:8-10
Now Stephen, a man full of God's Grace and power, did great wonders and miraculous signs among the people. Opposition arose, however, from members of the Synagogue... These men began to argue with Stephen, but they could not stand up against *his wisdom or the spirit by whom he spoke.*

Stephen's account of historical events in Acts 7:2-53, which is contained in the longest speech in the book of Acts, diverges considerably from the historical record of the Jewish Scriptures. Some Christian apologists have sought to address these conflicts by suggesting that inerrancy need only be attributed to the author of Acts and not to Stephen as a character in the narrative.[1] This solution, however, is untenable because the author of the Book of Acts insisted that Stephen's speech was inspired by the Holy Spirit (6:8-10).

Among the significant errors in Stephen's speech is his assertion that Joseph called for his father and all his relatives to join him in Egypt, which we are told was seventy-five people:

Acts 7:14
"And Joseph sent word and invited Jacob his father and all his relatives to come to him, seventy-five persons in all."

In three distinct passages, however, the Torah records that seventy people went down to Egypt, not seventy-five:

Genesis 46:27
And the sons of Joseph who were born to him in Egypt were two persons. All the persons of the house of Jacob who went to Egypt were seventy.

Exodus 1:5
All those who were descendants of Jacob were seventy persons, for Joseph was in Egypt already.

Deuteronomy 10:22
Your fathers went down to Egypt with seventy persons, and now the Lord your God has made you as the stars of heaven in multitude.

The editors of the Septuagint employed a different method to solve the discrepancy between the Jewish Scriptures and Stephen's speech: they changed the text of the Greek "translation" of the Torah so that these verses appear to conform to Steven's claim that seventy-five people went down to Egypt. Although they changed the Greek Septuagint to read "seventy-five" in Genesis 46:27 and Exodus 1:5, these editors overlooked Deuteronomy 10:22. As a result, the Septuagint correctly reads that seventy (ἑβδομήκοντα) people went to Egypt in Deuteronomy 10:22.

[1] Richard N. Longenecker, *The Acts of the Apostles* [EBC; Grand Rapids: Zondervan, 1981] p. 341, E. F. Harrison, *Acts: The Expanding Church* [Chicago: Moody, 1975] p. 115.

Where is the Tomb of the Patriarchs, in Hebron or Shechem?

Hebron is most notable for containing the burial site of the biblical Patriarchs and Matriarchs, and is therefore considered the holiest city in Judaism after Jerusalem.

We are told in Acts 7:16, however, that Stephen made the baffling claim that the tomb of the Patriarchs is located in Shechem. The historical record in the Torah states that the Tomb of the Patriarchs is located in Hebron, which is in Judea, rather than Shechem, which is in Samaria (Genesis 23:17-19; 50:13).

The distance between Hebron and Shechem is about 90 kilometers. Many thousands of pilgrims visit this ancient tomb each year in Hebron.

Cave of the Patriarchs in Hebron

I Chron. 1-3	Matthew 1	Luke 3
1 Abraham	1 Abraham	1 Abraham
2 Isaac	2 Isaac	2 Isaac
3 Jacob	3 Jacob	3 Jacob
4 Judah	4 Judah	4 Judah
5 Perez	5 Perez	5 Perez
6 Hezron	6 Hezron	6 Hezron
7 Ram	7 Ram	7 Ram
8 Amminadab	8 Amminadab	8 Amminadab
9 Nahshon	9 Nahshon	9 Nahshon
10 Salma	10 Salma	10 Salma
11 Boaz	11 Boaz	11 Boaz
12 Obed	12 Obed	12 Obed
13 Jesse	13 Jesse	13 Jesse
♛ 14 David	14 David	14 David
♛ 15 Solomon	15 Solomon	15 Nathan
♛ 16 Rehoboam	16 Rehoboam	16 Mattatha
♛ 17 Abijah	17 Abijah	17 Menna
♛ 18 Asa	18 Asa	18 Melea
♛ 19 Jehoshaphat	19 Jehoshaphat	19 Eliakim
♛ 20 Jehoram	20 Jehoram	20 Jonam
♛ 21 Ahaziah	* Omitted	21 Joseph
♛ 22 Jehoash		22 Judas
♛ 23 Amaziah		23 Symeon
♛ 24 Azariah	21 Uzziah	24 Levi
♛ 25 Jotham	22 Jotham	25 Matthat
♛ 26 Ahaz	23 Ahaz	26 Jorim
♛ 27 Hezekiah	24 Hezekiah	27 Eleizer
♛ 28 Manasseh	25 Manasseh	28 Jesus
♛ 29 Amon	26 Amon	29 Er
♛ 30 Josiah	27 Josiah	30 Elmadam
♛ 31 Jehoiakim	** Omitted	31 Cosam
♛ 32 Jeconiah	28 Jeconiah***	32 Addi
33 Shealtiel	29 Shealtiel	33 Melchi
34 Zerubbabel	30 Zerubbabel	34 Ner****
35 Hananiah	31 Abiud	35 Shealtiel
36 Jeshaiah	32 Eliakim	36 Zerubbabel
37 Rephaiah	33 Azor	37 Rhesa
38 Arnan	34 Zadok	38 Joanan
39 Obadiah	35 Achim	39 Joda
40 Shecaniah	36 Eliud	40 Josech
41 Shemaiah	37 Eleazar	41 Semein
42 Neariah	38 Matthan	42 Mattathias
43 Elioenai	39 Jacob	43 Maath
	40 Joseph	44 Naggai
	41 Jesus	45 Esli
		46 Nahum
		47 Amos
		48 Mattathias
		49 Joseph
		50 Jannai
		51 Melchi
		52 Levi
		53 Matthat
		54 Heli
		55 Joseph
		56 Jesus

See chapter: **'Unraveling Matthew's Genealogy – Was Jesus a Descendant of a Cursed Ancestry?'** Volume 2 page 3.

Matthew 1:17
So all the generations from Abraham to David are fourteen generations; and from David until the carrying away into Babylon are fourteen generations; and from the carrying away into Babylon unto Christ are fourteen generations.

Luke 1:27
To a virgin betrothed to a man whose name was Joseph, of the house of David.

I Chronicles 3:11-12*, 15**, 16-17***

Joram his son, Ahaziah his son, Joash his son, [12] Amaziah his son,* Azariah his son, Jotham his son, [15] And the sons of Josiah** were, the firstborn Johanan, the second Jehoiakim, the third Zedekiah, the fourth Shallum. [16] And the sons of Jehoiakim: Jeconiah his son, Zedekiah his son. [17] And the sons of Jeconiah;*** Assir, Shealtiel his son.

The Davidic Covenant Passes Exclusively Through King Solomon, not Nathan

I Chronicles 22:9-10
"But you will have a son who will be a man of peace and rest, and I will give him rest from all his enemies on every side. **His name will be Solomon**, and I will grant Israel peace and quiet during his reign. [10] He is the one who will build a house for my Name. He will be my son, and I will be his father. And I will establish the throne of his kingdom over Israel forever."
(See also II Sam 7:12-16, I Chr. 17:11-14, 28:6-7; Ps. 89:29-38)

Only Patrilineal Descent Determines Tribe Affiliation

Numbers 1:18
And they assembled all the congregation together on the first day of the second month, and they declared their pedigrees after their families, **by their fathers' houses**, according to the number of names, from twenty years old and upward, by their polls.

The Curse on Jeconiah and His Descendants***

Jeremiah 22:30
Thus saith the Lord, "Write ye this man [Jeconiah] childless, a man that shall not prosper in his days: for **no man of his seed shall prosper, sitting upon the thone of David, and ruling anymore in Judah**."

I Timothy 1:4
Neither give heed to fables and endless genealogies, which minister questions, rather than godly edifying which is in faith: so do.

A Ready Defense by Josh McDowell, page 188

> Moreover, if Jesus had been sired by Joseph, He would not have been able to claim the legal rights to the throne of David. According to the prophecy of Jeremiah 22:28-30, there could be no king in Israel who was a descendant of King Jeconiah, and Matthew 1:12 relates that Joseph was from the line of Jeconiah. Jesus would have been of the cursed lineage.
>
> The virgin birth of Christ is not only an historical fact, but it was also a *necessary* historical fact when one considers all the data.

The Ryrie Study Bible (NIV), page 1,315

1:1 *Jesus Christ.* The name "Jesus" is from the Greek (and Latin) for the Hebrew "Jeshua" (Joshua), which means "the Lord is salvation." "Christ" is from the Greek for the Hebrew *Meshiah* (Messiah), meaning "anointed one." *son of David* was a highly popular messianic title of the times. The genealogy is here traced through Joseph, Jesus' legal (though not natural) father, and it establishes His claim and right to the throne of David (1:6). The genealogy in Luke 3:23–38 is evidently that of Mary, though some believe it is also Joseph's, by assuming that Matthan (Matt. 1:15) and Matthat (Luke 3:24) were the same person and Jacob (Matt. 1:16) and Heli (Luke 3:23) were brothers (one being Joseph's father and the other his uncle). See note at Luke 3:23.

1:11 *Jeconiah.* Jehoiachin, king of Judah, who was taken into captivity by Nebuchadnezzar in 597 B.C. In the Heb., Jeremiah contracted "Jeconiah" to "Coniah" (Jer. 22:24, 28; 37:1). A curse was pronounced on Coniah that none of his descendants would prosper sitting on the throne of David. Had our Lord been the natural son of Joseph, He could not have been successful on the throne of David because of this curse. But since He came through Mary's lineage, He was not affected by this curse.

1:16 *of whom.* The word is feminine singular, indicating clearly that Jesus was born of Mary

Martin Luther on the Genealogy of Jesus (and the Jews) — 1543

From the beginning of the gospel, as St. Luke and St. Mark wrote it, the question has arisen: why the two apostles have told the story of the origins of the family of our Lord Jesus Christ so differently (or, as many have explained it, so contradicted by one another?) and it is peculiar that both agree upon the lineage or origins of these persons and end with Joseph and not with Mary and Christ; from this the wise sought to conclude it is not proved that Christ is of the family of David, because he does not come from Joseph, whom the apostles trace as coming directly from the line of David, and then suddenly abandon the same Joseph and substitute Mary....

First, to answer the Jews, if anyone even wants to get into an argument with them. Since the Jew moved me the last time to write about the Jews and touched upon this point: it cannot be proved that Jesus is of the tribe of Judah, because the apostle Matthew traces the tribe of Judah to Joseph and not to Mary; therefore he could not be Messiah as proved by the tribe of Judah and David. Prickly and poisonous are the snakes and make every effort to make our books appear wrong. For they do not ask because they wish to learn from us and know the truth, but to bother and heckle us with such questions—with scorn and derision of our beliefs as if we could not prove it.

Therefore one should step on the heads of these poisonous snakes and answer in the coarsest and rawest manner, defying the Devil, that Mary, the mother of Jesus, is of the tribe of Judah and the House of David says not only the apostle Matthew, (about whom they laugh) but even Moses, the first to say it after whom all the prophets agreed together. And if we Christians otherwise had nothing of the Old Testament, other than Moses, then we would have enough, easily enough, to prove that Mary must be of the tribe of Judah and the House of David so that all devils and the whole world cannot overthrow. (Keep quiet, the miserable, screaming Jews.)

Yes, here one encounters resistance from the Jews: they don't want to have Jesus as the Messiah, therefore they bother us with their poisonous, slanderous goads about Joseph, Mary; for they are hardly concerned as to whether Mary is of the House of David or not. And even if they had seen it themselves, that she was born of David, like Solomon and his other Children, still they would not believe that Jesus, her son, was the Messiah. They are concerned with the son, whom they do not want; they know, the knaves and lying mouths, that if Jesus is the Messiah, then there is no question that Maria is of the house of David.

Excerpts from "Vom Schem Hamphoras Und Vom Geschlecht Christi," By Martin Luther; The Jew in Christian Theology, Gerhard Falk, McFarland and Company, Inc., Jefferson, NC and London, 1931.

	Matthew	**Mark**	**Luke**	**John**
Who carried the cross?	Simon of Cyrene (27:32)	Simon of Cyrene (15:21)	Simon of Cyrene (23:26)	Jesus alone (19:17)
A) At what time was Jesus crucified? B) On which day was Jesus crucified?	A) Not mentioned B) First day of Passover, 15th of Nissan.* (26:20-30)	A) 9:00 am — at the 3rd hour." (15:25) B) First day of Passover, 15th of Nissan.* (14:17-25)	A) Not mentioned B) First day of Passover, 15th of Nissan.* (22:14-23)	A) 12:00 noon — after the 6th hour! (19:14-15) B) Passover eve, 14th of Nissan.* (18:28, 19:14)
A) Did Jesus drink? B) What kind of drink?	A) Yes B) Wine & gall (27:34)	A) No B) Wine & myrrh (15:23)	A) Not mentioned B) Vinegar (23:36)	A) Yes B) Vinegar (19:29-30)
Did the two thieves believe in Jesus?	Neither believed in Jesus. (27:44)	Neither believed in Jesus. (15:32)	One thief didn't believe, *but one does!* (23:39-41)	Not mentioned in John
What were Jesus' last dying words on the cross?	"*Eloi, Eloi, lama sabachthani?*" (My God, my God, why did you forsake me?) (27:46)	"*Eloi, Eloi, lama sabachthani?*" (My God, my God, did You forsake me?) (15:34)	"Father, into thy hands I commend my spirit." (23:46)	"It is finished" (19:30)
When did Mary prepare the spices?	Not mentioned in Matthew	Mary prepared spices Saturday night (16:1)	Mary prepared spices on Friday (23:56)	Nicodemus prepared spices on Friday (19:39)
Had the sun risen when the women arrived at the tomb?	It was toward dawn of the first day of the week. (28:1)	YES — They came to the tomb when the sun had risen. (16:2)	At early dawn they went to the tomb (24:1)	No — Mary came to the tomb, while it was <u>dark</u> (20:1)
How many days was Jesus in the tomb?	3 days and 2 nights** (28:1)	3 days and 2 nights** (16:2)	3 days and 2 nights** (24:1)	2 days and 2 nights** (20:1)
A) How many people came to the tomb? B) Who were they?	A) TWO B) Mary Magdalene and the other Mary (28:1)	A) THREE B) Two Marys and Salome (16:1)	A) FOUR+ B) Two Marys, Joanna and other women (24:10)	A) ONE B) Mary Magdalene came alone. (20:1)
Was the stone removed when the women arrived at the tomb?	NO — An angel rolled the stone away after the women arrived (28:1-2)	YES — The stone had already been rolled away when they arrived (16:4)	YES — The stone had already been rolled away when they arrived. (24:2)	YES — The stone had been rolled away when Marry arrived (20:1)
A) How many angels were at the tomb? B) What were they (was he) doing? C) Where were they?	A) One angel B) Sitting (28:2) C) <u>On the stone, which he rolled away from the tomb</u>	A) One young man B) Sitting (16:5) C) <u>On the right side, inside the tomb</u>	A) Two men B) Standing (24:4) C) <u>By them, inside the tomb</u>	A) No angels at first B & C) The second time Mary arrived at the tomb, two angels are <u>sitting inside</u> (20:1-12)
What are the angels' instructions at the tomb?	Go to the Galilee to meet Jesus – "He is not here; for he has risen... Tell his disciples he is going before you to the Galilee!"*** (28:6-7)	Go to the Galilee to meet Jesus – "Do not be amazed...he has risen.... Tell his disciples and Peter he is going before you to Galilee!"*** (16:6-7)	The women were specifically instructed not to go to the Galilee, but to "Stay in Jerusalem!" (24:5-7; 49) "He commanded them that they should not leave Jerusalem!" (Acts 1:4)***	The angels ask Mary, "Why are you weeping?" Before she could respond, she noticed Jesus, but assumed he was a gardener. Contradicting all the other Gospels, John claims that Mary had no idea what happened to Jesus' body when she returned from the tomb (20:2). On the contrary, according to John's version of the events, it was Jesus, *not* the two angels, who told Mary about the resurrection during her second visit to the tomb! (20:13-17)

*Matthew, Mark, and Luke claim that the Last Supper was a Passover Seder. Accordingly, their version of the crucifixion story occurred on the first day of Passover, rather than the eve of Passover as John claims (see Volume 2, 213-226).

**Although Jesus claimed that he would be in the tomb for "three days and three nights!" (Mat. 12:40)

***Matthew (28:16) and Mark (16:7) claim that the apostles immediately went to the Galilee following the crucifixion, which is an 80-mile journey from Jerusalem. Luke, on the other hand, insists that the apostles were never told to go to the Galilee and never departed Jerusalem! According to the author of the Book of Luke and Acts, the disciples were specifically warned to remain in Jerusalem after the crucifixion in order to form the new Jerusalem church (Luke 24:5-7, 49; Acts 1:4). Luke, therefore, prevents the followers from leaving Jerusalem because the apostles need to stay in Jerusalem for Pentecost. (Acts 2:1)

	Matthew	**Mark**	**Luke**	**John**
Does Mary wish to tell the disciples what occured?	YES—"They departed... and ran to tell the disciples." (28:8)	NO—"They said nothing to anyone, for they were afraid." (16:8)	YES—"Returning from the tomb, they told all this to the 11..." (24:9)	YES—Mary Magdalene told them "I have seen the Lord." (20:18)
After encountering the angel(s) at the tomb, who did Mary meet first, Jesus or the disciples?	Jesus (28:9)	Jesus (16:9)	The disciples (24:4-9)	Jesus (20:14)

Contradicting Luke's resurrection story, Matthew (28:8), Mark (16:9) and John (20:14) all claim that Mary met Jesus before she was able to tell any of the disciples what had happened at the tomb, whereas Luke asserts that Mary told the disciples what occurred before ever encountering Jesus! (Luke 24:4-10)

	Matthew	**Mark**	**Luke**	**John**
To whom and where does Jesus make his first appearance?	Both Marys, on their way to Jerusalem, after leaving the tomb (28:9).	Jesus makes no appearances following the crucifixion	Cleopas and an other in Emmaus (24:13-18).	To Mary Magdalene at the tomb (20:1, 11-14). Paul claims Jesus appeared first to Peter (I Cor. 15:5).

Originally, the Book of Mark abruptly ended without any description of Jesus encountering Mary or the disciples following the crucifixion. Early church scribes were so alarmed by Mark's disappointing conclusion that they added their own, appending 12 additional verses (16:9-20) which describe some of Jesus' appearances to Mary and the disciples after Mary fled the tomb (16:8-9).

Luke claims that the 11 disciples said: "It is true!" when two followers who met Jesus on the road to Emmaus related to them about their encounter (24:34). Mark claims, however, when the two reported their encounter, the disciples did not believe them! (16:13)

	Matthew	**Mark**	**Luke**	**John**
Is Mary permitted to touch Jesus after the resurrection?	YES —"they came and held him by his feet, and worshiped him." (28:9)	Not mentioned in Mark	YES—"Behold my hands and my feet... handle me and see...." (24:39)	NO—Jesus said to her, "Touch me not; for I am not yet ascended to my Father...." (20:17)
How many times does Jesus appear after the resurrection?	Two Times 28:9-20	Three Times 16:9-18 (*See above*, right)	Two Times 24:13-51	Four Times 20:14-21:23
Paul				
Six Times 1 Cor. 15:5-8				

Contradicting Luke's story, John insists the apostles received the Holy Spirit on the first Easter Sunday when Jesus breathed on them following the resurrection (20:22). Luke, on the other hand, insists that the Holy Spirit was bestowed on them during Pentecost, fifty days later! (Acts 1:5, 8; 2:1-4)

	Matthew	**Mark**	**Luke**	**John**
Before whom, and in what chronological order, do these appearances take place?	1st) Mary Magdalene and the other Mary (28:9) 2nd) 11 disciples (28:16)	1st) Mary Magdalene (16:9) 2nd) Two followers (16:12) 3rd) 11 disciples (16:14)	1st) Cloepas and another unknown follower. (24:13) 2nd) 11 disciples "...and those that were with them." (24:33)	1st) Mary Magdalene (20:14) 2nd) Ten disciples (Thomas was not there) (20:24) 3rd) 11 disciples (20:26) 4th) Peter, Thomas, the two sons of Zebedee (James and John), Nathanael and two other disciples. (21:2)

Paul

1 Corinthians
1st) Peter 15:5
2nd) All 12 apostles 15:5
3rd) 500 people 15:6
4th) James 15:7
5th) All 12 apostles

According to Matthew, Mark and Luke, Jesus appeared to 11 disciples. This event, however, occurred in the presence of all 12 apostles according to Paul (1 Cor. 15:5), although Judas should have long been dead (Matthew 27:5; Acts 1:18). In contrast, there are only 10 disciples at the scene in John's story, because Thomas was absent! (John 20:24)

	Matthew	**Mark**	**Luke**	**John**
Where do these appearances take place?	1st) Leaving the tomb, going to the disciples (28:8) 2nd) On a mountain in the Galilee (28:16) – "but some doubted it!" (28:17)	1st) After they fled the tomb (16:8-9) 2nd) As they walked to the country (16:12) 3rd) At a meal (16:14)	1st) Emmaus (24:13) 2nd) Jerusalem (24:33, 49), not in the Galilee, as Matthew claims (28:6-7, 16)	1st) At the tomb (20:14) 2nd & 3rd) Jerusalem, behind closed doors (20:18-29) 4th) Sea of Tiberias (21:1)

For error is manifold, truth but one

Why did later Gospels contradict the Passion narrative of earlier Gospels?

We are told by each of the four Gospels—Matthew, Mark, Luke, and John—the story of Jesus' death, with each version strikingly different from the others. The extensive inconsistencies in these Passion narratives are well known and widely noted. Christians who believe in the inerrancy of the New Testament are, understandably, unnerved by the discrepancies found in all the Gospels' accounts. For example, it is clear that the synoptic Gospels—Matthew, Mark, and Luke—claim that the Last Supper was a Passover Seder, and Jesus was crucified on the first day of Passover, the 15th day of Nissan. In sharp contrast, there is no Passover Seder in the Book of John, and according to this last Gospel, Jesus was not crucified on Passover. Rather, Jesus was crucified on the day before Passover, the 14th of Nissan. This is the day that the Passover lambs were sacrificed (19:17-37). In essence, all four Gospels agree that Jesus was crucified on Friday, but they cannot agree on which day of the month this occurred. The chart on the previous pages highlight numerous contradictions found in the Gospels' Passion narrative.

This raises a pressing question: How did these variegated stories develop? Moreover, the significance of these inconsistent accounts are, relatively speaking, inconsequential when we examine the vastly different ways the Gospels portray Jesus as he faced his execution.

In the Book of Mark, the oldest and least embellished of the four Gospels, Jesus is portrayed as deeply troubled and emotionally lost as he faced death. We are told by Mark that following the Last Supper, Jesus goes to the Garden of Gethsemane in a state of unbearable agony. Mark depicts Jesus as one who is in the throes of despair and loneliness. As his execution draws near, he is distressed and faltering as he cries over his fate. Mark produced a despondent portrait of Jesus, who "began to be distressed and agitated" (14:33) when he said to his disciples, "My soul is deeply troubled, even unto death" (14:34), as he fell to the ground in anguish (14:35). Mark's Jesus is traumatized and mournful before his death, and asks his followers to keep him company, while pleading to God three times that "this cup" (meaning, his death) might pass from him (14:36, 39, 41). As Jesus is on the cross, his desperation and bewilderment only deepens in Mark's version of the events, as Jesus cries despondently, "My God, My God, why have you forsaken me?" (15:34). Here, Jesus is broken, dumbfounded, and utterly confused by his predicament. Mark "borrowed" this phrase from King David in Psalm 22 and placed them in the mouth of Jesus.

The Book of Luke was written about 15 years after the Book of Mark (c. 85 CE), and its author borrowed heavily from this earlier Gospel (Luke copied well over half of the Book of Mark). Despite this, the author of the Book of Luke was so disappointed by Mark's unsatisfying Passion narrative that he wanted little to do with his meek portrayal of Jesus entering his passion filled with fear, trembling over his coming fate. In fact, Luke went to great lengths to counter this weak view of Jesus. And he accomplished this task by expunging the passion from the Passion narrative.

Accordingly, Luke completely eliminated the aforementioned passages from the Book of Mark regarding Jesus' distress and anguish. Texts like "My soul is deeply troubled, even unto death" (Mark 14:34) disappeared in the Book of Luke. Jesus doesn't fall to the ground in anguish in Luke's narrative. Instead, Jesus is stalwart and focused as he bows to his knees to pray (Luke 22:41). As expected, there is no trace of Jesus whining about his impending death in the Book of Luke because its author stripped away any trace of Jesus' distress and suffering from his story. Everyone else is in distress and filled with anguish in the Book of Luke, but not Jesus.

In fact Luke's Jesus tells a group of wailing women as he is led to the Crucifixion, "weep not for me, but weep for yourselves and your children" (Luke 22:27). No other Gospel mentions this brief but significant anecdote; it is unique to the Book of Luke.

In Mark's narrative Jesus cries out three times to God that "this cup might pass from me." In Luke's story, however, Jesus remains calm and steady, and asks God only one time "remove this cup from me" (22:42). However this entire scene in the Book of Luke has an almost businesslike feel to it. Luke is able to paint this confident portrait of Jesus, who is completely at peace in the face of death, by bracketing this request with an important condition, "If it be Your will...nevertheless, not my will, but thine, be done."

Luke's Jesus has no fear of death.

On the contrary, Jesus is resolute and self-confident in Luke's Gospel. On the other hand, in Mark's Gospel, Jesus is mocked, broken, anguished, and so bewildered by his predicament on the cross that he cries out as he is dying, "My God, My God, why hast Thou forsaken me." In Luke's version of the events, however, Jesus is completely lucid and in control, conducting intelligent conversations on the cross with the two thieves who were crucified with him. And only in the Book of Luke (23:43), Jesus promises one of the two thieves that "Today, you shall be with me in paradise." (In Matthew's story, neither of the thieves believed in Jesus). Luke's Jesus is confident and knows exactly where he is going; Mark's Jesus is shattered, dumbfounded, and has no clue why he is on the cross.

Most importantly, instead of Mark's cry of Dereliction, "My God, My God, why have you forsaken me," Luke's Jesus is steady and reserved. And instead of asking God why he was abandoned on the cross, in Luke's version, Jesus is self-confident as he proclaims at his crucifixion, "Father, into your hands I commit my spirit" (23:26). Interestingly, both Mark and Luke quote the Book of Psalms. Yet, whereas Mark cites a desperate passage from Psalm 22, Luke quotes Psalm 31, a chapter that conveys confidence and victory.

In essence Luke's Passion narrative didn't just change the events, but he completely altered Jesus' demeanor and conduct. Compare Mark 14:32-36 and Luke 22:39-45 for yourself. You will find it striking that Luke radically changed historical datum in order to make a theological point about Jesus' fearless personality as he approached his death.

The only exception to Luke's courageous portrayal of Jesus is found in a famous scene where Jesus is sweating blood (this is where the saying comes from) just prior to his arrest (Luke 22:43-44). This story is found in no other Gospel, and, as you might suspect, it doesn't appear in the earliest and best ancient manuscripts of the Book of Luke.[1] The story of Jesus in anguish, sweating blood, was added later. These verses were, therefore, omitted by the Revised Standard Version, and their validity is questioned in the margins of many Christian Bibles, including the New International Version, the New King James Version, and the New English Bible.

This passage was later interpolated into the Book of Luke by scribes who opposed popular docetic Christian groups that flourished during the first few centuries of the Christian church. The word docetic derives from the Greek, meaning an "apparition" or a "phantom." Early docetic Christian groups such as the Marcionites and Gnostics taught that what appeared to be Jesus' body was just an illusion. Both of these groups abhorred what they regarded as the inferior Jewish Creator God. In other words, they believed that Jesus could not have been the product of a world which was created by the God of the Jews, whom they loathed. They insisted that Jesus was so divine that he could not really have human characteristics. He only "appeared" to be human. Luke's Passion narrative fit perfectly with this christology, because Jesus exhibited no fear of death. These sects were labeled as heretics by other Christian groups who attacked their doctrines. Accordingly, the opponents of the Marcionites and Gnostics inserted Luke 22:43-44 in order to show that contrary to their claims, Jesus was a human being, who experienced very real human emotions, displayed by his sweating blood in agony. They therefore altered Luke's betrayal-and-arrest scene in order to stress Jesus' humanity to the docetic Christian sects who denied it.

This pattern of portraying Jesus as steady and confident in his last hours is pushed further by the author of the Book of John, which was written about 15 years after the Book of Luke. The last Gospel portrays Jesus as so strong and confident that he is cast as one who confronts Pontius Pilate, the Roman prefect, head-on, as in no other Gospel. Furthermore, in the Book of John, Jesus doesn't require the assistance of Simon of Cyrene to carry his cross to Calvary, as he does in Mark 15:21 and Luke 23:26. With no help from others, Jesus carries his own cross all the way to Calvary in John's story. Accordingly, Simon of Cyrene is never mentioned in the Book of John.

Mark's portrait of a frail and anguished Jesus didn't escape the attention of early critics of Christianity.

The second-century pagan scholar, Celsus, a well known critic of Christianity, assesses this portrayal when he asked, "Why does [Jesus] howl, lament, and pray to escape the fear of destruction, expressing himself in a manner like this: 'Oh father, if it be possible, let this cup pass?'"[2]

Luke's passionless Passion narrative was fashioned to address the sort of criticism found in Celsus' critique.

---

[1]These ancient sources include Papyrus 69, Papyrus 75, Codex Sinaiticus1, Codex Alexandrinus, Codex Vaticanus, Codex Petropolitanus Purpureus, Codex Nitriensis, Codex Borgianus, Codex Washingtonianus, and Georgian mss.

[2]Origen, *Contra Celsum* 6.10.

Deuteronomy 4:32-40

You might inquire about times long past, going back to the time that God created man on earth, [exploring] one end of the heavens to the other, see if anything as great as this has ever happened, or if the like has ever been heard. ³³Has any nation ever heard God speaking out of fire, as you have, and still survived? ³⁴Has God ever done miracles, bringing one nation out of another nation, with tremendous miracles, signs, wonders, war, a mighty hand and outstretched arm, and terrifying phenomena, as God did for you in Egypt before your very eyes? ³⁵**You are the ones who have been shown, so that you will know** that God is the Supreme Being, and there is none besides Him. ³⁶From the heavens, He let you hear His voice admonishing you, and on earth He showed you His great fire, so that you heard His words from the fire. ³⁷It was because He loved your fathers, and chose their children after them, that [God] Himself brought you out of Egypt with His great power. ³⁸He will drive away before you nations that are greater and stronger than you, so as to bring you to their lands, and give them to you as a heritage, as [He is doing] today. ³⁹Realize it today and ponder it in your heart: God is the Supreme Being in heaven above and on earth beneath—there is no other. ⁴⁰Keep His decrees and commandments that I am presenting to you today, so that He will be good to you and your children after you. Then you will endure for a long time in the land that God your Lord is giving you for all time.

No ancient people of the East has had a stranger history than the Jews...The history of no ancient people should be so valuable, if we could only recover it and understand it... Stranger still, the ancient religion of the Jews survives, when all the religions of every ancient race of the pre-Christian world have disappeared...

Again it is strange that the living religions of the world all build on religious ideas derived from the Jews... This then is the problem offered by the Jews to the historian. The great matter is not, "What happened?" but "Why did it happen?" Why does this race continue? Why does Judaism live? How did it really begin? These questions will not be answered here... There lay the uniqueness of the Jews.

Glover, T.R., Professor at Queen's University Kingston, Ontario, *The Ancient World*. Penguin Books: Baltimore, 1964. Pages 184-191.

The following related articles can be found in Volume 2 of *Let's Get Biblical! Why doesn't Judaism Accept the Christian Messiah?*

I. Unraveling Matthew's Genealogy – Was Jesus a Descendant of a Cursed Ancestry?. . . . . Page 3

II. Jewish Genealogy. . . . . Page 181

III. The Christian Messiah?. . . . . Page 185

IV. Mary's Genealogy. . . . . Page 189

V Who Killed Jesus?. . . . . Page 205

VI. Did Jesus Rise From the Dead? What is the Evidence?. . . . . Page 213

VII. Who Was Jesus?. . . . . Page 229

Part X

The Oral Law

Oral Torah and the Church

It was in the wilderness, more than 3,300 years ago, when Moses gave his people 613 commandments accompanied by oral instructions. These instructions illuminated and conveyed the rules and methods to accurately read and understand the Written Torah. In addition, these teachings, maxims and interpretations were indispensable, because they shed light on the meaning of obscure Scriptural passages. This requisite body of oral tradition was initially transmitted by Moses to the nation that cried out "We will do and we will listen!" through a chain of disciples, by word of mouth, and is therefore called תורה שבעל פה, meaning the "Oral Torah."

What is the Oral Torah, and why was it later recorded in writing?

A perfect text must, by definition, be totally unambiguous, requiring no additional information to be understood. Since the Torah is "perfect" (Psalms 19:8), the Torah must not contain any ambiguities. The Written Torah, however, is pregnant with startling ambiguities!

Therefore, although all 613 commandments are identified in the Written Torah, the Oral Torah supplies the necessary, detailed information that has enabled us throughout Jewish history to perform these commandments.

Although originally the Oral Law was not transcribed, but instead was transmitted from father to son and from teacher to disciple, the system used to convey these sacred oracles was radically changed approximately 1,800 years ago.

The destruction of the Temple and the end of the Jewish commonwealth in the year 70 CE resulted in an unprecedented upheaval of Jewish social and legal norms. The Rabbis were faced with the new reality of a Jewish people displaced, shattered and exiled throughout the Roman Empire. Following the Bar Kokhba revolt (132–135 CE), Jewish life was further traumatized and decimated. It is during this bitter period that Rabbinic discourse began to be recorded in writing.

During this traumatic century, a revolutionary innovation was carried out by the central leader of the Jewish community during the Roman occupation of Judea. This reform was enacted by Rabbi Judah the Prince (135-220 CE), who was a direct descendant of the royal line of King David.

Fearing that the oral traditions might be forgotten as a result of this upheaval, "Rabbeinu HaKadosh," as he was reverently called, assembled the scholars of his generation and undertook the mission of compiling the Oral Law in what became known as the "Mishnah" (from the Hebrew word which means: "repetition," from the verb *shanah*, "to study and review"). The Mishnah consists of 63 tractates codifying Jewish law, which are the basis of the Talmud.

This was the first major written redaction of the Oral Torah (circa 200 CE). Other oral traditions from the same time period not entered into the Mishnah were recorded as "Baraitot" (*external teaching*), and the Tosefta (Aramaic: *Additions, Supplements*). Other traditions were written down as Midrashim.

This massive work emerged as the written authority (codex) and companion to the Tanach, which together formed the basis for passing judgments, a source and a tool for illuminating laws, and the first of many vital works to complement the Hebrew Scriptures.

The Mishnah is also called *Shas* (an acronym for *Shisha Sedarim*—the "six orders"), in reference to its six main divisions.[1] Rabbinic commentaries on the Mishnah over the next three centuries were redacted as the *Gemara*, which, coupled with the Mishnah, comprise the Talmud. The word "*Gemara*" is derived from the Aramaic word "*gamar*," which literally means "[to] study" or "learning by tradition."

Unlike the Talmud, the majority of the Mishnah is written in Hebrew, while the Talmud, which was compiled in Babylon, is written in Aramaic, and was edited in approximately 600 CE. The sages in Israel also collected their traditions and compiled them into the Jerusalem Talmud in approximately 450 CE. In general, the terms "*Gemara*" or "Talmud," without further qualification, refer to the Babylonian recension. Both the Babylonian and the Jerusalem versions of the Talmud are arranged according to the order of the Mishnah, which they expound and elaborate.

Since that time, the Oral Law has ceased to be "oral." As time passed under the harsh conditions of the Roman Empire, more and more of the previously oral tradition was recorded. For many centuries prior to this period, only the Tanach appeared as a sacred written text.

Why was the Oral Law necessary?

As mentioned earlier, many verses in the Torah require explanation and interpretation. Numerous passages even presuppose that the reader understands what is being referred to in the text. Many terms used in the Torah are undefined, incomprehensible, and many procedures are mentioned without explanation or instructions, assuming familiarity on the part of the reader.

The significance of the Oral Law is that it was the result of a long chain of tradition dating back to the revelation at Mt. Sinai, and therefore its teachings are binding and authoritative.

The following are just a few of the numerous striking examples of commandments (*mitzvot*), where the Written Torah does not supply the necessary information which would explain how to fulfill these ordained commandments highlighted in the Torah:

- Moses instructed the Jewish people to perform kosher slaughter כַּאֲשֶׁר צִוִּיתִךָ, "as I have commanded you" (Deuteronomy 12:21). Yet nowhere in the written text of the Torah do we find even a hint of one of the intricate and demanding rules of kosher slaughter. Where can we find these instructions that God demanded?

- The Torah states that "It is a law for all time, throughout the ages, in all your settlements: you must not eat any fat or any blood" (Leviticus 3:17). To what type of fat was Moses referring? What exactly is fat? Are there different types of animal fat, some which are permitted and some which are forbidden? How are these fats differentiated?

- The Ten Commandments states that it is forbidden to perform any "work" on the Sabbath (Exodus 20:10). What does the Torah mean when it states that it is prohibited to "work" on the Sabbath? What work is proscribed and what is permitted? Is a man allowed to carry a heavy chair up a flight of stairs, from the dining room to the bedroom within his own home, on the Sabbath day? There can be little doubt that this chore would require some grueling work! Without an oral explanation of the details of this forbidden work, it is impossible to know what the Torah means by this cardinal prohibition.

  To be sure, the Torah states that the consequences for violating the Sabbath are severe. Thus, it is certain that direction was provided as to how exactly such a serious and core commandment should be upheld. However, there is little to no information in the Written Torah as to what can and cannot be performed on the Sabbath. Without the oral tradition, keeping this law would be impossible. Accordingly, it was vital that Moses supply the Jewish people with very specific laws delineating activities that are permitted from those that are forbidden on this holy day. This detailed information is contained in the Oral Law, which identifies 39 specific categories of forbidden work on the Sabbath (Mishnah Tractate Sabbath Chapter 7, Mishnah 2).

Moreover, numerous prophets who lived many centuries after Moses explicitly refer to these forbidden actions which are outlined exclusively in the Oral Torah.[2]

- When the Jews returned to Jerusalem following a 70-year Babylonian exile, with permission from the Persian government to rebuild the Temple, the prophet Haggai tested the priests on their knowledge of the laws of purity. He asked them the following two questions:

    > If a man is carrying a sacrificial flesh in a fold of his garment, and with that fold touches bread, stew, wine, oil, or any other food, will the latter become holy?... If someone defiled by a corpse touches any of these, will it be defiled?
    >
    > (Haggai 2:12-13)

    The answers to these two questions are not found anywhere in the Torah. How were the priests to know the answers if not from an oral tradition?

- The very first commandment given to Israel is the sanctification of the New Moon, an indication that the concept of *Rosh Chodesh* (Hebrew: ראש חודש; trans. *Beginning of the Month*; lit. *Head of the Month*) is very meaningful. For without a precise accounting of the New Months, which are marked by the New Moon, there can be no Jewish calendar, and without a calendar there can be no festivals. Thus, this first national commandment regulated and affected much of Jewish life.

    What does the Torah mean when it states, "This month shall mark for you the beginning of the months"? (Exodus 12:2) To which months is this passage referring? The Written Torah is completely silent on this crucial matter. Is this passage speaking of the Egyptian months (where the Jews were living at the time), or Chaldean months (from where their patriarch Abraham was born)?

Without an oral tradition, it would be impossible to know to which month this verse referred.

- In spite of the unambiguous declaration in the Torah, the Oral Torah states that the phrase "An eye for an eye, a tooth for a tooth, a hand for a hand, a foot for a foot" (Ex 21:22–27) is not to be understood literally. Instead, these punishments are held in the oral tradition to imply monetary compensation —as opposed to a literal *Lex talionis*, where the person who has injured another person receives the same injury in compensation. Logically, since the Torah requires that penalties be universally applicable, the phrase cannot be interpreted literally; it would be inapplicable to blind or eyeless offenders. The Oral Torah explains that this concept entails monetary compensation in tort cases (Talmud Bava Kama 84a).

- Yom Kippur, the Day of Atonement, is the holiest and most solemn day of the year for the Jewish people. Its central themes are atonement and repentance. Jews traditionally observe this holy day with a 25-hour period of self-introspection and intensive prayer, often spending most of the day in synagogue services. Yom Kippur completes the annual period known in Judaism as the High Holy Days or *Yamim Noraim* ("Days of Awe").

In Leviticus 16:29, 23:27 and Numbers 29:7, the Torah mandates establishment of this holy day on the 10th day of the 7th month as the day of atonement for sins. It is called the "Sabbath of Sabbaths" and a day upon which we are commanded to "afflict your souls." Furthermore, the Torah warns that the penalty for violating this commandment is most severe:

> For any person who is not afflicted in soul on that same day
> shall be cut off from his people.
> (Leviticus 23:29)

Scripture explicitly states that it is a capital crime to transgress this commandment. Yet, how are we to comply with this cardinal law when the Written Torah is silent on the meaning of this ambiguous *mitzvah*? How, specifically, do you afflict your soul? It is inconceivable that Moses warned us that it was a capital offence to violate this commandment without conveying specific details on how to comply with these passages! It is inconceivable that the meaning of this passage was meant to be subjective if the penalty for violating this commandment is so severe. These instructions, however, are not recorded anywhere in the Torah.

The Oral Law conveys this essential information. The Mishnah (Yoma 8:1) explains that the commandment to "afflict your souls" entails five specific prohibitions that must be observed on Yom Kippur. The Talmud identifies these forbidden activities as follows:

1. No eating and drinking (Eruvin 4b; Yoma 76a, 79b-81a; Succah 5b-6a)
2. No wearing of leather shoes (Yoma 78b)
3. No bathing or washing (Yoma 76b, Sabbath 86a)
4. No anointing oneself with perfumes or lotions (Yoma 76b, Sabbath 86a)
5. No marital relations (Yoma 77a; Pesachim 53b)

A few years ago, a Christian missionary, who was a fierce opponent of the Oral Torah, presented the following argument to disprove that fasting on Yom Kippur could only be derived from the Oral Torah. He explained that the Jewish Scriptures, rather than the Oral Law, explicitly states that afflicting one's soul meant that it is forbidden to eat on Yom Kippur. In other words, he argued that the source for the commandment to fast on Yom Kippur is not the Oral Law but instead the Hebrew Bible.

To support his contention, he cited the following passages from the Book of Isaiah where the prophet severely castigates Jews who technically comply with the commandment of fasting on Yom Kippur, but do nothing to change their immoral behavior:

> Is it a fast that I have chosen, a day for a man to afflict his soul? Is it to bow down his head like a bulrush, And to spread out sackcloth and ashes? Would you call this a fast, And an acceptable day to the Lord? Is this not the fast that I have chosen: To loose the bonds of wickedness, To undo the heavy burdens, To let the oppressed go free, and that you break every yoke?
>
> (Isaiah 58:5-6)

He insisted, therefore, that the source for fasting on Yom Kippur was not the rabbis, but instead the Written Tanach.

I replied to his novel argument by asking him a simple question: "Did the Jewish people fast on Yom Kippur from the moment Moses gave the Torah until the time that the Prophet Isaiah lived? "After all," I pointed out, "Isaiah lived more than 600 years after Moses led the Jews out of Egypt." He immediately conceded that the Jewish people fasted on Yom Kippur during those intermediate six centuries. "If, as you claim, there was no Oral Law that accompanied the Torah," I asked, "on which source did the Jews who lived between the prophets Moses and Isaiah rely to determine that the cardinal commandment to 'afflict one's soul' specifically meant abstaining from eating on Yom Kippur?"

He shrugged his shoulders and changed the topic.

Isaiah's passing mention of fasting on Yom Kippur provides incontrovertible proof from the Jewish Scriptures that Moses gave the Written Torah with oral instructions.

Numerous other examples illustrate that Oral instructions accompanied the Torah.

Furthermore, the necessity of the Oral Law is eminently clear from incontrovertible attestations in the Jewish Scriptures.

The following are a just few simple examples of this empirical evidence:

- It would be impossible to read and understand the words of the Jewish Scriptures without the Oral Law regarding the vowelization and punctuation of the words. A simple reading of the text requires this Oral tradition passed down to us by Moses, our Teacher. Since the only existing tradition regarding the text includes a tradition about the concepts and laws, one who accepts the vowelization and punctuation must also accept the Oral Law.

  Bear in mind that the Hebrew נְקֻדּוֹת (*nikkudot*), which literally means "dots" or "points," is a system of diacritical signs used to represent vowels or distinguish between alternative pronunciations of letters of the Hebrew alphabet. Several such written diacritical systems were developed in the early Middle Ages. The most widespread system, and the only one still used to a significant degree today, was created by the Masoretes of Tiberias in the second half of the first millennium in the Land of Israel. The word "*Masorete*" is derived from the Hebrew word which denotes those who "passed down" the oral tradition. Before this written *nikkudot* system was created 1,200 years ago, how did people know the meaning and vocalization of the words of the Hebrew Bible? After all, if the vowels of a Hebrew word are changed, both the meaning and the pronunciation are radically altered. They relied on the Oral Law.

For example, Exodus 23:19, among other places in the Torah, states that a young goat may not be boiled in its mother's milk. In addition to numerous other problems with understanding the ambiguous nature of this law, the lack of vowelization characters in the Torah creates a monumental problem in understanding this particular commandment. The Hebrew word for milk חלב is identical to the word for animal fat when vowels are absent. Without the oral tradition, it is not known whether the violation is in mixing meat with milk or with fat.

The handwritten Torah scrolls that are used in the synagogue lack vowelization points because the strict and meticulous laws that govern the writing of a Torah scroll on parchment date back to the biblical period. The vowels which appear in printed Hebrew Bibles are a relatively recent innovation, dating back a little more than a thousand years. These innovations cannot be inserted into a sacred Torah scroll used for public worship services. The Dead Sea Scrolls, therefore, contain no *nikkudot* because they were written about two thousand years ago, during the period when Hebrew vowels were only known through the Oral Law.

Strangely, the entire Christian world depends entirely on the Jewish Oral Torah to read their own Bibles, which all rely on our Jewish oral tradition.

- The marriage of Boaz to Ruth, who was a Moabite as described in the Book of Ruth, directly contradicts the prohibition found in Deuteronomy 23:3-4, where the Torah emphatically states that it is forbidden for a Jew to marry a Moabite. In fact, Scripture explicitly states that a Moabite may never become a member of the Jewish Nation! In view of this prohibition in the Written Torah, how is it possible that direct descendants of Ruth—all the Davidic kings, including King David and the messiah—could become leaders of the Jewish people?

  The Oral Torah, however, explains that this prohibition is limited to Moabite men, not women. Thus, only the Oral Law enabled Ruth to become the progenitor of the most illustrious men in Jewish history.

  Once again, Christendom is forced to rely entirely on the Oral Torah to advance the core tenet of its belief.

- The Torah relates that Jethro advised Moses to appoint judges. Jethro told Moses,

> Enjoin upon them the laws and the teachings, and make known to them the way they are to go, and the practices they are to follow.
>
> (Exodus 18:20).

What did Jethro's suggestion mean? If the Written Law is all that was given, then there would have been nothing more for Moses to instruct these judges. What was Moses supposed to tell them, if not the Oral Law?

Moreover, the Torah states:

> If a matter of judgement is **hidden from you**, between blood and blood, between verdict and verdict, between plague and plague, matters of dispute in your cities—you shall rise up and ascend to the place that the Lord, your God, shall choose. You shall come to the priests, the Levites, and to the judge who will be in those days; you shall inquire and they will tell you the word of judgement. You shall do according to the word that they will tell you, from the place that God will choose, and you shall be careful to do according to everything that they will teach you. According to the teaching that they will teach you and according to the judgement that they will say to you, shall you do; you shall not deviate from the word that they will tell you, right or left.
>
> (Deuteronomy 17:8-11)

What knowledge could possibly be "hidden" if the Written Torah was the only revelation conveyed at Mt. Sinai? If there was no Oral Law, the only basis for judgement is contained in the Written Torah, which is available and open for anyone to study.

Clearly, the pressing need for the above judicial process of following the ruling of the central court illustrates that there was an elaborate oral tradition which served as the basis for adjudicating cases.

The implication of all of these examples is clear: There is a companion to the Written Torah, an Oral Law, without which many of the commandments enumerated in the Written Torah are virtually incomprehensible, and can be twisted and misinterpreted beyond recognition, as indeed it has been done by heretical movements down through the centuries.

Oral Law predates the Written Torah

Critics of the Jewish faith often claim that the Oral Torah was an "after-thought" interpretation of the Written Torah. They argue that the rabbis invented these laws long after the Torah was given, and claimed that its origins were from Mount Sinai. In fact, the giving of the Oral Torah actually preceded the giving of the Written Torah we have today. When the Jewish people stood at Mount Sinai 3,300 years ago, Moses conveyed the 613 commandments, along with the Oral Law, which contained the detailed, practical explanation of how to fulfill them. At that point in time, the teachings were entirely oral.

It wasn't until 40 years later, just prior to Moses' death and the Jewish people's entering the Land of Israel, that Moses wrote the scroll of the Written Torah, the Five Books of Moses, and gave it to the Jewish people. Following the death of Moses, Joshua added the final eight verses to the Book of Deuteronomy.

In fact, this chain of oral tradition dates back long before Moses' encounter with God at Mount Sinai. For example, God instructed Noah to board the ark with his family, seven pairs of the birds and the clean animals, and one pair of the unclean animals (Genesis 7:1-5). How did Noah, who lived 1,000 years before the Torah was given in written form, know how to distinguish between clean and unclean animals? Nowhere in the Written Torah does God instruct Noah how to identify clean and unclean species. The Laws of the Torah were orally conveyed to Noah and other saints of the distant past long before the children of Israel experienced their national revelation in the wilderness.

Rabbi Aryeh Kaplan explains why the system of both a Written and Oral Law was necessary:

The Oral Torah was meant to cover the infinitude of cases which would arise in the course of time. It could never have been written in its entirety. It is written (Ecclesiastes 12:12), "Of making many books there is no end." God therefore gave Moses a set of rules through which the Torah could be applied to every possible case. If the entire Torah would have been given in writing, everyone would be able to interpret it as he desired. This would lead to division and discord among people who followed the Torah in different ways. The Oral Torah, on the other hand, would require a central authority to preserve it, thus assuring the unity of Israel...

(Handbook of Jewish Thought – Moznaim 1979)

The Church's attitude toward the Oral Law

Although over the past 1,800 years virtually all Christian denominations virulently rejected the Oral Torah, generally regarding it with utter contempt, the New Testament clearly attests that the earliest Christians took the Mosaic origin of the Oral Law for granted, never questioning its authenticity and authority.

During the last two centuries of the Second Temple period, the Jewish people in the Roman province of Judea were divided into several movements. Numerous sources, including the Talmud, Flavius Josephus, the Christian Bible, and recovered fragments of the Dead Sea Scrolls,[3] attest to the ancient schisms and divisions among Jews at this time.

Josephus, the Roman-Jewish historian, identifies three[4] Jewish sects during the early first century: the Pharisees, Sadducees, and the Essenes.[5] While there is significant uncertainty regarding the precise beliefs of the Essenes, this relatively small, apocalyptic, reclusive group is not mentioned in the Christian Bible, and to some extent was ignored until the 20th century. However, the Essenes have gained fame in modern times as a result of the discovery of an extensive group of religious documents in 1947 known as the Dead Sea Scrolls. Many scholars believe that these ancient, well-preserved texts were written by the Essenes, thus linking this obscure, ascetic group to the Qumran community.

The two major sects during the first century were the Pharisees and Sadducees, whose core beliefs as well as their numerous disagreements are well known and widely documented. The furious conflicts between them took place in the context of broad social and religious issues which dated back to the second century BCE, when the Sadducees sect began. Their discord was further exacerbated by the Roman conquest. Josephus described the many arenas in which they clashed.[6] He characterized one conflict as a class warfare, between the wealthy and the poor, as the Sadducees included mainly the priestly and aristocratic families. Another conflict was cultural: the Sadducees favored hellenization and Pharisees resisted it. The Sadducees emphasized the importance of the Second Temple rituals, and the Pharisees emphasized the importance of other Mosaic laws and prophetic values.

The final, and most significant clash was theological, and centered on different interpretations of the Torah and how to apply it to current Jewish life. The Sadducees recognized only the Written Torah and vehemently opposed the Oral tradition. They claimed the soul is not immortal and insisted that there is no afterlife or rewards or penalties after death, and rejected belief in the resurrection of the dead.

Each of these tenets the Sadducees discarded were the cardinal and cherished beliefs of the widespread Pharisaic community.

Josephus records that the Pharisees received the backing and goodwill of the common people, in contrast to the more elite Sadducees. Pharisees claimed prophetic or Mosaic authority for their interpretation of Jewish laws, while the Sadducees represented the authority, priestly privileges and prerogatives of the priesthood.

Following the destruction of the Second Temple in the year 70 CE, the Pharisees produced the normative, traditional Judaism which is the basis for contemporary forms of Judaism. The Sadducees, who were the main Jewish antagonists of the Pharisees, became extinct sometime after the destruction of Herod's Temple in Jerusalem in 70 CE.

The Oral Law in the Christian Bible

Although the conflict between the Church and the Synagogue began almost immediately after the birth of Christianity, and this clash of long duration expressed itself extensively on cardinal doctrines, members of the newly emerging Jesus-centered movement did not question the authenticity and divine origins of the Oral Law. In fact, even in a chapter of the New Testament which is widely regarded as one of the most anti-Jewish in the Christian canon, where we would least expect to find any approval of the traditions passed down by the Pharisees, the Gospels explicitly endorsed the divine origin of Judaism's Oral Law.

Many Jews and Christians trace 2,000 years of anti-Jewish persecution directly back to certain pronouncements placed in the mouth of Jesus by the authors of the New Testament. Although the Church widely considers the Gospel of Matthew to be the "most Jewish" of the Gospels, it contains some of the most anti-Jewish passages found in the New Testament. As Matthew's narrative marches toward the Passion, the anti-Jewish rhetoric increases. In chapter 23, Jesus launched a series of virulently hostile accusations against the Jews. These bitter charges were not just against those in his audience, but rather against all the Jews collectively, of all generations:

> You testify against yourselves that you are descendants of those who murdered the prophets...You snakes, you brood of vipers! How can you escape being sentenced to hell?... O Jerusalem, Jerusalem, killing the prophets and stoning those who are sent to you... Behold, your house is forsaken and desolate.
>
> (Matthew 23:31, 33, 37)

These and other passages in the New Testament stereotyped the Jewish people for all time as an icon of unredeemed humanity: the image of a blind, stubborn, carnal and perverse nation. This dehumanization, no doubt, is the vehicle that formed the psychological prerequisite to the Church's unrelenting atrocities against Jewish communities centuries later.

Although similar passages can be found in the Gospels of Luke (11:37-54) and Mark (12:35-40), Matthew's portrayal of Jesus' assault on the character of the Jewish people is by far the most elaborate and maligning.

Yet, although the end of this fuming chapter collectively charges the Jews with all of the innocent spilt blood in history (Matthew 23:35)—including the death of Abel, who was murdered by his brother Cain—this chapter opens with Jesus conceding that the Pharisees were the most expert and accurate expositors of Jewish law, and they received their authority directly from Moses! Therefore, Jesus insisted, their ruling and interpretation on matters of Jewish Law must be followed. At this juncture of his speech—literally in mid-sentence—Jesus warns, "do as they say, but not as they do..."

> Then Jesus spoke to the multitudes and to His disciples, saying: "The scribes and the Pharisees sit in Moses' seat. Therefore whatever they tell you to observe, that observe and do, but do not do according to their works; for they say, and do not do.
>
> (Matthew 23:1-3)

Jesus' message in this chapter, as portrayed by Matthew, may be deeply offensive, yet it is unmistakably clear: the Written and Oral Law taught by the Pharisees originated at Mt. Sinai. And although the Jews are responsible for the most loathsome crimes in history, a clear distinction is asserted between the authentic and authoritative teachings conveyed by the Pharisees and the detestable character of the Jew.

In essence, Jesus asserts in the first Gospel that notwithstanding the fact that the Pharisees are abhorrent, their teachings are genuine, for they received their authority directly from Moses.

The following are a few of many examples in the New Testament which illustrate that the earliest Christians took the Oral Law for granted, and never questioned its authority:

- The three synoptic Gospels state that Jesus celebrated a Passover Seder during the Last Supper with his disciples, which included oral traditions not found anywhere in the Written Torah. Passover rituals do not appear at the Last Supper in the Book of John (chapter 13) because the fourth Gospel claims that Jesus was crucified on the day of the slaughtering of the lambs, which is the 14th day of Nisan, a day earlier than the synoptic Gospels, who date Jesus' crucifixion on the 15th of Nisan.

- According to the synoptic Gospels Jesus wore *tzitzit*, "fringes" (Mark 6:56, Matt. 9:21). The commandment in the Torah (Numbers 15:38 and Deuteronomy 22:12) to wear *tzitit* lacks the detailed instructions necessary to perform this commandment. How many strings and knots do the *tzitis* require? Which garments require such fringes? Are both men and women required to observe this commandment? Is a person permitted to wear a four cornered garment made of linen but having *tzitzis* made of wool? After all, the Torah states in Deuteronomy 22:11 that it is forbidden to wear *shaatnez*, a garment made of a mixture of wool and linen!

  The answer to these questions and many more meticulous instructions on this central commandment are enumerated only in the Oral Law.

- Acts 1:12 states that the disciples traveled only "a Sabbath day's journey," when returning to Jerusalem from the Mount of Olives, which is located just across the Kidron Valley, on the eastern side of the Temple Mount. What distance is a Sabbath day's journey? This information is not found anywhere in the Written Law. The Torah simply states:

  > Remember! The Lord has given you the Sabbath; therefore on the sixth day he gives you bread for two days. Remain each of you in his place; let no one go out of his place on the seventh day."
  >
  > (Exodus 16:29)

  What does the Torah mean by this prohibition that one may not "go out of his place on the seventh day"? Curiously, members of heretical sects of Judaism which fiercely rejected the Oral Law would not leave their homes throughout the entire Sabbath based on their literal reading of this prohibition! According to the Oral Law, however, on the seventh day it is forbidden to walk farther than a Sabbath day's journey beyond the city limits, which is defined as up to 2,000 cubits (about one-half of a mile). Clearly, the author of the

Book of Acts, who also penned the Book of Luke, considered the Oral Law authoritative and authentic.

The Christian Bible often reflects the world of Israel's sages. Other examples include Paul, who took for granted the Jewish tradition that the children of Israel were enslaved in Egypt for 210 years rather than 400 years (Galatians 3:17), and the author of the gospel of Luke recorded the Jewish custom of giving a boy his name during his circumcision ceremony (1:59-64).

The Oral Law is vital to exegesis of the Christian Bible

While I could list numerous other examples of oral traditions recorded in the Christian Bible, the anecdotal evidence is astounding. In order to best clarify this point, I will share a little about my surprising first exposure to Christian canonical literature. It was an eye-opening, unexpected experience that I will not forget.

I recall preparing myself to read the New Testament for the first time. It was more than thirty years ago; I was a young product of the yeshiva, trained and steeped in the traditional, deeply Orthodox Jewish world. My education was rigorous, but not unusual for my community. All the boys who attended yeshiva studied Scripture, and spent many hours each day expounding and probing the Talmud. We were deeply immersed in the timeless works and commentaries penned by the sages—the giants of the Torah world.

I was sure that no one in my community ever touched a Christian Bible, let alone read one. This aspect didn't bother me; I readily accepted the fact that I would be alone in this venture. My situation was different; I believed I had a calling. I didn't see any visions or hear any voices from God. There came a point in my life, however, when I realized that I was to fulfill an unusual mandate: My purpose in this world was to help Jews who were lost in the Church return to their God and their people.

How did I know this was my mission? I just knew.

Nothing in my formative years could have prepared me for this lifelong endeavor. A bomb exploded in my soul, however, when I encountered Christian missionaries on the streets of New York and the holy places in Israel. They were targeting Jews for conversion. I had to do something to help my brethren recover their faith. But how could I bring them home? They all seemed so entrenched in Christianity. They were zealous and unyielding in their new-found religion. My agonizing conversations with them went nowhere. We were clearly talking past each other when we discussed fundamental theological teachings. I could not stop wondering how these Jews could have betrayed their faith. What possessed them to cross that line? Did they not know that their ancestors sacrificed everything to remain Jewish? After all, no one forced them to be baptized on the pain of death. Why did they do what was unthinkable to their grandparents?

It quickly became clear that I was missing something in my endeavor that was very important. I realized that I could not coherently reach out to Jews who had converted to Christianity without a thorough knowledge of Church teachings. I had to understand what this New Testament had to say and the ideas it sought to convey.

I found it particularly difficult to grasp why people, who appeared to be rational in other aspects of their lives, believed that Jesus was the messiah, and was worthy of worship.

As I prepared myself to read the New Testament, everything inside of me screamed that this task was going to be unpleasant and strange. I was deeply aware that unimaginable atrocities were committed against my people over the past two millennia by those who embraced the teachings of this book. I was certain that I was about to encounter an unfamiliar and hostile world.

I still remember peeking into a local Church when I was a young child; it was the first time I ever looked inside. I must have been eight or nine years old at the time. The doors of the Holy Ghost Catholic Church were wide open as I walked by one Sunday morning. It was the only church in Boro Park, Brooklyn—a neighborhood that is home to the largest Orthodox Jewish community in North America. I was curious about what went on in there. From where I stood on the sidewalk I could see statues, icons, crosses, and an altar. I could feel my stomach churning. I was horrified. What struck me as more bizarre, the priest seemed to be wearing a yarmulka on his head.

After a few moments I felt as though I had seen enough; I was deeply shaken and very perplexed.

I knew that their elaborate worship rituals resembled nothing found in the Torah. How could these parishioners not know that it was forbidden to worship any graven images, I wondered? How could normal people believe in this? Why do priests wear a yarmulka? While I had so many unanswered questions about what I witnessed that morning, one thing crystallized in my mind: I now understood why my grandparents were willing to die rather than convert to Christianity. I felt that if given the choice, I would have likely done the same.

When I opened the King James Bible for the first time, I wondered if I would understand it. Would any of it make sense? Perhaps I needed an annotated Christian Bible with some sort of a commentary in order to understand what I was reading? There was no doubt in my mind that this endeavor was going to be a strange experience. Yet I knew that I had to move ahead. How else would I help Jews who believed in Jesus if I didn't know what was written in the New Testament?

Nothing surprised me as I probed Matthew's opening chapters. I was just astounded that none of the millions of Christians in the world were aware that Matthew's numerous quotes from the Jewish Scriptures were spurious. "Surely some curious Christian must have discovered that the passage in Isaiah 7:14, which Matthew quoted (1:23) to support Jesus' virgin birth, had been mistranslated and taken out of context," I thought. I wondered why parishioners hadn't noticed that Matthew 2:6 expunged the final modifying segment of Micah 5:1 (5:2 in a Christian Bible), which is vital to understanding the meaning of this passage. Although I found it perplexing that churchgoers didn't question the validity of the Gospel's fantastic claims, I was well acquainted with these famed "proof-texts" because they regularly appeared in the missionary tracts that I had read.

I was, however, shocked by the nature of the conflicts between Jesus and the Pharisees. Their bitter confrontations are strewn throughout the Gospels. I was not surprised that Jesus was portrayed as the winner of all these heated debates. After all, the Christian Bible was not going to cast Jesus as the loser. I was, however, completely unprepared to discover that the theological construction of these arguments could be fully understood only by those familiar with Talmudic literature which had not yet been recorded in writing during the first century! The New Testament incorporated the Oral Law into its narratives during a period when the Oral Law was still only transmitted verbally.

Rabbinic literature has an oral pre-history which has never been apart from the sacred written texts. The first issue is that of historical and methodological legitimacy: the earliest redaction of Tannaitic texts is not prior to the third century CE. The first *haggadic* Midrashim[7] appear towards the fourth century. Talmudic studies commenced in the fifth century. Is it possible for such late texts to clarify the New Testament, which was written during the first century? The answer is yes. Thus, the New Testament contains the earliest written attestations of the Oral Law! I was astounded by this discovery. Jesus' many rancorous debates with his opponents are, in fact, incomprehensible without the framework of Jewish oral traditions, which had not yet been committed to writing.

Moreover, throughout these testy conflicts, Jesus was essentially seeking to out-Pharisee the Pharisees! Thus, one could only comprehend the substance of the discussions between Jesus and his interlocutors with an understanding of the Oral Torah. The early Christians clearly considered the Oral Law sacred and accepted its teachings as authentic and authoritative.

How strange to discover that Christians could not comprehend many passages in their own Bible without a thorough yeshiva education. As it turned out, rabbinic literature was essential to the exegesis of the New Testament. This conclusion was incontrovertible and completely unexpected.

Moral imperatives mirroring nine of the Ten Commandments are repeated in the New Testament, but the commandment regarding the Sabbath is notably absent. Instead, rancorous debates between the Jews and Jesus regarding the Sabbath commandments underscore much of the New Testament narratives and discussion. For example, in one of the many controversies about the Sabbath found in the Gospels, Jesus argues:

> Moses ordered you to circumcise your sons (although it was not Moses but your ancestors who started it), and so you circumcise a boy on the Sabbath.
>
> (John 7:22)

Here, Jesus is seeking to demonstrate to his opponents that he was not violating Jewish Law by healing on the Sabbath. Employing a *"kal v'chomer,"*[8] which is a common Talmudic hermeneutic meaning "from the lighter to the stronger case," Jesus continues his argument:

> If a boy is circumcised on the Sabbath so that Moses' Law is not broken, why are you angry with me because I made a man completely well on the Sabbath?
>
> (John 7:23)

The argument Jesus is making is that if circumcision, which affects a small limb, justifies overriding a Sabbath prohibition, certainly a healing procedure that affects the entire man should do so.

While the antecedent of this conflict in John 7:22-23 is preposterous, the argument presented in these two verses is incomprehensible without the Oral Torah. For critics of the Oral Law, these passages raise numerous insurmountable problems.

Jesus' point in these passages is that although performing a circumcision would require activities that are, under other circumstances, forbidden on the Sabbath, there is a special authorization to carry out these tasks for the purpose of circumcision (Talmud Sabbath 79a, 105b, 106a, 107b). Given that there is a special *heter* (permission) for a *mohel* (a man who performs circumcision) to carry out tasks that are otherwise forbidden on the Sabbath, which perfect only one organ of a child, Jesus argues that it is certainly permitted to heal a person's entire body on the Sabbath.

Critics of "Rabbinic Judaism," an appellation that missionaries frequently employ derisively, insist that the Oral Torah is manmade. They argue that the third century rabbis who redacted the Mishnah and other early rabbinic literature contrived the notion that the texts they codified emerged from a oral pre-history which dated back to Moses.

Bearing in mind that the New Testament was written during the first century, those who question the veracity of the Jewish oral tradition must answer the following questions: Relying only on the Written Law, on what basis is it forbidden to cause a blood-letting wound on the Sabbath? Furthermore, where does the Written Torah provide special dispensation to carry out a circumcision on the Sabbath, in spite of this prohibition?

In essence, where is this prohibition written in the Torah regarding Sabbath? Where is this exemption regarding circumcision written in the Torah?

There are no references in the Written Torah that address any of these issues. Indeed, the practice of circumcision on the Sabbath was expressly authorized in the Mishnah, and, as the Gospels cite, it is an ancient praxis: "Everything implied by circumcision may be done on the Sabbath" (Mishnah Sabbath 18:3; 19:2, 3, 5; Talmud Sabbath 106a, 132a-133a; Yoma 85b; Nedarim 31b). This demonstrates that the law recorded in the Mishnah during the third century was widely understood to be a normative, integral part of Judaism during the first century.

The teachings embedded in the Gospels that cast Jesus as antagonistic to the Pharisees are found nowhere in the Written Torah, and are themselves uniquely Pharisaic teachings. The New Testament author did set up Jesus' authority against the Pharisees but, as the evidence shows, the Book of John and other Gospels sought to portray Jesus as one who had mastered Pharisaic law more than his interlocutors had, and taught in accordance with rabbinic authority.

Stories of Pharisees enraged with Jesus for healing the sick on the Sabbath appear frequently in the Gospels. The authors of the New Testament recognized that these anecdotes were very provocative. They employed these potent stories in order to portray Jesus as the godly miracle worker, healing the infirm, while having to fend off the pestering, small-minded Pharisees who sought to impede the compassionate, miraculous wonders of the son of God.

In reality, these gripping narratives in which Jesus is described as fending off Pharisees who supposedly criticized him for healing on Sabbath could never have occurred. There is no prohibition that would prevent a rabbi from healing someone through prayer on the Sabbath. Even unlearned Jews are well aware that it is permitted to call upon God to heal the sick on the Sabbath. If fact, this practice is performed publicly on every Sabbath day in virtually every synagogue throughout the world!

Jewish tradition ordains that whenever the Torah is read we are granted a special and uniquely opportune moment to invoke blessing for those in need of divine intervention. Therefore, from time immemorial it has been the custom to recite a "*Mi-Sheberach*" (prayer for the sick) on behalf of people who are ill when the Torah is read in the synagogue. The notion that Jesus would have been condemned for praying for the sick on the Sabbath is preposterous.

Thus, the New Testament accounts of these disputes over Sabbath-healing are fictitious.

These narratives, however, play a central role in the Christian canon. The Gospel writers manufactured these carefully constructed stories in order to portray Jesus as the merciful, all-knowing son of God, and his opponents as ignorant, cruel, heartless villains who are obsessed with the cold letter of the Law rather than the compassionate spirit of grace. The authors of the New Testament repeatedly employed this same provocation, contrasting imagery in many of their other narratives in order to depict the Jews as acting collectively as the enemy of God. This prevalent, perverse icon of the Jew in Church literature would become fixed in the Christian mind.

While the numerous stories in the New Testament where Jesus is criticized for healing on the Sabbath are fictitious, these narratives were not manufactured out of thin air.

Interestingly, there is a Rabbinic prohibition related to healing on the Sabbath which is, no doubt, the antecedent for these stories.

The Talmud states that under certain circumstances, when a person is not seriously ill, it is forbidden to take non-vital medications during the Sabbath (Sabbath 109a, 111a,140a, 156a; Shulchan Aruch, Orach Chaim 328). This prohibition was enacted out of concern that a person might grind herbs to prepare the medicine. Since grinding constitutes one of the 39 categories of work forbidden on the Sabbath, it is prohibited to take non-essential medication as a safeguard against Sabbath desecration.

Thus, even New Testament fiction cannot be fully understood without Rabbinic teachings!

The Oral Law is essential to the exegesis of virtually all New Testament vitriolic accounts of Jesus' conflicts with the Pharisees over the Sabbath. Another example, is the episode in which the disciples are rebuked by the Pharisees for plucking ears of corn on the Sabbath (Mark 2:23-28; Matthew 12:1-8; Luke 6:1-5), the Written Torah does not proscribe such activity. So the entire narrative can only be understood with knowledge of the Talmud (Beitzah 2b-3a; Pesachim 56b; Sabbath 73b, 125b).

Rabbinic prohibitions in the Christian Bible

There is, however, a striking anecdote in the Gospels where a rabbinic injunction regarding the Sabbath, which is not even one of the 39 categories of forbidden activity outlined in the Oral Law, is taken for granted as authoritative by the early Church. In order to grasp the significance of this point, a brief overview of Rabbinic decrees and "fences" is essential, because these injunctions were not conveyed at Mount Sinai.

The Jewish sages instituted precautionary decrees as a safeguard to protect Jews from transgressing Torah laws. In fact, the sages encourage everyone to build personal fences where they know that they are weak.

The Sabbath presents special concerns in this regard, since it proscribes actions and activities which people are in the habit of doing all other six days of the week. Jews at all times, conscious of what is at stake, have been determined not to stumble on account of habit or forgetfulness. To this end, they sought methods of protection against unintentional desecration of the Sabbath.

Moreover, since in every case the reason for the decree lies in the frailty and forgetfulness of human nature, the decrees must remain binding for as long as human nature remains unchanged. For these reasons, the sages prohibited on the Sabbath many activities which, although themselves are not biblically proscribed, could very easily lead to unintentional profaning of the Sabbath.

The *Anshei Knesset Hagedolah* ("Men of the Great Assembly"), a gathering of 120 prophets and sages assembled about 2,500 years ago (during the last generations of the biblical prophets), said, "And you shall make a fence for the Torah." (Mishnah, Pirkei Avos 1:1).

> Upon the founding of the modern State of Israel in 1948, the first independent Jewish state in almost 2,000 years, its political leadership was aware of Jewish history's once Great Assembly that consisted of 120 members, and therefore decided to call its newly-established parliament the Knesset, i.e., "Assembly," which would also consist of 120 elected members.

Maimonides explains that these "fences" refer to the precautionary decrees that our sages instituted as a safeguard to protect us from transgressing the Torah laws. Maimonides quotes from the Talmud (Yevamos 21a) that these rabbinic safeguards are alluded to in the Torah itself. In the portion that deals with immorality and intimate relationships, Scripture states:

> And you shall guard My guard in order not to perform any of the abominable customs that were done before you and not contaminate yourselves.
>
> (Leviticus 18:30)

Our sages teach that there must be a clear distinction between God's command and man's "protective fence" around it. When the Torah instructs that we may neither add to nor subtract from the commandments, it means that the rabbis may not say that God gave us in the Torah 613 commandments and we add another few commandments, such as lighting the Hanukkah menorah and reading the Megillah on Purim. The sages, however, do have the authority to add rabbinic commandments *as long as they are clearly defined as such*. The Talmud (Megillah 7a; see also the commentary of the Ritva on Rosh Hashanah 16a) explains that even these rabbinic commandments were instituted only when the rabbis found a hint or source in the Torah itself. In the same way, when the rabbis instituted added prohibitions in connection with intimate relationships, they are clearly based on the words of the Torah itself. Nevertheless, they are established as rabbinic injunctions, distinct from the actual Written or Oral Torah commandment that the injunctions are protecting.

If the safeguards are taken seriously and observed as an integral part of the Sabbath law, the probability of actual desecration of the Sabbath is greatly lessened.

In Jewish thought, one's attitude to this safeguarding legislation is an indicator of one's attitude to the whole institution of the Sabbath—indeed to the divine Torah as a whole. The Jew who treats the rabbinic fences lightly has already decided in his heart to treat the Torah itself lightly.

The rabbis, however, in their great practical wisdom, restricted this type of legislation to the minimum that is necessary in order to prevent transgression of the actual Torah laws. It is a rule of Jewish law that 'A protective measure is never enacted to safeguard another protective measure' (Talmud, Bava Metzia, 5b).

Generally speaking, many objects have been designated by our sages as *muktzah* (the Hebrew word מוּקצה means "separated," or "set aside")—it is forbidden to touch or move them during the Sabbath. For example, because it is forbidden to write letters or light a fire on the Sabbath day, the rabbis enacted a decree which forbids one from even touching a pen or a kindling instrument on the Sabbath.

Moreover, any object which offers no immediate practical use on the Sabbath is considered *muktzah* as well and may not be handled on the Sabbath. According to conventional Jewish law, animals, too, fall into this category. Household pets are an exception—as will be explained shortly. Let us first discuss conventional *halachah* (Jewish Law) with regards to handling animals.

It is forbidden to pet, hold, or stroke an animal on the Sabbath day.[9] An exception to the no-handling rule is if the animal is in pain or discomfort; in such an instance it is permitted to touch it in order to ease its pain. For example, one is allowed to apply oil or an ointment to a wound,[10] or help an animal which is having difficulty walking.[11] This exception only applies to the rules of *muktzah*. The laws of *muktzah* are of rabbinic origin, and were waived by the rabbis in an instance where an animal is in pain or danger.

All of the above, as we said, is the conventional law pertaining to touching animals on the Sabbath. According to Rabbinic opinion, however, it is permitted to handle household pets because they are not included in the category of *muktzah*, because pets do have an "immediate practical use"—namely, providing people with pleasure and companionship.[12]

The Synoptic Gospels make it clear that even the injunctions of *muktzah*, which are prohibitions enacted by the sages alone, were considered by first century Christians to be authoritative and an integral part of Judaism. This is evident from a another conflict between Jesus and the Pharisees over Sabbath-healing.

In Matthew 12:9-13, Mark 3:1-5, and Luke 6:6-10, Jesus is criticized by the Pharisees for healing a man on the Sabbath. Employing the Talmudic *kal v'chomer* logic (*a fortiori* argument), Jesus illustrates that his actions are permissible, not based on the Written or Oral Torah, but rather upon the authority of the rabbinic prohibition of *muktzah*!

> And behold, there was a man who had a withered hand, and they asked Him, saying, "Is it lawful to heal on the Sabbath?"—that they might accuse Him. Then he said to them, "What man is there among you who has one sheep, and if it falls into a pit on the Sabbath, will not lay hold of it and lift it out? Of how much more value then is a man than a sheep? Therefore it is lawful to do good on the Sabbath."
> (Matthew 12:10-12)

Jesus' point here is that although there is a rabbinic prohibition against handling an animal on the Sabbath, nevertheless, to alleviate the pain and suffering of an animal, the sages specifically enacted a special dispensation permitting a Jew to rescue an animal that is stuck in a ditch. Employing rabbinic reasoning, Jesus claims that if it is permitted to rescue a distressed sheep on the Sabbath, how much more so is it permitted to heal an infirm person on the Sabbath.

What is the source for the framework and logic of this argument? Where does it state in either the Written or Oral Law that it is forbidden to handle an animal on the Sabbath? What is the source for the special dispensation to handle a distressed animal in order to rescue it from a ditch? The source for both the rabbinic prohibition and dispensation is conveyed verbatim in the Babylonian Talmud, which was written 500 years after this supposed argument between Jesus and the Pharisees took place!

The passages dealing with alleviating the pain of a distressed animal on the Sabbath are found in the Talmud (Sabbath 128b), where the sages teach that if an animal falls into a pit, one should provide food and water so that it does not suffer and perish. If despite this effort the animal remains in distress, one is permitted to place pillows and bolsters beneath it in order for it to climb out of the pit. Simply put, Jesus was employing the authority of the rabbinic injunction and exception to prove that it is permitted to heal on the Sabbath.

Clearly, this account is fictitious because, as mentioned earlier, there is no prohibition against praying for someone's recovery on the Sabbath. Nevertheless, the New Testament authors used rabbinic praxis to fashion their fanciful stories.

Once again, these passages create insurmountable problems for critics of rabbinic Judaism. Moreover, it is doubtful that the intricate argument in this Gospel narrative makes sense to ordinary churchgoing Christians. Yet, although they do not grasp the story's underlying logic, parishioners are reassured by these passages that Jesus was the wise and compassionate son of God, and his interlocutors were the merciless, blind, stubborn opponents of God.

Given that the Oral Law was considered sacred by the first Christians, how did it eventually come to be reviled, slandered, and consigned to the flames countless times in the Middle Ages, and why has it has been subjected to similar indignities in the recent past?

Why did Christendom reject the Oral Law?

While the Written Law is inscribed on parchment, the Oral Torah is inscribed on the hearts, minds, and lips of the children of Israel. The chain of oral tradition was conveyed at Mount Sinai, and transmitted from father to son and master to disciple.

In essence, the Jewish people are the living, breathing vessel in which God chose to bear, protect and convey these sacred oracles. Because the Church would regard the Jewish people as accursed for committing the most serious and outrageous crime in history, they had to reject the notion that such an odious nation can be the repository of the sacred teachings of the God whom they murdered.

Although the earliest Christians regarded the Oral Law as authoritative, there was a decisive, anti-Jewish trend that quickly developed during the first few centuries of the Church. By the second century, theologians and Church Fathers became more concerned with making the break with anything Jewish, and pursued an uncompromising posture of theological and political opposition to their elder rival.

The trajectory of growing anti-Jewish emphasis can be observed in the New Testament itself. Looking chronologically at the Gospels, as time passed, the fact that the Romans killed Jesus retreats into the background, and the Jewish people are portrayed as increasingly guilty for Jesus' crucifixion.

The Book of Mark, the earliest Gospel, indicates that both the Jewish leaders and the Roman governor, Pontius Pilate decided to execute Jesus. Even in Mark's account, the Jews are prodding Pilate who is reluctant. In the Book of Luke, written about 15 years after Mark, Pontius Pilate repeatedly insists that Jesus is innocent. In this account, the culpability for the crucifixion falls squarely upon the Jewish people who demanded it. Pilate not only agrees that Jesus did not conspire against Rome, but Herod Antipas, the tetrarch of the Galilee, also finds nothing treasonable in Jesus' actions.

In the Book of Matthew, which was written at about the same time as Luke, Pilate washes his hands in order to demonstrate that he is blameless for Jesus' fate. The culmination of this gruesome spectacle, and arguably the one verse that has caused more Jewish suffering than any other New Testament passage, is the uniquely Matthean attribution to the Jewish people: "His blood be on us and on our children!" (27:25).

The Passion Narrative in the Book of John, which was written about 15 years after Luke and Matthew, takes the grizzly story to a whole new level of indictment against the Jews:

> Then Pilate said to Him, "Are You not speaking to me? Do You not know that I have power to crucify You, and power to release You?" Jesus answered, "You could have no power at all against Me unless it had been given you from above. Therefore the one who delivered Me to you has the greater sin." From then on Pilate sought to release Him, but the Jews cried out, saying, "If you let this Man go, you are not Caesar's friend. Whoever makes himself a king speaks against Caesar." When Pilate therefore heard that saying, he brought Jesus out and sat down in the judgment seat in a place that is called The Pavement, but in Hebrew, Gabbatha. Now it was the Preparation Day of the Passover, and about the sixth hour. And he said to the Jews, "Behold your King!" But they cried out, "Away with Him, away with Him! Crucify Him!" Pilate said to them, "Shall I crucify your King?" The chief priests answered, "We have no king but Caesar!" Then he delivered Him to them to be crucified. So they took Jesus and led Him away.
>
> (John 19:10-16)

In this last canonical Gospel, Jesus explicitly tells Pilate that the sin of the Jews is greatest, for the Roman governor is powerless to halt the execution. In John's story, the Jewish people reject Jesus as their King, proclaiming "we have no king but Caesar!" With this odious declaration, John portrays the Jews as simultaneously rejecting God as their King as well! The fourth Gospel then claims that Pilate "handed Jesus over to them [the Jews] to be crucified" (19:16). In this outlandish story, it is the Jews who actually take custody of Jesus to be executed!

According to some Eastern Orthodox traditions, Pilate committed suicide out of remorse for having sentenced Jesus to death. The Ethiopian Orthodox Church actually recognized Pilate as a saint in the 6th century based on these claims.

Second century Christian epistles, which were widely read and came close to being included in the New Testament canon, are even more extreme in their depiction of the Jews. For example, the *Gospel of Peter*, which was written in the early second century, explicitly states that "none of the Jews" would wash their hands of Jesus' blood. Moreover, this Gospel claims that it was the Jewish king Herod rather than Pilate who orders the crucifixion. This is followed by the Jews expressing responsibility for Jesus' death, and anticipating that God will punish them for their crime by destroying Jerusalem and the Temple.

Another book that was nearly included into the Christian canon is the *Epistle of Barnabas*, which was written anonymously in about the year 135 CE. This book launches some of the most vile, spiteful assaults on the Jewish people from the early Christian period. Strangely, in an effort to demonstrate the superiority of the Church over the Synagogue, the author maligns Judaism as a religion that is and always has been false, going all the way back to the time of Moses! According to the author, the Jews lost the covenant when Moses descended from Mount Sinai and smashed the Ten Commandments to pieces. In essence, as the Church grew older, the Jews were increasingly demonized, and the Roman culpability for Jesus' execution quickly evaporated.

Thankfully, these books were not included in the New Testament canon. Had they been included, Jewish-Christian relations would have been worse, if that was even possible.

The second century Church embraced Replacement Theology and was now the "New Israel." Accordingly, Christendom was compelled in every way to discredit the Old Israel. It did so by making anti-Jewish theology an integral part of Christian apologetics, thus entirely rejecting the Jewish oral tradition, casting it as profoundly noxious. The Church Fathers turned out volumes of literature to prove that Christians were the true people of God, and that Judaism had only been a prelude to, or in preparation for, Christianity.

The Jews were no more the Chosen People. Instead, they were the Christ-killers, and as a result, lost the covenant that they once possessed. The Church was now the embodiment of the "New Covenant," heir to all the blessings originally bestowed upon the Old Israel.

The war of the Christian Church against the Jews continued with the Church Fathers' relentless attacks on both the faith and peoplehood of the Jewish people. Early Christian commentators taught that the Old Covenant was fulfilled and replaced (superseded) by the New Covenant in Christ.

For instance, the Church Father Tertullian (ca.160 – ca.220 CE), the prolific Christian apologist and theologian, declared:

> Who else, therefore, are understood but we, who, fully taught by the new law, observe these practices—the old law being obliterated, the coming of whose abolition the action itself demonstrates.... Therefore, as we have shown above that the coming cessation of the old law and of the carnal circumcision was declared, so, too, the observance of the new law and the spiritual circumcision has shone out into the voluntary observances of peace.[13]

As the Church came into power in the 4th century under Rome's first Christian emperor, Constantine, it turned on the Synagogue with even greater intensity. Jewish civil and religious status was deteriorating thanks to the influence that the bishops had in the political arena. Laws were passed making it a capital offense for any Jew to make a convert, they were excluded from various professions, denied all civil honors, and their autonomy of worship was severely threatened. In every way, they were being discriminated against.

Christians felt that their belief in divine punishment was now supported by this growing evidence of Jewish misery.

Saint Ambrose, who was a bishop of Milan and became one of the most influential ecclesiastical figures of the 4th century, defended fellow bishops and monks for burning a synagogue at Callinicum and asked, "Who cares if a synagogue—home of insanity and unbelief—is destroyed? What real wrong is there, after all, in destroying a synagogue, a home of perfidy, a home of impiety, in which Christ is daily blasphemed?"[14]

When did the Church officially reject the Oral Law?

The first Christians, Jewish and Gentile, followed the Hebrew calendar (Acts 2:1; 12:3; 20:6; 27:9; 1 Cor. 16:8), and did not celebrate any specifically Christian annual festivals. Direct evidence for the Easter festival begins to appear in the mid-2nd century, when this feast emerged as the central Church holiday of the Christian liturgical year.[15] The conflict between the Latin and Eastern churches over the date of Easter erupted in the years that would follow. This schism was resolved at the Council of Nicaea, where the Church officially rejected the Jewish calendar, and thereby the Oral Torah. In order to fully comprehend the link between the ecumenical conflict over Easter (called *Pascha* in Greek and Latin) and the Oral Torah, a brief overview of the Jewish calendar is essential.

The Oral Law Contained the information necessary to produce a precise Jewish calendar

The first commandment given to the Jewish people instructed them to sanctify the new moon, necessitating the construction of their own calendar (Exodus 12:2). What resulted is the most precise calendar ever produced. Where did the Jews acquire the vital information that enabled them to produce the most accurate calendar created by any civilization? Even NASA and the U.S. Naval Observatory have to throw in a leap-second now and again to "fix" the civil (solar) calendar. The Jewish people, on the other hand, have no need to add a split second to correct their calendar, which is far more complex than a simple solar calendar. Where did the Children of Israel obtain this unique knowledge?

While it is beyond the scope of this book to present a complete explanation of the Jewish calendar, I will briefly explain how its structure and calculations are based on the Oral Torah.

People frequently ask, "When does Passover come out this year?" The answer is simple: on the 15th day of Nisan. In reality, however, this common question and its snap answer raises an important point: the date of Jewish holidays does not change from year to year. Although holidays are celebrated on the same day of the Jewish calendar every year, the Jewish year is not the same length as a solar calendar used by most of the western world, so the date shifts on the civil calendar.

Therefore, the Jewish calendar or fixed lunar year, which is based on twelve lunar months of twenty-nine or thirty days, requires an intercalary lunar month added about seven times every nineteen years (once every two to three years). This is necessary in order to synchronize the twelve monthly lunar cycles with the slightly longer solar year. Each Jewish lunar month starts with the new moon. Although originally the new lunar crescent had to be observed and certified by witnesses, the birth of the new moon is now assessed arithmetically.

The Jewish calendar is a *lunisolar* calendar based on three astronomical phenomena: the rotation of the Earth about its axis (a day); the revolution of the moon about the Earth (a synodic month); and the revolution of the Earth about the sun (a solar year).

These three phenomena are not contingent upon each other, so there is no direct correspondence between them. On average, the moon revolves around the Earth in about 29½ days. The Earth revolves around the sun in about 365¼ days, that is, about 12.4 lunar months.

With the exception of the Islamic world, which uses the pure lunar *Hijri Qamari* calendar, the civil calendar used by most of the world has abandoned any correlation between the moon cycles and the month, arbitrarily setting the length of months to 28, 29, 30 or 31 days.

Thus, the Jewish calendar coordinates all three of these astronomical phenomena. Months are either 29 or 30 days, corresponding to the 29½-day lunar cycle. Years are either 12 or 13 months, corresponding to the 12.4 month solar cycle. (The Islamic calendar makes no attempt to harmonize with the solar cycle. As a result, Islamic holidays can and do appear in all different seasons from year to year.)

The lunar month on the Jewish calendar begins when the first sliver of moon becomes visible after its dark phase of the moon. But in ancient times, the new months were determined by observation. When people observed the new moon, they would notify the Sanhedrin.[16] Once the Sanhedrin heard testimony from two independent, reliable eyewitnesses that the new moon occurred on a certain date, they would declare the *Rosh Chodesh* (first of the month) and send out messengers to inform to Jewish communities worldwide when the next month had begun.

Adherence to a strictly lunar calendar would create a monumental problem for Jews. Herein lies the difficulty: The Torah states that Passover, which begins on the 15th day of the first month of Nisan, must occur during the "springtime" (Deuteronomy 16:1). The lunar calendar, however, does not determine the seasons. "Springtime" is influenced by the solar calender alone. There are approximately 12.4 lunar months in every solar year, so a 12-month lunar calendar, which is 354 days, is about 11 days shorter than a solar year and a 13-month lunar is about 19 days longer than a solar year. The months would then drift around the seasons on such a calendar. On a 12-month lunar calendar, the month of Nisan, which is supposed to occur in the spring, would occur 11 days earlier in the season each year, eventually occurring in the winter, the fall, the summer, and then the spring again. If no adjustments were made to a pure lunar calendar, in eight years for Passover were to fall out in the winter! On a 13-month lunar calendar, the same thing would happen in the other direction, and much sooner. For good reason there is no commandment in the Torah that a year must have only 12 months.

Therefore, to compensate for this drift, the Jewish calendar uses a 12-month lunar calendar with an extra month occasionally added. The month of Nissan occurs 11 days earlier each year for two or three years, and then jumps forward 30 days, balancing out the drift. In ancient times, this month was added by observation: the Sanhedrin observed the conditions of the weather, the crops and the livestock, and if these were not sufficiently advanced to be considered "spring," then the Sanhedrin inserted an additional month into the calendar to make sure that Passover would occur in the spring, as mandated in the Torah. A year with 13 months is referred to in Hebrew as a *shanah me'uberet*, literally, "a pregnant year." In English, we commonly call it a leap year.

As mentioned earlier, by the fourth century, the Jews were subject to bitter persecution under Constantine, who, following the tyranny of Hadrian, forbade the Jews from holding meetings in order to determine intercalations. The increasing despotism of Rome forced the Jews to determine the time of the new moons and feasts independently of eye witnesses. Yet the entire Jewish nation, the vast majority of which lived in the diaspora, depended upon the calendar sanctioned by the Sanhedrin in the land of Israel. By the fourth century, significant danger had threatened the communication required for fixing the Jewish holidays. Without a fixed calendar, the life-cycle of the Jews would have been shattered. It is in the context of this religious and political upheaval that Hillel II established a fixed calendar based on a special calculation. The adoption of the fixed calendar, at about the middle of the fourth century, made it possible for Jews everywhere to determine the first day of the month without actual visual observation. The Jewish calendar is regarded to be the most brilliant achievement of its kind.

Where did this brilliance come from? What essential knowledge did Hillel II require in order forge an accurate calendar that would be precise for thousands of years, until the messianic age?

One critical piece of information was essential in order to perfectly align the lunar cycle with the solar years: The exact average length of a lunar month. This information is found in the Oral Torah:

> Rabban Gamaliel said to them: "I have it on the authority of the house of my father's father that the renewal of the moon takes place after not less than twenty-nine days and a half and two-thirds of an hour and seventy-three *halakim*."
>
> (Talmud, Rosh Hashanah 25a)

The accuracy of the Jewish lunisolar calendar is fixed by the value of the mean lunation period coupled to the 19 year cycle of 235 lunar months. This is called a *molad* (new moon), which is, according to the Oral Torah, exactly 29 days, 12 hours and 793 *halakim* (parts), or 3 1\3 seconds. There are 1080 *halakim* in each hour; thus, one *helek* is 3 1/3 seconds. Therefore, 793/1080 = 0.734529 hours = 0.03059 days. Accordingly, if we add 29.5 days with 0.03059 days, we receive an exact total of 29.53059 days. This computation transmitted by the Talmud is so precise that any mean lunar conjunction can be found within 1 day in 14,000 years! A 1-day error in 14,000 years! (Gregorian: 1 day per 3,300 years error; Julian: 1 day in 128 years error). This calendar, still in use, standardizes the length of months and the addition of months over the course of a 19-year cycle, so that the lunar calendar realigns perfectly with the solar years (see pages 307 - 309).

Who could have access to this sort of information? According to Jewish tradition, the Almighty supplied this knowledge to the Children of Israel so that their covenant with God can be maintained wherever they are scattered. Accordingly, the prophet Jeremiah umbilically connects the One Who set the celestial ordinances in their place with His eternal covenant with Israel:

> Thus says the Lord, Who gives the sun for a light by day, the ordinances of the moon and the stars for a light by night, Who disturbs the sea, and its waves roar. The Lord of hosts is His name. If those ordinances depart from before Me," says the Lord, "Then the seed of Israel shall also cease from being a nation before Me forever.
> (Jeremiah 31:35-36)

The message of the prophet is simple: Look up at the sun, the moon and the stars. The covenant that God forged with the nation of Israel is intact if these bodies are properly aligned in their place.

It is an eternal covenant.

Students have asked why God would give His people a calculation that was only accurate to one day in 14,000 years. After all, the Almighty could have conveyed a calculation that is even more accurate, perhaps to one day in 100,000 years, or eternity! Why did He stop short precisely at a calculation that is accurate for only one day in 14,000 years? The answer to this question is eye-opening: The Talmud,[17] Midrash,[18] and the Kabbalistic work, the Zohar,[19] state that the "deadline" by which the Messiah must appear is 6,000 years from creation, and therefore no more precise information was needed.

The great schism between the Latin and Eastern Church over the date of celebrating Easter

The violent controversy that exploded in the ancient church regarding the time of the Easter feast—the most important holiday on the Christian liturgical calendar and the fast connected with it—erupted into a warring confrontation almost as fierce as the later schism that challenged the primacy of Rome.

The Easter/Paschal controversies of the ante-Nicene age grew in stages and intensity, and are a very complicated chapter in ancient Church history. Strangely, the contention was purely ritualistic and disciplinary, and involved no dogma. All the interlocutors completely embraced the teachings of Paul. And yet this polarizing division threatened to split the churches; all the opposing parties demanded external uniformity. Quite directly, however, the conflict involved the question of the dependence of Christianity on Judaism and its all-important Jewish Calendar.

During the second century, most Christians in Asian Minor celebrated Easter on the 14th of Nisan, the eve of the Jewish festival of Passover, even though this date fell on a day other than Sunday. They based this date on the Book of John, which linked the crucifixion day with the killing of the lambs. However, Roman and most other Christians celebrated Easter on the Sunday following the 14th of Nisan, to coincide with the day of resurrection. Although Victor I, who was the Pope from 189 to 199 CE, required the churches of Asian Minor to follow the day of Easter with the Latin Church, they refused to abandon their tradition. Then, the conflict regarding this issue became more and more serious between the Latin and Eastern churches.

Around 195, Pope Victor I attempted to excommunicate the *Quartodecimans*, turning the divergence of practice into a full-blown ecclesiastical controversy. "Quartodecimanism," a word not used in Eusebius' account (which was written in Greek), is the Latin term for the practice of fixing the celebration of Passover for Christians on the fourteenth (Latin: *quarta decima*) day of Nisan in the Hebrew Calendar (Lev. 23:5). According to the Gospel of John (for example John 19:14), this was the day that Jesus was crucified.

According to Eusebius,[20] synods were convened and letters were exchanged, but in the end, having overstepped his mark, Pope Victor was rebuked and had to back down.

Bishops Polycarp (69 – 155 CE) and Melito (d. 180 CE), of Sardis (Asia Minor), were both regarded by the Church Fathers as among the most esteemed early Christian leaders, were notable Quartodecimans.

The Synoptic Gospels place the day of Jesus' Crucifixion on the 15th day of Nisan, a day later than the Book of John. Accordingly, some sects calibrated Easter a day later than the rest. This fierce, manifold schism had severely divided the early Church into many camps. Essentially, Christians in Rome who came from Asia Minor were celebrating Easter on one date, while others were celebrating it on another date. Some were fasting while others were not.

Moreover, many bishops of Rome considered it detestable to follow the Jewish tradition altogether and struggled to solve this problem. The Easter dating dispute was an explosive issue in Christendom and became one of the important reasons for the division of churches.

It is not known how long the Nisan 14 practice continued. But both those who followed the Nisan 14 custom, and those who set Easter to the following Sunday (the Sunday of Unleavened Bread) had in common the custom of consulting their Jewish neighbors to learn when the month of Nisan would fall, and setting their festival accordingly.

By the 3rd century, however, Christian leaders openly expressed disgust with the custom of relying on the Jewish community to determine the date of Easter. Brewing beneath the surface was the unresolved question whether Christians should follow Jewish practices altogether. As the bitter conflict continued through the 4th century, the strident anti-Jewish tone of the confrontation was reaching a feverish pitch. In essence, a growing number of powerful Christian leaders thought that it was undignified for Christians to depend on Jews to set the date of their most holy Christian festival, and sought out a method for calculating the date for Easter which was not linked in any manner to the Jews and their calendar.

Constantine's Council of Nicaea officially rejected the Jewish Calendar and thereby the Oral Torah

This controversy between those who advocated independence from the Jews, and those who wished to continue the custom of relying on the Jewish calendar, was formally resolved by the First Council of Nicaea in 325 CE, which endorsed the move to independent computations, effectively requiring the abandonment of the old custom of consulting the Jewish community in those places where it was still used.

Bear in mind that Constantine was by no means a devout Christian. This council was the first effort to attain a consensus within a deeply divided Church, as he sought to unify his empire. Moreover, the emperor's disdain for the Jews was shared by the church leaders during his reign. Accordingly, the Council of Nicaea ruled that all churches should follow a single rule for Easter, which should be computed independently of the Jewish calendar.

Thus, in a hate-filled letter to all churches concerning the date of Easter, Constantine did not conceal the fact that the Council of Nicaea's decision was born out of contempt for the Jews and their tradition:

> At the council we also considered the issue of our holiest day, Easter, and it was determined by common consent that everyone, everywhere should celebrate it on one and the same day.... In the first place, it seemed very unworthy for us to keep this most sacred feast following the custom of the Jews, a people who have soiled their hands in a most terrible outrage, and have thus polluted their souls, and are now deservedly blind.... Therefore have nothing in common with that most detestable people, the Jews. We have received another way from the Savior. In our holy religion we have set before us a course which is both valid and accurate. Let us unanimously pursue this. Let us, most honored brothers, withdraw ourselves from that detestable association. It is truly most absurd for them to boast that we are incapable of rightly observing these things without their instruction. On what subject are they competent to form a correct judgment, who, after that murder of their Lord lost their senses, and are led not by any rational motive, but by an uncontrollable impulsiveness to wherever their innate fury may drive them? Why then should we follow the example of those who are acknowledged to be infected with serious error? Surely we should never allow Easter to be kept twice in one and the same year! But even if these considerations were not laid before you, you should still be careful, both by diligence and prayer, that your pure souls should have nothing in common, or even seem to do so, with the customs of men so utterly depraved.[21]

> "Therefore have nothing in common with that most detestable people, the Jews"
> — Emperor Constantine, 325 CE

The First Council of Nicaea thus established the date of Easter as the first Sunday after the full moon following the northern hemisphere's vernal equinox, therefore severing Christendom's ecclesiastical attachment to the Jewish people and their Oral Torah.

The Roman Catholic Church discovers the Talmud

During the early centuries of the Middle Ages, as the Roman Catholic Church solidified its hegemony over western Christendom, Jews constituted only a tiny minority of the European population. With the remarkable growth of western Christendom from the year 1000 CE. onward, large numbers of Jews were both absorbed through Christian conquests and attracted by the civilization's dynamic expansion and development. As Jewish numbers increased, the Church and the Christian populace became increasingly cognizant of and concerned with western Christendom's Jewish minority. For a number of centuries, however, that awareness did not include genuine familiarity with Jewish religious thinking and practice. Jews continued to be viewed essentially in terms of what Christians knew from their New Testament and the writings of the Church Fathers and apologists rather than through direct knowledge of the religious beliefs and practices of the Jews living in Christian society.

From Christianity's inception, its critique of Judaism focused primarily on the failure of Jews to grasp the true meaning of the Jewish Scriptures. Church apologists insisted that the Hebrew Bible was filled with incontrovertible evidence that Jesus was the promised messiah, and yet the stiff-necked Jews stubbornly ignored these proof-texts.

During the Middle Ages, however, this modus operandi of long duration underwent a dramatic change. When Christian polemicists became cognizant of the existence of the Talmud, they began to identify this text as the greatest barrier to Jewish conversion. The Christian encounter with the Talmud did not merely add another focus to anti-Jewish polemic; it caused the Church to reevaluate its understanding of Judaism's role in a Christian world, and to reformulate its Jewry policy.

Up until this turning point, Augustine's perspective had set the tone: Jews in Christian lands could be subjected to legal and civil constraints, but they were not to be killed. After all, reasoned Augustine, while the Jews in their blindness failed to acknowledge that certain Scriptural prophecies had already been fulfilled, their tenacious adherence to Torah and miserable existence in exile bore witness to Scripture's truthfulness and authenticity. Moreover, wrote Augustine, if Jews were allowed to live unharmed, and were shown the error of their way, they might well come to acknowledge the truth of Christianity.[22]

The Christian encounter with the Talmud in the Middle Ages challenged the very assumptions of Augustine's doctrine and the policy that stemmed from it. It was now becoming apparent to Christians that the Church, over the course of centuries, had not taken into account the looming presence of the Talmud in Jewish life, nor reckoned with the fact that this text constituted a monumental, and perhaps insurmountable, impediment to Jewish conversion. In other words, when the Church discovered the Talmud, it felt compelled to reconsider its attitude toward the Jews.

Christians, however, knew little of the Oral Law that the Jews had committed to writing in recent centuries.

Since knowledge of the Talmud necessitated considerable linguistic mastery of Hebrew and Aramaic, Jews who converted to Christianity played a special role in early Christian knowledge of the Talmud. Moreover, the Jewish apostates were well aware of the central value of the Talmud for the Jews, and incited the Church to condemn and exploit the Talmud. They believed that Judaism could be eviscerated if they succeeded at destroying the Talmud.

The Talmud on Trial:
Contrasting two 13th century Christian-Jewish debates

In 1236, a Jew who converted to Christianity named Nicholas Donin appeared at the papal court. Details of his background are scant. Years earlier, Donin was excommunicated from the Jewish ghetto of Paris in the presence of the whole community. Having for ten years lived in the state of excommunication, he was baptized into the Roman Catholic Church and joined the Franciscan Order.[23]

Donin had a score to settle with the Jews.

As a Franciscan, Donin's first act of retaliation against his former coreligionists was to stir up some Crusaders to the bloody persecutions in Brittany, Poitou, and Anjou, in which 3,000 Jews were killed, 500 accepting the alternative of baptism.

Little is known as to how he made his way into the papal court. However he achieved his entrée, the message he brought was deeply disturbing to Church leadership. Donin made a number of damning allegations against the Talmud.

It appears that these serious accusations were studied carefully, since a three-year period elapsed between Donin's initial appearance at the papal court and the first concrete actions taken as a result of his claims.

Donin's accusations against the Talmud in his presentation before Pope Gregory IX were very serious, and stunned the Church. He presented 35 articles in which Donin stated his charges that the Talmud contained virulent blasphemy, vicious attacks on the virginity of Mary, and horrendous assaults against Jesus.

In June of 1239, Pope Gregory IX sent to the bishop of Paris, via Nicholas Donin, a set of letters addressed to the ecclesiastical and lay leadership of western Christendom. He requested that the bishop of Paris examine the letters and transmit them to the archbishops and the kings of France, England, Aragon, Navarre, Castile, Leon, and Portugal.[23] The letters to be transmitted contained wide-ranging indictments against the Talmud, including the following:

> If what is said about the Jews of France and of the other lands is true, no punishment would be sufficiently great or sufficiently worthy of their crime. For they, so we have heard, are not content with the Old Law which God gave Moses in writing; they even ignore it completely and affirm that God gave another law which is called the "Talmud," that is, "Teaching," handed down to Moses orally. Falsely, they allege that it was implanted in their minds, and unwritten, was there preserved until certain men came, whom they call "Sages" and "Scribes," men who, fearing that this law may be lost from the minds of men through forgetfulness, reduced it to writing. And the volume of this far exceeds the text of the Bible. In this contained matters so abusive and so unspeakable that it arouses shame in those who mention it and horror in those who hear it. Wherefore...this is said to be the chief cause that holds the Jews obstinate in their perfidy.[24]

The packet of letters carried by Donin also included a missive addressed to the bishop, the Dominicans, and the Franciscans of Paris, ordering them to scrutinize the books of the Jews, confiscated with the assistance of the lay authorities of all the kingdoms addressed. Books in which such errors existed, the Pope ordered, "you will cause to be burned at the stake."[25]

The routing of the papal letters through the bishop of Paris, and the special role of the Dominicans and Franciscans of the same city, suggest that Pope Gregory IX likely anticipated that the anti-Talmud initiative would be confined to the realm of the King Louis IX of France, who was by all standards a zealous, fanatical Christian and the only canonized king of France. The papal directive commanded that all the books of the Jews were to be confiscated on the first Sabbath of Lent in the following year

(March 3, 1240) while Jews attended their synagogue services, and then transferred to the mendicant friars for safekeeping. They were scrutinized by agents of the French monarchy, with Nicholas Donin seemingly playing a major role. A detailed bill of indictment was drawn up, with translated Talmudic passages adduced to substantiate each charge.[26] The suspicions of Pope Gregory IX about King Louis IX of France were proved correct because his order was generally ignored, except in France, where the Jews were compelled under pain of death to surrender their Talmuds (March, 1240).

Paris debate of 1242: The Talmud is put on trial

Louis IX ordered four of the most distinguished rabbis of France—Yechiel of Paris, Moses of Coucy, Judah of Melun, and Samuel ben Solomon of Château-Thierry—to answer Donin in a public debate. This was the first debate of its kind in medieval northern Europe, and was attended by religious and political notables of the Christian world. In vain, however, did the rabbis argue against the charges of blasphemy and immorality which were the main points of Donin's arraignment.

On June 25 and 26, 1240, Friar Nicholas Donin and Rabbi Yechiel of Paris confronted one another publicly in Paris. What emerged was an ecclesiastical show trial. The structure of the Paris debate was lopsided, favoring Nicholas Donin. The French rabbis were severely restricted in their responses at the Paris debate: Although they were permitted to defend the Talmud against the serious charge of blasphemy, they were forbidden to express anything during the proceedings that could be construed as offensive to Christianity. Donin, on the other hand, was given free reign to excoriate Judaism in any way he saw fit.

Few were therefore surprised at the outcome of the debate when the commission condemned the Talmud to be burned. The Jews managed to forestall implementation of the sentence, but after a number of delaying machinations, twenty-four wagon loads of Talmudic manuscripts—approximately 12,000 volumes of handwritten works—were publicly burned in Paris in the Place de Grève (the execution site which symbolized medieval French justice) over the course of one and a half days in 1242.

The loss of the holy works and resulting disruption of study among Jews contributed to the decline of the Jewish schools in northern France. Equally demoralizing for northern French Jewry was the vision of the Talmud, a symbol of Jewish faith, history, accomplishment, tradition, and values going up in flames. The Jews regarded the destruction of the Talmud as an almost unparalleled national catastrophe. After the Debate, Rabbi Yechiel left Paris for the Land of Israel in 1259.

The investigations of the Talmud in Paris in the 1240s along with the resulting confiscation and burning of Jewish books in France had a lasting impact on ecclesiastical policy as well. Previously, Jewish practices had been to some extent left to the Jews, so long as they had not interfered with Christian ritual or society. Now, Christian investigation into Jewish texts reflected a radical departure from established Jewry policy. Pope Gregory IX's intrusion into internal Jewish affairs had a negative impact upon the Church's established concept of some form of toleration of Jews and Judaism. Moreover, the public burnings of the Talmud demeaned Jews and Judaism in the eyes of the Christian populace who witnessed these public events. The very assertion that the Church had the right to confiscate, examine, and destroy Jewish literature—specifically the Talmud—set a new tone for Christian-Jewish relationships in centuries to come.

In the decade following this edict, many copies of the Talmud were publicly burned across Europe. The harsh policy launched by Pope Gregory IX, at the original instigation of the Nicholas Donin, was to be maintained and, if possible, expanded.[27]

Similar decrees were issued several times in the course of the 13th century, on one occasion by Pope Clement IV in 1264, when thousands of copies of the Talmud were consigned to the flames. The decree did not encompass all of Europe; in the Iberian Peninsula, for example, the Talmud was not burned but merely censored by statements considered derogatory to Christianity being removed. A Church synod in Basel in 1431 reaffirmed the stringent ban on the Talmud as well. In 1553, as the result of the Counter-Reformation, and due to the intense efforts of several Jewish converts to Christianity, Pope Julius III ordered the work burned again. This decree, carried out in various Italian states, resulted in the destruction of tens of thousands of copies of the Talmud.

At approximately the same time that Nicholas Donin appeared at the papal court and elicited papal condemnation of the Talmud, a second important 13th-century convert from Judaism to Christianity impacted Jewish life. Though, again, information is scarce, it is at least clear that this second convert grew up in the Jewish world of southern France. After converting to Christianity and joining the Dominican Order as Pablo Christiani, he began a preaching campaign among his former coreligionists, which was grounded in his knowledge of the Jewish faith and psyche.

Pablo Christiani, however, adopted an entirely opposite approach to exploiting the Talmud than Nicholas Donin. The major innovation of Pablo Christiani was his utilization of rabbinic sources for making the case for the Christian truth. Unlike the argument made by Donin that the Talmud had to be destroyed because it contained unspeakable blasphemies against Mary and Jesus, and was the major impediment to the conversion of the Jews, Christiani claimed that passages in the Talmud and other Rabbinic literature proved that Jesus was a divine messiah!

Pablo Christiani was well aware that the historic Christian-Jewish argument focused on the Hebrew Bible. More than most Christians, he was also aware that Jews were relatively immune to Christian argumentation rooted in key biblical verses, since Jews had their own powerful tradition of exegesis. Pablo Christiani was determined to show Jews that their rabbis in fact understood key biblical verses in ways similar to Christians. He attempted to argue that a close look at rabbinic exegesis—and indeed freestanding rabbinic dicta as well—would indicate acknowledgment of Christian truths by the rabbis. Therefore, Christiani adopted the opposite line of argumentation than that of Donin's.

Barcelona debate of 1263

Like Donin, Christiani sought an epic public debate with a renowned Jewish scholar to prove his point, and he chose the world's most illustrious sage as his opponent. This debate between Dominican Friar Pablo Christiani, the convert from Judaism to Christianity, and Rabbi Nachmanidies (whose full name, Rabbi Moshe ben Nahman Gerondi, is often abbreviated as Ramban). After all, he reasoned, if he could covert the greatest rabbinic luminary to Christianity, scores of other Jews would follow. This led to the most famous Jewish-Christian debate in history. The Disputation of Barcelona (July 20–24, 1263) was held at the royal palace of King James I of Aragon in the presence of the King, his court, and many prominent ecclesiastical dignitaries and knights.

Nachmanidies (b. Girona, 1194 – d. Land of Israel, 1270) was a towering Jewish figure in Spain, and was widely regarded as the greatest Jewish scholar of his generation. Aside from his position as the Catalan rabbi, he was a renowned philosopher, physician, kabbalist, and biblical commentator.

Until the Disputation of Barcelona, Nachmanidies seems to have led a largely untroubled life. He was well advanced in years when King James I of Aragon interrupted his life requesting that he participate in this debate, an event which eventually made him leave his family and country and wander in foreign lands. This was the religious disputation in which he was called upon to defend his faith in 1263. The debate was initiated by the apostate Pablo Christiani, who had been sent by the Dominican Master General, Raymond de Penyafort, to King James I of Aragon, with the request that the king order Nachmanidies to respond to charges against Judaism.

The stature of Nachmanidies made the encounter all the more meaningful. If the new argumentation advanced by Pablo Christiani could not be decisively rebutted by such a distinguished Jewish thinker, then the Jews of western Christendom would stand in very great danger.

Pablo Christiani had been trying to make the Jews abandon their religion and convert to Christianity. Relying upon the reserve his adversary would be forced to exercise due to fear of offending the feelings of the Christians, Pablo assured the King that he would prove the truth of Christianity from the Talmud and other rabbinical writings. Nachmanidies answered the order of the King, but demanded that he must be accorded complete freedom of speech during the debate.

Unlike the prior Paris debate that occurred only two decades earlier, King James I granted Nachmanidies permission to freely express himself during the proceedings. This authorization granted by the king to Nachmanidies was unprecedented, and enraged his Christian opponents. The debate turned on the following questions:[28]

1. whether the messiah had appeared or not
2. whether the messiah is divine or human
3. whether the Jews or the Christians held the true faith.

Based upon several *aggadic* passages (homiletic, non-legalistic exegetical texts), Christiani argued that Pharisaic sages believed that the Messiah had lived during the Talmudic period, and that they must therefore have believed that Jesus was the Messiah.

Nachmanidies countered that Christiani's interpretations of Talmudic passages were per-se distortions; the rabbis would not hint that Jesus was Messiah while, at the same time, explicitly opposing him as such:

> "Does he mean to say that the sages of the Talmud believed in Jesus as the messiah, and believed that he is both human and divine, as held by the Christians? However, it is well known that the incident of Jesus took place during the period of the Second Temple. He was born and killed prior to the destruction of the Temple, while the sages of the Talmud, like Rabbi Akiva and his associates, followed this destruction. Those who compiled the Mishnah, Rabbi and Rav Nathan, lived many years after the destruction. All the more so Rav Ashi who compiled the Talmud, who lived about four hundred years after the destruction. If these sages believed that Jesus was the

> messiah and that his faith and religion were true, and if they wrote these things from which Friar Paul intends to prove this, then how did they remain in the Jewish faith and in their former practice? For they were Jews, remained in the Jewish faith all their lives, and died Jews —they and their children and their students who heard their teachings. Why did they not convert and turn to the faith of Jesus, as Friar Paul did? ... If these sages believed in Jesus and in his faith, how is it that they did not do as Friar Paul, who apparently seems to understand their teachings better than they themselves do?"[29]

Nachmanidies noted that prophetic promises of the Messianic Age, a reign of universal peace and justice had not yet been fulfilled. On the contrary, since the appearance of Jesus, the world had been filled with violence and injustice, and among all religions the Christians were the most warlike. He asserted that questions of the Messiah are of less dogmatic importance to Jews than most Christians imagine, because it is more meritorious for the Jews to observe the precepts of the Torah under a Christian ruler, while in exile and suffering humiliation and abuse, than under the rule of the Messiah, when every one would perforce act in accordance with the Law.

Nachmanidies then demonstrated from numerous biblical and Talmudic sources that traditional Rabbinic Jewish belief ran contrary to Christiani's postulates, and showed that the Biblical prophets regarded the future messiah as a human, a person of flesh and blood, without ascribing to him divine attributes:

> "It seems most strange that the Creator of Heaven and Earth resorted to the womb of a certain Jewish lady, grew there for nine months and was born as an infant, and afterwards grew up and was betrayed into the hands of his enemies who sentenced him to death and executed him, and that afterwards... he came to life and returned to his original place. The mind of a Jew, or any other person, simply cannot tolerate these assertions. You have listened all your life to the priests who have filled your brain and the marrow of your bones with this doctrine, and it has settled into you because of that accustomed habit. I would argue that if you were hearing these ideas for the first time, now, as a grown adult, you would never have accepted them."

Christiani then claimed:

> "Behold the passage in Isaiah, chapter 53, tells of the death of the

messiah and how he was to fall into the hands of his enemies and how he was placed alongside the wicked, as happened to Jesus. Do you believe that this section speaks of the messiah?"

Nahmanides replied:

"In terms of the true meaning of the section, it speaks only of the people of Israel, which the prophets regularly call 'Israel My servant' or 'Jacob My servant.'"

As the disputation turned in favor of Nachmanidies, the Jews of Barcelona, fearing the resentment of the Dominicans, entreated him to discontinue; but the King, whom Nachmanidies had acquainted with the apprehensions of the Jews, desired him to proceed. At the end of the disputation it was clear that Nachmanidies had won the debate. King James awarded Nachmanidies a prize of 600 gold coins for his endeavors[30] and declared that never before had he heard "an unjust cause so nobly defended."[31] On the Sabbath after the debate, the king also attended the synagogue and addressed the Jewish congregants there, a thing unheard of during the Middle Ages.

Thus, in fundamentally divergent ways, the aggressiveness of medieval western Christendom brought the Talmud into majority consciousness.

On the one hand, making it the target of efforts to eradicate sacred Jewish literature deemed blasphemous and harmful, and, on the other hand, advancing the intensified Christian missionizing enterprise.

In essence, the Christian anti-Jewish polemic is not monolithic. Here too, a comparison of the methods of Christiani and Donin will prove instructive.

Both Donin and Christiani confronted their interlocutors based on Talmudic sources. Instead of seeking to merely undermine the Jewish presence in Christian Iberia (as Donin tried to do in northern Europe), Pablo attempted to prove the truth of Christianity to the Jews from the Talmud itself—that is, if rabbinic texts demonstrated the Christian truth, Jews would have no choice but to convert.

In contrast, Donin did not seem to have a positive goal in mind for his former coreligionists; he just wanted to defeat them.[32] Donin's purpose was destructive in nature. By pointing out Talmudic passages offensive to Christians, Donin sought to outlaw rabbinic texts so that Jewish survival would be untenable.

Thus we have two authors of polemical documents who based their anti-Jewish arguments on the same set of texts, the Talmud. Yet each Christian polemicist had a different goal, and accordingly, chose a different stratagem. Until this day, these two different approaches would sum up the Church's attitude toward the Talmud.

In the aftermath of the tumultuous Barcelona Debate, Nahmanides left Aragon and sojourned for three years in southern France. In 1267, seeking refuge in Muslim lands from Christian persecution, he made *aliyah* to Jerusalem. There he established a synagogue in the Old City that exists until this present day, known as the Ramban Synagogue. His reestablishment of Jewish communal life in Jerusalem, which had been decimated by the Crusaders, is notable in that it marked the beginning of more than 700 consecutive Jewish years in Jerusalem.

To arouse the interest of the Israeli Jews in the exposition of the Bible, Nahmanides wrote the greatest of his works, his commentary on the Torah. Nahmanides died after having passed the age of seventy-six.

According to tradition, his remains were interred as he requested, next to the building housing the Tomb of the Patriarchs and Matriarchs in Hebron.

Today, the attitude of fundamentalist Christians toward the Talmud has not changed much since the Paris and Barcelona Debates, and embrace the position of both Donin and Christiani. They regard Rabbinic works derisively, as an impediment to the conversion of the Jews, and at the same time their missionaries frequently quote the Talmud to prove that the ancient rabbis embraced the central tenets and interpretations of Christianity.

A Christian scholar defends the Talmud against the damning charges of an apostate Jew

I would be remiss if I failed to mention one of the strangest twists in Church history regarding the Talmud. In 1509, a Jewish convert to Christianity named Johannaes Pfefferkorn tried to incite Church leaders to burn the Talmud in all countries under the rule of Charles V. Born a Jew, possibly in Nuremberg,[35] Pfefferkorn moved to Cologne after many years of wandering. After committing a burglary, he was imprisoned and released in 1504.[36] He converted to Christianity in 1505 and was baptized together with his family.

Pfefferkorn became an assistant to the prior of the Dominican friar order at Cologne, Jacob van Hoogstraaten, and under the auspices of the Dominicans published several libelous pamphlets in which he tried to demonstrate that Jewish religious writings were hostile to Christianity. Pfefferkorn's animus toward his former coreligionists appeared shocking, even by Christian standards.

In his book *Der Judenspiegel* (Cologne, 1507), he demanded that the Jews should give up the practice of usury, attend Christian sermons, and do away with the Talmud. In his book *Judenfeind* (1509), he insisted that every Jew considers it a good deed to kill, or at least to mock, a Christian; therefore he deemed it the duty of all true Christians to expel the Jews from all Christian lands; if the law should forbid such a deed, they do not need to obey it: "It is the duty of the people to ask permission of the rulers to take from the Jews all their books except the Bible...."[37] He preached that Jewish children should be taken away from their parents and educated as Catholics. In conclusion he wrote: "Who afflicts the Jews is doing the will of God, and who seeks their benefit will incur damnation." He insisted the only way to get rid of the Jews was either to expel or enslave them; the first thing to be done was to collect all the copies of the Talmud found among the Jews and to burn them.

Through the help of the Elector and Archbishop of Mainz, Uriel von Gemmingen, the Jews asked the emperor to appoint a commission to investigate Pfefferkorn's damning accusations. A new imperial mandate of November 10, 1509, gave the direction of the whole affair to Gemmingen, with orders to secure the opinion from Johann Reuchlin. Professor Reuchlin (January 29, 1455 – June 30, 1522) was a leading German scholar of Greek and Hebrew. For much of his life, he was the real center of all Greek and Hebrew teaching in Germany. As one of the world's most renowned Christian Hebraists of his time, he mastered and commented on Rabbinic literature. Due to his extraordinary credentials, Ruchlin was appointed by Emperor Maximilian to a commission which was convened to review Pfefferkorn's grave charges against the Jews and the Talmud.

Ruchlin's final answer is dated October 6, 1510. In his response, he divides Jewish books into six classes—apart from the Bible which no one proposed to destroy—and, going through each class, he shows that the books openly insulting to Christianity are very few and viewed as worthless by most Jews themselves, while the others are either works necessary to the Jewish worship, which was licensed by papal as well as imperial law, or contain matter of value and scholarly interest which ought not to be sacrificed because they are connected with another faith than that of the Christians. He proposed that the emperor should decree that for ten years there be Hebrew chairs at every German university for which the Jews should furnish books.

As a result of Reuchlin's report, which favored the Jews and humiliated Pfefferkorn, the emperor suspended his edict of November 10, 1509, and the books were returned to the Jews on June 6, 1510. A fuming battle of pamphlets between Pfefferkorn and Reuchlin ensued for many years.

As it turned out, during a moment of great turmoil for the Jewish people, a champion of the Jews emerged in the form of a Christian.

The Messianic movement's attitude toward the Oral Law

"Messianic Judaism," a movement that emerged in the late 1960s in an in an effort to convert to Christianity Jews who would otherwise resist a straightforward Christian message, holds the same theological positions as fundamentalist Christians, but with a twist. Members of this Christian sect, who use Jewish culture and rituals in order to witness to Jews, regard the Talmud and other Rabbinic literature with contempt. Messianic leaders refer to normative Judaism derisively as "Rabbinic Judaism," and identify the beliefs of their own movement as "Biblical Judaism." Yet since its inception, the Messianic movement has produced countless booklets and tracts which quote the Talmud in order to prove that the rabbis believed that Jesus is the "Jewish" messiah—just as Pablo Christiani did nearly eight centuries ago.

There is, however, a strange irony with regard to the Messianic movement and groups like "Jews for Jesus." As I mentioned, there is no theological difference between these groups who target Jews for conversion and other fundamentalist Christians. In fact, most of the leaders of these groups are trained and indoctrinated in the same evangelical seminaries as other Christian clergy.

What then is the difference between a Messianic congregation and a Southern Baptist church down the same street? After all, they both embrace the identical doctrines. The distinction is that Messianic congregations employ Rabbinic traditions in their worship and Southern Baptist churches do not.

Herein lies the irony: the Messianic movement tactically uses Rabbinic Judaism, which they fiercely reject, in order to lure Jews into the baptismal pool. Moreover, although members of the Messianic movement routinely observe Rabbinic traditions like lighting Sabbath candles and wearing a yarmulka, they do not observe Scriptural prohibitions that appear explicitly in the Torah. Virtually all members of the Messianic movement cook with fire on the Sabbath day and wear clothing made of both wool and linen. In essence, Jews for Jesus-type groups routinely parade Rabbinic practices in an effort to convince Jews that it is "Jewish to believe in Jesus," but ignore Scriptural commandments because Paul insisted that the Law was replaced by faith in Jesus.

In spite of the efforts of the Church, the Torah remains an eternal gift to our nation that no fire can quench. After the Torah was given, the Oral Law enabled Jews to properly understand the Written Torah, to derive from the laws the principles that should be applied to new situations. That human intellect is capable of divining a degree of God's wisdom is one of His greatest gifts to man.

> He declared His *words* to Jacob, His statutes and His ordinances to Israel. He has not dealt so with any other nation; and therefore they do not understand His ordinances. Halleluyah!
>
> (Psalm 147:19-20)

Footnotes:

1. The term *Shas* is also used to refer to a complete Talmud, which follows the structure of the Mishnah. The six orders of the Talmud are:

   - Zeraim ("Seeds"), dealing with prayer and blessings, tithes and agricultural laws (11 tractates)
   - Moed ("Festival"), pertaining to the laws of the Sabbath and the Festivals (12 tractates)
   - Nashim ("Women"), concerning marriage and divorce, some forms of oaths and the laws of the nazirite (7 tractates)
   - Nezikin ("Damages"), dealing with civil and criminal law, the functioning of the courts and oaths (10 tractates)
   - Kodashim ("Holy things"), regarding sacrificial rites, the Temple, and the dietary laws (11 tractates) and
   - Tohorot ("Purities"), pertaining to the laws of purity and impurity, including the impurity of the dead, the laws of food purity and bodily purity (12 tractates).

   In each order (with the exception of Zeraim), tractates are arranged from biggest (in number of chapters) to smallest.

2. In all the passages in the Pentateuch regarding the Sabbath, none of them ever forbids carrying objects out of one's dwelling. . . . According to the book of Jeremiah, however, Jerusalem was destroyed for violating this oral tradition.

> Thus says the Lord: "Take heed to yourselves, and bear no burden on the Sabbath day, nor bring it in by the gates of Jerusalem; nor carry a burden out of your houses on the Sabbath day, nor do any work, but hallow the Sabbath day, as I commanded your fathers. But they did not obey nor incline their ear, but made their neck stiff, that they might not hear nor receive instruction. And it shall be, if you heed Me carefully," says the Lord, "to bring no burden through the gates of this city on the Sabbath day, but hallow the Sabbath day, to do no work in it, then shall enter the gates of this city kings and princes sitting on the throne of David, riding in chariots and on horses, they and their princes, accompanied by the men of Judah and the inhabitants of Jerusalem; and this city shall remain forever. And they shall come from the cities of Judah and from the places around Jerusalem, from the land of Benjamin and from the lowland, from the mountains and from the South, bringing burnt offerings and sacrifices grain offerings and incense, bringing sacrifices of praise to the house of the Lord. But if you do not listen to me, to keep the Sabbath day holy, and not to bear a burden and enter by the gates of Jerusalem on the Sabbath day, then I will kindle a fire in its gates, and it shall devour the palaces of Jerusalem and shall not be quenched."
>
> (Jeremiah 17:21-27)

3. The work, *Understanding the Dead Sea Scrolls* (Ktav, 2003), now contains Professor Lawrence H. Shiffman's article which explores this topic.

4. Josephus identifies three main Jewish sects at this time, the Pharisees, the Sadducees, and the Essenes. The Zealots were a "fourth sect," founded by Judas of Galilee (also called Judas of Gamala) and Zadok the Pharisee. The Zealots emerged as a political movement in 1st century, and sought to incite the Jews to rebel against the Roman Empire and expel it from the Holy land by force of arms, most notably during the Great Jewish Revolt (66-70). Theologically, they "agree in all other things with the Pharisaic notions; but they have an inviolable attachment to liberty, and say that God is to be their only Ruler and Lord." (*Jewish Antiquities* 18.1.6)

5. Josephus, *Jewish War* 2.119.

6. Josephus states, "The Sadducees have their support only among the rich, and the people do not follow them, while the Pharisees have the people for their ally." Josephus, Jewish Antiquities 12.298.

7. The Midrash (Hebrew: מדרש – meaning "to investigate" or "study") is a homiletic method of biblical exegesis. The term also refers to the whole compilation of homiletic teachings on the Bible. Midrash is a way of interpreting biblical stories that goes beyond simple distillation of religious, legal or moral teachings. It fills in many gaps left in the biblical narrative regarding events and personalities that are only hinted at.

8. A *kal v'chomer*, known in Latin as an argument *a fortiori*, is a tool of logic where the "heavier" case is derived from the "lighter case." For example, if the blood alcohol level at which a person is considered to be legally impaired for the operation of a vehicle in the state of New York is .1%, a person is certainly considered impaired with a blood alcohol level of .2%.

9. *Shulchan Aruch Harav*, Orach Chaim 308:78.

10. Interestingly, although many non-critical medicines and cures are forbidden on Sabbath for humans, for animals they are permitted.

11. There are two exceptions to this rule: 1) One may not lift the animal entirely. For that reason a bird's feet may not be moved because that will cause it to automatically lift off from the ground. 2) This is only permitted in a "private domain."

12. Rabbi Moshe Feinstein (Responsa *Igrot Moshe*, Orach Chaim vol. 5, responsa 22)

13. Tertullian, *An Answer to the Jews*, Chapter 3

14. *Epistolæ*, xl. xvi. 1101 et seq.

15. Cheslyn Jones, Geoffrey Wainwright, Edward Yarnold, and Paul Bradshaw, Eds., *The Study of Liturgy*, Revised Edition, Oxford University Press, New York, 1992, p. 474.

16. The Sanhedrin was the assembly appointed in the Biblical Land of Israel.

17. Talmud, Rosh Hashana 31a and Sanhedrin 97a

18. *Pirke De Rabbi Eliezer*, Gerald Friedlander, Sepher-Hermon Press, New York, 1981, p. 141.

19. Zohar (1:117a) and Zohar Vayera 119a

20. Eusebius of Caesarea (*Church History*, V, xxiv)

21. Eusebius, *Life of Constantine*, 3.18, in A Select Library of Nicene and Post-Nicene Fathers of the Christian Church, Second Series, Volume 14: *The Seven Ecumenical Councils*, Eerdmans, 1956, p. 54. *Socrates, Church History* 1.9, W. Bright, Socrates' ecclesiastical history, 2nd edition (Oxford: Clarendon Press, 1893)

22. Augustine, *City of God*. Trans. Demetrious B. Zema and Gerald G. Walsh (New York, 1950-1954), Book 18.

23. Eisenberg, Saadya, R., *Reading Medieval Religious Disputation: The 1240 "Debate" Between Rabbi Yehiel of Paris and Friar Nicholas Donin*, University of Michigan – 2008.

24. This letter in its Latin original and English translation is available in Solomon Grayzel (ed. and trans.), *The Church and the Jews in the XIIIth Century* (2 vols.; Philadelphia and New York: Dropsie College and Jewish Theological Seminary, 1933–1989), 1:238–241.

25. *Ibid.*, 1:240–243.

26. *Ibid.*, 1:242–243.

27. For full discussion of the bill of indictment, see Judah Rosenthal, "The Talmud on Trial," Jewish Quarterly Review 47 (1956–57), pp. 58–76 and 145–169.

28. Grayzel, *The Church and the Jews in the XIIIth Century*, 1:250–253.

29. "Disputations" (Jewish Encyclopedia, 1906 ed.)

30. *The Disputation of Barcelona (1263)*. Report of Moses Nahmanides, translated from Hebrew, and Anonymous Report, translated from Latin.

31. Wein, Berel (1993). *Herald of Destiny: The story of the Jews in the Medieval Era 750–1650*. Shaar Press. p. 171.

32. Slater, Elinor & Robert (1999): *Great Moments in Jewish History*. Jonathan David Company, Inc. p.168.

33. Eisenberg, Saadya, R., *Reading Medieval Religious Disputation: The 1240 "Debate" Between Rabbi Yehiel of Paris and Friar Nicholas Donin*, University of Michigan - 2008.

34. *Ibid*, pg. 10

35. Carlebach, Elisheva (2001). *Divided Souls: Converts from Judaism in Germany*, 1500-1750. Yale University Press. p. 52.

36. *Reuchlin, Pfefferkorn, and the Talmud in the Sixteenth and Seventeenth Centuries in The Babylonian Talmud.* The History of the Talmud translated by Michael L. Rodkinson. Book 10 Vol. I Chapter XIV (1918) p.76.

37. *Ibid*

Torah Exhorted Israel to Keep More than One Torah

Leviticus 26:46 ➡ These are the decrees, the ordinances, and the ***Torahs*** וְהַתּוֹרֹת (*plural*) that the Lord gave, between Himself and the Children of Israel, at Mount Sinai, through Moses.

Rosh Hashanah
(A "Day of Blowing"?)

Numbers 29:1
And in the seventh month, on the first day of the month, you shall have a holy convocation, you shall do no manner of work; it is a **day of blowing** for you.

Yom Kippur
(How do you "afflict Your soul"?)

Leviticus 16:31
It is a Sabbath of solemn rest for you, and *you shall **afflict your souls**,* it is a statute forever.

Zechariah Enumerates Four Rabbinic Fast Days

Zechariah 8:19
So said the Lord of Hosts: The fast of the fourth [month][1], and the fast of the fifth [month][2], the fast of the seventh [month][3], and the fast of the tenth [month][4] shall be for the house of Judah for joy and happiness and for happy holidays; so love truth and peace.

[1] The fast of Tammuz, which commemorates the breaching of the wall of Jerusalem.
[2] The fast of Av, when both Temples were destroyed.
[3] The fast of the assassination of Gedaliah.
[4] The fast of Teveth, which commemorates the siege of Jerusalem by the king of Babylon.

Sabbath Observance
(What kind of "work" is forbidden on Sabbath?)

Exodus 20:8-11
Remember the Sabbath day to sanctify it. Six days shall you work and accomplish all your work; but the seventh day is Sabbath to the Lord, your God; you shall **not do any work**...for in six days the Lord made the heavens and the earth, the sea and all that is in them, and He rested on the seventh day. Therefore, the Lord blessed the Sabbath day and sanctified it. *(see Exodus 31:12-17)*

(How do you not "leave Your place" on Sabbath?)

Exodus 16:29-30
Let every man **remain in his place; let no man leave his place** on the seventh day. The people rested on the seventh day.

(How do you "restrain Your foot" on Sabbath?)

Isaiah 58:13-14
If you **restrain your foot** because of the Sabbath, from performing your affairs on My holy day, and you call the Sabbath a delight, the holy of the Lord honored, and you honor it by not doing your wonted ways, by not pursuing your affairs and speaking words. Then you shall delight with the Lord...for the mouth of the Lord has spoken.

God Clearly Conveyed His Teachings to His People

Isaiah 45:19
I [God] **have not spoken in secret**, or in a place of the land of darkness. I did not say to the seed of Jacob "seek me in vain." I, Hashem, speak righteousness, I declare things that are upright.

Daniel Observed Prohibition Against Consuming Food and Wine Prepared by a Gentile

Daniel 1:3-16

King [Nebuchadnessar] told Ashpenaz, the chief of his officers, to bring from the children of Israel, from the royal seed, and from the nobles, youths in whom there was no blemish; good-looking, skillful in all wisdom, discriminating in knowledge, perceptive in learning, and who had the stamina to stand in the king's palace; and to teach them the script and language of the Chaldeans. And the king provided for them a daily portion from the king's food and from his wine to nurture them for three years, after which they should stand before the king. Among them, from the children of Judah, were Daniel, Chananyah, Mishael, and Azaryah... Daniel resolved not to be defiled by the king's food nor by his wine, and he asked the chief officer that he not be defiled. God granted Daniel favor and mercy before the chief officer, and the chief officer said to Daniel, "I fear my lord the king, who has provided you food and your drinks. For why should he see your faces more depressed than the youths like yourselves, and you will forfeit my head to the king?" So Daniel said to the steward whom the chief officer had assigned to Daniel, Chananyah, Mishael, and Azaryah, "Please test your servants for ten days, and let them give us pulse [raw seeds, peas, beans, etc.] to eat and water to drink. Then let our appearance and the appearance of the youths who eat the king's food be seen by you; in accord with what you will see, act toward your servants." He heeded them in this matter and tested them for ten days. At the end of ten days they looked better and fatter than all the youths eating the king's food. The steward would take their food and wine, and give them pulse.

Daniel Risked his Life in Order to Observe the Duty to Pray Three Times Each Day

Daniel 6:4-13

At this, the administrators and the satraps tried to find grounds for charges against Daniel in his conduct of government affairs, but thy were unable to do so. They could find no corruption in him, because he was trustworthy and neither corrupt nor negligent. Finally these men said, "We will never find any basis for charges against this man Daniel unless it has something to do with the law of his God...." The advisors and the governors have conferred that the king should issue an edict and enforce the decree that anyone who prays to any god or man during the next thirty days, except to you, O king, shall be thrown into the lions' den. Now, O king, issue the decree and put it in writing so that it cannot be altered.... So King Darius put the decree in writing. Now when Daniel learned that the decree had been published, he went home to his upstairs room where the windows opened toward Jerusalem. **Three times a day he got down on his knees and prayed**, giving thanks to God, just as he had done before. Then these men went as a group and found Daniel praying and asking God for help. So they went to the king and spoke to him about his royal decree: "Did you not publish a decree that during the next thirty days anyone who prays to any god or man except to you, O king, would be thrown into the lions' den?"... Then they said to the king, "Daniel, who is one of the exiles from Judah, pays no attention to you, O king, or to the decree you put in writing. **He still prays three times a day**."

Moses Admonished the Jewish Nation to Obediently Follow the Authority of the Sages of Israel

Deuteronomy 17:8-11

If a matter arises that is too hard for you to judge, between degrees of guilt of bloodshed, between one judgement or another, or between one punishment or another, matters of controversy within your gates, then you shall arise and go up to the place which the Lord your God chooses. And you shall come to the priests, the Levites, and to the judge in those days, and inquire of them; they shall pronounce the word of judgement. You shall do according to the sentence which they pronounce upon you in that place which the Lord chooses. And you shall be careful to do according to all that they order you. According to the teaching that they will teach you and according to the judgement that they will say to you, shall you do; do not deviate from the word that they will tell you, right or left.

Shechitah — Ritual Slaughtering

Deuteronomy 12:21
If the place that the Lord, your God, will choose to place His Name will be far from you, you may slaughter from your cattle and your flocks that the Lord has given you as I have commanded you, and you may eat in your cities according to your heart's entire desire.

The special method of slaughtering animals, called *Shechitah*, consists of an incision made across the neck of the animal or fowl by a qualified person especially trained for ritual slaughter, with a special knife that is razor-sharp and has a smooth edge with absolutely no nicks. The cutting must be made by moving the knife in a single swift and uninterrupted sweep, and not by pressure or by stabbing. The cut severs the main arteries, rendering the animal unconscious and permitting the blood to drain from the body. The slaughterer (*shochet*) recites a prayer before the act of *shechitah*.

Objection has sometimes been raised to this method of slaughter on grounds of cruelty. The sight of the struggling animal aroused the concern of humane societies, and in some European countries this resulted in legislation forbidding *shechitah*. Scientific opinion indicates, however, that severance of the carotid arteries and jugular vein by one swift movement results in almost immediate loss of consciousness, and the after-struggle is reflex muscular action.
Britannica Encyclopedia, "Kosher," 1990, vol 6, page 969.

Tefillin

Exodus 13:9
And it shall be for you a **sign** (לְאוֹת) on your arm and a reminder between your eyes — so that the Lord's Torah may be in your mouth — for with a strong hand the Lord removed you from Egypt.

Exodus 13:16
And it shall be a *sign* (לְאוֹת) upon your arm, and an **ornament** (לְטוֹטָפֹת) between your eyes, for with a strong hand the Lord removed us from Egypt.

Deuteronomy 6:8
Bind them as a *sign* (לְאוֹת) upon your arm and let them be **ornaments** (לְטוֹטָפֹת) between your eyes.

Deuteronomy 11:18
You shall place these words of Mine upon your heart and upon your soul; you shall bind them for a **sign** (לְאוֹת) upon your arm and let them be an **ornament** (לְטוֹטָפֹת) between your eyes.

(L) Earliest remains of Tefillin, both the leather containers and scrolls of parchment, found at Qumran among the Dead Sea Scrolls in 1955. The dig revealed the dating of the Tefillin to be approximately 2,100 years old. The source texts for Tefillin in the Torah are completely obscure. For example, the following verses from the *Shema* (Deut. 6:8) states: "And you shall bind them as a sign upon your arm, and they shall be as '*totafot*' between your eyes." The verse does not designate what specifically to "bind upon your arm," and the definition of *totafot* is not obvious — the only other appearances of this word are in identical contexts (Ex.13:16 and Deut.11:18). But the authoritative Oral Torah explains that it is these scriptural passages themselves (including the *Shema*) that are to be bound to the body in the form of Tefillin. It is only the Oral Torah that provides the details of the construction and application of Tefillin. What are a sign and a frontlet made of? What do they look like? Exactly where on the hand shall they be placed? Where is "Between the eyes"? Who must put on Tefillin and when? This vital information is contained only in the Oral Law.

First Century Christianity Did Not Question the Authority of The Oral Law

Matthew 23:1-3
Then Jesus spoke to the multitudes and to his disciples, saying, "**The scribes and the Pharisees sit in Moses' seat**: therefore all that they tell you, do and observe...."

Mark 2:23-26
And it came about that he [Jesus] was passing through the grainfields on the Sabbath, and his disciples began to make their way alone while picking the heads of grain. And the Pharisees were saying to him, "See here, why are they doing what is not lawful on the Sabbath?" And he said to them, "Have you never read what David did when he was in need and became hungry, he and his companions: how he entered the house of God in the time of **Abiathar** the high priest, and ate the consecrated bread, which is not lawful for anyone to eat except the priests, and he gave it also to those who were with him?"

I Samuel 21:1-4
Then David came to Nob to *Ahimelech the priest*; and Ahimelech came trembling to meet David, and said to him, "Why are you alone and no one with you?" And David said to **Ahimelech** the priest, "The king has commissioned me with a matter, and said to me, 'Let no one know anything about the matter on which I am sending you and with which I have commissioned you; and I have directed the young men to a certain place.' Now therefore, what do you have on hand? Give me five loaves of bread, or whatever can be found." And the priest answered David and said, "There is no ordinary bread on hand, but there is consecrated bread...."

"Salvation is of the Jews"

John 4:19-22
The [Samaritan] woman said to him, "Sir, I perceive that you are a prophet. Our fathers worshiped on this mountain [Mount Gerizim], and you Jews say that in Jerusalem is the place where one ought to worship." Jesus said to her, "....You worship what you do not know; we know what we worship, for salvation is of the Jews."

The Prophets Warn the Jewish People to Keep the Oral Law

The Prohibition of Purchasing and Selling on the Sabbath Day

Nehemiah 10:30-32

They held with their brethren, their noblemen, and entered the curse and the oath to follow the Law of God, which was given through Moses, the servant of God, and to keep and perform all the commandments of the Lord our God, and His ordinances and His statutes. And that we shall not give our daughters to the peoples of the land, and we shall not take their daughters for our sons. And as for the peoples of the land who bring merchandise and all grains on the Sabbath day to sell—we shall not purchase from them on the Sabbath or on holy days, and we shall abandon [the land] during the seventh year [and] the loan given by every hand.

Jews Warned that they Violated Sabbath Prohibitions Not Found In the Written Torah: Treading Winepresses, Carrying, and Selling Merchandise — the Oral Torah Lists these Restrictions

Nehemiah 13:15-18

In those days, I saw in Judea [people] treading winepresses on the Sabbath and bringing stacks [of grain] and loading them on donkeys, and also wine, grapes, figs, and all types of loads and bringing them to Jerusalem on the Sabbath day, and I warned them on the day they sold provisions. The Tyrians [who] sojourned there were bringing fish and all [types of] merchandise and selling on the Sabbath to the people of Judea and Jerusalem. I quarreled with the dignitaries of Judea, and I said to them, "What is this bad thing that you are doing—profaning the Sabbath day? Did not your ancestors do this, and our God brought upon us all this calamity, and upon this city, and you are increasing the wrath upon Israel by profaning the Sabbath?"

Jewish Identity Passes Exclusively Through the Mother

Ezra 10:2-3

We have betrayed our God, and we have taken in foreign wives of the peoples of the land, but now there is hope for Israel concerning this. Now, let us make a covenant with God to cast out all the wives and their offspring, by the counsel of the Lord, those who hasten to [perform] the commandment of our God, and according the Law it shall be done.

Jeremiah Reminds the Jewish People that it is forbidden to Carry on the Sabbath Day — A Prohibition Not Mentioned in The Written Torah

Jeremiah 17:19-24

So said the Lord to me. "Go and stand in the gate of the children of the people, in which the kings of Judah come, and out of which they go, and in all the gates of Jerusalem. And you shall say to them: 'Hearken to the word of the Lord, O kings of Judah and and all the inhabitants of Jerusalem, who come into these gates. So said the Lord: Beware for your souls and carry no burden on the sabbath day, nor bring into the gates of Jerusalem. Neither shall you take a burden out of your houses on the Sabbath day nor shall you perform any labor, and you shall hallow the Sabbath day as I commanded your forefathers. But they did not listen, neither did they bend their ears, and they hardened their nape not to listen and not to receive instruction. And it shall be if you listen to Me, says the Lord, not to bring any burden unto the gates of this city on the Sabbath day and to hallow the Sabbath day not to perform any labor thereon, then shall there enter into the gates of this city kings and princes sitting on David's throne...."

Identifying Signs of Clean Animals

Leviticus 11:1-8
God spoke to Moses and Aaron, telling them: ²Speak to the children of Israel, saying : These are the creatures that you may eat from among all the animals that are upon the earth. Everything among the animals that has a split hoof, which is completely separated into double hooves, and brings up its cud—that one you may eat. But this is what you shall not eat from among those that bring up their cud or that have split hooves: The camel, for it brings up its cud, but its hoof is not split—it is unclean to you; and the shafan, for it brings up its cud, but its hoof is not split—it is unclean to you;

and the arnevet, for it brings up its cud, but its hoof is not split—it is unclean to you; and the pig, for its hoof is split and its hoof is completely separated, but it does not chew its cud—it is unclean to you.

Was Moses a Zoologist?

Was Moses a hunter or an archer? This refutes those who maintain that the Torah was not divinely revealed. (Talmud, Hulin 60b)

Maimonides Laws of Forbidden Foods Chapter 1:2-3
2. The identifying signs of the clean animals are specified in the Torah as two: the true cloven hoof and the chewing of the cud (rumination). Both must be present. In addition, all ruminants have no incisor teeth in the upper jaw. All ruminants have cloven hoofs, with the sole exception of the camel. And all cloven hoofed animals ruminate, with the exception of the pig.
3. Consequently, if a person finds an animal in the wilderness whose species he cannot identify, he should examine its hoofs. If, however, the hoofs are missing (mutilated), he should examine the mouth. If it has no incisor teeth in its upper jaw he may be certain that it is a clean animal provided he can recognize a camel. If he finds an animal whose muzzle had been mutilated, he should examine the hoofs. If they are cloven, the animal is clean provided he can recognize a pig.

Identifying Signs of Clean Fish

Leviticus 11:9-12

This may you eat from everything that is in the water: everything that has fins and scales in the water, in the seas, and in the streams, those may you eat. That which does not have fins and scales in the seas and in the streams—from all that teems in the water, and from all living creatures in the water—they are an abomination to you. And they shall remain an abomination to you; you shall not eat of their flesh and you shall abominate their carcass. Everything that does not have fins and scales in the water—it is an abomination to you.

Was Moses a deep sea diver?

Mishnah: <u>Whatsoever has scales has fins</u>, but there are some that have fins and no scales.

Mishnah — Nida 6:9

Talmud: Then why did not the All Merciful write scales and there would be no need for the mention of fins? Rebbe Abbahu replied and so it was also taught at the school of Rebbe Yeshmael: *"To make the teaching great and glorious* (Isaiah 42:21 — ‏(יַגְדִּיל תּוֹרָה וְיַאְדִּיר‎)."

Maimonides: Laws of Proscribed Foods 1:24

24. With fish there are but two tokens, fins and scales. The fin is the organ with which it swims, and the scales form the covering over its whole body. *Every fish which has scales necessarily has also fins.* If it possesses none at the moment, but is known to possess them when fully grown, or if it has scales while it is in the sea, but sheds them when out of the water, it is deemed permitted. If its scales do not cover its whole body, it is still permitted. Even if it has only one scale or only one fin, it is deemed permitted.

The Jewish Calendar

Passover Must Occur in the Spring Time
You shall observe the month of springtime and perform the Pesach offering for the Lord, your God, for in the month of springtime the Lord, your God, took you out of Egypt at night. *(Deuteronomy 16:1)*

Pesach Offering Must Occur On 14th Day of the 1st Month (Nissan)
The Lord spoke to Moses, in the Wilderness of Sinai, in the second year from their exodus from the land of Egypt, in the first month, saying: "The Children of Israel shall make the Pesach offering in its *appointed time*. On the fourteenth day of this month in the afternoon shall you make it, in its *appointed time*; according to all its decrees and laws shall you make it." *(Numbers 9:1-3)*

Instructions for Calculating Month Were Transmitted as *a Secret*
My hand will be against the prophets who see vanity and who divine falsehood. *They shall not share the secret of My people*, and in the roll of the Family of Israel shall they not be written, and to the land of Israel shall they not enter. Then you shall know that I am the Lord God. *(Ezekiel 13:9)*

"They Shall not be in the council of My people," which refers to the council for intercalation. ***Talmud Ketubot 112a***

Hashem said to Moses and Aaron... "This month shall mark for you the beginning of the months..." (Ex. 12:1-2) At the moment when Moses received this commandment, the Holy One blessed be He, transmitted to him the precise rules of calculating the new moon. He made known to him the way to intercalate the year and establish the months, in order to fulfill the verse "Observe the spring month and offer a Passover sacrifice..." ***Midrash Sod Ha'Ibbur (see Talmud, Rosh Hashanah 25a)***

Maimonides' Laws of Sanctifying the Moon (6:2-3)

2. The day and the night consist of 24 hours, 12 for the day and 12 for the night, in any season. The hour is divided into 1,080 parts. The reason for dividing the hour into this number of parts is that this number may be divided without a remainder by two, four, eight, three, six, nine, five, and ten, and with these denominators the fractions may again be divided into many other parts.
3. By these figures, the interval between two conjunctions of moon and sun according to their mean motion is 29 days and 12 hours of the 30th day, beginning with the night of this day, and 793 parts of the 13th hour. That is the time which elapses between one (mean) conjunction and the other, and that is the duration of the lunar month.

According to the Oral Torah which was handed down by the sages of blessed memory, the time between one new moon and the next is 29 days 12 hours and 793 parts of an hour (the hour is divided into 1080 parts, see Maimonides).

$$\frac{793}{1080} = \underset{Hours}{(0.734529)} = \underset{Days}{(0.03059)}$$

If we add 29.5 days, we receive a total of 29.53059 days.

How does the figure 29.53059 compare with scientific calculations today?

"Facts of File Dictionary of Astronomy"

241   **moon**

month	reference point	length (days)
tropical	equinox to equinox	27.32158
sidereal	fixed star to fixed star	27.32166
anomalistic	apse to apse	27.55455
draconic	node to node	27.21222
synodic	new moon to new moon	29.53059

sky (see table). The differences in the monthly periods result from the complicated motion of the moon.

moon (or **Moon**). The only natural satellite of the earth, visible by virtue of reflected sunlight. It has a diameter of 3476 km, lies at a mean distance from the earth of 384,400 km, and completes one orbit around the earth in 27.322 days (*see* sidereal month; month). Its mass in relation to that of the earth is 1 : 81.3, i.e. 0.0123. It is in *synchronous rotation, i.e. it keeps the same face—the *nearside—toward the earth, although more than 50% of the moon's surface can be seen as a result of *libration. The same face is not however always turned towards the sun, the length of the solar day on the moon being equal to the moon's *synodic period, i.e. 29.53059 days. During this period —the *synodic month—the moon exhibits a cycle of *phases, reaching an apparent magnitude of -12.7 at full moon. It can also undergo *eclipses and produce *occultations.

The moon's mean orbital velocity is 10 km s^{-1}. Its orbital mo-

Ellingsworth, "*Facts of File Dictionary of Astronomy*," New York: 1985.

The New Encyclopedia Britannica
Volume 2, Micropeadia, 1990, Page 740

Calendar, any system for dividing time over extended periods, such as days, months, or years, and arranging such divisions in a definite order. A calendric system is essential for regulating the basic affairs of civil life—*e.g.*, agricultural, business, and domestic—and for reckoning time for religious observances and scientific purposes.

A brief treatment of calendars follows. For full treatment, *see* MACROPAEDIA: Calendar.

There are several standard units common to virtually all calendric systems. The day is the fundamental unit of computation in any calendar. It is to some extent a natural division of time, but its subdivision into a number of equal intervals of, for example, 24 hours is purely artificial.

The week, too, is an artificial division of time and cannot be correlated with any astronomical or natural phenomena except insofar as it is a closed cycle of days. The seven-day week that is now universally used may have been derived from the mystical significance attached to the number seven. Support of this view may perhaps be derived from the use of the names of gods and goddesses for each of the days (*see* week).

The month is a calendric period derived from lunation, the time interval in which the Moon completes a full cycle of its phases. This period, known as the synodic month, consists of 29.53059 days. As the earliest adopted of the longer calendar periods, it had a significance in religious observance. The age-old Jewish calendar, for instance, is a lunar one, as are the calendric systems still used by Islam and the Christian Church.

The year is based on the length of time it takes the Earth to orbit the Sun. There are several ways to measure this period, but the most common is the tropical year, which is the interval between successive passages of the Sun through the vernal equinox. The year thus computed consists of 365.242199 mean solar days, each of which is 24 hours 3 minutes 56.55 seconds long. The mean solar day is the average time it takes the Sun to cross the meridian twice.

Unfortunately, the tropical year and the synodic month are incommensurable: 12 lunations come to 254.36706 days, almost 11 days less than a tropical year. In addition, neither the tropical year nor the synodic month is evenly divisible by the length of the day. Therefore, to compile or maintain any calendar that keeps in step with the Moon's phases or with the seasons, it is necessary to insert days at appropriate intervals. These extra days are know as intercalations. The most familiar example of an intercalation is the additional day given to February every fourth year - *i.e.*, leap year.

The origin of the calendric system in general use today—the Gregorian calendar—can be traced back to the Roman republican calendar, which is thought to have been introduced by the fifth king of Rome, Tarquinius Priscus (616-579 BC). Although somewhat similar in style to the dating system of the ancient Greeks, this calendar was more likely derived from an earlier Roman calendar—a lunar calendric system of 10 months—that supposedly was devised around 738 BC by Romulus, traditionally the founder of Rome. The Roman republican calendar consisted of 12 months with a total of 355 days. Like its model, it was basically a lunar system, short by 10¼ days of the 365¼-day tropical year. To keep it in step with the seasons, a special month was supposed to be intercalated between February 23 and 24 once every two years; but because of negligence and political interference, the intercalations were made irregularly. As a result, by 46 BC the calendar had become so hopelessly confused that Julius Caesar was forced to initiate a reform of the entire system. Caesar invited the Alexandrian astronomer Sosigenes to undertake this task. Sosigenes suggested abandoning the lunar system altogether and replacing it with a tropical year of 365¼ days. Further, to correct the accumulation of previous errors, a total of 90 intercalary days had to be added to 46 BC, meaning that January 1, 45 BC, occurred in what would have been the middle of March. To prevent the problem from recurring, Sosigenes suggested that an extra day be added to every fourth February. The adoption of such reformatory measures resulted in the establishment of the Julian calendar, which was used for roughly the next 1,600 years.

During that time, however, the disagreement between the Julian year of 365.25 days and the tropical year of 365.242199 gradually produced significant errors. The discrepancy mounted at the rate of 11 minutes 14 seconds per year until it was a full 10 days in 1545, when the Council of Trent authorized Pope Paul III to take corrective action. No solution was found for many years. In 1572 Pope Gregory III agreed to issue a papal bull drawn up by the Jesuit astronomer Christopher Clavius. Ten years later, when the edict was finally proclaimed, 10 days in October were skipped to bring the calendar back in line. The length of the year was redefined was 365.2422 days, a difference of 0.0078 days per year from the Julian count, which produced a discrepancy between them amounting to 3.12 days every 400 years. Clavius had allowed for such a discrepancy in his suggestion that three out of every four centennial years, which would ordinarily be leap years, should be regarded as common years instead. This led to the practice that no centennial year could be a leap year unless it was divisible by 400. Following this rule, 1700, 1800, and 1900 were common years, but 2000 would be a leap year. These reform measures gave rise to an extremely accurate calendric system; the difference between the Gregorian calendar year and the solar year was less than half a minute. The Gregorian calendar, firmly establishing January 1 as the beginning of its year, was widely referred to as the new style calendar, with the Julian known as the old style calendar.

Although the Gregorian calendar is used throughout much of the world today, it was not immediately accepted everywhere. Most of the Roman Catholic states adopted the improved dating system by 1587. Some Protestant states embraced it around the beginning of the 18th century, but a number of others, such as Great Britain and its colonies, did not do so until the 1750s. Japan, China, and the Soviet Union, to name only a few, adopted the Gregorian rules much later. A few dating systems besides

God's Covenant With the Nation of Israel Is Eternal

Genesis 17:7

And I will establish My covenant between Me and you and your descendants after you throughout their generations, an *eternal covenant*; to be your God and the God of your descendants after you.

Genesis 17:19

And God said, Sarah thy wife shall bear thee a son indeed; and thou shalt call his name Isaac: and I will establish my covenant with him for an everlasting covenant, and with his seed after him.

Genesis 26:3-4

Stay in this land, and I will be with you and will bless you [Isaac]. For to you and your descendants I will give all these lands and will confirm the oath I swore to your father Abraham. ⁴I will make your descendants as numerous as the stars in the sky and will give them all these lands, and through your offspring all nations on earth will be blessed.

More than three centuries ago, King Louis XIV of France asked Blaise Pascal, the great French philosopher of his day, to give him proof of the existence of miracles. Without a moment's hesitation, Pascal answered, "Why, the Jews, your Majesty—the Jews." We don't have to speculate what Pascal meant when he gave this answer, because he took the trouble to spell it out.

In his masterwork, *Pensees*, he explained that the fact that the Jewish people had survived until the seventeenth century—the time period in which he lived—was nothing short of a supernatural phenomenon.

From Abraham to the Holocaust, and the birth of the State of Israel the Jewish people's progress through time violates all the laws of human history. How did this people survive against all the odds?

The pages of Tanach contain the promise that God chose the Children of Israel, in His wisdom and for His purpose, and made His eternal covenant with them.

Although the covenant God forged with the nation of Israel is eternal, and therefore it can never be broken, no individual Jew is guaranteed a place among corporate Israel.

The children of Israel were charged with a divine mission to be a "light unto the nations," and transmit an eternal message to the world. Historically, those Jews who rejected this sacred mandate were quickly lost among the gentiles over the course of just a few generations.

If Jesus was the messiah, why did God only preserve those Jews who, in spite of relentless persecution, did not believe this claim? Where are the descendants of the first Jews who followed Jesus 2,000 years ago? Why are none of them among us today as Jews? Why did God not preserve those Jews who adopted the tenets of Christianity over the course of history? Why did God only preserve those Jews who tenaciously remained loyal to the Written and Oral Law, and rejected the claims of the Church? What eye-opening message did the Almighty convey through His unique covenant with Israel?

Genesis 28:12-15

And he [Jacob] dreamed, and behold, there was a ladder set up on the earth, and the top of it reached to heaven. And behold, the angels of God were ascending and descending on it! [13]And behold, the Lord stood above it and said, "I am the Lord, the God of Abraham your father and the God of Isaac. The land on which you lie I will give to you and to your offspring. [14]Your offspring shall be like the dust of the earth, and you shall spread abroad to the west and to the east and to the north and to the south, and in you and your offspring shall all the families of the earth be blessed. [15]Behold, I am with you and will keep you wherever you go, and will bring you back to this land. For I will not leave you until I have done what I have promised you."

Leviticus 26:44-45

Yet even while they are in the land of their enemies, I will not reject or spurn them, lest I break My covenant with them by destroying them, for I am their God. [45]I will remember them because of the covenant I made with their forefathers, whom I brought out of the land of Egypt under the very eyes of the nations, so that I might be their God.

Deuteronomy 7:6-9

For you are a holy nation unto the Lord your God. The Lord your God has chosen you to be a special nation unto Himself, above all people upon the face of the earth. [7]The Lord did not set His love upon you, nor choose you, because you were more in number than any people, for you were the fewest of all the people. [8]But because the Lord loved you, and because He would keep the oath which He had sworn unto your fathers, has the Lord brought you out with a mighty hand, and redeemed you out of the house of bondmen, from the hand of Pharaoh king of Egypt. [9]Know, therefore, that the Lord your God, He is God, the faithful God, Who keeps His covenant and mercy with them that love Him and keep His commandments to a thousand generations....

2 Samuel 7:21-24

For the sake of your word and according to your will, you have done this great thing and made it known to your servant. [22]"How great you are, O Sovereign Lord! There is no one like you, and there is no God but you, as we have heard with our own ears. [23] And who is like your people Israel—the one nation on earth that God went out to redeem as a people for himself, and to make a name for himself, and to perform great and awesome wonders by driving out nations and their gods from before your people, whom you redeemed from Egypt? [24] You have established your people Israel as your very own forever, and you, O Lord, have become their God.

Continued

Joshua 1:3-6

I will give you every place where you set your foot, as I promised Moses. ⁴ Your territory will extend from the desert to Lebanon, and from the great river, the Euphrates—all the Hittite country—to the Great Sea on the west. ⁵ No one will be able to stand up against you all the days of your life. As I was with Moses, so I will be with you; I will never leave you nor forsake you. ⁶ Be strong and courageous, because you will lead these people to inherit the land I swore to their forefathers to give them.

Isaiah 43:1-7

But now thus saith the Lord Who created thee, O Jacob, He that formed thee, O Israel: Fear not, for I have redeemed thee, I have called thee by thy name, thou art Mine. ² When thou passeth through the waters, I will be with thee, and through the rivers, they shall not overflow thee; when thou walkest through the fire, thou shalt not be burned, neither shall the flame kindle upon thee. ³ For I am the Lord thy God, The Holy One of Israel, thy Savior; I have given Egypt as thy ransom, Ethiopia and Seba for thee. ⁴ Since thou art precious in My sight, and honorable, and I have loved thee; therefore will I give men for thee, and peoples for thy life. ⁵ Fear not, for I am with thee; I will bring thy seed from the east, and gather thee from the west; ⁶ I will say to the north: 'Give up,' and to the south: 'Keep not back, bring My sons from far, and My daughters from the end of the earth; ⁷ Every one that is called by My name, and whom I have created for My glory, I have formed him, yea, I have made him.'

Isaiah 49:13-15

Shout for joy, O heavens; rejoice, O earth; burst into song, O mountains! For the Lord comforts his people and will have compassion on his afflicted ones. ¹⁴ But Zion said, "The Lord has forsaken me, the Lord has forgotten me." ¹⁵ "Can a mother forget the baby at her breast and have no compassion on the child she has borne? Though she may forget, I will not forget you!"

Isaiah 54:10

For the mountains may move and the hills be shaken, but My love shall never move from you, nor My covenant of peace be shaken, said God, Who has compassion on you.

Isaiah 54:17

No weapon fashioned against you shall prevail; and every tongue that launches an accusation against you, you shall prove false. This is the heritage of the servants of God, their vindication from me, says God.

Isaiah 59:21

As for Me, this is My covenant with them, says God. My spirit, which rests upon you, and *My words which I have put in your mouth*, shall not depart from your mouth nor from the mouths of your children, nor from the mouths of your children's children, says God, from now on to all eternity.

Jeremiah 31:35-37

Thus saith the Lord, Who giveth the sun for a light by day, and the ordinances of the moon and of the stars for a light by night, who stirreth up the sea, that the waves thereof roar, the Lord of hosts is His name: [36] If these ordinances depart from before Me, saith the Lord, then the seed of Israel also shall cease from being a nation before Me for ever. [37] Thus saith the Lord: If heaven above can be measured, and the foundations of the earth searched out beneath, then will I also cast off all the seed of Israel for all that they have done, saith the Lord.

Jeremiah 33:25-26

Thus says the Lord: "If My covenant is not with day and night, and if I have not appointed the ordinances of heaven and earth, then I will cast away the descendants of Jacob and David My servant, so that I will not take any of his descendants to be rulers over the descendants of Abraham, Isaac, and Jacob. [26] For I will cause their captives to return, and will have mercy on them."

Jeremiah 46:27-28

But fear not O Jacob My servant, neither be dismayed, O Israel, because I shall redeem you from afar, and your children from the land of their captivity; and Jacob will again be quiet and at ease and none shall make him afraid. [28] Fear not, O Jacob My servant, said God, for I am with you. For I will topple all the nations to which I have driven you. But of you I will not make a full end. I will correct you in just measure, but I will not utterly destroy you.

Ezekiel 16:60

Yet I will remember the covenant I made with you in the days of your youth, and I will establish an everlasting covenant with you.

Ezekiel 37:25-28

They will live in the land I gave to my servant Jacob, the land where your fathers lived. They and their children and their children's children will live there forever, and David, my servant, will be their prince forever. [26] I will make a covenant

Continued

of peace with them; it will be an everlasting covenant. I will establish them and increase their numbers, and I will put my sanctuary among them forever. ^{27} My dwelling place will be with them; I will be their God, and they will be my people. ^{28} Then the nations will know that I, the Lord, make Israel holy, when my sanctuary is among them forever.

Ezekiel 39:22-29

So the house of Israel shall know that I am the Lord their God, from that day and forward. ^{23}And the nations shall know that the house of Israel went into captivity for their iniquity, because they broke faith with Me, and I hid My face from them; so I gave them into the hand of their adversaries, and they fell all of them by the sword. ^{24}According to their uncleanness and according to their transgressions did I unto them; and I hid My face from them. ^{25}Therefore thus saith the Lord God: Now will I bring back the captivity of Jacob, and have compassion upon the whole house of Israel; and I will be jealous for My holy name. ^{26}And they shall bear their shame, and all their breach of faith which they have committed against Me, when they shall dwell safely in their land, and none shall make them afraid; ^{27}when I have brought them back from the peoples, and gathered them out of their enemies' lands, and am sanctified in them in the sight of many nations. ^{28}And they shall know that I am the Lord their God, in that I caused them to go into captivity among the nations, and have gathered them unto their own land; and I will leave none of them any more there; ^{29} neither will I hide My face any more from them; for I have poured out My spirit upon the house of Israel, saith the Lord God.'

Joel 3:1-3

"For behold, in those days and at that time, when I restore the fortunes of Judah and Jerusalem, ^{2}I will gather all the nations and bring them down to the Valley of Jehoshaphat. ^{3}And I will enter into judgment with them there, on behalf of my people and my heritage Israel, because they have scattered them among the nations and have divided up my land."

Malachi 3:6

For I am God, I do not change; you are the children of Jacob, you will not cease to be.

Psalms 105:6-10

O descendants of Abraham his servant, O sons of Jacob, his chosen ones. ^{7} He is the Lord our God; his judgments are in all the earth. ^{8} He remembers his covenant forever, the word he commanded, for a thousand generations, ^{9} the covenant he made with Abraham, the oath he swore to Isaac. ^{10} He confirmed it to Jacob as a decree, to Israel as an everlasting covenant.

Psalm 125:1-2

Those who trust in the Lord are like Mount Zion, which cannot be moved, but abides forever. ²As the mountains are round about Jerusalem, so the Lord is round about His people [Israel], from this time forth and forever.

1 Chronicles 16:14-19

He is the Lord our God; his judgments are in all the earth. ¹⁵He remembers his covenant forever, the word he commanded, for a thousand generations, ¹⁶the covenant he made with Abraham, the oath he swore to Isaac. ¹⁷He confirmed it to Jacob as a decree, to Israel as an everlasting covenant: ¹⁸"To you I will give the land of Canaan as the portion you will inherit."

1 Chronicles 17:22-26

"You made your people Israel your very own forever, and you, O Lord, have become their God. ²³And now, Lord, let the promise you have made concerning your servant and his house be established forever. Do as you promised, ²⁴so that it will be established and that your name will be great forever. Then men will say, 'The Lord Almighty, the God over Israel, is Israel's God!' And the house of your servant, David, will be established before you. ²⁵You, my God, have revealed to your servant that you will build a house for him. So your servant has found courage to pray to you. ²⁶O Lord, you are God! You have promised these good things to your servant. ²⁷Now you have been pleased to bless the house of your servant, that it may continue forever in your sight; for you, O Lord, have blessed it, and it will be blessed forever."

2 Chronicles 20:7

O our God, did you not drive out the inhabitants of this land before your people Israel and give it forever to the descendants of Abraham your friend?

The Passover Haggadah
"Blessed is He who keeps His promise to Israel!"

This is what has stood up for our fathers and for us!
Not one alone has stood up against us,
but in every generation they rise up to finish us—
and the Blessed Holy One saves us from their hand!

The Eternal Jew

This people are not eminent solely by their antiquity, but are also singular by their duration, which has always continued from their origin till now. For, whereas the nations of Greece and of Italy, of Lacedaemon, of Athens and of Rome, and others who came long after, have long since perished, these ever remain, and in spite of the endeavors of many powerful kings who have a hundred times tried to destroy them, as their historians testify, and as it is easy to conjecture from the natural order of things during so long a space of years, they have nevertheless been preserved (and this preservation has been foretold); and extending from the earliest times to the latest, their history comprehends in its duration all our histories (which it preceded by a long time).

Blaise Pascal, *Pensées*. Paragraph 620, page 285, Encyclopedia Britannica, 1952.

The Jews have played an all-important role in history. They are preeminently an historical people and their destiny reflects the indestructibility of the divine decrees. Their destiny is too imbued with the "metaphysical" to be explained either in material or positive-historical terms.

I remember how the materialist interpretation of history, when I attempted in my youth to verify it by applying it to the destinies of peoples, broke down in the case of the Jews, where destiny seemed absolutely inexplicable from the materialistic and positivist criterion, this people ought long ago to have perished. Its survival is a mysterious and wonderful phenomenon demonstrating that the life of this people is governed by a special predetermination, transcending the processes of adaptation expounded by the materialistic interpretation of history; all these point to the particular and mysterious foundations of their destiny.

The history of the Jews is not only a phenomenon; it is also a noumenon in that special sense of the word to which I drew attention when speaking of the phenomenal-nominal historical antithesis. I said that the historical not only represented man's external relations, but that it might also reveal the very noumenon and essence of his being. The peculiarity of Jewish destiny consists in its incommensurability with either the pre-Christian or the Christian era. Scientific criticism applied to traditional Biblical history can neither discredit the universal role played by the Jews nor offer a satisfactory explanation of their mysterious destiny. Nor does this criticism grapple with the absolutely peculiar tie existing between the Jews and the 'historical', and their extraordinarily intense feeling for history.

Professor Nicholai Berdyaev, *The Meaning of History*. London: Moscow Academy

Six hundred and twenty letters, which comprise the Ten Commandments, represent six hundred and thirteen scriptural and seven Rabbinic commandments

Exodus 20:2-17
The Ten Commandments

"Although it may appear that God only gave Ten Commandments on Mount Sinai, those who know the truth realize that these Ten included all the Commandments."

Yalkut Me'am Lo'ez, quoting from BeMidbar Rabbah, Nasso, Chapter 13

Scriptural commandments = 613
Rabbinic commandments = 7
620

7 Rabbinic Commandments
1. Washing hands for bread
2. Hanukkah candles
3. Megillah reading
4. Sabbath Candles
5. Blessing before eating
6. Reciting Hallel
7. Eruv (Sabbath enclosure)

"Rabbi Meir (who was a scribe) was cautioned by Rebbi Yeshmael: 'My son, be careful in your work as a scribe, for it is a sacred task. Perhaps you will delete one single letter or add one single letter and thereby destroy the entire world.'"

Talmud, Ervin, 23b

The Eternal Nation of Israel Throughout History

The history of Jews and Judaism is a unique phenomenon. It is the most long-lived historical continuum in the emergence, development and spread of western civilization. Since its appearance as a differentiated entity in the ancient Near East about four thousand years ago, Jews and Judaism have been active participants in every phase of the development of the civilizations of Egypt, Babylonia, Assyria, and Persia. They are tightly interconnected with the rise and fall of the Hellenistic monarchies and the waxing and waning of Roman hegemony. They gave birth to Christianity and successfully warded off the rivalry of their offspring. They sustained a creative and differentiated identity under the Sassanians despite the challenge of Zoroastrianism.

They played a vital role in the launching of Islam, even as they spawned a variety of novel forms to cope with the creative expansiveness of this world-girdling religion. And most remarkably, this history not only did not remain confined to either Palestine or the Near East, but spread throughout the western world forming viable and significant communities in Africa, Asia Minor, the Balkans, Greece, Italy, Spain, France, Germany, England, the Slavic lands, even reaching as far east as India and China. This diaspora history is all the more remarkable, because it represents the bulk of the history of the Jews and Judaism during the past two thousand years and because it demanded adaptive powers that border on the phenomenal. In any given century Jews would be living simultaneously in as many as three or four radically different societies, each of which demanded a distinctive form of Jewish adaption if survival was to be sustained. Not only was this challenge met, but it was met without annulling a distinctive Jewish identity.

But this variety by no means fully exposes the uniqueness of Jewish history. Not only did it successfully traverse the ancient and medieval worlds, but it preserved itself as a viable strand within the modern world — a strand so viable as to (1) excite the wish to annihilate it - as Hitler did indeed attempt to do — (2) give birth to the modern nation state of Israel, (3) sustain flourishing communities and multiple Jewish identities throughout the western world, (4) be deemed worthy of sharing with Christianity the responsibility for the highest values of western civilization.

This is the empirical record. The facts as stated are not open to refutation. The uniqueness is there for all to verify. It is not a projection of some religious or ethnic wish.

Ellis Rivkin, *The dynamics of Jewish History*. H.U.C. New College 1970, pp.1-2.

Part XI

Bethlehem and The Messiah: What's the Connection?

Two Christmas Stories in Bethlehem

Everything that Christians believe about Jesus' birth is derived exclusively from two narratives found in the opening chapters of Matthew and Luke. Mark and John make no mention of anything unusual surrounding the events of Jesus' birth, and in both of these Gospels Jesus is first introduced to us as an adult. In fact, no other writer in the Christian Bible mentioned Jesus' conception, birth, or the city in which he was born. When Christians gather to celebrate Midnight Mass each December, the story they are told is a fusion of the accounts presented only in Matthew and Luke. Churchgoers, no doubt, feel more acquainted with the details of the Christmas story than practically any other narrative in the New Testament. Some Christians are aware that there are disparities between Matthew and Luke's infancy narratives, but they feel confident that the stories told each Christmas combine the details of both Gospels to create one elaborate, congruous story. Matthew and Luke's stories of Jesus' birth, however, are anything but congruous. In fact, the manifold contradictions in the Gospels' crucifixion/resurrection narratives pale in comparison to the stunning discrepancies found in the New Testament's two infancy narratives. Moreover, many details in the accounts found in Matthew's and Luke's stories about Jesus' birth are historically untenable.

Matthew and Luke agree only that Jesus was born in the city of Bethlehem to a virgin named Mary. These Gospels do not agree on any other detail in their accounts. This raises an important question: Why do both Matthew and Luke want Jesus to be born in Bethlehem? The answer here is simple: Bethlehem is the birthplace of King David, the progenitor of the messiah. What is most striking is that these two Gospels contain completely contradictory accounts, as they each seek to explain how Jesus came to be born in Bethlehem. In fact, all of the specific details found in Luke' Gospel are not found in Matthew's account, just as none of Matthew's details appear in Luke. Most importantly, the problem with these infancy narratives is not simply that they differ from one another. Rather, they do so in a way that makes them hopelessly irreconcilable.

Bear in mind that the Gospels frequently contradict each other about many of the details told about Jesus in the New Testament. Some of the stories contain small, less significant contradictions while others are enormous. And some of the stories are so convoluted that they were obviously made up out of whole cloth. The infancy narratives found in Matthew and Luke fall into this last category. There is little doubt that if Jesus ever existed, he was born in Nazareth, which was a rustic town that virtually no one had ever heard of. This tiny hamlet tucked away in the Galilee was so insignificant that it is not mentioned even one time in the Jewish Scriptures, the Talmud, or Josephus. Matthew and Luke wanted to have Jesus born in Bethlehem, the birthplace of King David, the royal ancestor of the messiah, and therefore they independently made up a story that struck each of them as believable.

In other words, Matthew and Luke changed an historical datum in order to make a theological point: Jesus was born in the birthplace of King David. And in order to convey this theological point, Matthew and Luke independently crafted their own story of Jesus' birth. The problem is that their accounts are entirely different from one another and, interestingly, the discrepancies are highlighted by their one overarching desire to place Jesus' birthplace in Bethlehem rather than Nazareth.

The discrepancies between these two accounts can easily be understood by examining the area where each of their stories begin. Where did Joseph and Mary originally reside? Most people think that Nazareth was their hometown. In fact, only Luke makes this claim. According to Matthew, Joseph and Mary were originally from Bethlehem where Jesus was born, not Nazareth. We are told in this account that the couple made their way to Nazareth only years after Jesus' birth when they return from Egypt following the death of Herod (2:23). Therefore, Jesus was born in his home in Matthew's story (2:11), not a stable as we are told by Luke. Remember, according to Matthew, Joseph and Mary had no need to look for an inn because the couple's hometown was Bethlehem! Would you sleep in an inn or a barn down the block from your own house? Thus, only in Luke's nativity scene, where the couple's hometown is Nazareth, way up north in the Galilee, is Mary forced by necessity to give birth in a stable in Bethlehem, which is 80 miles south of Nazareth (Luke 2:7).

A brief side-by-side overview of the two accounts illustrates the conspicuous internal and historical problems embedded in their narratives. Matthew's nativity story (1:18-2:23) goes something like this: Mary is betrothed to Joseph when she discovers that she is pregnant. Joseph is set to divorce her because he assumed she was unfaithful. An angel then informed Joseph that Mary miraculously conceived through the holy spirit. Sometime following Jesus' birth, wise men from the East follow a star to Jerusalem and inquire of Herod where the king of the Jews is to be born (found only in Matthew). Jewish leaders inform King Herod that the king of the Jews is to be born in Bethlehem. The wise men then travel from Jerusalem to Bethlehem following the same star, which then stops precisely over Jesus' house and, bearing gifts, they worship the child. After the wise men are warned not to return to Herod with information about Jesus' whereabouts, they return home using a different route.

We are told by Matthew that Herod ordered his troops to kill every baby boy born in Bethlehem because he feared that one day this child will usurp his throne. In advance of the slaughter, Joseph is warned by an angel to escape with his family to Egypt. Following Herod's death, Joseph learns that he cannot return from Egypt to his hometown in Bethlehem because Herod's son, Archelaus, a ruler worse than his father, is now the ruler of Judea. So he decides instead to settle in Nazareth, which is in the northern Galilee. We are told that Jesus is raised in this small town.

Luke also seeks to place Jesus' birth in Bethlehem, but his version of the events is very different than Matthew's. In fact, their stories are reversed. In Luke's account, the couple originally came from Nazareth and, due to an empire-wide census, is compelled to make their way to Bethlehem. According to Matthew, however, Joseph and Mary's hometown is Bethlehem, and it is years later when they are forced to move to Nazareth.

In Luke's infancy narrative, which is far more elaborate than Matthew's, we are told that after the angel tells Mary that she will miraculously conceive, the emperor, Augustus, decrees that everyone in his empire must register for a worldwide census. In order to register for the census, every citizen must return to their ancient ancestral home. This, Luke claims, occurred while Quirinius was the governor of Syria. Since Joseph is a descendant of King David, he and Mary travel from Nazareth to Bethlehem in order to comply with the decree of Augustus. Matthew, of course, makes no mention of any census because a census compelling people to move would ruin his version of the story: Mary and Joseph already resided in Bethlehem, and Matthew doesn't want the couple to leave for another zip code before Jesus' birth!

While Mary and Joseph are staying in the stable in Bethlehem—which is at least a four-day journey south of their home in Nazareth ("for there is no room for them in the inn")—she gives birth to Jesus and places the infant in a manger (Luke 2:1-7). We are told that local shepherds, alerted by an angel that the messiah was born in Bethlehem (rather than wise men following a star from the East, as in Matthew), visit and worship the baby Jesus. Following Jesus' circumcision eight days later, he is brought to the Temple in Jerusalem, and his parents offer the sacrifice prescribed in the Torah (Lev. 12) thirty-three days after the child's birth. After they perform their sacrificial duties, "they returned to Galilee, to their own city, Nazareth," where Jesus is raised (Luke 2:39-40).

These two stories raise serious problems. Before we explore the striking contradictions between these two accounts, I should point out some of the historical problems with these narratives. There is no record whatsoever in any source—Jewish, Roman, or even any other author in the New Testament—to support Matthew's claim that

Herod killed baby boys born in Bethlehem or anywhere else. The "Slaughter of the Innocents" never happened. Matthew invented this story in order to fashion two theological points.

First, Matthew sought to cast Jesus as the "new Moses," and therefore we are not surprised to discover that what happened to Jesus in the Book of Matthew mirrors the events that took place during the life of Moses. Therefore, just as Moses was saved when Pharaoh, king of Egypt, sought to kill all the Jewish newborn baby boys (Exod. 1:16-19), Jesus was saved from King Herod, who sought to slaughter all the boys born in Bethlehem (Matt. 2:13-15). Jesus escaped Herod by fleeing to Egypt, the land where Moses rescued his people. Just as Moses led the Jews out of Egypt into the Holy Land, Jesus left Egypt and settled in the Holy Land as well. While fleeing the Egyptians, Moses and his people traveled through the Red Sea. So too, the first thing Jesus did as an adult is get baptized in the waters of the Jordan River (Matt. 3:16-17). God tested the Jewish nation for forty years in the desert, and so too was Jesus tempted in the wilderness for forty days (Matt. 4:1-11). Moses delivered the Law at Mt. Sinai to the Jewish people, and Jesus delivered his Sermon on the Mount, where he expounded on the Law of Moses to his followers (Matt. 5-7).

What is Matthew's point? Jesus is the new Moses, savior of the Jewish people. You will not find stories like this anywhere else in the New Testament. This parallelism is unique to Matthew. There is no king trying to kill Jesus, the slaughter of the innocents, flight to Egypt, Sermon on the Mount, etc. in any of the other Gospels. Matthew crafted stories in his Gospel to make this theological point.

The second reason that Matthew inserted the story of the Slaughter of the Innocents into his Infancy narrative is far more ominous. The visit of the Magi (Matt. 2:1-12) is an intriguing story and unique to the Book of Matthew. These men from a distant land in the East are presumably pagans, who are for some reason searching for the newborn king of the Jews. People often wonder what sort of star could move in a way that Magi could follow it into Jerusalem and on to Bethlehem. Matthew obviously had in mind a magical star that could do far more than stop, move, and then hover over somebody's home. Matthew's star had a spectacular Global Positioning System far more advanced than the most sophisticated Android. It could locate the home of the messiah without an address!

Matthew's magic star raises an important question that readers often overlook: If the star was so extraordinary that it was able to pick out Jesus' home without an address, why did the wise men need to stop off at Herod's palace to find out where the king of the Jews was supposed to be born? After all, if the star could identify Jesus' home, it could have guided the Magi from the East directly to Bethlehem without stopping off at Herod's for some advice from the Jews along the way. Why did the wise men have to make a detour into Jerusalem, then make their inquiries of priests and Jewish scholars before heading off to Jesus' home in Bethlehem? Why did Matthew weave this seemingly unnecessary and trivial scene into his story?

The answer should be obvious. Recall when the Magi first inquired in Jerusalem where the king of the Jews is to be born, Herod consulted the Jewish chief priests and rabbis, and here we encounter the key irony of the account. We are told that the Jewish leaders and scholars know exactly where the messiah is to be born: the city of Bethlehem. They are even able to quote a verse from the Book of Micah to support their conclusion. Who, then, goes to worship Jesus? Was it Herod, the priests, the rabbis? Not at all. Rather, it is the non-Jews from the East who come to Jesus bearing gifts and worship him. In stark contrast to the gentiles from the East, Herod, the king and representative of the Jews, conspires to murder Jesus.

In the Book of Matthew, this powerful short tale sets the stage for what will subsequently happen to Jesus leading up to his crucifixion. Jesus claims that he fulfilled the Scriptures, yet his own people reject him and conspire to have him killed. They scream, calling for his death. According to Matthew, the Jewish priests and leaders are fully responsible for the blood of Jesus.

Others at the scene—specifically the gentiles—react differently than the Jews. In Matthew's account of the events leading up to the crucifixion, Pontius Pilate fights more vigorously than in the Book of Mark for Jesus' vindication and release (27:15-18). Moreover, in the New Testament, the only reference to Pilate's wife exists in a single sentence by Matthew. According to Matthew 27:19, she sent a message to her husband pleading with him not to condemn Jesus to death: While Pilate was sitting in the judgment hall, his wife sent him a message: "Have nothing to do with that innocent man, because in a dream last night, I suffered much on account of him."

The gentile couple, Pilate and his wife, ardently defend Jesus against the bloodthirsty Jewish crowd. The conflict intensifies quickly in Matthew's Passion narrative. Pilate insists that Jesus is innocent of any wrongdoing and does not deserve any punishment; however, the Jews are relentless, and demand his crucifixion (27:22-23).

This is followed by a horrific scene found only in the Book of Matthew where Pilate publicly washes his hands of Jesus' blood, declaring, "I am innocent of the man's blood; see to it yourselves" (27:24). Pilate placed himself on the side of Jesus and against the Jewish hordes. The crowd then utters a cry with the chilling words that would cast the Jews as "Christ-killers" to this day: "His blood be on us and our children" (27:25). Now the Jewish responsibility for Jesus' crucifixion is absolute. The first ominous narrative in the Book of Matthew set the stage for the last dire narrative. From the beginning until the end of Matthew's Gospel, it is the Jews alone who seek to kill Jesus. In stark contrast, the gentiles in Matthew's Gospel—both the Magi at Jesus' birth and Pilate at Jesus' death—are firmly on Jesus' side.

Not to be outdone, the details surrounding Jesus' birth in the Book of Luke contain serious historical problems in addition to the difficulties raised by a detailed comparison of the two nativity stories found in the New Testament. In fact, historically, Luke's nativity story is more problematic than Matthew's.

Contrary to what we are told by Luke, it widely known from every early historian that Quirinius became governor of Syria in 6 CE, a full decade after Herod the Great died in 4 BCE. This slice of Roman history is straightforward. Archelaus replaced his father as the ruler of Judea following Herod's death in 4 BCE. Due to Archelaus' despotic cruelty, he was banished and replaced by Quirinius who became governor over Syria and Judea in 6 CE. Simply put, it is impossible for both Herod and Qurinius to have governed Judea at the same time. Therefore, if Jesus was born during Herod's lifetime, as Matthew insists, then Quirinius was not the Syrian governor when Jesus was born. Conversely, if Matthew is correct that Jesus and Herod were contemporaries, then Luke's claim that Jesus was born during a census when Quirinius was governor of Syria is false. Moreover, it is unimaginable that Caesar Augustus imposed a worldwide tax when Jesus was born, in which everyone in the Roman Empire had to register by returning to the town where their ancestors once lived. It is inconceivable that this actually occurred. For one thing, we have numerous records for the reign of Caesar Augustus, and there is no mention, even in passing, anywhere of an empire-wide census, let alone one in which everyone in the Roman Empire had to register in the town from which their ancient ancestors had come.

Are we to believe that Joseph had to travel from Nazareth to Bethlehem because his distant ancestor, King David, who lived 1,000 years earlier, was born there? Is it possible that everyone in the Roman empire had to migrate to the town their ancestors lived in a thousand years earlier? If Australians were ordered to return to where their ancestors lived one thousand years ago, where would they go? Furthermore, is it possible that apart from Luke, no ancient author or historian—not even Matthew—mentions this supposed census and resulting mass migration

Why then did Luke fashion this story of a worldwide census? Like Matthew, he did not want Jesus born in the one-horse town of Nazareth. He wanted Jesus to be born in the city in which David was born although he was aware that Jesus was said to have come from Nazareth. Matthew sought to accomplish the same task; however, he crafted an entirely different plot device.

Christian apologists frequently argue that Matthew and Luke were somehow not contradicting each other. Rather, they were each supplying different parts of the whole Christmas story. Their accounts, however, are impossible to reconcile.

If Matthew is correct that Jesus was born while Herod was alive, then Luke's claim that Jesus was born when Quirinius was the governor of Syria is untenable. If Luke is correct that Nazareth was the hometown of Mary and Joseph, then Matthew's claim that Bethlehem was the couple's hometown is false. Remember, Joseph and Mary were from Bethlehem in Matthew's version of Jesus' nativity story. Joseph, we are told, wanted to return home to Bethlehem from Egypt. He was forced to abandon his plan and move instead to Nazareth because Archelaus, a potentate worse than his father Herod, became the ruler of Judea. Read Matthew 2:13-23 for yourself! Accordingly, Jesus was either born in his home in Bethlehem, as Matthew states, or was born in a stable "because there was no room at the inn" as Luke claims. If Joseph and Mary fled to Egypt after Jesus was born, as Matthew insists, how can Luke be correct that they returned to Nazareth a month after his birth?

Why are there astonishing contradictions between Matthew's and Luke's Christmas stories? As mentioned earlier, they both were aware that Jesus came from Nazareth, but each Gospel writer needed a story in which Jesus grew up in Nazareth but was born in Bethlehem. Matthew and Luke then independently crafted a story in order to make the same theological point: Jesus was born in the city of David. Why didn't Luke simply open a New Testament to make sure that his story was consistent with Matthew's? Because the New Testament didn't exist during the first century! Some Christians believe that the entire New Testament somehow fell out of heaven shortly after Jesus' crucifixion. In fact, the earliest list of 27 books which comprise the official canon of the New Testament was not compiled until 367 CE, nearly three centuries after the Books of Matthew and Luke were written. This list was composed by Athanasius, the influential bishop of Alexandria, Egypt, who forty-two years earlier played a central role at the Council of Nicea.

On eleven occasions Matthew employs "fulfillment citations," where he claims the events in the life of Jesus fulfilled a prophecy in the Jewish Scriptures. Among all the four Gospels, Matthew is the only author to implement this approach. Here in his nativity story, Matthew claims that the birthplace of the messiah was foretold in the Jewish Scriptures:

> And thou Bethlehem, land of Judah, Art in no wise least among the princes of Judah: For out of thee shall come forth a governor, Who shall be shepherd of my people Israel.
>
> (Matthew 2:6)

Here, Matthew cites Micah 5:1 (5:2 in a Christian Bible) to prove that the Jewish prophet foretold many centuries earlier that the messiah is to be born in Bethlehem. I will not address the imperfections in Matthew's translation. Rather, we will examine what Matthew chose not to translate. If you read his quote out of context, as it is cited in Matthew 2:6, it appears pretty straightforward that Micah foretold that the messiah would be born in Bethlehem. In quoting Micah, however, Matthew deliberately expunged the last phrase of the original passage. And this last clause of Micah 5:1 was eliminated for good reason: It is the modifier of the passage which dramatically impacts the meaning of the prophecy; and Matthew considered this modification unwelcome. The complete verse in Micah 5:1 reads:

> But you, Bethlehem Ephrathah, though you are small among the clans of Judah, out of you will come for me one who will be ruler over Israel, **whose origins are from old, from ancient times**.

Micah 5:1	But you, Bethlehem Ephrathah, though you are small among the clans of Judah, out of you will come for me one who will be ruler over Israel, *whose origins are from old, from ancient times*.
Matthew 2:6	And thou Bethlehem, land of Judah, Art in no wise least among the princes of Judah: For out of thee shall come forth a governor, *Who shall shepherd my people Israel*. ← *Interpolated*

Where did "whose origins are from old, from ancient times" go? Why didn't Matthew include these words in his quote? Why did he replace them with other words that do not appear anywhere in the original verse in Micah? Look up Micah 5:1 (5:2 in a Christian Bible) for yourself. Why did Matthew tamper with Jewish Scriptures? The answer is obvious to the reader. Micah, who lived approximately 2,700 years ago—about three centuries after King David—foretold that the "original" link which connects the Messiah to Bethlehem is "from old, from ancient times." This was not the message that Matthew sought to convey, so Matthew deliberately interpolated the words, "Who shall shepherd my people Israel." The original passage stripped of the modifying phrase appears to foretell that the messiah would be born in Bethlehem, rather than King David, the messiah's ancestor, who was born there. Here we have another striking example where Matthew manipulated a passage in Tanach so that its message appears christological.

Few chapters in the Bible more clearly illustrate that Jesus could not be the messiah than the fifth chapter of Micah. Examine the prophecies that fill the rest of this chapter (5:2-14). It is here that Micah foretold that the Jewish people will be led by the messiah to defeat their enemies. Jesus failed to fulfill these vital prophecies.

The New Jerusalem Bible

(Christian)

5:1   MICAH   1550

↗Mt 2:6
↗Jn 7:42

5 But you (Bethlehem) Ephrathah,
the least *a* of the clans of Judah,
from you will come for me
a future ruler of Israel
whose origins go back to the distant past,
to the days of old. *b*
Hence Yahweh *c* will abandon them

Is 7:14
only until she who is in labour gives birth, *d*
and then those who survive of his race
will be reunited to the Israelites.

Is 40:11
He will take his stand and he will shepherd them
with the power of Yahweh,
with the majesty of the name of his God,
and they will be secure, for his greatness will extend
henceforth to the most distant parts of the country.

---

5 a. 'the least' Gk; 'little' Hebr.

b. Ephrathah (to which Micah apparently attaches the etymological meaning of 'fruitful', connecting it with the birth of the liberator) originally indicated a clan related to Caleb, 1 Ch 2:19,24,50, and settled in the district of Bethlehem, Rt 1:2; 1 S 17:12; the name later came to be used of the town itself, Gn 35:19; 48:7; Jos 15:59; Rt 4:11, hence the gloss in the text. Micah is thinking of the ancient origin of the dynasty of David, Rt 4:11,17,18–22; 1 S 17:12. The evangelists later interpreted this passage as a prophecy of Christ's birthplace.

c. lit. 'he'.

d. Reference to the mother of the Messiah. Micah is perhaps thinking of the famous prophecy of the *'alma,* delivered by Isaiah some 30 years previously, Is 7:14g.

e. This fragment announces a future victory over Assyria. It is attributed to the descendant of David (beginning of v. 4, end of v. 5) and to the chieftains of Judah (vv. 4b–5a, an old fragment re-used).

f. 'in our land' Gk. Syr.; 'in our palaces' Hebr.

g. 'with naked blade' one Gk MS and Lat.; 'in its entrances' Hebr.

h. This saying, in two symmetrical strophes, announces the function of the 'remnant' in the salvation of the peoples (cf. vv. 1–4; 7:12) and in their punishment (4:13; 5:8,14). The first theme, occurring only at the end of the Exile, suggests a date later than Micah.

i. Hebr. adds 'among the nations'.

j. The prophecy of vv. 9–13 declares that Yahweh will tear (lit. 'cut off') from his people all their spurious human supports (cf. Is 2:7–8; 30:1–3,15–16; 31:1–3; Ho 3:4; 8:14; 14:4): military power, apparatus of divination and of the cult on the 'high places'. But the threat also implies an era of peace and of true faith. This prophecy is applied by vv. 8 and 14, to the nations, enemies of Yahweh; it is a subsequent adjustment.

6 a. After Yahweh's indictment in which he recalls his goodness to Israel, vv. 3–5, his repentant worshipper enquires what his God demands of him, vv. 6–7. The prophet replies, v. 8.

b. The mountains are God's favourite place of meeting with his people (Sinai, Nebo, Ebal and Gerizim, Zion, Carmel). They are changeless witnesses and often personified, Gn 49:26; 2 S 1:21; Ps 68:15–16; Ezk 35–36.

c. 'give ear' *weha'azinu* conj.; Hebr. *weha'etanim* 'you solid ones'.

d. 'have I been a burden to you' (*hele'etika*) and 'I brought you up' (*he'elitika*) are similar in sound • In response to Israel's complaint that God has abandoned them, Yahweh recalls his past kindnesses.

e. There is a lacuna in the Hebr. text. The reference is to the crossing of the Jordan. • 'you to know' versions. 'knowledge of Hebr. Yahweh's 'saving justice' are those great events of sacred history by which Yahweh demonstrated his loyalty to the covenantal promises. Since the covenant itself was the issue of a divine initiative, God's 'saving justice' is freely bestowed, not in any sense deserved.

Compare

Micah 5:1 (5:2 in a Christian Bible)
And you, Bethlehem Ephrathah, you should have been the lowest of the clans of Judah, from you shall emerge for Me, to be a ruler over Israel; **and his origin is from old, *from ancient days*** (מִימֵי עוֹלָם).

Matthew 2:6
But you, Bethlehem, in the land of Judah, are by no means least among the rulers of Judah; for out of you will come a ruler who will be the shepherd of my people Israel [Omitted]. *Interpolated*

Part A

וְאַתָּה בֵּית לֶחֶם אֶפְרָתָה צָעִיר לִהְיוֹת בְּאַלְפֵי יְהוּדָה מִמְּךָ לִי יֵצֵא לִהְיוֹת מוֹשֵׁל בְּיִשְׂרָאֵל

And you, Bethlehem Ephrathah, you should have been the lowest of the clans of Judah, from you shall emerge for Me, to be a ruler over Israel;

> The Book of Matthew (2:6) deliberately omitted the last phrase (Part B) of Micah 5:1 (2), "and his origin is from old, from ancient days," to conceal that the prophet Micah was describing the ancient birthplace of King David, rather than that of the messiah. Matthew replaced the omitted text with the interpolated phrase "who will be the shepherd of my people Israel," which appears nowhere in the original Hebrew text of the Book of Micah.

Part B (Matthew expunged this phrase)

וּמוֹצָאֹתָיו מִקֶּדֶם מִימֵי עוֹלָם:

and his <u>origin</u> is from old, **from ancient days**.

וּמוֹצָאֹתָיו	מִקֶּדֶם	מִימֵי עוֹלָם:
and his origin	from old	from ancient days

King David was a Bethlehemite	Ruth was the great grandmother of King David	Ruth a Moabite, was a descendant of a condemned nation
I Samuel 17:58 And Saul said to him, "Whose son are you, young man?" And David said, "The son of your bondsman, Jesse the **Bethlehemite**." *(see also I Sam. 16:1-3)*	**Ruth 4:13-22** And so, Boaz took Ruth and she became his wife; and he came to her. Hashem let her conceive, and she bore a son...and **Boaz begot Oved; and Oved begot Jesse, and Jesse begot David.**	**Ruth 1:4** **Moabite** women, one named Orpah, and the other Ruth... **Deuteronomy 23:3** No Ammonite or **Moabite** shall enter the assembly of the Lord...

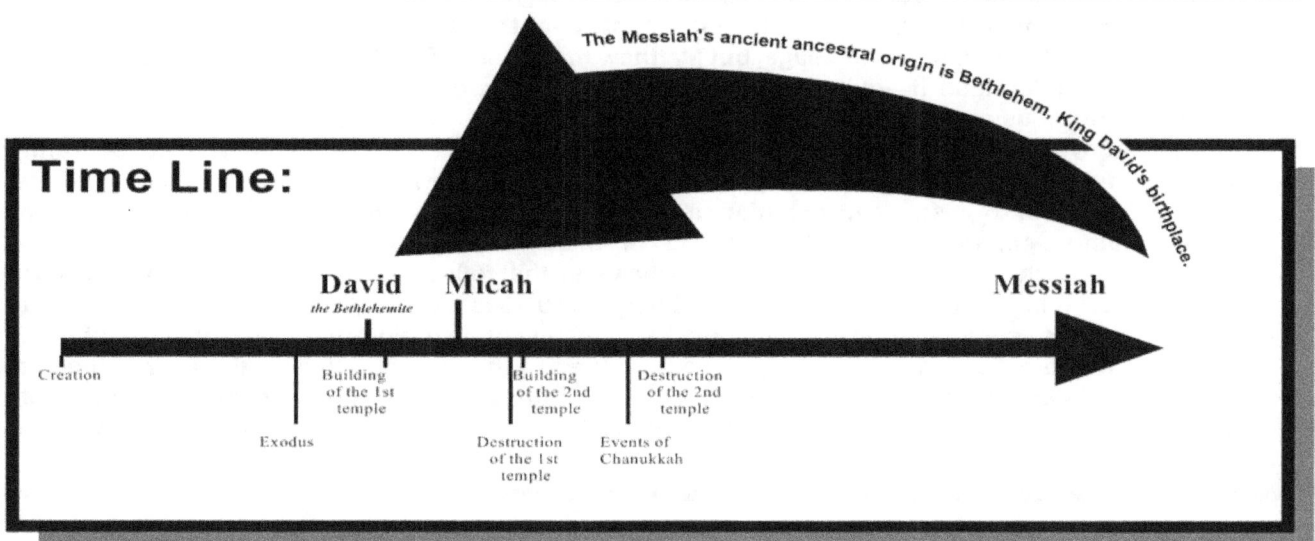

Matthew 21:1-7	Zechariah 9:9-10	Luke 19:29-35
Then Jesus sent two disciples, saying to them, "Go into the village opposite you, and immediately you will find a **donkey tied and a colt** with her. Loose **them** and bring **them** to me. And if anyone says anything to you, you shall say, 'The lord has need of **them**,' and immediately he will send **them**... So the disciples went and did as Jesus commanded them. They brought the donkey and the colt, laid their clothes on **them**, and set him on **them**. *(also compare Matthew 20:29-34 with Luke 18:35-43.)*	Be exceedingly happy, O daughter of Zion; Shout, O daughter of Jerusalem. Behold, your king shall come to you. He is just and victorious; humble, **riding a donkey, the colt, the foal of a donkey**. ¹⁰And I will remove the chariots from Ephraim, and the horses from Jerusalem; and the bow of war shall be removed. And he shall speak peace to the nations, and his rule shall be from the sea to the west and from the river to the ends of the earth.	He sent two of his disciples, saying, "Go into the village opposite you, in which as you enter you will find **a colt** tied, on which no one yet has ever sat; untie **it**, and bring *it* here. And if anyone asks you, 'Why are you untying **it**?' thus shall you speak, 'The lord has need of **it**'" And those who were sent went away found *it* just as he had told them. And as they were untying the colt, its owners said to them, "Why are you untying the colt?" And they said the lord has need of *it*." And they brought *it* to Jesus, and they threw their garments on the colt, and put Jesus on **it**.

How many animals did Jesus ride when he entered Jerusalem during his Triumphal Entry into Jerusalem? It seems like there should be an obvious answer: he rode one animal. And that is what three out of the four Gospels claim, including Mark 11:7, Luke 19:29-35, and John 12:14. These New Testament authors constructed their narratives to have Jesus fulfill Zechariah's notable prophecy of the messiah entering Jerusalem on a colt, the foal of a donkey.

The author of the Book of Matthew, however, lacked familiarity with the Hebrew language, which led to a rather bizarre result: He misconstrued the messianic prophecy in Zechariah 9:9 and assumed that the messiah was to ride into Jerusalem on two animals, rather than one ("the colt, the foal of a donkey"). In other words, Matthew claimed in his Palm Sunday narrative that Jesus straddled two animals riding into Jerusalem.

Those who are familiar with Biblical Hebrew are aware that there is a common poetic prophecy structure in Tanach where the third line of the text restates what is said in the second line. This is called "synonymous parallelism"—where two lines of poetry say basically the same thing in different words:

...Behold your king shall come to you. He is just and victorious;
humble, riding a donkey,
the colt, the foal of a donkey. (Zechariah 9:9)

It is clear that the author of Matthew could not read the Jewish Scriptures in Hebrew, and therefore was unfamiliar with the poetic convention in this passage. His lack of understanding of the Hebrew Scriptures in its original language led him to write his story so that Jesus' disciples procured *two* animals for him; a donkey and a colt; they spread their garments over the two of them, and Jesus rode into town straddling both of them. It's an odd image, but Matthew made Jesus fulfill the prophecy of Scripture—as he thought he understood it—quite literally! As mentioned above, this story contradicts the other Gospels, where Jesus rode into Jerusalem on one animal.

The above conflicting accounts reveal how the authors of the Christian Bible went about crafting and writing their stories about Jesus: They read a prophecy in the Jewish Scriptures and then projected these prophecies onto Jesus and manufactured their narratives. This technique, which the New Testament authors employed frequently, is called "prophecy historicized."

Unfortunately, many Christians fail to read the verse that follows Zechariah 9:9, which begins with the word "And." This conjunction indicates that Zechariah 9:10 is umbilically connected to the previous verse. The prophet completed this prophecy in Zechariah 9:10 declaring that, "he [the messiah] shall speak peace to the nations, and his rule shall be from the sea to the west and from the river to the ends of the earth." Jesus did not bring peace to the world (see Matthew 10:34-35; Luke 12:51-53) nor did he rule over anyone. It is therefore no coincidence that Christian "Old Testament Fulfilment Charts" always quote Zechariah 9:9 but never 9:10.

Why does the King James Version (KJV) correctly translate the phrase יְמֵי עוֹלָם in every other place in the Bible as "days of old"?

Isaiah 63:9 (King James)	**Isaiah 63:11** (King James)	**Amos 9:11** (King James)	**Micah 7:14** (King James)	**Malachi 3:4** (King James)
In all their affliction he was afflicted, and the angel of his presence saved them: in his love and in his pity he redeemed them; and he bare them, and carried them all the ***days of old*** (יְמֵי עוֹלָם).	Then he remembered the ***days of old*** (יְמֵי עוֹלָם), Moses and his people, saying, where is he that brought them up out of the sea with the shepherd of his flock? Where is he that put his holy Spirit within him?	In that day will I raise up the tabernacle of David that is fallen, and close up the breaches thereof; and I will raise up his ruins, and I will build it as in ***days of old*** (כִּימֵי עוֹלָם).	Feed thy people with thy rod, the flock of thine heritage, which dwell solitarily in the wood, in the midst of Carmel: let them feed in Bashan and Gilead, as in the ***days of old*** (כִּימֵי עוֹלָם).	Then shall the offering of Judah and Jerusalem be pleasant unto the Lord, as in the ***days of old*** (כִּימֵי עוֹלָם), and as in former years.

Why does the KJV and many other Christian translators render יְמֵי עוֹלָם as "eternity" in Micah 5:1 (2)?

King James Version	**New American Standard**	**Living Bible**	**Amplified Bible**	**Modern Language**
But thou, Bethlehem Ephratah, though thou be little among the thousands of Judah, yet out of thee shall he come forth unto me that is to be ruler in Israel; whose goings forth have been from old, from ***everlasting***.	But as for you, Bethlehem Ephratah, too little to be among the clans of Judah, from you One will go forth for Me to be a ruler in Israel. His goings forth are from long ago, from the ***days of eternity***.	O Bethlehem Ephrathah, you are but a small Judean village, yet you will be the birthplace of my King who is alive from ***everlasting***.	But you, Bethlehem Ephratah, you are little to be among the clans of Judah; yet out of you shall one come forth for Me who is to be ruler in Israel, Whose goings forth have been from of old, from ancient days ***(eternity)***.	As for you, Bethlehem Ephratah, little as you are among the thousands of Judah, from you shall He come forth to Me, who is to be ruler over Israel, His goings forth are from of old, from days of ***eternity***.

All Christian translations below render the Hebrew words מִימֵי עוֹלָם in Micah 5:2 correctly.

Revised Standard Version But you, O Bethlehem Ephrathah, who are little to be among the clans of Judah, from you shall come forth for me one who is to be ruler in Israel, whose origin is from old, **from ancient days**.	**New International Version** But you, Bethlehem Ephrathah, though you are small among the clans of Judah, out of you will come for me one who will be ruler over Israel, whose origins are from of old, **from ancient times**.
Modern Reader's Bible But thou, Bethlehem Ephrathah, which art little to be among the thousands of Judah, out of thee shall one come forth unto me that is to ruler in Israel; whose goings forth are from of old, **from ancient days**.	**New English Bible** But you, Bethlehem in Ephrathah, small as you are to be among Judah's clans, out of you shall come forth a governor for Israel, one whose roots are far back in the past, in **days gone by**.
The Bible: An American Translation And you, O Bethlehem Ephrathah, too little to be among the clans of Judah, from you, one shall come forth for me, who shall be ruler over Israel, whose origins are from old, **from ancient days**.	**A New Translation of the Bible — James Moffatt** O Bethlehem Ephrathah, tiniest of townships in all Judah, out of you a king shall come to govern Israel, one whose origin is of old, **of long descent**.
Good News Bible The Lord says, "Bethlehem Ephrathah, you are one of the smallest towns in Judah, but out of you I will bring a ruler for Israel, **whose family line goes back to ancient times.**	**The Revised English Bible** But from you, Bethlehem in Ephrathah, small as you are among Judah's clans, from you will come a king for me over Israel, one whose origins are far back in the past, **in ancient times**.
The New American Bible (Catholic) But you, Bethlehem-Ephrathah, too small to be among the clans of Judah, from you shall come forth for me one who is to be ruler in Israel; whose origin is from of old, **from ancient times**.	**New Revised Standard Version** But you, O Bethlehem of Ephrathah, who are one of the little clans of Judah, from you shall come forth for me one who is to rule in Israel, whose origin is from of old, **from ancient days**.
The Jerusalem Bible But you (Bethlehem) Ephrathah, the least of the clans of Judah, out of you will be born form me the one who is to rule over Israel; his origin goes back to the distant past, to the **days of old**.	**The New Jerusalem Bible** But you (Bethlehem) Ephrathah, the least of the clans of Judah, from you will come form me a future ruler of Israel whose origins go back to the distant past, to the **days of old**.
The International Critical Commentary And thou, Bethlehem Ephrathah, the least among the clans of Judah, from thee one will come forth for me, who will be ruler over Israel, whose origins are from of old, **from ancient days**.	**Young's Literal Translation of the Holy Bible** And thou, Bethlehem Ephratah, little to be among the chiefs of Judah! From thee to Me he cometh forth — to be ruler in Israel, from the **days of antiquity**.

Part XII

Who is the Messiah?

Did the Patriarch Jacob Predict that the Davidic Kingdom would Continue, Uninterrupted?

Blessings occupy a prominent place in the Torah and particularly in the Book of Genesis.

When Jacob felt his death approaching, he gathered his twelve sons to his side and gave each a blessing mingled with prediction, suited to their character. Using powerful imagery of the tribes of which his sons were to be the ancestors, he sketched pictures in a grand outline of the future history of the covenant nation that would emerge from them. Of all of Jacob's sons, Judah received the most extensive blessings, suited to his preeminence and leadership among his brothers (Genesis 49:8-12).

> **Genesis 49:10**
> The scepter shall not depart from Judah, nor a lawgiver from between his feet, until Shiloh comes; And to Him *shall be* the obedience of the people.

Citing the opening words of Genesis 49:10, "The scepter shall not depart from Judah, nor a lawgiver from between his feet, until Shiloh comes," missionaries insist that this passage predicts that a king from the tribe of Judah would rule without interruption over the Jewish people. Based on their rendering of this verse, they argue that Judaism, as practiced for the past 2,000 years, is therefore a defective religion, having no king, blood sacrifice, or high priest, as outlined in the Bible. Accordingly, they insist, Christianity is the world's only valid faith, because it alone recognizes and embraces the reign of Jesus as king, sacrifice, and high priest.[1]

Is this a legitimate claim? Is the Church the only valid heir to the biblical faith, which the Jews have long abandoned? Can Christendom claim authenticity because it recognizes the uninterrupted reign of Jesus as king, high priest and sacrifice?

> **Hosea 3:4-5**
> For the children of Israel shall abide many days without king or prince, without sacrifice or sacred pillar, without *ephod* or *teraphim*. ⁵Afterward the children of Israel shall return and seek the Lord their God and David their king. They shall fear the Lord and His goodness in the latter days.

This Christian interpretation of Genesis 49:10 is erroneous and misleading. This passage in the Torah does not suggest that the Davidic dynasty would continue without interruption.

To be sure, all Christians concede that no king from the tribe of Judah reigned during the Babylonian exile or Second Temple period, which spanned five centuries!

The blessing that Judah received from his father bestowed upon his descendants the preeminent role of leadership: they alone would reign as legitimate kings over the children of Israel. Jacob recognized that Judah was unique among his sons. He displayed the uncommon character of leadership among the ten eldest brothers: Judah spoke up against killing Joseph, negotiated with his father regarding Joseph's demand that Benjamin be brought down to Egypt, and pleaded with Joseph after the latter placed the silver cup into Benjamin's bag. Jacob did *not* predict that the descendants of Judah would reign as king for all time without interruption. In fact, the Bible promised that no king would reign over the Jewish people during their long exile which would precede the messianic age. The destruction of the First and Second Temple was responsible for seismic changes in communal Jewish life. Hosea predicted that the nation of Israel would endure "many days"—an exile of long duration—without a king, sacrifice, or high priest (*ephod,* the vestment of the high priest) until the End of Days (3:4-5). This prophecy utterly disproves the contention raised by missionaries. Hosea foretold that his people would persist without a king, sacrificial system, or high priest. Most importantly, these passages refute the chief claim of the Church: Jesus is king, sacrifice, and high priest (see Volume 2, page 237).

Hosea 6:6
For I desire mercy and not sacrifice, And the knowledge of God more than burnt offerings.

Micah 6:6-8
With what shall I come before the Lord and bow down before the exalted God? Shall I come before him with burnt offerings, with calves a year old? ⁷Will the Lord be pleased with thousands of rams, with ten thousand rivers of olive oil? Shall I offer my firstborn for my transgression, the fruit of my body for the sin of my soul? ⁸He has shown you, O mortal, what is good. And what does the Lord require of you? To act justly and to love mercy and to walk humbly] with your God.

I Kings 8:46-50
"If they sin against You, for there is no man who does not sin, and You will be angry with them, and deliver them to the enemy, and their captors will carry them away captive to the land of the enemy, far or near. ⁴⁷And they shall bethink themselves in the land where they were carried captive, and repent, and make supplication to You in the land of their captors, saying, 'We have sinned, and have done perversely, we have committed wickedness. ⁴⁸And they shall return to You with all their heart, and with all their soul, in the land of their enemies, who led them away captive, and pray to You toward their land, which You gave to their fathers, the city You have chosen, and the house which I have built for Your name. ⁴⁹And You shall hear their prayer and their supplication in heaven, in Your dwelling place, and maintain their cause. ⁵⁰And forgive Your people for what they have sinned against You, and all their transgressions that they have transgressed against You....'"

Furthermore, there is not a single instance in Tanach in which the Jewish people are instructed to worship or place their faith in a crucified messiah or demigod.[2] Did Hosea simply forget to mention that one day the messiah would die for our sins?

Moreover, the notion that an innocent person can die in order to atone for the behavior of the wicked is found nowhere in the Tanach. In fact, this idea is widely condemned in the Jewish Scriptures.[3]

The Almighty will forgive the sins of Israel if they confess and repent directly to God (I Kings 8:46-50). This core teaching is conveyed throughout Tanach. Hosea imparted a dramatic and comforting message to his people as they were set to wander the world's nations: you will replace the sacrificial system with prayer during your expansive future exile.

What about all the animal sacrifices prescribed in the Book of Leviticus? Can mankind survive spiritually without the shedding of blood for an atonement? Missionaries claim that this is an impossible task. The Bible disagrees. With three words, Hosea discredited the central creed of the Church: He instructed the Jewish people to replace the sacrificial system with devotional prayer during their long exile: "Render for bulls the offering of our lips (וּנְשַׁלְּמָה פָרִים שְׂפָתֵינוּ)."

The fundamentalist, Christian translators of the popular New International Version Bible were so alarmed by Hosea's disappointing conclusion—"let us render for bulls the offering of our lips"—that they concealed the prophet's last words of the text to read instead, "that we may offer the fruit of our lips," thereby effacing Hosea's inspiring message.

> **Psalm 68:35**
> Awesome is God in His sanctuary, the God of Israel; He gives power and strength to His people. Blessed be God! (see also Isaiah 45:5-6)
>
> **Isaiah 43:10-11**
> "You are My witnesses," declares the Lord, "And My servant whom I have chosen, In order that you may know and believe Me, And understand that I am He. Before Me there was no God formed, And there will be none after Me. [11]I, I am the Lord, and besides me there is no savior!"
>
> **Hosea 14:2-3**
> Return O Israel to the Lord your God, for you have stumbled in your iniquity. Take with you words and return to the Lord. Say: You shall forgive all sin and teach us the good way, **and let us render for bulls the offering of our lips** (וּנְשַׁלְּמָה פָרִים שְׂפָתֵינוּ).

> The translators of the widely-read New International Version Bible were so troubled by the conclusion of this passage that they replaced it with their own, appending instead, "that we may offer the fruit of our lips."

---

[1]Mat. 27:11, 37; Acts 17:7; Eph. 5:2; Heb. 2:17, 3:1, 4:14, 9:26 [2]Ex. 20:2-3; Deut. 4:35; 6:14; 32:39; Hos. 13:4   [3]Ez. 18:1-23; Ex. 32:33

The Prophets of Israel Conveyed the Salvation plan of God to the Jewish Nation

The Hebrew Scriptures frequently present salvation in the form of a story that describes the outworking of God's eternal plan to deal with the problem of human frailty and sin. The events recorded in Tanach are set against the background of the turbulent history and spiritual struggles of God's chosen people, and reaches its climax in the writings of the Prophets of Israel.

With a clear and warm message, these men, speaking in the name of God, remind us that our personal relationship with the Creator allows us to turn directly to Him at any time. As Malachi 3:7 says, "Return to Me and I shall return to you." Ezekiel asks, "Have I any pleasure at all that the wicked should die? said the Lord God: and not that he should return from his ways, and live?... When the wicked man turns away from his wickedness that he has committed, and does that which is lawful and right, he shall save his soul alive" (18:23-27).

Daniel reassures us that the Almighty is compassionate and forgives those who come before Him. "We do not present our supplications before You because of our righteousness, but because of Your abundant mercy," declares the prophet "beloved by God," (Daniel 9:18).

In the Book of Ecclesiastes, King Solomon tells his listeners that without God, all earthly pleasures are meaningless. After the listeners take this message to heart, then true happiness can be achieved with a personal relationship with God and obedience to the *mitzvot* (commandments).

> **Ecclesiastes 12:13**
> Let us hear the conclusion of the whole matter: Fear the Lord, and keep His commandments: for this *is* the whole *duty* of man.

While this teaching is the core message of the Jewish faith, it is utterly inconsistent with cardinal teachings of the Church. If, as Paul and other New Testament authors insist, man is incapable of keeping the commandments of the Torah, why does Solomon insist that "this is the whole duty of man"?

Furthermore, if the claims of the Church are valid, why didn't King Solomon state that the purpose of man is to believe that Jesus died for our sins? (John 3:16; 17:3)

For example, according to Christian teachings, it would have been impossible for God to have forgiven the sins of the people of Nineveh. The uplifting conclusion in the Book of Jonah clearly demonstrates that bloodless repentance expiates sin and is the desire of God:

> And God saw their works, that they turned from their evil way; and God repented of the evil, that he had said that he would do unto them; and he did *it* not.
>
> (Jonah 3:10)

In spite of this clear message, the Church insists that man cannot atone for his sins through his own repentance or initiative. The human race is incapable of achieving salvation by its own deeds (Romans 3:10). No person born to this world can save himself through his own initiative, missionaries routinely argue.

Man's only hope to cleanse his iniquity and receive salvation is through the Cross. Outside of Calvary, man is utterly hopeless and spiritually lost. Nothing but believing in Jesus will save you, the New Testament argues (Mark 16:16, John 3:16, 14:6).

While this teaching is the centerpiece of Christian theology, it is controverted by the teachings of the Jewish Scriptures.

Moreover, the Hebrew Bible explicitly states that human sacrifice is an abomination in the sight of God (Lev. 18:21, 20:2-5, Deut. 12:31, Jer. 32:34-35).

The Book of Isaiah's first chapter (1:16-18) reveals the sacred path to purity and atonement.

The Book of Isaiah opens with a harsh censure of the nation of Israel. Few chapters in the Bible are as brutally critical of the Jewish people as the prophet Isaiah is in his opening sermon.

Almost unexpectedly, however, the prophet soothes his wayward people as he conveyed both the essence of atonement, and the way to regain a life of purity. He assures his disobedient nation that if they turn from their sinful ways and care for the downtrodden, their sins will be completely forgiven.

> Wash, cleanse yourselves, remove the evil of your deeds from before My eyes, cease to do evil. [17]Learn to do good, seek justice, strengthen

the robbed, perform justice for the orphan, plead the case of the widow. ¹⁸Come now, let us reason together, says the Lord. If your sins prove to be like crimson, they will become white as snow....

(Isaiah I:16-18)

Isaiah's message, like the other Jewish prophets, stands in stark contrast to the declaration in the Book of Hebrews that "without the shedding of blood there is no atonement."[1]

If, as missionaries insist, belief in Jesus is the only conduit to atonement and salvation, then Isaiah's first chapter would have been an ideal place for the prophet to inform us that in order to expiate our sins we must all believe in Jesus and be covered in the blood of the Cross.

Why does this core Christian doctrine appear nowhere in the Jewish Scriptures?

In contrast, the Jewish prophets, as if with one clear voice, testify that repentance alone atones for sin.[2]

Thus, according to traditional Jewish thought, one should not despair on account of his or her sins, for every penitent sinner is graciously received by the Merciful One (Isa. 55:6-9; Jer.31:9). It is never too late to return to God with sincere repentance for "as the sea is always open for every one who wishes to cleanse himself, so are the gates of repentance always open to the sinner,[3] and the hand of God is continually stretched out to receive the penitent.[4] The Talmud states, therefore, that a repentant sinner attains a more exalted spiritual eminence than one who has never sinned.[5]

> **Micah 6:6-8**
> With what shall I come before the Lord and bow down before the exalted God?
> ⁷Shall I come before him with burnt offerings, with calves a year old? Will the Lord be pleased with thousands of rams, with ten thousand rivers of oil? Shall I offer my firstborn for my transgression, the fruit of my body for the sin of my soul? ⁸He has showed you, O man, what is good. And what does the Lord require of you? To act justly and to love mercy and to walk humbly with your God.

[1]Hebrews 9:22 [2]Deuteronomy 4:26-31; I Kings 8:46-50; Isaiah 55:6-9; Jeremiah 7:3-23; Ezekiel 18:1-23; Hosea 6:6; 14:2-3; Psalm 40:7-9 (6-8); 51;51:16-19; Proverbs 10:2; 11:4; 16:6; Daniel 4:24; II Chronicles 6:36-39 [3]Pesiqta., ed. Buber, xxv. 157; Midrash Deuteronomy Rabbah ii.; Midrash Psalms lxiii [4]Talmud Pesachim 119a; Deuteronomy Rabbah ii [5]Talmud Berachoth 34b

Why Doesn't Judaism Accept the Christian Messiah?

Ezekiel 37:1-28

Ezekiel's Vision of the Valley of Dry Bones

The hand of the Lord was upon me, and He brought me out by the spirit of the Lord and set me down in the middle of the valley; and it was full of bones. ²And He caused me to pass among them round about, and behold, *there were* very many on the surface of the valley; and lo, *they were* very dry. ³And He said to me, "Son of man, can these bones live?" And I answered, "O Lord God, Thou knowest." ⁴Again He said to me, "Prophesy over these bones, and say to them, 'O dry bones, hear the word of the Lord.' ⁵Thus says the Lord God to these bones, 'Behold, I will cause breath to enter you that you may come to life. ⁶And I will put sinews on you, make flesh grow back on you, cover you with skin, and put breath in you that you may come alive; and you will know that I am the Lord.'" ⁷So I prophesied as I was commanded: and as I prophesied, there was a noise, and, behold, an earthquake; and the bones came together, bone to its bone. ⁸And I looked, and behold, sinews were on them, and flesh grew, and skin covered them; but there was no breath in them. ⁹Then said he unto me, "Prophesy unto the wind, prophesy, son of man, and say to the wind, 'Thus saith the Lord God: Come from the four winds, O breath, and breathe upon these slain, that they may live.'" ¹⁰So I prophesied as He commanded me, and the breath came into them, and they came to life, and stood on their feet, an exceedingly great army.

Ezekiel's Vision Is Explained: the Jewish People Will Be Restored

¹¹Then He said to me, "Son of man, these bones are the whole house of Israel; behold, they say, 'Our bones are dried up, and our hope has perished. We are completely cut off.'"

The Resurrection of the Dead: "Then You Will Know That I Am Lord"

¹²"Therefore prophesy, and say to them, 'Thus says the Lord God,' Behold, I will open your graves and cause you to come up out of your graves, My people; and I will bring you into the land of Israel. ¹³Then you will know that I am the Lord, when I have opened your graves and caused you to come up out of your graves, My people. ¹⁴And I will put My Spirit within you, and you will come to life, and I will place you on your own land. *Then you will know* that I, the Lord, have spoken and done it,'" declares the Lord.

The Restoration of the Ten Lost Tribes (Judah and Israel Will be Reunited)

¹⁵The word of the Lord came again to me saying, ¹⁶ "And you, son of man, take for yourself one stick and write on it, 'For Judah and for the sons of Israel, his companions'; then take another stick and write on it, 'For Joseph, the stick of Ephraim and all the house of Israel, his companions.' ¹⁷Then join them for yourself one to another into one stick, that they may become one in your hand. ¹⁸And when the children of thy people shall speak unto thee, saying, 'Wilt thou not show us what thou meanest by these?' ¹⁹say to them, 'Thus says the Lord God, 'Behold, I will take the stick of Joseph, which is in the hand of Ephraim, and the tribes of Israel, his companions; and I will put them with it, with the stick of Judah, and make them one stick, and they will be one in My hand.' ²⁰And the sticks on which you write will be in your hand before their eyes. And say to them, ²¹'Thus says the Lord God, Behold, I will take the sons of Israel from among the nations where they have gone, and I will gather them from every side and bring them into their own land; ²²and I will make them one nation in the land, on the mountains of Israel; and one king will be king for all of them; and they will no longer be two nations, and they will no longer be divided into two kingdoms. ²³And they will no longer defile themselves with their idols, or with their detestable things, or with any of their transgressions; but I will deliver them from all their dwelling places in which they have sinned, and will cleanse them. And they will be My people, and I will be their God.'"

The Davidic Kingdom Will be Restored and the Commandments Observed

²⁴"And My servant David will be king over them, and they will all have one shepherd; and they will walk in My ordinances, and keep My statutes, and observe them. ²⁵And they shall live on the land that I gave to Jacob My servant, in which your fathers lived; and they will live on it, they, and their sons and their sons' sons, forever; and David My servant shall be their prince forever. ²⁶And I will make a covenant of peace with them; it will be an everlasting covenant with them.

The Third Temple will Stand Forever: "Then the Nations Will Know that I am Lord"

And I will place them and multiply them, and will set My sanctuary in their midst forever. ²⁷My dwelling place also will be with them; and I will be their God, and they will be My people. ²⁸And the nations will know that I am the Lord who sanctifies Israel, when My sanctuary is in their midst forever."

> The 37th chapter of the Book of Ezekiel contains one of the most detailed descriptions of the Final Redemption. Here, the prophet illustrates the events that will occur in the messianic age, employing unusual intensity.
>
> Why, in these famed passages, is there not even a hint that the messiah will die or come twice? Bear in mind, the prophet explicitly speaks of the messiah in this celebrated chapter. Why doesn't Ezekiel discuss the Cross or a single core Christian tenet anywhere in his renowned oracle? Yet these are the things you *will* find here: The ingathering of the Jewish exiles, the resurrection of the dead, the messiah's reign on the throne of David, the Jewish people faithfully keeping the commandments of the Torah, and the building of the final Temple that will stand forever in Jerusalem.
>
> So, if anyone should ever ask you why Judaism doesn't accept the Christian messiah, ask him to read Ezekiel 37.

The following related article can be found in Volume 2 of *Let's Get Biblical! Why doesn't Judaism Accept the Christian Messiah?*

I. Why Doesn't Judaism Have a King?
   Where is Our Messiah?. . . . . Page 237

Part XIII

Judaism and Christianity On Satan:
Why We Differ

Is Satan a Servant of God, or Is he God's Arch Enemy?

According to Jewish teachings, Satan is an agent of God and has no independent agency or autonomy. God created Satan in His wisdom and for His purpose, to test man's faith.

In sharp contrast, we are told by the Church that Satan is a synonym for the Devil. Christian theology insists that Satan is an angel who rebelled against God. His ultimate goal is to draw people away from the love of God, and lead them to fallacies which God opposes.

According to the Church, before Satan's insurrection, he was among the highest of all angels and the brightest in the sky. His pride is considered a reason why he would not bow to the Almighty as all other angels did, and instead sought to rule heaven himself, as the chief adversary of God.

Jewish and Christian teachings on the person, nature, and function of Satan are diametrically different.

In the instances where Satan is discussed in the Jewish Scriptures, Satan is consistently described as a loyal servant of God, rather than a disobedient angel.

Throughout Tanach, angels are merely messengers, created without free will of their own, whose purpose is to carry out assignments from God. At times, they assume human form in order to carry out their divinely appointed mission.

For example, at the beginning of the Book of Job, Satan is an angelic member of the divine council, the "sons of God" who are subservient to God. Job is a good person "...who feared God and turned away from evil" (Job 1:1) and has therefore been rewarded by God. When the divine council meets, God informs Satan about Job's blameless and morally-upright character.

Between Job 1:9–10 and 2:4–5, Satan points out that Job had been loyal to God because the Almighty gave Job everything that a man could want. If all Job was given—even his health—were to be taken away from him, Satan reasoned, his faith would likely collapse. God therefore grants Satan the chance to test Job.

Satan is under the complete sovereignty of God, and cannot act without the authority of the Almighty.

This is further illustrated in the epilogue in which God is speaking to Job. Satan is absent from these dialogues. For Job, his friends, and for the narrator, it is ultimately God Himself who is responsible for Job's suffering (Job 2:3).

And it is God Who removes Job's protection, allowing Satan to take his wealth, his children, and his physical health, in order to tempt Job to curse God.

Despite his travails, Job does not curse God, but instead curses the day of his birth. And although Job protests his plight and pleads for an explanation, he stops short of accusing God of injustice. Although perplexed by his predicament, Job remains righteous—faithful to God—and is restored to an even better condition than his former wealthy state. The Book of Job is the most widely-known formulation in Jewish thought addressing the reason for the existence of suffering.

Judaism teaches that Satan is an angel who faithfully serves God as a prosecuting attorney, one who accuses men of wickedness and impiety. At the direction of God, Satan may be permitted to test these accusations, such as in the Book of Job. Thus, Satan's ultimate goal is not to lead mankind away from their faithfulness to God, but merely to reveal the true depths of their devotion.

According to core Christian teachings, however, none of the events described in the Book of Job could have occurred. By his own actions, Job could not have remained faithful to God. The Church argues that as a result of the Original Sin, man is totally depraved, and can do nothing to merit his own salvation. We are told by both the Church Fathers and Reformers that humans—quite literally—inherit the guilt of Adam and Eve, and are sinful from the moment of conception. This inherently sinful nature results in a complete alienation from God and the total inability of humans to achieve reconciliation with God based on their own abilities. Job's ultimate virtue and vindication would have not been possible according to Church teachings.

Moreover, in contrast to the portrayal of Satan by the Church as a fallen angel and the chief blasphemer and enemy of God, the Book of Job reveals that Satan is a loyal servant of the Almighty, created to test the morality of man. In essence, without Satan, true virtue would be impossible.

The following seemingly conflicting accounts between two parallel reports in the Tanach also illustrate that Satan is an *instrument* of God, rather than His adversary.

Was it God or Satan?	
II Samuel 24:1	**I Chronicles 21:1**
And again the anger of the Lord was kindled against Israel, and He moved David against them to say, "Go, number Israel and Judah."	And Satan stood up against Israel, and provoked David to number Israel.

At first glance, the parallel verses above (II Samuel 24:1 and I Chronicles 21:1) appear contradictory. Although these two accounts are found in different books of the Bible, they both describe the same event: King David's ill-fated census of the Jewish people.

In the Book of Exodus, the Torah forbids the act of performing a head count of the Jewish people. Scripture warns that if this commandment is violated, a devastating affliction will descend upon the people.

> Then the Lord said to Moses, [12]"When you take a census of the Israelites to count them, each one must pay the Lord a ransom for his life at the time he is counted. Then no plague will come on them when you number them. [13]Each one who crosses over to those already counted is to give a half shekel, according to the sanctuary shekel, which weighs twenty *gerahs*. This half shekel is an offering to the Lord.
>
> (Exodus 30:11-13)

David ignored this commandment and, as a result, David's census brought about a dreadful plague.

It is difficult to miss a glaring difference between these two narratives. Who provoked King David to perform this ill-fatted head count? Whereas in II Samuel 24:1, God aroused David to number the Jewish people, in I Chronicles 21:1, it was Satan who provoked David to perform the census.

Which account is accurate? Was it God or Satan who induced David to perform a perilous headcount of the Jewish people?

This question is not trivial.

Satan is not mentioned frequently in the Jewish Scriptures; therefore, a careful study of this rare occurrence will prove invaluable. Can these two conflicting passages be harmonized?

For the Church, this glaring contradiction is hopelessly irreconcilable.

According to Christian theology, Satan is the chief enemy and arch opponent of God. The New Testament casts him as the secret power of lawlessness,[1] the Dragon,[2] and the author of all evil.[3] Accordingly, Christendom insists that the chief adversary of God has no inclination to fulfill the will of God. Quite the contrary, Satan opposes all of the Father's goals. In mainstream Christian teachings, he is called "the ruler of the demons" (Matt. 12:24). In essence, the New Testament portrays Satan as a being who relentlessly works *against* God and His plan. If the Christian portrayal of Satan was accurate, these two passages would be hopelessly in conflict and contradict all Christian doctrines concerning Satan.[4]

For the Jewish faith, these two passages are in complete harmony: Satan is only an angelic agent of God with no independent existence or authority. Throughout the Hebrew Scriptures, Satan is under the sovereignty of the Almighty so, like all other angels, he cannot act autonomously. As a servant, Satan faithfully carries out all of his tasks in obedience to the divine will of his Creator. The Book of I Chronicles' mention of Satan gives us insight into how the Almighty moved the heart of King David: Satan was used as the agent of God in order to provoke King David to perform a census.

Satan is only one of the many angels mentioned in the Bible. The Hebrew word for angel is מַלְאָךְ (*malach*), meaning "messenger." The same is true for the English word *angel*, derived from the Greek word ἄγγελος (*angelos*), which also means "messenger."

In essence, an angel is a courier of God who merely carries out the divine will of the Almighty. Throughout the corpus of the Jewish Scriptures, there is not a single instance in which any angel, Satan included, opposes the sovereign will of God.

How did Satan become evil?

Christians believe that Satan is a fallen angel who rebelled against the Almighty, and emerged as the archenemy of God. He is a decidedly malevolent entity (devil) who possesses demonic god-like qualities. This idea fed the widely held Christian belief that Satan was once a prideful angel who "fell" because of his insurrection and arrogance. It was then, we are told, Satan rebelled against God.

In addition, unlike the Hebrew Bible, which teaches that God is involved in everything in the universe, the New Testament claims that God did not create evil: "God is light, and in Him there is no darkness at all" (1 John 1:5). "God is not the author of confusion" (1 Corinthians 14:33). Accordingly, the Church argues, God cannot in any way be the author of evil.

Instead, Christendom teaches that Satan was originally the most anointed and highest cherub. Yet because of his pride, he went from being only good to being only evil. He wanted to be like God. The fallen angel was therefore permanently exiled and banished from Heaven for disobeying and rebelling against God. From that moment, the Church teaches, Satan never had one good thought.

The Gospels claim that Satan is "the ruler of the demons" (Matt. 12:24) who was cast out of heaven: "I was watching Satan fall from heaven like lightning." (Luke 10:18)

Yet this sensational teaching is nowhere to be found in the Jewish Scriptures. On the contrary, the Tanach teaches that God originally created evil so that virtue and free will could flourish. Not a single prophet suggested that Satan rebelled against God or was banished from Heaven. On the contrary, Satan appears preeminently in God's heavenly court in both Job 1:6-7 and Zechariah 3:1-2.

Moreover, the Book of Isaiah testifies that it was God Himself Who created "evil" as an integral feature in the world:

> I form the light, and create darkness; I make peace, and create evil.
> I am the Lord, that does all these things.
>
> (Isaiah 45:7)

The translators of several Christian Bibles, however, sought to conceal Isaiah's message. They accomplished this task by mistranslating the Hebrew word רָע (*rah*) as "a calamity" or "natural disaster," rather than "evil."

Isaiah 45:7

King James Version	New International Version
"I form the light, and create darkness: I make peace, and **create evil** (רָע): I the Lord do all these things."	"I form the light and create darkness, I bring prosperity and **create disaster**; I, the Lord, do all these things."

Many conservative Christian Bibles, including the King James Version and the New American Standard, resisted the temptation to tamper with this unambiguous passage in the Book of Isaiah.

God created both good and evil and presented these two powerful forces to mankind, so that man could then freely choose his spiritual path. This cardinal principle is clearly expressed in the Torah:

> **See, I have set before you today life and good, death and evil**, [16]"in that I command you today to love the Lord your God, to walk in His ways, and to keep His commandments, His statutes, and His judgments, that you may live and multiply; and the Lord your God will bless you in the land which you go to possess.... [19]"I call heaven and earth as witnesses today against you, that I have set before you life and death, blessing and cursing. Therefore, choose life, that both you and your descendants may live.
>
> (Deuteronomy 30:14-19)

Why does the Church claim that the Almighty did not create evil, when the Torah explicitly states that God laid out before man both good and evil?

It is a core teaching in the Jewish faith that man can attain virtue only if he possesses the free will to reject it and choose evil.

Contradicting this creed in the Torah, the Church holds that as a consequence of the Fall of Man, every person born into the world is enslaved to Satan and, apart from the efficacious or prevenient grace of God, is utterly unable to choose to follow God or choose to accept salvation as it is offered. The human race is spiritually feeble due to the fallen state of man, which is the result of Original Sin. Missionaries argue, therefore, man is powerless to resist Satan's strength and blandishments.

This core Church teaching, however, is contravened by the Torah.

Immediately after the sin in the Garden of Eden, the Almighty declares that although Satan is lurking behind the door, one can master over him:

> **Genesis 4:7**
> "If you do well, will you not be accepted? And if you do that which is not well, sin lieth at the door. Unto you shall be his desire, and **you shall rule over him**."

Footnotes

1. 2 Thessalonians 2:7

2. Revelations 12:9

3. Luke 10:19; Acts 5:3; 2 Corinthians 11:3; Ephesians 2:2

4. Christian Bible commentators struggle considerably in their attempt to reconcile this problem. Although their explanations vary, the common theme in their responses is almost always a regurgitation of the problem itself. They maintain that both the Satan of the Jewish Scriptures and the Satan in Christian theology are true; Satan is both the servant of God and at the very same time the enemy of God. For example, the *New International Version Study Bible's* commentary on I Chronicles 21:1 (Zondervan: 1985) states:

   "Although Scripture is clear that God does not cause anyone to sin, it is also clear that man's and Satan's evil acts are under God's sovereign control."

   While this is a remarkable and necessary concession, it doesn't begin to resolve the original irreconcilable problem of the nature of Satan in Christian theology.

In Whose Merit Will Israel Be Saved?

Isaiah 59:20	Romans 11:26
And the Redeemer shall come to Zion, and **unto them that turn from transgression in Jacob**, saith the Lord.	And so all Israel shall be saved: even as it is written, "There shall come out of Zion the Deliverer; **He shall turn away ungodliness from Jacob**."

Isaiah 59:21	Romans 11:27
As for Me, this is My covenant with them, saith the Lord; My spirit that is upon thee, and my words which I have put in thy mouth, shall not depart out of thy mouth, nor out of the mouth of thy seed, nor out of the mouth of thy seed's seed, saith the Lord, from henceforth and for ever.	For this is my covenant with them, **when I shall take away their sins**.

Pauline interpolation → "when I shall take away their sins"
Original Isaiah text → "For this is my covenant with them"

In an epic passage, the prophet Isaiah brings into view an inspiring and uplifting picture of the messianic age. In 59:20, Isaiah describes the End of Days, when the messiah will come to his people who have turned away from transgression. These stirring passages set the stage for the extraordinary prophecies in the following chapter where Isaiah holds up the picture of a pious remnant of Israel, a righteous people, with a light that will serve as a guide for all the surrounding gentile nations (60:1-22).

For Christians, however, Isaiah 59:20 presents a serious theological problem. In the third chapter of the Book of Romans, Paul insists that man cannot merit his own salvation. One of the most fundamental underpinnings of Christian doctrine regarding salvation is the Pauline teaching that the cross alone, not our own good deeds and heart-felt repentance, can save.[1] Who then would the Redeemer come to if no one can turn from transgression?

Paul therefore rearranges the words of Isaiah 59:20 in the Book of Romans (11:26) so that the text appears to predict that the Redeemer [Jesus] will turn away sin from Jacob. This, of course, is not what the prophet actually predicts. As mentioned above, the original verse declares that the messiah will come to those who have repented of transgression. It is not difficult, therefore, to understand why Paul found it necessary to alter Isaiah's original message.

In the following verse, Paul continues to tamper with the text so that it remains consistent with his alterations in the previous verse. Romans 11:27 was designed to appear as a continuation of Isaiah's message when he writes, "And this is my covenant unto them, when I shall take away their sins." Although the first half of this verse, "And this is my covenant with them," is correctly quoted from the first part of Isaiah 59:21, the second half has disappeared. Paul expunged the latter half of Isaiah's verse and instead inserted a contrived text, "When I shall take away their sins." Paul interpolated this segment in order to support his modifications of Isaiah's previous verse (11:26).

---

[1] Paul bases this assertion primarily on the verse from Genesis 15:6, *"And he [Abram] believed in the Lord; and he counted it to him for righteousness."* In both Romans 4:3 and Galatians 3:6, Paul sets out to prove from this verse that faith alone is what saves man—not his observance of the Law. Paul insists that this verse clearly demonstrates that Abraham was considered righteous through faith alone and not by his deeds.

Paul, however, ripped this quote completely out of context. A little further on in the Book of Genesis, the Torah brings to light the very fabric of Abraham's faith. In Genesis 26:5, the Bible declares that *"Because Abraham obeyed Me and kept My charge, My commandments, My statutes and My laws."* It was Abraham's unwavering obedience to the commandments of the Almighty in spite of the challenging tests placed before him that revealed his unyielding faith in God.

Who is the 'Morning Star,' Jesus or Satan?

Isaiah 14:12	Revelation 22:16
"How you have fallen from heaven, O **morning star**, son of the dawn! You have been cut down to the earth, You who have weakened the nations!"	"I Jesus have sent mine angel to testify unto you these things in the churches. I am the root and the offspring of David, and the bright and **morning star**." *(See II Peter 1:19)*

Isaiah 27:9
Therefore through this Jacob's iniquity will be forgiven; and this will be the full price of the pardoning of his sin: When he makes all the altar stones like pulverized chalk stones; when *Asherim* and incense altars will not stand.

Isaiah proclaims that the "full price" of Jacob's iniquity will be fully atoned when the Jewish nation finally destroys the altars and idols of heathens.
   This prophecy completely contradicts Christianity's most cherished doctrine: The blood of Jesus alone atones for man's manifold sins. According to Christian theology, destroying idolatry and heathen altars is irrelevant to salvation.

The Devil and the Jews

John 8:44	Revelation 2:9
"**Ye [Jews] are of your father the devil**, and the lusts of your father ye will do. He was a murderer from the beginning, and abode not in the truth, because there is no truth in him. When he speaketh a lie, he speaketh of his own: for he is a liar, and the father of it."	"I know your works, tribulation, and poverty (but you are rich); and I know the blasphemy of those who say they are Jews and are not, but are a **synagogue of Satan**." *(See also Revelations 3:9)*

Matthew 28:11-15
Now while they were going, behold, some of the guard came into the city and reported to the chief priests all the things that had happened. When they had assembled with the elders and consulted together, they gave a large sum of money to the soldiers, saying, **"Tell them, 'His disciples came at night and stole Him away while we slept.'** And if this comes to the governor's ears, we will appease him and make you secure." So they took the money and did as they were instructed; **and this saying is commonly reported among the Jews until this day**.

In Jewish thought, Satan is seen as an agent of God whose job is to tempt one into sin, and then turn around and accuse the sinner on High. An additional understanding of Satan is from a parable to a prostitute who is hired by the King (God) to tempt his son (a Jew). The prostitute has to do the best she can to tempt the son; but deep down she hopes the son will pass the test. Similarly, Jewish thought sees Satan in the same situation. His job is to tempt us as best he can; turn around and accuse us; but deep down, his wish is that we would resist his blandishments.

The following related article can be found in Volume 2 of *Let's Get Biblical! Why doesn't Judaism Accept the Christian Messiah?*

I. Who is Satan?........................ Page 249

Part XIV

Paul and the Christian Corruption of the Jewish Scriptures

Why did the author of the Book of Luke interpolate the phrase "Recovery of sight to the blind" into the mouth of the Prophet Isaiah?

Luke 4:18-19

The Spirit of the Lord is upon me, because he has anointed me to preach the gospel to the poor; he has sent me to heal the brokenhearted, to proclaim liberty to the captives and **recovery of sight to the blind**, to set at liberty those who are oppressed; ¹⁹to proclaim the acceptable year of the Lord.

Isaiah 61:1-2 *(KJV)*

The Spirit of the Lord God is upon me; because the Lord hath anointed me to preach good tidings unto the meek; he hath sent me to bind up the brokenhearted, to proclaim liberty to the captives, and the opening of the prison to them that are bound; ²to proclaim the acceptable year of the Lord,

Romans 9:24-26

Even us, whom he also called, not only from the Jews but also from the Gentiles? As he says in Hosea: "I will call them 'my people' who are not my people; and I will call her 'my loved one' who is not my loved one, and, it will happen that in the very place where it was said to them, 'You are not my people,' they will be called 'sons of the living God.'"

Hosea 1:3-9

So he went and took Gomer the daughter of Diblaim; which conceived, and bare him a son. And the Lord said unto him, "Call his name **Jezreel**; for yet a little while, and I will avenge the blood of Jezreel upon the house of Jehu, and will cause to cease the kingdom of the house of Israel. And it shall come to pass at that day, that I will break the bow of Israel in the valley of Jezreel." And she conceived again, and bare a daughter. And God said unto him, "Call her name **Lo-rachamah**: for I will no more have mercy upon the house of Israel; but I will utterly take them away. But I will have mercy upon the house of Judah, and will save them by the Lord their God, and will not save them by bow, nor by sword, nor by battle, by horses, nor by horsemen." Now when she had weaned Loruhamah, she conceived, and bare a son. Then said God, "Call his name ***Lo-ammi***: for ye are not my people, and I will not be your God."

Hosea 2:25 *(Christian Bible 2:23)*

And I will sow her for Myself in the land. I will also have compassion on her who had not obtained compassion, And I will say to those who were not My people, 'You are My people!' And they will say, "*Thou art* my God!"

Isaiah 7:14-16

Therefore the Lord himself will give you a sign. Look, the young woman is with child and shall bear a son, and shall name him Immanuel. He shall eat curds and honey by the time he knows how to refuse the evil and choose the good. For before the child knows how to refuse the evil and choose the good, the land before whose two kings you are in dread will be deserted.

Hosea served as a prophet primarily to the Northern Kingdom of Israel, and was given children whose names made them like walking prophecies of doom—foreboding the fall of the ten northern tribes and their severed covenant with God.

The name of Hosea's son, "Lo-ammi," which translates as "not my people," was chosen by God as a sign of the Almighty's displeasure with the people of the Northern Kingdom for following other gods (see Hosea 1:8-9).

Later, the Almighty showed pity on the Northern Kingdom of Israel and promised that they will be restored (Hosea 2:25). The name of Hosea's son was then changed to "Ammi," which translates as "My people."

In Romans 9:25, however, Paul erroneously attributed this famed prophecy in the Book of Hosea to the gentiles, who, he insisted, were originally not God's people, yet would be called "My people" under Christ. This assertion is completely contrived as evidenced from the first two chapters of Hosea.

Paul deliberately ripped Hosea 2:25 completely out of context. The first two chapters of the Book of Hosea are clearly referring to the future restoration of the ten exiled tribes of the Northern Kingdom of Israel who will finally be called "My people" in the messianic age; not the gentiles, as Paul claims.

Isaiah 7:3-4

Then the Lord said to Isaiah, "Go out to meet Ahaz, you and your son **Shear-yashuv**, at the end of the conduit of the upper pool on the highway to the Washer's Field, ⁴and say to him, 'Take heed, be quiet, do not fear, and do not let your heart be faint because of these two smoldering stumps of firebrands, because of the fierce anger of Rezin and Aram and the son of Remaliah.'"

Isaiah 8:18

"See, I and the children whom the Lord has given me are signs and portents in Israel from the Lord of hosts, who dwells on Mount Zion."

As mentioned above, the name designated to a prophet's child symbolizes the destiny of the people to whom he was preaching. Therefore, the names assigned to Hosea's children expressed God's displeasure with the Northern Kingdom of Israel, i.e. "Lo-Amee," meaning, "You are not My people."

In contrast, the names of Isaiah's children symbolize the divine preservation and protection the Almighty would bestow upon the Southern Kingdom of Judah (Isaiah 8:18). For example, the name of Isaiah's son Shear-Yashuv means "The remnant will remain."

Galatians 3:6-9

Just as Abraham "believed God, and it was accounted to him for righteousness." Know ye therefore that they which are of faith, the same are the children of Abraham. ⁸And the scripture, foreseeing that God would justify the heathen through faith, preached before the gospel unto Abraham, *saying*, In thee shall all nations be blessed. ⁹So then they which be of faith are blessed with faithful Abraham.

Genesis 15:5-6

And he brought him forth outside, and said, "Look now toward heaven, and tell the stars, if thou be able to number them: and he said unto him, So shall thy **seed** be." ⁶And he [Abraham] believed in the Lord, and He counted it to him for righteousness.

Genesis 26:4-5

And I will make thy seed to multiply as the stars of heaven, and will give unto thy seed all these countries; and in thy seed shall all the nations of the earth be blessed; ⁵**Because Abraham obeyed My voice, and kept My charge, My commandments, My statutes, and My laws**.

Genesis 12:2-3

"I will make you into a great nation and I will bless you; I will make your name great, and you will be a blessing. ³I will bless those who bless you, and whoever curses you I will curse; and all peoples on earth will be blessed through you."

Genesis 15:2-5

Abram said, "O Lord God, what will You give me, since I am childless, and the heir of my house is Eliezer of Damascus?" ³And Abram said, "Since You have given no offspring to me, the one born in my house is my heir." ⁴Then behold, the word of the Lord came to him, saying, "**This man will not be your heir; but one who will come forth from your own body, he shall be your heir**." ⁵And He brought him forth outside, and said, "Look now toward heaven, and tell the stars, if thou be able to number them: and He said unto him, So shall thy **seed** be."

Were Paul's Teachings Divinely Inspired?

Although Paul's influence on Christian thinking has been more significant than that of any other New Testament author, there is no existing evidence that he possessed more than a perfunctory knowledge of the Hebrew language. He virtually never used it, and when he used the Greek text he misquoted and misappropriated it. He mistranslated Scriptures in order to convey his contrived story, and craft the DNA of Christian theology.

In fact, Paul more accurately quoted Greek philosophers, playwrights and poets than the Jewish prophets. Moreover, if, as Christians insist, the writings of Paul were divinely inspired and Heaven-breathed, why would God quote from godless, Greek writers? Would God quote Voltaire or Russell?

For example, Paul quoted Plato in I Cor. 13:12, the Greek poets Epimenides of Crete, who worshiped Zeus, and Aratus of Cilicia in Acts 17:28. In I Cor. 15:33, he quoted the comedy playwright Menander, who frequently used vulgarities in his plays. Would God quote from an off-color playwright who oftentimes used the filthy phrase "Sh_ _-eaters" in his plays?

In the Book of Galatians, Paul addressed an illiterate, non-Jewish audience in Asia Minor. He advanced a contrived teaching about the Abrahamic Covenant, which portrays gentile Christians as children of Abraham. He sought to turn the father of circumcision into the father of the uncircumcised because that is his unambiguous agenda.

He argued that the repeated promises throughout the Book of Genesis are to "you and to your seed," which he insisted can only mean Jesus (Gal. 3:16).

To make his case, he pointed out, "notice it doesn't say the word 'seeds' which is plural." Using deeply flawed theological craftsmanship, he argues that "the promise is to you and your seed, and that seed is Christ."

> **Galatians 3:16**
> [16]Now the promises were spoken to Abraham and to his seed. He does not say, "And to seeds," as referring to many, but rather to one, "And to your seed," that is, Christ.

The apostle to the gentiles is definitely trying to convince his unlettered audience that the word, "seed," in the Torah is speaking of a single individual.

"Seed" is like the word "sheep" in the English language. If I were a farmer, would I command my herdsmen, "Feed my sheeps"? In this context, "sheep" is a plural word, and in the context where Abraham is told the promise is "to you and to your seed,"[1] it refers to the generations to come. It does not mean a single person or Jesus.

Paul's writings illustrate that he was either profoundly ignorant or a charlatan. Regardless, Paul had the good fortune to be addressing an audience who knew less about Scripture than he did. The Torah uses the word "seed" rather than the word "seeds" only when referring to the entire nation of Israel. This page contains numerous examples of the Torah referring to the nation of Israel with the word "seed."

While missionaries suggest that he was making some sort of analogy, Paul's famed analogies turn the Jewish Scriptures on its head. In the following chapter, he turned Sarah, the mother of the Jewish people, who received the Torah at Mt. Sinai, into a metaphor for those who are free from the curse of the Law. According to Paul's twisted theology, the bondwoman Hagar, the mother of the Arab nation, represents the Jews who are bound by the Law (Gal 4:22-31).

Why does this "Pharisee of Pharisees" misquote the Jewish Scriptures when he said he was the smartest person in his class?

[1]Gen. 13:16; 15:5-6; 16:10; 17:19; 18:18; 22:17; 26:46; II Ki. 11:1; Mal. 2:15; 2 Chron. 20:7

Genesis 13:16
And I will make thy **seed** (זַרְעֲךָ) as the dust of the earth: so that if a man can number the dust of the earth, then shall thy **seed** (זַרְעֲךָ) also be numbered.

Genesis 15:5
He brought him forth abroad, and said, Look now toward heaven, and tell the stars, if thou be able to number them: and He said unto him, So shall thy **seed** (זַרְעֲךָ) be.

Genesis 16:10
And the angel of the Lord said unto her, I will multiply thy **seed** (זַרְעֲךָ) exceedingly, that it shall not be numbered for multitude.

Genesis 17:19
And God said, Sarah thy wife shall bear thee a son indeed; and thou shalt call his name Isaac: and I will establish my covenant with him for an everlasting covenant, and with his **seed** (לְזַרְעוֹ) after him.

Genesis 22:17
That in blessing I will bless thee, and in multiplying I will multiply thy **seed** (זַרְעֲךָ) as the stars of the heaven, and as the sand which is upon the sea shore; and thy **seed** (זַרְעֲךָ) shall possess his enemies gates; (See Genesis 18:18, 26:46, 2 Kings 11:1, Malachi 2:15 and 2 Chronicles 20:7.)

Genesis 3:15

And I will put enmity between thee and the woman, and between thy **seed** (זַרְעֲךָ) and her seed; he shall bruise thy head, and thou shalt bruise his heel.

I John 3:8

He that committeth sin is of the devil; for the devil sinneth from the beginning. For this purpose **the son of God was manifested, that he might destroy the works of the devil.**

Hebrews 2:14

Forasmuch then as the children are partakers of flesh and blood, he also himself likewise took part of the same; that **through death he might destroy him that had the power of death, that is, the devil**;

I Samuel 2:20

And Eli blessed Elkanah and his wife, and said, "The Lord **give thee seed** (זֶרַע) **of this woman** for the loan which is lent to the Lord." And they went unto their own home.

Genesis 4:7

If you do that which is well, would that not be accepted? And if you do that which is not well, sin lies by the door, you shall be his desire, and you shall rule over him.

Genesis 3:20

And Adam called his wife's name Eve; because she was the mother of all living.

I Thessalonians 2:18

Wherefore we would have come unto you, even I Paul, once and again; **but Satan hindered us**.

The assertion that the singular "seed" in Genesis 3:15 is an allusion to Jesus' destiny to destroy Satan is erroneous. As mentioned above, the Torah exclusively uses the word "seed," in the singular, for the Jewish nation (see, for example, Genesis 15:5 and 16:10). Moreover, if, as Christians frequently argue, Genesis 3:15 is interpreted to mean that the messiah's central role is to destroy Satan, Jesus clearly failed at this monumental task.

Satan thrives among Christians in the New Testament. More importantly, the state of mankind was not transformed for the better following the advent of Christianity. How has the condition of the world improved as a result of the Cross? On the contrary, it is reasonable to conclude that some of the most odious crimes in history were carried out in the name of Jesus.

The prophets of Israel foretold that the coming of the true messiah would usher in a world that will be radically changed for the better. War will cease, and the knowledge of God will cover the world as the water covers the sea (see pages 232-235). None of these epic prophecies occurred as a result of any event in the New Testament.

The word "seed" in Genesis 3:15 is not referring to a single individual. Rather, this verse is speaking of every faithful member of mankind, and its message is clear. Mankind, Eve's descendants, will be confronted with temptation, and will have the ability to conquer Satan, who manifests himself in our nagging, evil inclination. While many would fail at this task, others like Abraham, Joshua, Caleb, and Daniel would succeed.

In essence, although Satan lies crouched behind the door seeking to seduce man, Eve's children have the power to "crush his head" (Genesis 3:15), and "rule over him [Satan]" (Genesis 4:7).

Part XV

Bearers of the Torch

"Jews Go Home"
- By William Eiken -
The Gazette Telegraph of Colorado
(reprinted in more than 250 newspapers throughout North America)

"Jews Go Home!" – Well, now this is nothing new. Never in the past have you taken this gentle suggestion to move on. But Heaven forbid, suppose just this once you thought that this expression of a few sick people actually expressed the conviction of all the people in this wonderful land of ours, and all of you started to pack your bags and leave for parts unknown.

"Jews Go Home, we don't want Jews, we want oil!" But before you leave, could you do me a favor? Would you leave behind your formula for the Salk Vaccine with me before you leave? You wouldn't be so heartless as to let my children contract polio?

And would you please leave behind your knack for government, politics, persuasion, literature, and your good food. And would you please leave me with the secret of your desire to succeed?

And please have pity on us. Please show us the secret of how to develop such geniuses as Einstein and Steinmetz, and so many others who have helped us all. After all, we owe you a lot for the atomic bomb, most of our rocket research, and perhaps the fact that we are alive today. Instead, we could have been looking up from our chains and from our graves at Hitler, old but glad, driving slowly by in one of our Cadillacs had he succeeded in reaching the atom bomb and not us.

On your way out, Jews, will you do me another favor? Will you please drop by my house and pick me up too? I'm not sure I could live too well in a land where you were not to be found. For if ever you were to leave, love goes with you, democracy and morality goes with you, everything I and my buddies fought for in World War II goes with you. God goes with you.

Just pull up in front of my house, slow down and honk because so help me, I'm going with you too.

Yours sincerely,

William Eikin.

"You Are My Witnesses!"

1. *"You have been shown so that you will know"*

Only take heed to yourself, and diligently keep yourself, so that you do not forget the things your eyes have seen. Do not let [this memory] leave your hearts all the days of your lives. Teach them to your children and your children's children, ¹⁰about the day you stood before the Lord your God in Horeb...¹¹Then you came near and stood at the foot of the mountain, and the mountain burned with fire to the midst of heaven, with darkness, cloud, and thick darkness. ¹²And the Lord spoke to you out of the midst of the fire. You heard the sound of the words, but saw no form; you only heard a voice.

Deuteronomy 4:9-12

You might inquire about times long past, going back to the time that God created man on earth, [exploring] one end of the heavens to the other, see if anything as great as this has ever happened, or if the like has ever been heard. ³³Has any nation ever heard God speaking out of fire, as you have, and still survived? ³⁴Has God ever done miracles, bringing one nation out of another nation, with tremendous miracles, signs, wonders, war, a mighty hand and outstretched arm, and terrifying phenomena, as God did for you in Egypt before you very eyes? ³⁵You are the ones who have been shown, so that you will know that God is the Supreme Being, and there is none besides him. ³⁶From the heavens, He let you hear His voice admonishing you, and on earth He showed you His great fire, so that you heard His words from the fire. ³⁷ It was because He loved your fathers, and chose their children after them, that [God] Himself brought you out of Egypt with His great power. ³⁸He will drive away before you nations that are greater and stronger than you, so as to bring you to their lands, and give them to you as a heritage, as [He is doing] today. ³⁹Realize it today and ponder it in your heart: God is the Supreme Being in heaven above and on earth beneath — there is no other.

כִּי שְׁאַל־נָא
לְיָמִים רִאשֹׁנִים...

Deuteronomy 4:32-39

If your brother, the son of your mother, your son or your daughter, the wife of your bosom, or your friend who is as your own soul, secretly entices you, saying, 'Let us go and serve other gods,' which you have not known, neither you nor your fathers, ⁷of the gods of the people which are all around you, near to you or far off from you, from one end of the earth to the other end of the earth, ⁸you shall not consent to him or listen to him, nor shall your eye pity him, nor shall you spare him or conceal him;

Deuteronomy 13:6-8

2. *A Nation Bears Testimony*

Everyone who is called by My name, whom I have created for My glory; I have formed him, yes, I have made him. Bring out the blind people who have eyes, and the deaf who have ears. Let all the nations be gathered together, and let the people be assembled. ⁹Who among them can declare this, and show us former things? Let them bring out their witnesses, that they may be justified; Or let them hear and say, 'It is truth.' ¹⁰ "You are My witnesses!" says the Lord, "And My servant whom I have chosen, That you may know and believe Me, And understand that I am He. Before Me there was no God formed, nor shall there be after Me. ¹¹I, even I, am the Lord, And besides Me there is no Savior. ¹²I have declared and saved, I have proclaimed, And there was no foreign god among you; therefore you are My witnesses," says the Lord, "that I am God."

Isaiah 43:8-12

"Remember — Do Not Forget"

3. *<u>Remember the Slavery in Egypt</u>*

And you shall <u>remember</u> that you were a slave in the land of Egypt, and the Lord your God redeemed you; therefore I command you this today.
Deuteronomy 15:15 (see also 16:12)

You shall not pervert the justice due an alien or an orphan, nor take a widow's garment in pledge. [18]But you shall <u>remember</u> that you were a slave in Egypt, and that the Lord your God redeemed you from there; therefore I am commanding you to do this thing.
Deuteronomy 24:17-18

> The nation of Israel is commanded to remember the events that they were witness to and personally experienced. Only when it becomes evident that the Torah was not written at a later date or dates, but at the time the events themselves occurred, is it conceivable that the entire nation would shoulder the responsibility to remember.

4. *<u>Remember the Events in Egypt</u>*

You shall not be afraid of them; you shall well <u>remember</u> what the Lord your God did to Pharaoh and to all Egypt: [19]the great trials which your eyes saw and the signs and the wonders and the mighty hand and the outstretched arm by which the Lord your God brought you out.
Deuteronomy 7:18-19

5. *<u>Remember the Exodus</u>*

And Moses said to the people, "<u>Remember this day</u> in which you went out from Egypt, from the house of slavery; for by a mighty hand the Lord brought you out from this place. Nothing leavened shall be eaten."
Exodus 13:3

You shall not eat leavened bread with it; seven days you shall eat with it unleavened bread, the bread of affliction (for you came out of the land of Egypt in haste), in order that you may <u>remember</u> all the days of your life the day when you came out of the land of Egypt.
Deuteronomy 16:12

> The Torah turns to the Nation of Israel in the first person and emphatically commands: "You shall remember, you shall remember!" No nation would have accepted such a detailed command to remember that which was seen and experienced had these events not actually occurred. The emphasis which is placed on remembering demonstrates that the memory of these events carved itself deeply in the consciousness of the nation.

6. *<u>Remember Receiving the Torah at Sinai</u>*

But take care and watch yourselves closely, so as <u>neither to forget the things that your eyes have seen nor to let them slip from your mind all the days of your life</u>; make them known to your children and your children's children.
Deuteronomy 4:9

7. *<u>Remember the Journey in the Wilderness</u>*

And you shall remember all the way which the Lord your God has led you in the wilderness these forty years, that He might humble you, <u>testing you, to know what was in your heart</u>, whether you would keep His commandments or not.
Deuteronomy 8:2

Holocaust Revisionism

Mahmoud Abbas
Chairman of the PLO and President of the Palestinian Authority and Fatah. Abbas earned his PhD at the University in Moscow. The theme of his doctoral dissertation was *"The Other Side: The secret relations between Nazism and the leadership of the Zionist movement"* in which he attempted to prove that the Nazi Holocaust of Jews never happened.

Austin J. App
Former associate professor of English at LaSalle College, Philadelphia, is the author of numerous neo-Nazi pamphlets, one, for example, called *"Did Six Million Really Die? The Truth at Last."*

Arthur Butz
Professor of engineering at Northwestern University and author of *"The Hoax of the Twentieth Century,"* denying the death camps and the extermination of millions of Jews. Claims of fabrication of the Holocaust by Jews seeking to enlist support for Israel by appealing to popular guilt feelings.

Willis Carto
Founder of the Institute for Historical Review (1978) in Torrance, CA. The I.H.R. Publishes journals and sponsors conventions designed to whitewash Nazi war crimes by denying the Holocaust. Carto is also the treasurer of the "Liberty Lobby" in Washington D.C. Which publishes the *"Spotlight,"* a weekly publication long known for its diatribes against Israel and the American Jewish community.

Thies Christopherson
64 year-old journalist and leader of the Christians and Farmers Initiative, continues to write and lecture in the Federal Republic of Germany in defense of the Nazi regime and in propagation of the canard that there was no Holocaust. In addition to leading his group, he publishes tracts and pamphlets under the auspices of Critical Review Publications. A close associate of the American Hitlerite George Dietz, he has been a frequent visitor and lecturer in the USA and Canada.

Leon Derelle
Author of articles in praise of the S.S. of which he was a member...currently hiding in Spain to escape a death sentence for war crimes committed in his native Belgium...contributor to the I.H.R. journal.

Robert Faurisson
Holds a PhD from the Sorbonne in Paris...was dismissed from his position as professor of French at Lyons University for revisionist views and convicted by a French court for defaming the victims of the Holocaust. He claims that the Nazi gas chambers never existed and that facts about the Holocaust and the number of victims have been grossly exaggerated.

David McCalden
Also known as Lewis Brandon, co-founder of the Institute for Historical Review....sponsor of "Truth Missions," a front for the defamation of Simon Wiesenthal and the propagation of Holocaust revisionism in Manhattan Beach, Ca.

George Pape
President of the German-American Committee of Greater New York (a cultural organization with over 50 branches in the metropolitan area) objected to the introduction of teaching the Holocaust in the school system with the words: "there is no real proof that the Holocaust actually happened."

Paul Rassinier
French author and a pioneer of this revisionist approach, speaks of "The Lie of Auschwitz."

Manfred Roeder
A 57 year-old disbarred lawyer is the leader of the 100 member German Citizens Initiative. Without a steady income and facing imprisonment because of his neo-Nazi activities, Roeder became a fugitive from justice who found refuge with friends and associates in North and South America. While a fugitive, he established a working relationship with the "Aryan Nations," a small vitriolic, violence-prone American anti-Semitic group located in Idaho. Currently he is serving his sentence in a German prison, having been taken into custody by German authorities in September 1980, as he sought surreptitiously to return to the Federal Republic.

Charles Weber
Professor of German at the university of Tulsa...author of "The Holocaust: 120 Questions and Answers," a conglomeration of distortions and half-truths trivializing Nazi guilt during World War II. Contributor to the I.H.R. journal. Article authored by Weber recently appeared in an "Aryan Nations" pamphlet.

Ernst Zundel
German-Canadian revisionist and major international publisher of anti-Semitic material and distributor of pro-Nazi literature convicted for knowingly spreading false information about the Holocaust.

Trials of War Criminals Before the Nuernberg Military Tribunals
Opening statement of the Prosecution
by Brigadier General Telford Taylor, December 9, 1946

We need look no further than the law which the Nazis themselves passed on the 24th of November 1933 for the protection of animals. This law states explicitly that it is designed to prevent cruelty and indifference of man towards animals and to awaken and develop sympathy and understanding for animals as one of the highest moral values of a people. The soul of the German people should abhor the principle of mere utility without consideration of the moral aspects. The law states further that all operations or treatments which are associated with pain or injury, especially experiments involving the use of cold, heat, or infection, are prohibited, and can be permitted only under special exceptional circumstances. Special written authorization by the head of the department is necessary in every case, and experimenters are prohibited from performing experiments according to their own free judgment. Experiments for the purpose of teaching must be reduced to a minimum. Medico-legal tests, vaccinations, withdrawal of blood for diagnostic purposes, and trial of vaccines prepared according to well-established scientific principles are permitted, but the animals have to be killed immediately and painlessly after such experiments. Individual physicians are not permitted to use dogs to increase their surgical skill by such practices. National Socialism regards it as a sacred duty of German science to keep down the number of painful animal experiments to a minimum.

If the principles announced in this law had been followed for human beings as well, this indictment would never have been filed. It is perhaps the deepest shame of the defendants that it probably never even occurred to them that human beings should be treated with at least equal humanity.

"The Medical Case", Volume I, page 71

"The receptivity of the great masses is very limited, their intelligence is small, but their power of forgetting is enormous. In consequence of these facts, all effective propaganda must be limited to a very few points and must harp on these in slogans until the last member of the public understands what you want him to understand by your slogan. As soon as you sacrifice this slogan and try to be many-sided, the effect will piddle away, for the crowd can neither digest nor retain the material offered. In this way the result is weakened and the end entirely canceled out...

The magnitude of a lie always contains a certain factor of credibility, since the great masses of the people in the very bottom of their hearts tend to be corrupted rather than consciously and purposely evil, and that, therefore, in view of the primitive simplicity of their minds, they more easily fall a victim to a big lie than to a little one, since they themselves lie in little things, but would be ashamed of lies that were too big."

Adolf Hitler, Mein Kampf

"The Jews inflicted two scars on mankind. Circumcision on his body and a conscience on his soul."

Adolf Hitler, Mein Kompf

Historical Parallels — "Our eyes have seen!"

In Jerusalem, June 14th to 18th, 1981,
the World Gathering of Jewish Holocaust Survivors:

Ernest Michel, Chairman of the World Gathering:

My name is Ernest Michel. Auschwitz number one zero four nine nine five. Like many of you I had a dream that one day — if we live — we could come and stand together.

This is a reunion of a special group of people for which there is no parallel anywhere. We want to stand together once more before time runs out, united in freedom as we were in slavery. We want to see in each others eyes and in the eyes of our children the proof of our survival and the joy that comes from being alive and free. But there is more than that. We survivors want to tell those who try to rewrite the history and deny that the Holocaust ever happened: <u>Our eyes have seen. Our ears have heard. Our nostrils were filled with the acrid fumes</u> from the gas chambers drifting over our camp. Day after day. Week after week. Year after year. These hands [Michel holds his hands up in the air] have carried more corpses than I care to remember. So don't tell us it never happened. <u>We were there</u>.

This gathering could not have taken place 10 or 20 years ago. It took time for wounds to heal enough for us to meet. <u>This is why this event took almost 40 years to come into being, and that is why we shall never meet as one group again</u>. It has become fashionable to invoke the memory of the Holocaust - so much has been written, so much has been dramatized. <u>It is *we* who have lived it, *we* who have survived it, *we* of whom they write, *we* of whom they speak</u>. So, today, it is our turn. Today, *we* speak. Despite the memories of the past, we have built new lives. Many of us have second families — so many of the first were exterminated. We have children, grandchildren. We have sanctified the names of those we lost — we have contributed to Jewish tomorrows. A number of people have asked: Why are you doing this? Why do you want to meet? Why recall a past such as you've had. Why not leave it alone? Our response, straight and simple: we survived for a purpose. Already something constructive has emerged from this gathering.

<u>Represented here are almost 1,000 members of the Second Generation. I am pleased to announce that they have formed here in Jerusalem a Second Generation International Network whose major purpose will be to carry on the memory of the Holocaust</u>. Like you, I will never forget this week, the seeking, the finding, then that first look of recognition. Aren't you? Aren't you? Weren't you? Block 14? Commando 35? From the ghetto? The embrace — the touch — God, how good it felt to see each other, to be together — the tears, the smiles, the memories, the stories: It will take a while to climb down from the mountain of this emotional high of this unforgettable and unrepeatable week. As long as I live the faces of this four days will be indelibly etched in my memory, when our tears turned to laughter and our sadness to joy.

Lucy Dawidowicz

Can all these lies change the truth? Can a honest and intelligent person believe in a criminal and absurd falsehood which claims that Nazi Germany never murdered 6 million Jews? Who can give credence to the monstrous lie that Auschwitz never housed a gas chamber? To our chagrin, these are not merely rhetorical questions. While writing this article, a young man who works on a radio program in North America approached me and asked if I would be willing to debate Robert Faurisson on the air. When I replied angrily that it would be a travesty of justice and decency to give such a man a public platform, the young man answered: "<u>Why are you opposed to dealing with a problem which is up for debate?!</u>" I asked him if, in his opinion, the murder of European Jewry was included in the category of "up for debate." Has it not been proven as a historical fact? "I wouldn't know," he answered, "<u>I wasn't born yet; I am only 30.</u>"

(From an article by Lucy Dawidowicz in Ma'ariv, April 30, 1981 - Hebrew)

"Some of the Israelis claim that God gave them this country. First, I do not believe that God loves Jews fore than He loves Christians and Moslems. Secondly, who were the witnesses?"
(Dr. Mahmoud, Arab Journalist, East Jerusalem)

Elie Wiesel, speaking at a press conference:

"<u>The Second Generation is the most meaningful aspect of our work.</u> <u>Their role in a way is even more difficult than ours</u>. They are responsible for a world they didn't create. They who did not go through the experience <u>must</u> <u>transmit it</u>."

Hillel Goldberg, "A Holocaust Theology: The Survivors' Statement - Part I" Tradition 20(2) 1982

Thousands of Holocaust Survivors at the Western Wall for the final ceremony of the World Gathering of Jewish Holocaust Survivors and the reading of "The Legacy"

Remember

זָכוֹר אֵת
אֲשֶׁר־עָשָׂה
לְךָ...

Deuteronomy 25:17

This day, 16 Sivan 5741 Anno Mundi (18.6.81), in the 36th year of our liberation from the hands of the Nazis, we are all standing before the remnant of our Sanctuary in Jerusalem, to transmit the legacy of this generation to future generations to come.

We are members of the generation which lived through the Holocaust. "One of a city, two of a family" survived. Some are scattered amongst the nations, from Holocaust to Dispersion; others came to Zion, from Holocaust to Redemption.

Ours is the generation of our children; they are standing here with us today, children without grandparents. And the generation of our children's children is also with us.

The memory of the six million, burnt in the fires of the Holocaust, is with us here as we transmit our everlasting legacy: Remember, and let nothing be forgotten! Remember what evil men did to us! Remember, we are a people scattered and dispersed amongst the nations in all countries - forget not!

Let memory be turned into deed! Let our broken fragments be brought together and become one people! Let our dispersed ones be brought together to one country, to become one amongst the nations, our State one amongst other states.

Let the desolation be rebuilt until our people can dwell securely in its land, in Israel, and there shall be no one to make us afraid; until it can "eat the fruits of its own labors and be content."

Let <u>every Jew view himself as through he had been scorched in the fires of the Holocaust, for the obligation lies on him to remember and not to forget</u>, to turn memory into action — to restore the life and culture of our people.

Thursday evening. The closing ceremony at the Western Wall. 6,000 memorial candles. 1,000 people per candle. Six million....This was the evening of the future: the transmission of the "legacy." In six languages (Hebrew, Yiddish, English, French, Ladino and Russian), <u>a survivor read the legacy and the son or grandson of a survivor received it</u>. For 45 minutes, 10,000 people sat in perfect silence as an Israeli, an Australian, a New Yorker, a Parisian, and another Israeli survivor read in each of the six languages:

The Legacy

"**We take this oath!** We take it in the shadow of flames whose tongues scar the soul of our people. We vow in the name of dead parents and children; we vow with our sadness hidden, our faith renewed; we vow we shall never let the sacred memory of our perished Six Million be scorned or erased.

We saw them hungry, in fear; we saw them rush to battle; we saw them in the loneliness of night - true to their faith. At the threshold of death; we saw them. We received their silence in silence; merged their tears with ours.

Deportations, executions, mass graves, death camps, mute prayers, cries of revolt, desperation, torn scrolls, cities and towns, villages and hamlets, the young the old, the rich, the poor, ghetto fighters and partisans, scholars and messianic dreamers, ravaged faces, fists raised like clouds of fire, all have vanished.

We take this oath! Vision becomes word to be handed down from father to son, from mother to daughter, from generation to generation.

Remember what the German killers and their accomplices did to our people. Remember them with rage and contempt. Remember what an indifferent world did to us and to itself. Remember the victims with pride and with sorrow. Remember also the deeds of the Righteous Gentiles.

We shall also remember the miracle of the Jewish rebirth of the land of our ancestors, in the independent State of Israel. Here pioneers and fighters restored to our people the dignity and majesty of nationhood. From the ruin of their lives, orphans and widows built homes and old-new fortresses on our redeemed land. To the end of our days we shall remember all those who realized and raised their dream, our dream, of redemption to the loftiest heights.

We take this oath here in Jerusalem, our eternal spiritual sanctuary. Let our legacy endure as a stone of the Temple Wall. For her prayers and memories burn. They burn and burn and burn and will not be consumed."

Abraham Zelezniakov

Reading the Legacy of Survivors and Response of the Second Generation

Menachem Rosensaft

Norbert Wollheim

Chaim Zlotogorski

Yaakov Lerner

Marcel Stourze

Mordecai Karasso

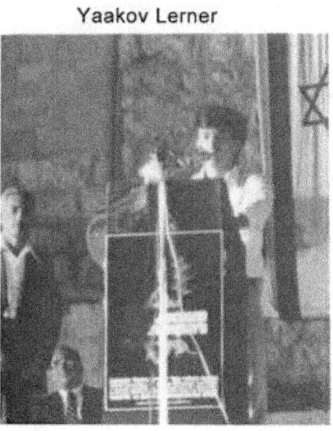

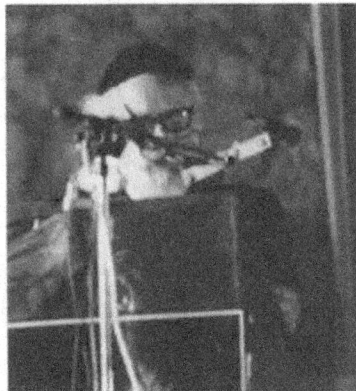

The Second Generation Accepts the Legacy

"We accept the obligation of this legacy.

We are the first generation born after the darkness. Through our Parents' memories, words and silence, we are linked to that annihilated Jewish existence whose echoes permeate our consciousness.

We dedicate this pledge to you, our parents, who suffered and survived; to our grandparents, who perished in the flames; to our vanished brothers and sisters, more than one million Jewish children, so brutally murdered; to all Six Million whose unyielding spiritual and physical resistance, even in the camps and ghettos, exemplifies our people's commitment to life.

We pledge to remember!

We shall teach our children to preserve forever that uprooted Jewish spirit which could not be destroyed.

We shall fight anti-Semitism and all forms of racial hatred by our dedication to freedom throughout the world.

We affirm our commitment to the State of Israel and to the furtherance of Jewish life in our homeland.

We pledge ourselves to the oneness of the Jewish people.

We are your children!"

Transmission to Future Generations: The Testimony

8. *<u>Gathering of the Survivors</u>*

And in the fortieth year, on the first day of the eleventh month, Moses spoke to the people of Israel according to all that the Lord had given him in commandment to them.

Deuteronomy 1:3

<u>Today, you are all standing before the Lord your God</u>; the heads of your tribes, your elders, and your officers, all the men of Israel, [10]your little ones, your wives, and the sojourner who is in your camp, both he who hews your wood and he who draws your water, [11]that you may enter into the covenant with the Lord your God, and into <u>His oath which the Lord your God is making with you today</u>.

Deuteronomy 29:9-11

9. *<u>The Testimony</u>*

You might inquire about times long past, going back to the time that God created man on earth, [exploring] one end of the heavens to the other, see if anything as great as this has ever happened, or if the like has ever been heard. [33]Has any nation ever heard God speaking out of fire, as you have, and still survived? [34]<u>Has God ever done miracles, bringing one nation out of another nation, with tremendous miracles</u>, signs, wonders, war, a mighty hand and outstretched arm, and terrifying phenomena, as God did for you in Egypt before your very eyes? [35]<u>You are the ones who have been shown</u>, so that you will know that God is the Supreme Being, and there is none besides Him.

Deuteronomy 4:32-35

And Moses summoned all Israel and said to them: "<u>You have seen all that the Lord did before your eyes in the land of Egypt</u>, to Pharaoh and to all his servants and to all his land, [2]the great trials which your eyes saw, the signs, and those great wonders; [3]but to this day the Lord has not given you a mind to understand, or eyes to see, or ears to hear. [4]<u>I have led you forty years in the wilderness; your clothes have not worn out upon you, and your sandals have not worn off your feet</u>; [5]you have not eaten bread, and you have not drunk wine or strong drink; that you may know that I am the Lord your God."

Deuteronomy 29:1-5

10. *<u>The Eyewitness Accounts</u>*

And Moses summoned all Israel, and said to them, "Hear, O Israel, the statutes and the ordinances which I speak in your hearing this day, and you shall learn them and be careful to do them. [2]The Lord our God made a covenant with us in *Horeb*. [3]<u>Not with our fathers did the Lord make this covenant, but with us, who are all of us here alive this day</u>. The Lord spoke with you face to face at the mountain, out of the midst of the fire."

Deuteronomy 5:1-3

<u>You must now realize that I am not speaking with your children, who did not know</u> and who did not see the lesson the Lord your God [taught] through His greatness and His mighty hand and His outstretched arm -- [3]His signs and His acts which He did in the midst of Egypt, to Pharaoh king of Egypt, and to all his land; [4]what He did to the army of Egypt, to their horses and their chariots: how He made the waters of the Red Sea overflow them as they pursued you, and how the Lord has destroyed them to this day; [5]what He did for you in the wilderness until you came to this place.... [7]<u>your eyes have seen every great act of the Lord which He did</u>.

Deuteronomy 11:2-7

Transmission to Future Generations: The Testimony

8. *Gathering of the Survivors*

And in the fortieth year, on the first day of the eleventh month, Moses spoke to the people of Israel according to all that the Lord had given him in commandment to them. ***Deuteronomy 1:3***

Today, you are all standing before the Lord your God; the heads of your tribes, your elders, your officers, all the men of Israel, [10]your little ones, your wives, and the sojourner who is in your camp, both he who hews your wood and he who draws your water, [11]that you may enter into the covenant with the Lord your God, and into His oath which the Lord your God is making with you today. ***Deuteronomy 29:9-11***

9. *The Testimony*

You might inquire about times long past, going back to the time that God created man on earth, [exploring] one end of the heavens to the other, see if anything as great as this has ever happened, or if the like has ever been heard. [33]Has any nation ever heard God speaking out of fire, as you have, and still survived? [34]Has God ever done miracles, bringing one nation out of another nation, with tremendous miracles, signs, wonders, war, a mighty hand and outstretched arm, and terrifying phenomena, as God did for you in Egypt before your very eyes? [35]You are the ones who have been shown, so that you will know that God is the Supreme Being, and there is none besides Him.
Deuteronomy 4:32-35

Moses summoned all Israel and said to them: "You have seen all that the Lord did before your eyes in the land of Egypt, to Pharaoh and to all his servants and to all his land, [2]the great trials which your eyes saw, the signs, and those great wonders; [3]but to this day the Lord has not given you a mind to understand, or eyes to see, or ears to hear. [4]I have led you forty years in the wilderness; your clothes have not worn out upon you, and your sandals have not worn off your feet; [5]you have not eaten bread, and you have not drunk wine or strong drink; that you may know that I am the Lord your God."
Deuteronomy 29:1-5

10. *The Eyewitness Accounts*

And Moses summoned all Israel, and said to them, "Hear, O Israel, the statutes and the ordinances which I speak in your hearing this day, and you shall learn them and be careful to do them. [2]The Lord our God made a covenant with us in *Horeb*. [3]Not with our fathers did the Lord make this covenant, but with us, who are all of us here alive this day. The Lord spoke with you face to face at the mountain, out of the midst of the fire." ***Deuteronomy 5:1-3***

You must now realize that I am not speaking with your children, who did not know and who did not see the lesson the Lord your God [taught] through His greatness and His mighty hand and His out-stretched arm—His signs and His acts which He did in the midst of Egypt, to Pharaoh king of Egypt, and to all his land; [4]what He did to the army of Egypt, to their horses and their chariots: how He made the waters of the Red Sea overflow them as they pursued you, and how the Lord has destroyed them to this day; [5]what He did for you in the wilderness until you came to this place.... [7]your eyes have seen every great act of the Lord which He did. ***Deuteronomy 11:2-7***

Kri and Kesiv - קרי וכתיב

What is to be read ↓ What is to be written ↓

Genesis 36:5 (Original Hebrew)
וְאָהֳלִיבָמָה יָלְדָה אֶת־(יְעִישׁ) [יְעוּשׁ] וְאֶת־יַעְלָם וְאֶת־קֹרַח אֵלֶּה בְּנֵי עֵשָׂו אֲשֶׁר יֻלְּדוּ־לוֹ בְּאֶרֶץ כְּנָעַן׃

Genesis 36:5 (King James Version)
And Aholibamah bare *Jeush*, and Jaalam, and Korah: these are the sons of Esau, which were born unto him in the land of Canaan.

What is to be written (kesiv)  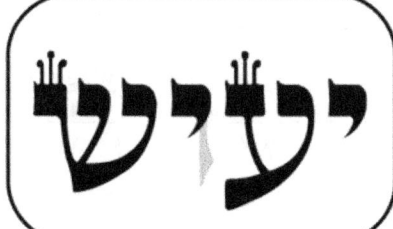 What is to be read (kri)

Josh McDowell
Evidence That Demands a Verdict

Geisler and Nix make the following comment about how textual variations are counted: "There is an ambiguity in saying there are some 200,000 variants in the existing manuscripts of the New Testament, since these represent only 10,000 places in the New Testament. If one single word is misspelled in 3,000 different manuscripts, this is counted as 3,000 variants or readings."

Although he was dealing with fewer manuscripts than we have today, *Philip Shaff* in *Comparison to the Greek Testament and the English Version* concluded that only 400 of the 150,000 variant readings caused doubt about the textual meaning, and <u>only 50 of these were of great significance</u>.

Here's Life Publishers, Inc.: San Bernardino, CA, 1979, page 44.

Transmission to Future Generations

16. *<u>Parents to Children</u>*

<u>Teach your children</u> to speak of them, when you are at home, when traveling on the road, when you lie down and when you get up.

Deuteronomy 11:19

These words which I command you today must remain on your heart. ⁷<u>Teach them to your children</u> and speak of them when you are at home, when traveling on the road, when you lie down and when you get up.

Deuteronomy 6:6-7

17. *<u>The Foundations of Morality</u>*

<u>You must show love toward the foreigner</u>, since you were foreigners in the land of Egypt.

Deuteronomy 10:19

<u>Do not pervert justice for the proselyte or orphan. Do not take a widow's garment as security for a loan.</u> ¹⁸You must remember that you were a slave in Egypt, and the Lord your God then liberated you. It is for that reason that I am commanding you to do this. ¹⁹<u>When you reap your grain harvest and forget a sheaf in the field, you must not go back to get it. It must be left for the foreigner, orphan and widow,</u> so that the Lord your God will bless you, no matter what you do.... ²²I am commanding you to do this because you must remember that you were a slave in Egypt.

Deuteronomy 24:17-22

18. *<u>Weekly Day of Spiritual Rejuvenation</u>*

Observe the Sabbath to keep it holy, as God your Lord commanded you. ¹³You can work during the six weekdays, and do all your work, ¹⁴but Saturday is the Sabbath to God your Lord, so do not do anything that constitutes work.... ¹⁵<u>You must remember that you were slaves in Egypt, when the Lord your God brought you out with a strong hand and an outstretched arm. It is for this reason that the Lord your God has commanded you to keep the Sabbath</u>.

Deuteronomy 5:12-15

19. *<u>Number Sign (Tattoo) on Body</u>*

This is My covenant between Me, and between you and your offspring that you must keep: <u>You must circumcise every male.</u> ¹¹<u>You shall be circumcised through the flesh of your foreskin.</u> This shall be the mark of the covenant between Me and you. ¹²Throughout all generations, <u>every male shall be circumcised</u> when he is eight days old....

Genesis 17:10-12

20. *<u>Special Garments — Yellow Badge With the Star of David</u>*

God spoke to Moses, telling him to speak to the Israelites and have them <u>make tassels on the corners of their garments for all generations</u>. They shall include a twist of sky-blue wool in the corner tassels. These shall be your tassels, and when you see them, you shall remember all of God's commandments so as to keep them....I am the Lord your God who brought you out of Egypt to be your God. I am the Lord your God.

Numbers 15:37-41

21. *Excerpt From the Scroll on Head and Heart*

[These words] shall be to you as a sign on your hand and as a memorial between your eyes, that the law of the Lord may be in your mouth; for with a strong hand the Lord has brought you out of Egypt.

Exodus 13:9

22. *Excerpt From the Scroll on Doorpost*

Write them on [parchments affixed to] the door posts of your houses and gates.

Deuteronomy 6:9

23. *Membership Sanctions*

Do not intermarry with them. Do not give your daughters to their sons, and do not take their daughters for your sons.

Deuteronomy 7:3

I see [this nation] from mountain tops, and gaze on it from the heights. It is a nation dwelling alone at peace, not counting itself among the nations.

Numbers 23:9

24. *Yearly Family Gathering: Transmission to the Next Generation*

When your son asks you in time to come, "What is the meaning of the testimonies and the statutes and the ordinances which the Lord our God has commanded you?" [21]then you shall say to your son, "We were Pharaoh's slaves in Egypt; and the Lord brought us out of Egypt with a mighty hand; [22]and the Lord showed signs and wonders, great and grievous, against Egypt and against Pharaoh and all his household, before our eyes; [23]and he brought us out from there, that he might bring us in and give us the land which he swore to give to our fathers.

Deuteronomy 6:20-23

25. *Commemoration of Deliverance: Potato Peels and Stale Bread*

You shall eat no leavened bread with it; seven days you shall eat it with unleavened bread, the bread of affliction — for you came out of the land of Egypt in hurried flight — that all the days of your life you may remember the day when you came out of the land of Egypt.

Deuteronomy 16:3

26. *Commemoration of Traveling to the Promised Land by Ship*

You shall dwell in booths for seven days; all that are native in Israel shall dwell in booths, [43]that your generations may know that I made the people of Israel dwell in booths when I brought them out of the land of Egypt: I am the Lord your God.

Leviticus 23:42-43

27. *Commemoration of Founding International Networks*

And you shall count from the morrow after the Sabbath, from the day that you brought the sheaf of the wave offering; seven full weeks shall they be.... [21]This very day shall be celebrated as a sacred holiday when no service work may be done. This is an eternal law for all generations, no matter where you may live.

Leviticus 23:15-21

By David Ben Gurion

About 300 years ago a ship set sail for the new world and its name was the Mayflower. Its passengers were Englishmen who had become disgusted with their government and their society. They set out in search of some deserted shore to establish a new life for themselves. They landed in America and they were the first founders of that land and that people. This was an important event in the history of both England and America. And for this reason, to this day, every American child knows of the Mayflower, the pilgrims, Plymouth Rock and November 25, Thanksgiving Day.

I am, however, very interested in knowing if any Englishman, or American for that matter, is aware of the hour and the day that the Mayflower set sail? Does any child or even adult know how many pilgrims there were on this historical voyage? What were the names of their families? What did they wear? What did they eat? Where did they get water to drink? What path did they navigate and what happened en route?

Behold, it was more than 3,300 years ago that the Jews set out from Egypt. Every Jewish child all over the world - in America, Soviet Russia, Yemen, and Germany - knows exactly how his ancestors left at dawn on the 15th of Nissan. What did they wear? "Their loins were girded, their sandals were on their feet and their staffs were in their hands? (Exodus 12:11). They ate matzot and they arrived at the Red Sea after a seven-day journey. These children also know the route that their ancestors traveled and what events transpired during their 40-year trek in the wilderness. They ate Manna and Quail, they drank water from the Well of Miriam. They arrived at the borders of the Promised Land on the banks of the Jordan River facing Jericho. They know the names of their ancestors and they can quote them to you from the Five Books of Moses.

Till this day, Jews the world over eat the same matzot for seven days starting from the 15th of Nissan each year. And they relate the story of the Exodus and the tribulation that the Jews have suffered from the day they left their land and wandered into exile. And they end by shouting two phrases that children and parents and grandparents have been saying for thousands of years: 'Now we are slaves. Next year we will be free men. Now we are here in exile. Next year we will be in Jerusalem....' in the land of Israel. This is the nature of the Jews."

From Ben Gurion's speech in front of the Anglo-American Investigation Committee of the United Nations, 1948

Credits:

The text used in *Bearers of the Torch* has been adapted from the Arachim source book, *Pathways to the Torah*.

Photographs on pages 326 and 329 were copied with permission from the book, *From Holocaust to Redemption: Bearing Witness*. Published by The World Gathering of Jewish Holocaust Survivors; 1984.

Scripture Index

Index of Scripture References

Parenthesis ( ) indicates scripture location in a Christian Bible

Jewish Scriptures

Genesis

Reference	Page
1:26-27	137
3:15, 20	364
4:7	353, 364
4:26	182
7:15	257
8:21	208
9:13-17	48
9:26	105
10:21	182
11:7	137
12:2-3	361
13:3	362
13:16	363
15:2-4	109, 361, 363
15:5-6	361
15:5	363-364
15:6	353
15:12	203
16:10	363-364
17:7	310
17:10-12	382
17:11	48
17:19	310, 363
18:18	363
22:17	363
23:17-19	235
26:3-4	310
26:4-5	214, 355, 361
26:46	363
28:12-15	311
30:23	203
33:20	183
34:2-4	51, 63
35:26	182
36:5	381
46:27	236-257
49:8-12	338
50:13	235

Exodus

1:5.	234-235
1:16-19.	325
4:16.	183
4:22.	97, 152, 168
7:1.	140, 183
12:1-2.	251, 276, 307
12:11.	376
12:46.	195-196
13:9.	302, 383
13:16.	302
14:31.	99
15:6.	99
16:29-30.	272, 300
18:20.	256
19:5-6.	109
20:2-3.	132, 340
20:2-17.	287-317
20:8-11.	300
20:10.	250
21:6.	140, 183
21:22-27.	252
22:8.	140, 183
23:19.	255
30:11-15.	350
31:12-17.	300
32:33.	340

Leviticus

1:1.	182
3:17.	250
4:1-2.	69
11:1-8.	305
11:9-12.	306
16:7-22.	70
16:16.	70-71
16:19.	252
16:30-31.	71
16:31.	300
17:10-11.	68-73
18:21.	342
18:30.	269
20:2-5.	342
23:5.	280
23:15-21.	383
23:27-29.	252
23:42-43.	383
25:1-22.	221
26:18.	221
26:42.	212
26:44-45.	311
26:46.	300

Numbers

1:18.	61, 236
9:1-3.	307
14:24.	214
15:24-31.	69
15:37-41.	382
15:38.	261
18:1.	110
23:9.	383
23:19.	132, 176, 206
25:12.	212
29:1.	300
29:7.	252

Deuteronomy

1:3.	379
4:2.	380
4:5-8.	209
4:9-12.	369-370, 380
4:11-12.	132
4:26-31.	76, 343
4:27.	213
4:32-40.	243, 369, 379
4:35.	132, 340
4:39.	132
5:1-3.	379
5:12-15.	382
6:4.	110, 132, 151, 155, 165, 179-180
6:6-7.	382
6:8.	302
6:9.	383
6:14.	340
6:20-23.	383
7:3.	383

7:6-9, 12	213, 321
7:18-19	370
7:19	99
8:2	364
10:12-13	209
10:19	382
10:22	234-235
11:2-7	379
11:18	302
11:19	382
12:21	250, 302
12:25	5
12:31	342
13:6-8	369
15:15	370
16:1	277, 307
16:3	383
16:12	370
17:8-11	256, 301
22:11-12	261
23:3-4	255, 331
24:17-18	370
24:17-22	382
25:17	375
29:1-5, 9-11	379
29:13-16	380
29:28 (29)	209
30:4	208
30:8-20	109
30:10-19	208
30:14-19	361
30:15-19	74
31:9, 19, 24-25	380
32:35	105
32:39	132, 340
33:2	105

Joshua

1:3-6	312

Judges

6:24	183

I Samuel

1:11	171
2:1-10	171
2:2	132
2:20	364
15:22	77
15:29	132
16:1-3	323
17:56	40, 60
17:58	331
20:22	40, 60
21:1-4	323

II Samuel

7:12-16	238
7:14	152, 165
7:21-24	321
12:13	68, 75
24:1	350

I Kings

8:27	133
8:46-50	76, 331-332, 339
8:60	133
15:11	214
17:17-23	199
22:19-23	137

II Kings

4:8-37	199
11:1	363
15:29-30	43
16:5, 9	43
19:19	133
19:30-34	183
19:31	182, 186
22:2	214

Isaiah

Reference	Pages
1:1	47
1:16-18	350-343
2:2-5	110
2:3	209
2:4	230
5:25	182
6:1-2, 8	137
6:7	112
6:8	137
7:1-16	41
7:3-4	44, 361
7:14-16	38-63, 73, 274, 360
8:2-4	44, 47, 49
8:18	47, 361
8:23-9:1-3 (9:1-4)	184
9:3 (4)	185
9:5-6 (6-7)	182-186
10:5	185
10:20-27	183
10:21, 24	185
10:26-27	185
11:1-5	233
11:6-9	230
11:11-12	231
14:12	356
16:4	105
21:8	184
23:1	105
23:3	182
23:12	61
26:19	199, 230
27:9	356
27:12-13	231
29:11	182
30:5	105
36:13	182
37:22	61
37:31-35	183
37:32	182, 186
38:13	37
40:2	101, 121, 126
40:18, 25	133
41:8-9	94, 97, 117, 121, 127
41:11	127
42:6	94, 109
42:8	133
42:21	306
43:1-7	312
43:8-12	369
43:10	94-97, 107, 127
43:10-11	340
43:5-6	231
43:7	120
43:10	94-97
43:10-11	109, 120-121, 133
44:1-2	94, 97, 117, 127
44:6-8	135, 155
44:7	105
44:21	97, 117, 127
44:24	134
44:28-45:1, 13	221, 223
45:1	202
45:4	95-97, 116, 127
45:5-7	134, 155, 332
45:18	156
45:7	352
45:11	109
45:19	109, 300
45:18-19	134
45:21-22	134
46:5, 9	134
47:1	61
48:11	134
48:12	135
48:20	95-97, 116, 129
48:21	104-105
49:3	95-97, 100, 117, 121, 129
49:5	120
49:6	100, 109-110
49:7-8	100
49:13-15	100, 312
51:21	121
52:1-2	97
52:4-5	101-102, 118
52:9-12	99
52:10	118
52:12	116
52:13-53:12	93-129
52:14	98, 125-126

Reference	Pages
52:13-53:1	94, 126
52:15	117-118
53:1	94, 99, 112, 116, 118
53:2	99
53:3	101, 118
53:4-5	94, 102, 117
53:6	103
53:7	103, 112
53:8	103-107, 118
53:9	107-108
53:10	106, 112, 119, 123
53:11	109
53:12	110, 119, 128
54:1	116
54:1-11	95-97
54:4-7	100
54:6-11	118
54:7-10	99
54:10	112, 312
54:11	100, 121
54:14	100
54:17	100, 272
55:6-9	85, 343
56:7-8	74, 79, 230
58:5-6	253
58:13-14	300
59:20-21	203, 313, 355
60:3	110, 124
60:1-22	355
60:14-15	101, 109
61:1-2	360
61:3	192
61:6-7	109
62:2-4, 12	101
62:5	61
63:9, 11	333
66:10	192

Jeremiah

Reference	Pages
7:3-23	343
7:7-23	74, 80
10:1-5	57
16:14-15	213
16:15	231
16:19-20	94, 127
17:19-24	304
17:21-27	296
22:26	137
22:30	236
23:3	231
23:5	233
23:7-8	212
23:18, 22	137
25:12	221
29:7	103
29:10	221
30:8-13	102
30:10	97
31:9 (10)	343
31:30-36 (31-37)	212, 279
31:33 (34)	212, 232
31:35-37 (36-38)	313
32:34-35	350
33:16	183
33:17-18	82
33:25-26	313
46:27-28	97, 313

Ezekiel

Reference	Pages
11:19-20	209
13:9	307
16:60	313
18:1-23	78-79, 340, 343
18:20-23	128
18:23-27	341
32:23-32	104
33:10-11	78
34:11-16	231
34:15-16	103
34:23-24	83, 209
34:27, 29-30	112
36:6-9, 15	104
36:24-28	232
37:1-28	344
37:12-13	231
37:21-22	232
37:24-25	83, 233
37:25-28	232, 313

39:22-29 ... 314
43:7 ... 232
43:22-25 ... 82-83
44:9 ... 209
44:27 ... 83
45:17-31 ... 83
46:16-18, 24 ... 83

Joel
1:2-13 ... 52
1:4, 8 ... 51
2:27 ... 135
4:1 (3:1) ... 232, 314

Amos
9:11 ... 333
9:15 ... 232

Hosea
1:8-9 ... 48, 360
2:23 ... 48
2:25 ... 360
3:4-5 ... 84, 336-338
6:6 ... 74, 79, 227, 338-339
11:1 ... 36, 97, 152, 168
13:4 ... 135, 340
14:2-3 ... 74-75, 332, 340
14:6-8 ... 99

Obadiah
1:17-18, 21 ... 192
1:8 ... 203

Jonah
3:5-10 ... 86-87
3:10 ... 68, 341

Micah
2:12 ... 232
2:15 ... 363
4:1-2 ... 231
4:3-7 ... 230
5:1 (2) ... 264, 321-334
5:2-16 ... 329
6:6-8 ... 74, 331, 339, 343
7:14 ... 333
7:15-16 ... 94, 127

Zephaniah
3:9 ... 124, 231
3:12-13 ... 121
3:12-20 ... 106-107, 230, 232

Habakkuk
2:7 ... 105

Haggai
2:12-13 ... 249

Zechariah
1:15 ... 101, 121
3:1-2 ... 352
4:7 ... 130
8:3-6, 20-23 ... 230
8:13 ... 112
8:19 ... 298
8:20-23 ... 230
8:23 ... 94, 109-110, 201
9:9-10 ... 332
10:6-10 ... 232
11:4-7 ... 103
12:1-9 ... 199
12:2-3 ... 197
12:8-14 ... 192
12:8-9 ... 197
12:10 ... 192-204
12:10-14 ... 199

12:11	198
13:1-6	36
13:8-9	121
14:9	230
14:16	209
14:21	82

Malachi
2:10	135
2:15	363
3:4	333
3:6	314
3:7	341
3:22 (4:4)	209
3:23-24 (4:5-6)	232

Psalms
2:3	203
2:4	105
2:7, 12	165, 219
8:6	183
17:8-12	37
18:20, 24 (21, 25)	219
18:28	103
19:8	248
19:8-9 (7-8)	209
19:9 (19:8)	219
22:13-22 (12-21)	37
24:4	219
33:15	136
35:17	37
40:7 (6)	71-74
40:7-9 (6-8)	343
44:4	105
44:11-15	121
44:12-22	103
51:7	208
51:16-19 (14-17)	74, 343
68:35	340
73:1	219
73:25	135
78:2-7	380
78:24	105
81:8-9	135
82:6	140
83:3	203
88:8	105
89:29-38	236
105:6-10	212
110:1	219
111:7-8	209
116:9	104
119:44, 97, 155, 163	209
119:165	105, 209
125:1-2	213
136:22	97
146:3	135
147:19-20	295

Proverbs
6:23	110
10:2	79, 343
11:4	79, 343
16:6	79, 343
21:3	79
30:18-20	39

Job
1:6	137
1:6-7	352
1:9-2:5	348
2:3	349
6:19	105
14:13-15	199
14:21	105
15:8	137
24:17	105

Song of Songs
5:1	119

Ruth
1:4	331
4:13-22	331

Lamentations
1:19. 105

Ecclesiastes
7:20. 208
12:12. 257
12:13. 341

Daniel
1:3-16. 301
4:24 (27). 79, 395
6:3-13. 301
9:1-27. 322-327
9:18. 341
11:2. 60
12:2. . . . . 199, 231

Ezra
1:1-3. 221
1:1-5. 223
10:2-3. 304

Nehemiah
9:6. 135
10:30-32. 304
13:15-18. 304

I Chronicles
3:11-12, 15, 16-17. 236
16:14-19. 315
17:11-14. 236
17:20. 135
17:22. 315
21:1. . . . . 350, 354
22:9-10. 236
28:6-7. 236

II Chronicles
6:36-39. 76, 343
20:7. . . . . 315, 375
29:2. 212
35:20-25. 198
35:22-24. 192
35:25. 200
36:21-23. 221

Christian Scriptures

Matthew
1:17. 236
1:18-21. 171
1:18-23. 323
1:20-23. . . . . 38-39, 266
2:1. 59
2:1-12. 325
2:6. 264, 328-331
2:11. 323
2:13-15. . . . . 36, 59, 97, 325
2:13-23. 328
2:22. 59
2:23. . . . . 37-63, 323
3:17. . . . . 138, 170
4:1-11. 325
4:7. 142
4:23. 84
9:21. 271
9:35. 84
10:34-36. . . . . 18, 233, 332
11:11-14. 233
12:1-8. 268
12:9-13. 271
12:24. 351
12:38-41. 87
12:40. 238
16:1-4. 87
16:21-22. 112
19:6-7. 148
20:20-23. 138
20:29-34. 324
21:1-7. 332

22:41-46.	219
23:1-3.	260, 303
23:31-37.	260
23:39.	19
24:14.	84
26:20-30.	238
26:36-46.	148, 157
26:39, 53.	138
27:5.	239
27:11, 37.	340
27:15-25.	327
27:22-25.	5, 201, 271
27:32, 34.	238
27:44.	238
27:46.	142
28:1-20.	238-239
28:11-15.	356
28:16-17.	238
28:17-20.	239

Mark

1:11.	148, 170
1:14.	84
1:15.	173
2:23-28.	268, 303
3:1-5.	271
6:56.	261
7:18-19.	210
7:21-23.	74
9:1.	173
10:17-20.	139, 148
11:7.	332
12:35-40.	260
13:32.	139, 173
14:17-25.	238
14:32-42.	148, 157, 240-241
15:21.	238
15:23, 25, 32.	238
15:34.	148, 170, 238, 241
16:1-8.	150-151, 238
16:8-18.	238-239
16:9-20.	150-151
16:13.	239
16:16.	74, 336, 350

Luke

1:6.	214
1:26-55.	171
1:27.	236
1:35.	171
1:59-64.	262
1:30-31.	46, 46
1:32-33.	84
2:1-7.	324
2:4, 11.	87, 331
2:39-40.	324
4:18-19.	360
6:1-5.	268
6:6-10.	271
10:18.	352
10:19.	3
11:29-32.	87
11:37-54.	260
12:51-53.	222
14:26.	233
18:28-29.	148
18:35-43.	230
19:14.	84
19:29-35.	230
22:14-23.	238
22:27.	241
22:37.	127
22:39-46.	148, 157
22:41.	241
23:26, 36, 39-41, 46, 56.	238, 242
24:1-10.	238-239
24:13-43.	239
24:49.	238-239

John

1:1-18.	172
1:8.	139
1:21.	196, 233
1:29.	83
1:36.	83, 196
3:14-16.	74
3:16.	341-350
3:19.	74
4:19-22.	303

Reference	Page
5:37	139
6:37	139
6:44	74
7:22-23	265
7:41-42, 52	172
8:17-18	139
8:44-45	6, 356
8:46	83
10:30-34	140
12:14	332
12:38	127
12:49	141
13:1	238
13:16	139
13:29	238
14:6	74, 342
14:26	139, 148
14:28	141, 160, 173, 178, 190
16:7	169
17:1-26	148
17:3	141, 341
17:11, 21-22	170
18:28	238
18:46	83
19:10-16	273-274
19:14	280
19:14-17, 29-30	238, 240
19:31	196
19:32-37	195-196, 240
19:34-37	192
19:37	196-197
20:1-18	238-239
20:17	141
20:24-29	239
21:1-24	239
21:24	177

Romans

Reference	Page
1:3-4	169
1:16	18
3:10-11	74, 87, 214, 342
3:20	208
3:23	77
4:1-4	87
4:3	355
5:12	214
5:27	77
6:10	81, 83
7:1, 4-6	208
8:7-8	74
9:24-26	360
10:4-8	208
11:26-27	355
15:6	142

Acts

Reference	Page
1:4	238
1:5, 8	239
1:12	261
1:18	239
2:1	276
2:1-4	238-239
5:3	354
6:8-10	234
7:14-16	235
8:28-34	127
10:11-16	210
11:5-10	210
12:3	276
13:14-15, 27	112
13:32-33	169
14:2	74
17:7	340
17:28	362
20:6	276
27:9	276

I Corinthians

Reference	Page
1:18-25	93
2:14	74
5:7	71, 83
8:4-6	142
9:19-22	3
9:22	335
11:3	142
13:12	362
14:33	352

15:5-8 . . . . 140, 238-239
15:12 77
15:22 214
15:28 142
15:33 362
16:8 276

II Corinthians
1:3 142
5:21 . . . . 74, 77, 83
11:3 354

Galatians
2:11-14 211
2:16, 21 208
3:6 355
3:6-9 361
3:13 208
3:16 362
3:17 272
4:22-31 375
5:2-3, 6 208-209

Ephesians
1:17 142
2:1-3 74
2:2 354
2:8-9 . . . . 77, 87
5:2 340

Philippians
3:8 211

Colossians
1:4 87
1:13 84
1:15 143
2:13-14 211
2:16-17 74

I Thessalonians
2:14-16 6
2:18 364

II Thessalonians
2:7 354

I Timothy
1:4 . . . . 38, 236
2:5 143
6:16 139
6:17 84

II Timothy
1:9 87

Titus
3:5-6 77

Hebrews
2:14 364
2:17 . . . . 84, 340
3:1 340
3:11 84
4:14-16 . . . . 84, 340
4:15 . . . . 83, 143
5:2 332
5:7-8 143
6:20 84
7:26 83
7:27 81
8:5 74
8:9 212
9:7-14 84
9:12 81
9:14 83
9:22 . . . . 68-73, 75, 335
9:26 340
10:1 74-75

10:4-5. 71-74
10:10, 18. 81
10:19-22. 84

James
1:13. 143

I Peter
1:3. 142
1:19. 83
2:22. . . . . 83, 127
2:24. 74
3:18. 74

II Peter
1:19. 348

I John
1:1. 239
1:5. 352
2:23. 74
3:5. 83
3:8. 364
4:10. 83
4:12. 139
5:7-8. 144-148

Revelation
1:6. 142
2:9. 356
3:9. 348
3:12. 171-172
5:6-8. 83
6:1-6. 83
7:9-17. 83
12:9. 354
22:16. 356

www.ingramcontent.com/pod-product-compliance
Lightning Source LLC
Chambersburg PA
CBHW080419230426
43662CB00015B/2146